Reading the Road, from Shakespeare's Crossways to Bunyan's Highways

Reading the Road, from Shakespeare's Crossways to Bunyan's Highways

Edited by Lisa Hopkins and Bill Angus

EDINBURGH
University Press

Edinburgh University Press is one of the leading university presses in the UK. We publish academic books and journals in our selected subject areas across the humanities and social sciences, combining cutting-edge scholarship with high editorial and production values to produce academic works of lasting importance. For more information visit our website: edinburghuniversitypress.com

© editorial matter and organisation Lisa Hopkins and Bill Angus, 2020, 2021
© the chapters their several authors, 2020, 2021

Edinburgh University Press Ltd
The Tun – Holyrood Road, 12(2f) Jackson's Entry, Edinburgh EH8 8PJ

First printed in hardback by Edinburgh University Press 2020

Typeset in 10.5/13 Adobe Sabon by
Servis Filmsetting Ltd, Stockport, Cheshire

A CIP record for this book is available from the British Library

ISBN 978 1 4744 5411 7 (hardback)
ISBN 978 1 4744 5412 4 (paperback)
ISBN 978 1 4744 5413 1 (webready PDF)
ISBN 978 1 4744 5414 8 (epub)

The right of Lisa Hopkins and Bill Angus to be identified as the Editors of this work has been asserted in accordance with the Copyright, Designs and Patents Act 1988, and the Copyright and Related Rights Regulations 2003 (SI No. 2498).

Contents

List of Illustrations vii
Acknowledgements viii

    Introduction: Allegories, Economies and Resonances of the Road 1
    Bill Angus and Lisa Hopkins

Part I Shakespeare's Roads

1. The Low Road and the High Road: *Macbeth* and the Way to Scotland 15
   Lisa Hopkins

2. Uncolting Falstaff: The Oats Complex and Energy Crisis in *1 Henry IV* 31
   Todd Andrew Borlik

3. The Night, the Crossroads and the Stake: Shakespeare and the Outcast Dead 51
   Bill Angus

4. Gender, Vagrancy and the Culture of the Early Modern Road in *As You Like It* 71
   Karalyn Dokurno

5. Traversing Monstrosity: Perilous Women and Powerful Men upon Shakespeare's Roads 87
   Sharon Emmerichs

Part II The Embodied Road

6. Not So Tedious Ways to Think about the Locations of the Early Playhouses   107
   Laurie Johnson

7. Wandering Fools and Foolish Vagrants: Folly on the Road in Early Modern English Culture   127
   Alice Equestri

8. 'Fallen Am I in Dark Uneven Way': Wandering from the Road in Early Modern Folklore and Drama   146
   Jennifer Allport Reid

9. 'I Must Abroad or Perish!': The Meta-theatre of the Road in Brome's *A Jovial Crew*   167
   Kim Durban

Part III Writing the Road

10. Staging the Road: Walking, Talking, Footing   185
    Robert Stagg

11. The Road to Damascus and the Road to Hell in Philip Massinger's *The Renegado*: Islamic England and the Pauline Crossroads   202
    Paul Frazer

12. How Margaret Cavendish Mapped a Blazing World   220
    Marion Wynne-Davies

13. 'The King's Highway': Reading England's Road in *The Pilgrim's Progress, Part I*   238
    Martha Lynn Russell

    Conclusion   252
    Lisa Hopkins and Bill Angus

Notes on Contributors   254
Index   258

List of Illustrations

Figure 2.1 John Taylor, *The World Runs on Wheels*, 1623. © The British Library Board. General Reference Collection C.30.d.29. 45

Figure 3.1 Roads outside London 3, Janelle Jenstad (ed.) (c. 1562), The Agas Map, University of Victoria, <http://mapoflondon.uvic.ca/map.htm> (last accessed 24 June 2019). 57

Figure 6.1 Newington Butts, Rocque Map (1746), reproduced courtesy of MOTCO Enterprises Limited. © MOTCO 2001. 114

Figure 9.1 Roads outside London 2, Janelle Jenstad (ed.) (c. 1562), The Agas Map, University of Victoria, <http://mapoflondon.uvic.ca/map.htm> (last accessed 24 June 2019). 166

Acknowledgements

With thanks to Michelle Houston, Ersev Ersoy and all at Edinburgh University Press, Pavel Drábek, Richard Dutton, Jill Le Bihan, Colm MacCrossan, Matt Steggle, Crosby Stevens, and all past and present colleagues at Sheffield Hallam University, UK, and Massey University, New Zealand; to Mark Houlahan, who organised the conference at which Bill and Lisa met and first thought of this collection; and to Chris, Sam, Sarah, Amy, Joe, Stephen, Sonny, Georgie, Aidan, Dan, Amelia, Jacob, Elin and Ciara.

Introduction: Allegories, Economies and Resonances of the Road

Bill Angus and Lisa Hopkins

This collection brings together thirteen essays by both established and emerging scholars that examine the most influential meanings of roads in early modern literature. Centred on the period from William Shakespeare's lifetime to John Bunyan's, these essays consider how the road is delineated in early modern Britain as both a physical and a metaphorical feature, develop our understanding of the place of the road in the early modern imagination, and thereby assess its contribution to shaping identity and culture.

The idea of the road may by its nature seem passing or trivial but, in an essential sense, the dominant ideas of the road in a given time underlie every journey narrative, every conception of geographical movement, and every personal voyage undertaken, whether dramatic, imaginary or physical. If we were to ask what an early modern road movie might look like, we might begin with the significance of the idea of the road as it has, in more modern times, helped to define the character and self-image of North America. In terms of its national identity, the USA has its own historical mythology of the road, taking in the idea of the great western journey and the exodus from slavery towards the promised land of civil rights, both configured biblically, though essentially opposed. Out of these fundamental tensions, and informed by many other transcontinental journeys from the Cherokee Trail of Tears to Kerouac's *On the Road*, come the preponderance of American road movies, books and songs, and the idea of America itself configured as movement/a movement. This collection asks how experiences and conceptions of the road might have contributed in a similar manner to early modern identity and culture in and around early modern Britain.

The new historical and literary research presented in these essays both engages with, and instances, the most recent scholarship in this area of critical studies, and draws on the kind of cultural geography established by the influential ideas of Henri Lefebvre and of Michel de Certeau.

This expanding body of work suggests that in any given time and place culture is more 'about routes than roots' (Cresswell 2006: 1) and the various ideologies of the road studied here certainly reflect this. The present collection negotiates both Lefebvre's concept of 'spatial practice' and de Certeau's 'spatial syntaxes', where journeys that map on to narrative structures are linked together by defining modalities, in this case those associated with freedom, danger, instability, performance, conversion or salvation (Lefebvre 1976: 31; de Certeau 1984: 115).

In Tim Cresswell's summary, the word 'place' itself is far from innocent, and has come to signify 'meaningful segments of space – locations imbued with meaning and power' (2006: 2). In this way, space may be understood as being 'both topographical and conceptual' (Dillon 2000: 6). Further in this vein, Lefebvre argues that while space is 'molded from historical and natural elements', it is equally 'literally filled with ideologies' not only in terms of 'the trivialised spaces of everyday life' but also via those 'made special by symbolic means' (1976: 31). In its significant 'turn towards movement', cultural geography has also produced theories of mobility that aim to comprehend how people move through particular kinds of landscapes. These further suggest that mobility plays a role in shaping those very cultural spaces (Merriman 2007; Urry 2000; Cresswell 2006). Within this understanding of experiential geographies, mobility is something that is 'practiced . . . experienced . . . [and] embodied' (Cresswell 2006: 5). To some extent this relatively new work builds upon that of cultural theorists such as Maurice Merleau-Ponty, who was arguing in this vein as far back as the 1960s that movement is not 'limited to submitting passively to space and time'; rather 'it actively consumes them, it takes them up in their basic significance' (Merleau-Ponty 1962: 102). In this context, the physical landscape is not understood as simply something to be moved through, but rather as a dynamic medium that is itself 'always in movement, always in making' (Cresswell 2006: 3). Without doing too much violence to the theory, we might extend this also to the human subject: as Joël Bonnemaison has said, 'no identity exists without a space that sustains it' (2005: 81). These sustaining interactions between physical environments and the moving human subject are the grounds upon which these essays consider the roads of early modern Britain as they were conceived of and experienced by contemporaries of William Shakespeare and those of John Bunyan.

Of recent historical work on the physical early modern road networks, Andrew McRae's practical approach to the road experience as producing and expressing a kind of communal knowledge may be representative. Janette Dillon and Julie Sanders meanwhile situate these experiences of the road within the early modern city, the court, and specifically dramatic contexts, while Alexandra Walsham has charted the shifting relations between landscape and religion. Drawing on such cultural-historical geographical and literary research, this collection aims to expand upon and nuance early modern ideologies of the road far beyond simply describing the experience of road travel in itself. The scope of our chapters takes in a broad range of aspects of the road experience, involving the intransigent roads of the north, Shakespeare's allusions to the dangerous and ambiguous nature of crossroads, the equine economics of the early modern road network, the historical understanding of the (literal) place of theatres on the roads of early modern London, the changing resonances and material effects of the physical road in depictions of Christian allegories of journeying, dramatic depictions of the nature of travelling communities, masterless wanderers and fools of the early modern road, the poetry of the staging of roads in early modern drama, and both literal and figurative roads in gendered perceptions of mobility. Rooted in the textual and material aspects of the culture's conceptions of this space, this collection also sheds new light on perhaps the most astonishing achievement of early modern plays: their use of one small, bare space to suggest an amazing variety of physical (and potentially even metaphysical) locations. It offers insight into the ways that writers used the typically bare boards of the early modern stage to invite audiences/readers to imagine road journeys and hence the transitional modes of public and private space.

Our chapters consider a number of indicative texts that reflect upon such conceptions, including *Macbeth*, *Cymbeline*, *A Midsummer Night's Dream*, *Hamlet*, *1 Henry IV*, *As You Like It*, *Twelfth Night*, *Titus Andronicus*, *A Jovial Crew*, *The Tempest*, *John a Kent and John a Cumber*, *The Renegado*, *The Blazing World* and *The Pilgrim's Progress*. These diverse studies offer rich suggestions on how such fundamental geographical features, and their related imaginary milieux, might have interacted. They therefore open new windows on a peculiarly British mythology of the road and illuminate our understanding of how this informs early modern British identity as a whole. The chapters are grouped under three broad thematic headings: 'Shakespeare's Roads', 'The Embodied Road' and 'Writing the Road', each of which allows us a particular angle of insight into early modern historical and cultural contexts in the depiction of physical and imaginary roads.

The first part, 'Shakespeare's Roads', gathers five essays which deal with topographical and ideological modalities of the road in Shakespeare's work and his historical context, including the perceived natural and supernatural perils of the roads heading north and elsewhere, looking at *Macbeth* and *Cymbeline*; the ecological impact of energy and transport crises on transportation networks in *1 Henry IV*; allusions to the crossroads as a site of rituals of transformation and binding in *A Midsummer Night's Dream* and *Hamlet*; the travelling woman's experience of gender and disorder in *As You Like It*; and female characters and the transformational properties of roads in *Titus Andronicus*.

Part two, 'The Embodied Road', covers the embodied experience of roads, beginning with the relationship between the King's Highway and contemporary theatres and the distinction between London performances and touring; it considers how early modern folklore shaped perceptions of wandering and the traumatic effects of losing the road in Munday's *John a Kent and John a Cumber* and *The Tempest*; it examines the subjectivities of vagrancy and the fool, reading narratives of the embodied experience of the road in Kemp's and Armin's jestbooks to explain how this affected their perception as performing legends; and it describes the meta-theatrical aspects of the road as a symbol of freedom, renewal and community, and an arena for performance, in Richard Brome's *A Jovial Crew*.

Part three, 'Writing the Road', combines spatial grammars with physical and metaphorical topography and examines the use of prosodic feet and 'gestic' verse to stage roads in early modern theatre; it explores how contemporary physical roads inform ideas of spiritual journey, and what resonances accrue to them, for instance in the conversion narrative of Saint Paul or Margaret Cavendish's *The Blazing World*, where the experience of road space undermines spiritual certainty; it probes the boundaries of confessional fidelity and conversion in *The Renegado* and addresses the notion of pilgrimage in *The Pilgrim's Progress*, where Bunyan's symbolic road may also be literal, Britain's Great North Road, its allegorical movement inflected by the physicality of contemporary transportation, drainage and fairs.

Beginning the first part, 'Shakespeare's Roads', Lisa Hopkins considers the perils posed by roads in *Macbeth*. She argues that roads in early modern Britain were not only arteries of communication but also possessed something of the inviolability of sanctuary. However, when Shakespeare represents roads in Celtic countries he figures them as also potentially haunted, dangerous or misleading, as in *Cymbeline*, where roads prove longer than expected. In Scotland, the chapter illustrates, it is even harder to find the way, and the roads hold danger of a not merely physical kind.

Putting a green twist on an old Marxist formula, Todd Borlik's chapter is an ecomaterialist study of mobility in the Shakespearean history play that aims to 'follow the energy'. The increasing complexity of road networks may be seen in the chorographical scope of the Second Henriad. This reflects the central role that road-building played in the development of modern nationhood, leading to the passing of the feudal demesnial system and laying the path for a more complex mercantile economy. These transformations had profound environmental effects. Composed during a period of dire scarcity, Shakespeare's *1 Henry IV* traces a link between political and ecological instability. In this, Shakespeare anticipates Lefebvre's understanding of the fundamental unity of space-time-energy by reminding us of the absolute necessity of oats and other crops to the movement of goods and persons, and the fact that access to such fuels could be easily disrupted by the variable English climate. The play's subversion of chivalric heroism initiates a corresponding interrogation of the horse's role on the roads of a post-chivalric society, raising prescient questions about the ethics of transportation. Here Borlik sees Shakespeare imagining English history from the point of view of an inadequately victualled horse. During the Great Dearth, at the time Shakespeare was writing *1 Henry IV*, the price of oats skyrocketed, exacerbated by a boom in personal mobility. In such a climate, it should not be surprising that the overconsumption of fodder might be a subject of moral concern. In the context of a late Elizabethan energy crisis, the play's insistent critiques of Hotspur's and Falstaff's over-reliance on horse-power carry an unmistakably ecocritical message.

Next, Bill Angus explores the idea that, in Shakespeare's lifetime and long after, to die as a traitor or in suicide meant, in burial, to be treated as refuse and interred in or by a roadway. It is probable that between the formative ages of eighteen and twenty-two, Shakespeare himself knew at least five people who were buried in unconsecrated ground, in a ceremony designed to arrest the unquiet spirit, and whose traditional elements were the night, the crossroads and the stake. The crossroads, a nexus where paths, movement and points of decision simultaneously converge and part, has long been the site of religious and magical rituals of transformation and binding. As the tri-via, the crossroads is literally one of 'the trivialised spaces of everyday life' but also one 'made special by symbolic means as . . . benevolent or malevolent' (Lefebvre 1976: 31). For Shakespeare and other early moderns, crossroads were haunted places, echoing with folk memory, but also spoke of new possibilities. When *A Midsummer Night's Dream*'s Puck refers to restless spirits that 'in cross-ways . . . have burial' (3.2.381), Shakespeare is therefore perhaps unwittingly referencing a history of crossroads as places whose function was to arrest the movement of unquiet spirits, of suicides, executed murderers and traitors, who might otherwise walk the roads of the night home to the scenes of their particular traumas. Here at the crossroads they may be fixed, sometimes literally staked, their movement arrested, paradoxically, in a place of permanent transit and transition. Although what happens at such places is largely unacknowledged in Shakespeare's imaginative world, the question of outcast burial in the roads of early modern Britain nevertheless emerges in hints and allusions found in the plays, like the shadowy revenants of unquiet thoughts. This chapter considers these hints from the edges of Shakespeare's imagination to argue that, despite the urge to exorcise such delinquents, they are often surprisingly inscribed into lasting cultural and geographical forms.

Karalyn Dokurno then investigates how Shakespeare's travelling heroines illustrate and complicate ideas about women's mobility and early modern road travel in general. She reads *As You Like It* to discover an enduring fascination with the constructive or reparative potential of the travelling woman, despite early modern censure of women's travel as culturally, politically and religiously disruptive. Given McRae's argument that 'roads had always coupled a promise of connection with a threat of disorder' (McRae 2009: 90), this chapter considers the conflicting social implications of Celia and Rosalind's recourse to the road in their travel to Arden. Building on work on mobility, vagrancy and female transgression, it explores how women's recourse to 'the common road' allows them to veer from prescribed gender, class and domestic roles. While their journey does this, it simultaneously helps to repair patriarchal structures within the play, thus reflecting the double nature inherent within early modern British road travel. Considering that Celia and Rosalind's habitation of 'the common road' is anything but easy or straightforward, and drawing on Lefebvrian notions of space as socially constructed, the chapter pays close attention to the ways in which the road opens a contradictory space in which Shakespeare's heroines move.

Sharon Emmerichs's chapter offers an ecofeminist analysis of the transformational properties of roads in Shakespeare's plays. Lefebvre describes urban spaces as transformative objects and this is certainly true of the circulatory system of the roads. Crime, vagrancy, the public nature of roads, and anxieties regarding how roads can facilitate invasion and vulnerability all serve to demonstrate their transformative power. Emmerichs shows how, in Shakespeare's plays, roads act not only as conduits for movement and change of place and action, but as a way to move characters from one state of being to another. Her chapter takes an ecofeminist approach to the meanings of roads and argues that in Shakespeare, interactions with roads cause a transformation from innocence to corruption. Roads then may represent potentially malignant spaces that ultimately produce gendered monstrosities by the end of one's journey. She identifies a dual-gendered tension of the road that survives in many of Shakespeare's works, where the road, both physical and metaphorical, becomes a space of physical, moral, economic and legal danger, particularly for female characters, as in *Titus Andronicus* when Aaron chooses the location for the assault upon Lavinia based on its roads. As Shakespeare negotiates both the power and the peril of the early modern road, these patterns serve to demonstrate the dangers inherent every time a woman leaves the private domestic sphere and ventures out into a public space.

Laurie Johnson begins Part II: The Embodied Road with the contention that roads have been largely invisible in the histories of the Elizabethan playhouses. A London-centric bias at the core of these histories tends to position roads as a key element in the lives of the travelling players, but roads disappear from the story of the rise of the purpose-built 'permanent' playhouses around London. Such a focus oscillates between what Lefebvre called 'paradigmatic' and 'symbolic' approaches to space: the playhouses are understood either as an expression of a binary opposition between travelling and permanence, or as symbols of the 'golden age' (Lefebvre 2009: 230). This chapter seeks to understand these playhouses according to Lefebvre's third term, the 'syntagmatic', by considering the movements of both players and audiences as key factors in decisions about where they were located. Importantly, the earliest playhouses (Red Lion, Newington Butts and Theatre) were all located on thoroughfares leading to the nearby fields in which archery was practised. With Elizabeth's mandate for all men to maintain skill with bows, the roads to the fields surrounding London provided a regular flow of potential customers. Both *Hamlet* and *Titus Andronicus* evidence the link between the players and the archery fields adjacent to their playing venues. By thinking of the playhouses as syntagmatic, that is, as links on a nodal sequence, it is possible to shift our view of the playhouses away from the image of a terminal location to which audiences flocked. The emergence of the permanent playhouses on both sides of London, alongside sites accommodating a state-mandated martial practice, therefore seems more of an inevitability than a bolt out of the blue.

Alice Equestri's chapter then explores ways in which the concept of folly interacts with vagrancy and mobility on early modern roads. Looking at the road through this lens enables us to see space as 'multi-level', as Bonnemaison has suggested, and this chapter illustrates how early modern ideas of folly work at different levels to expose a space that is formed of subjective and symbolic or cultural dimensions. In this world, Equestri argues, 'fools' were not only seen as luxury entertainers in rich households or as professional performers on London stages, and those termed 'idiots' were often free to roam the roads and possibly even to beg for alms. Both Erasmus and Alexander Barclay's *Ship of Fools* give such beggars a special prominence in their categorisation of the sins of humanity, in that they make 'imitation' their pitfall, a notion bound up with the performance of folly on the Elizabethan stage. Also, itinerant clowning had existed since the vices of medieval pageants and some Elizabethan and Jacobean stage clowns resituated this tradition to commercialise their artistic personae outside the playhouses on the roads to the provinces. The chapter thus contextualises William Kemp's and Robert Armin's work as itinerants: Kemp's nine-day morris dance from London to Norwich, and Armin's travel on the roads of England with Lord Chandos's Men. In these ways, it examines an image of the space of the roads that had both subjective and wider cultural qualities.

In Chapter 8, Jennifer Allport Reid asserts that religious belief and practice must be recognised as critical agents in the construction of the early modern road. She argues that folklore had a significant role in shaping perceptions of the landscape, and the roads which intersected and constituted it. The precise relationship between contemporary imaginings of the early modern road system and the lived practicalities of traversing it – what Lefebvre describes as 'the fragmented and uncertain connection between elaborated representations of space ... and representational spaces' (Lefebvre 1991: 230) – is never more equivocal than in the motif of the unwary traveller being led astray by supernatural tricksters, the malicious spirits more or less synonymous with the uncanny presences at crossroads examined in Chapter 3. Although local roads were often forged by local requirements, popular and folkloric depictions of the road indicate peril rather than utility or comforting familiarity. In their literalisation of the lived experience of getting lost, these will-o'-the-wisps embody everyday anxieties about wayfinding, casting disorientation as resulting from a purposefully deceptive external force, and the road as an active agent. This chapter reads a number of comedies concerning magic and the supernatural: *A Midsummer Night's Dream* and *The Tempest*, and Anthony Munday's *John a Kent and John a Cumber*. These plays' largely benevolent magical figures and trickster spirits tellingly remove their subjects' agencies, suggesting an equivalence to the misled traveller. This chapter therefore asks what it meant to wander from the road in early modern folklore, in the process recapturing, in Lefebvre's words, the experiences and representations of subjects that 'come together within a spatial practice' (Lefebvre 1976: 31).

Kim Durban then reads Richard Brome's *A Jovial Crew* (1641) to describe a road play in which the road is a symbol of freedom, a place to get money, an escape from parental control, a space of adventure for women, an arena for performance and a seductive natural environment apparently free from constraints. Or so the leading characters think, that is, until they run away to live with the beggars, leading them to ask, 'Is this the life that we admired in others, with envy at their happiness?' (3.1.349). This chapter explores the ways in which Brome's seminal play is rich in contemporary relevance, as the road provides a place where different communities can come together, their statuses intermingled. Durban investigates Brome's dramaturgical openness and generosity to suggest the ways that this seminal play is rich in contemporary relevance due to its characteristically democratic dramaturgy. She argues that the glossing over of Brome's repertoire may constitute a significant omission in understanding the early modern canon since importantly, as Christopher Hill suggests, *A Jovial Crew* articulates a view of the world seen from 'below' (Hill 1996: 4). Through an examination of a production of *A Jovial Crew* mounted in Ballarat, Australia, in 2013, this chapter also suggests that Brome's perception of the road as a place of play and renewal creates a complex example of early modern meta-theatre.

Robert Stagg's chapter in Part III: Writing the Road tracks how actors and characters walk roads on stage, and how, in a theatre uncommitted to absolute realism, characters travel onstage roads without those roads appearing ludicrously short, foreshortened or abbreviated. It shows early modern drama practising how to stage a road, and how it may often do so through the 'road' of metre. This, he argues, forms part of what Sanders calls the 'cultural geography' of the road (Sanders 2011), thinking with McRae about how both theatre and travel forge communal experience. In verse drama, characters walk roads not only on their physical feet but on their metrical feet too. If a foot can speak (*Troilus and Cressida*, 4.5.56), or can be a verb as well as a noun (*The Tempest*, 1.2.382), then playwrights can aspire to a drama of walking that effaces the need for a road to be staged according to the conventions of (something like) realism. The prosodic foot can sport a sense of distance which the physical stage lacks. This chapter dwells upon what de Certeau calls the 'poaching' of territory in *Coriolanus*, and how this is achieved through the play's feet (both metrical and material). It concludes by wondering whether we might think of plays as a sort of journey, as well as featuring kinds of journey – with the two hours' 'traffic' of a stage instancing not only a kind of 'bargaining' or 'trade' but also a 'voyage or expedition'.

In the next chapter Paul Frazer explores how the metaphor of the road was used in early modern Britain in relation to religious and political identity by exploring the conversion of Saint Paul on the Road to Damascus. He reads this in relation to Philip Massinger's *The Renegado* (1623–4), a play famed for its portrayal of Christians converting to Islam, or 'turning Turk', and vice versa. Analysing the play's interest in the mobility and transformation of Saint Paul, he argues that the conversion of Paul is not only an important indication of Massinger's understanding of Protestant and Muslim belief, but also inflects the early modern experience of the road.

Marion Wynne-Davies's chapter quotes John Speed's *A Prospect of the Most Famous Parts of the World* (1627), which asserts that 'Heaven was too long a reach for man to recover at one step and therefore God first placed him upon the earth' (Speed 1627: 1). Maps, and the roads they depicted, were therefore not only useful for navigation on earth, but also a guide on the spiritual road to 'heaven'. For Speed and his readers, the material and spiritual spheres merge inextricably on the page. This chapter considers Margaret Cavendish's fictional accounts of road travel which are derived not from scientific exploration or a quest for spiritual truth, but from political necessity and harsh personal experience. Wynne-Davies argues that in order to understand the roads and journeys of Cavendish's 'blazing world', it becomes necessary to consider her material experience of space in both its political and personal evocations. The Duchess's fantastical narrative alludes to a host of material journeys: Willem Barentsz's attempt to discover a North-East passage; the protective delta of Antwerp; and the journeys to London and to Welbeck Abbey. The final confluence of the worlds occurs on the road through Nottinghamshire, as the Empress and the Duchess – in spirit form – fly above what is the A60 today. While Speed claims that 'Heaven was too long a reach', Cavendish's 'blazing world' both challenges and undermines any certainty, political, spiritual or gendered, on the roads of early modern Britain.

Finally, Martha Lynn Russell's chapter builds on those of Paul Frazer and Marion Wynne-Davies by focusing on another religious road of the early modern period: John Bunyan's road to the Celestial City in *The Pilgrim's Progress, Part I*. Instead of viewing this road as merely allegorical, this chapter argues that Bunyan's road, from the City of Destruction to the Celestial City, also follows a literal journey – of the topography and spatial grammars of England's Great North Road. Russell considers three cultural conceptions of early modern road infrastructure – transportation, drainage and fairs – alongside Bunyan's political and Anabaptist theology and contemporary government roads policy. During the seventeenth century, England's dilapidated, deteriorating roads could not hold travellers' carriages and merchandise and the lack of drainage made fields unproductive and town flooding frequent. Throughout the course of Bunyan's life, he witnessed the English government attempt to fix these problems with various acts, which, though good for the roads, were not received well, since the Turnpike Act of 1663 imposed tolls and the Drainage Act of 1600 required land from citizens. *The Pilgrim's Progress* directly rejects tolls at gates, and the unfixable Slough of Despond reflects England's unfixable wetlands and correlates there with Anabaptist understandings of salvation and doubt. Furthermore, Vanity Fair parodies fairs of the time to demonstrate the belief that Christians must experience alienation before entering the Celestial City. Contextualising it alongside roads, drainage and fair systems is crucial to this chapter's understanding of Bunyan's unique religious and political vision.

Collectively, these essays show that early modern roads are associated with danger, vagrancy, beggary, thieves and prostitutes, but also with freedom from social constraints, the idea of the travelling and wandering, and the masterlessness of a world without boundaries or limits. They could carry a sense of social rejection but also confer a cast of legitimacy that we seem to see reflected in the self-confidence of various travelling groups, including actors in their peripatetic wanderings around areas outside London. The road at this time suggests ominous illegitimate otherness and locates this in very particular geographical locations, local and national, with international implications. Contradistinctively, it supports both a conventional site for Christian conversion and a fundamental rejection of the conventions of the Christian worldview. Its use as a religious metaphor could reflect the status of the pilgrim, which in itself was somewhat ambiguous at the time, but it was also inflected by the sense of the likelihood of, or even necessity for, a crisis-encounter on the road, with perhaps even Jesus playing a kind of highwayman waiting to waylay you on the route of your legitimate business. The early modern road can also be understood in terms of a wider geographic network which may be in crisis from an economic perspective, or in disrepair from a legislative one, but nevertheless functions powerfully in terms of its cultural resonance, and is freighted with symbolism.

Works cited

Bonnemaison, Joël (2005), *Culture and Space: Conceiving a New Cultural Geography*, New York: Palgrave.
Certeau, Michel de (1984), *The Practice of Everyday Life*, trans. Steven F. Rendall, Berkeley and Los Angeles: University of California Press.

Cresswell, Tim (2003), 'Landscape and the Obliteration of Practice', in K. Anderson, M. Domosh, S. Pile and N. Thrift (eds), *Handbook of Cultural Geography*, London: Sage, pp. 269–81.
—— (2006), *On the Move: Mobility in the Modern Western World*, London: Routledge.
Dillon, Janette (2000), *Theatre, Court, and City 1595–1610*, Cambridge: Cambridge University Press.
Hill, Christopher (1996), *Liberty against the Law*, London: Allen Lane, Penguin.
Lefebvre, Henri (1976), 'Reflections on the Politics of Space', *Antipode* 8, pp. 30–7.
—— (1991), *The Production of Space*, trans. Donald Nicholson-Smith, Oxford: Blackwell.
—— (2009), 'Space and the State', in Neil Brenner and Stuart Elden (eds), *State, Space, World: Selected Essays*, trans. Gerald Moore, Neil Brenner and Stuart Elden, Minneapolis and London: University of Minnesota Press, pp. 223–53.
McRae, Andrew (2009), *Literature and Domestic Travel in Early Modern England*, Cambridge: Cambridge University Press.
Merleau-Ponty, Maurice (1962), *The Phenomenology of Perception*, London: Routledge & Kegan Paul.
Merriman, Peter (2007), *Driving Spaces: A Cultural-Historical Geography of England's M1 Motorway*, London: Blackwell.
Sanders, Julie (2011), *The Cultural Geography of Early Modern Drama, 1620–1650*, Cambridge: Cambridge University Press.
Speed, John (1627), *A Prospect of the Most Famous Parts of the World*, London.
Urry, John (2000), *Sociology Beyond Societies*, London: Routledge.

# I. Shakespeare's Roads

Chapter 1

The Low Road and the High Road: *Macbeth* and the Way to Scotland

Lisa Hopkins

Roads in early modern Britain were not only means of travel and communication. The major arteries which traversed the country (in many cases the foundation of our own modern transport network) were generally understood as a legacy of the Romans, making them core markers of civilisation. Roads were also spaces in their own right, conceptually separate from the landscape they traversed: Caxton (quoted here in Marie Collins's modernisation) declared that 'Moliuncius [i.e. Molmutius] was the thirteenth King of the Britons and the first to give them laws. He ordained that the ploughs of farmers, the temples of gods and the highways leading people to cities and towns, should possess the inviolability of sanctuary, so that everyone going to any of them for help or because of an offence he had committed should be safe against pursuit by all his enemies' (Collins 1978: 54). Roads here are figured as both sacred and also surprisingly active: they 'lead' the people who use them rather than lying there passively, as if agency lay with roads rather than with those who used them. Moreover, they are privileged spaces, protected by the writ of the king; those who use them are, or ought to be, safe.

However, when Shakespeare's characters cross into Celtic countries, roads stop working for them. In the real world, Elizabethan troops in Ireland were finding themselves baffled and bewildered by bogs and pathless, perilous countryside. In *Cymbeline*, Imogen cannot understand how it can be so difficult to reach Milford Haven when at one point she could actually see it; now, though, the road simply does not seem to go there. Even if it did, it would be rendered mysterious by the strong association between Welsh roads and the legendary figure Elen Luyddog, Helen of the Ways, supposedly the wife of Magnus Maximus (the Macsen Wledig of the *Mabinogion*). Elen is persistently connected with the Sarn Helen, the name given to the Roman road which runs through Wales from Aberconwy to Carmarthen, but which is not readily identifiable as Roman because it is so very far from straight, and whose name marks it as no king's highway but an explicitly feminised space. In Scotland, it is even harder to find the way, and it is also dangerous. Charles Nicholl notes that 'in January 1586 [Thomas] Morgan was recommending [Robert] Poley to Ambassador Chateauneuf as the "fit man" to deliver a certain "packet" to Scotland. He had been there before, and "knoweth the best ways to pass into Scotland"' (Nicholl 2002: 171).[1] This was rare and valuable knowledge, and it remained so. In 1584 the Border Warden Henry Scrope explained to Secretary Walsingham that a microclimate had made it impossible for him to negotiate the frontier region of Liddesdale:

> I set furthe, the weather being verie fayre everie where in all the countrie, till we came to the boundes of Lyddesdale, wher their was growen suche a terrible and foggie myst as is wonderfull to be uttred ... wherin my companye were merveouslie seperated and dispersed from me ... and all guydes who were there verie well acqueynted, were utterlie voyde of any knowledge where they were. (Robb 2018: 76)

His son, the younger Lord Scrope, took up his post in August 1593 and promised the Privy Council 'to send them a map of the Debatable Land as soon as he could find one'; this took until April 1597, and even then the one he located 'was forty-five years out of date', since it did not show the Scots Dyke, which had been constructed in 1552 (Robb 2018: 151–2). When Elizabeth died in March 1603, Robert Carey, who set off to carry the news to James VI in Edinburgh, was one of the few men in London who actually knew how to get there. Carey (to whom I shall return) habitually presents himself in his *Memoir* as both outsider and insider, a man who is not from Scotland but nevertheless knows his way around it, and leaves the reader in no doubt that this makes him unusual and important (Mares 1972: 172).

There were two principal routes to Scotland, which diverged at Islington:[2] via Berwick, and via Carlisle, which was that taken by English players such as the Lady Elizabeth's Men, who were in Carlisle sometime between 25 May and 28 September 1620 (Boyle 2017: 28). In Greene's *James the Fourth*, Eustace mentions 'the Countess Elinor / From Carlisle, where we oft have merry been' (1.3.35–6), implying that he too has travelled by that route, and it is also the route to which *Macbeth* implicitly directs our attention by the mention of Malcolm's appointment as Prince of Cumberland. The road north of Carlisle led past some interesting locations, including the Scots Dyke and Arthuret Church. The first of these is remarkable for its unremarkableness: posing no real physical obstacle at all, it shows how nugatory and permeable the Border was in most places, and how little there was to protect against incursion and invasion. The second suggested that not only the border between nations but also that between past and future might not be fully secure. Though the present building (funded by public subscription because James I considered the area to be without faith) dates from 1609, there was a church before that which had a supposed holy well in its graveyard and claimed a connection to King Arthur, who was said to have fought a battle nearby. The site of the Battle of Solway Moss, fought in 1542 between the English and the Scots, was also close. This was thus a road which, like the Sarn Helen in Wales, spoke not of the king's writ but of challenges to it, reminding travellers of a Scots defeat, of powers other than Christian ones, and of a king other than James who was foretold to return to reign once more.

If this road had elements of the uncanny, though, at least it *was* a road. Outside the towns of Carlisle and Berwick, there might not be roads at all. General Wade's Military Road, which now takes visitors to the Roman forts of Vindolanda and Housesteads, is a legacy of the '45, built to facilitate troop movements between Carlisle and Newcastle; in the sixteenth century Camden found this area so forbidding that he never reached the Roman fort at Housesteads, deterred by the lawless, reiving members of the Armstrong clan who inhabited it. (The Armstrongs, sometimes said to be descended from Siward, were perhaps the most notorious of the Border clans.) As a result, many of those who wished to pass between England and Scotland simply did not attempt land travel. When Mary, Queen of Scots fled into England, she had herself rowed across the Solway rather than risk passing through the Debatable Land north of Carlisle, and the unnamed narrator of the recently discovered account of Ben Jonson's 'Foot Voyage' sailed home from Leith via Brunt Island (Loxley et al. 2015: 97). In *James the Fourth*, too, the Scots king says to his English bride after their wedding, 'Then, lovely Doll, and all that favour me, / Attend to see our English friends at sea' (1.1.67–8). The clear implication is that the watery route into Scotland is safer than the dry one. Indeed some Scottish roads might lead clean out of the world; the Scots folk tale of Thomas the Rhymer (mentioned in Camden's *Britannia*) told of a traveller who met the fairy queen, who showed him three roads, to heaven, to hell, and one which led into fairyland through a door in the Eildon Hills. In this chapter, I look at the representation of Scottish roads in English Renaissance drama, particularly *Macbeth*, and show that they are consistently imaged as perilous, untrustworthy, and dangerously connected with the supernatural.

The story of Thomas the Rhymer is not the only example of a hint of the uncanny attaching itself to the idea of travel between the north and the south. The suggestion of entry into a dark, unreliable and uncanny world is also found in connection with another, later voyage to Scotland: James Loxley, Anna Groundwater and Julie Sanders note that 'a poem surviving in a single manuscript copy suggests that current Anglo-Scottish tensions made their presence felt on at least one occasion. Attributed to "J. Joshnston" (*sic*), it figures Jonson as an Orpheus descending into the dark ("scotos") hell to England's north' (Loxley et al. 2015: 152). The verse 'O ye'll take the high road and I'll take the low road, and I'll be in Scotland afore ye' is generally taken to be connected, like the Military Road, to the unsuccessful Jacobite rising in 1745, and to imply that the dead, whose souls travelled north underground from their graves, had an easier route home than those who had to make the journey physically. The actual idea of a low road from north to south predates it, though: in Anthony Brewer's play *The Lovesick King*, the importance of Newcastle's underground wealth is confirmed when Grim the Collier offers to march his seven hundred miners underground to London, a journey which he affirms will take no more than six days.[3] There was however an anxiety attached to the idea of the low road. As Bill Angus discusses in his chapter, in Shakespeare's *Richard II*, the king, in one of his typically self-pitying moments, declares that he is happy for his subjects to 'trample' on him once he is buried (3.3.156); as in our modern idea of walking over someone's grave, there is clearly an implication here of something inappropriate and disrespectful about walking over burial spots, and a sense of the uncanny and the disturbing thus attaches to the idea of the low road.

Travel to Scotland was an unappetising prospect for more practical reasons too. As Camden found, the region of the Border was inhabited by Reivers, over whom neither the English nor the Scottish crown could exercise effective control. The situation became so bad that the English town of Haltwhistle was burned by the Scots in June 1601, and the accession of James by no means brought immediate peace to the region. There can be no doubt that London audiences were aware of the disordered state of the Border: in Robert Greene's *James the Fourth* we meet 'Bohan, a Scot, attired like a Redesdale man' (1.1.1 s.d.), and Sir Bartram says,

> As welcome is my honest Dick to me
> As morning's sun, or as the wat'ry moon
> In mirkest night when we the borders track. (1.3.8–10)

Greene clearly expected his audience to know what a Redesdale man looked like (the editor's note explains that 'Redesdale man' is an emendation of the Quarto's meaningless 'rid-stall' suggested by W. L. Renwick, whose own name points clearly to Border ancestry, and who observed that 'to a London audience of 1590 it would mean "a Border reiver, one who belonged to the wild and lonely No-man's land on the edges of Scotland" . . . Thus Bohan would look wild and ferocious' (Greene 1970); the emendation is a wholly convincing one). Moreover, Leland had already remarked of Redesdale and the surrounding area that 'these parishes are frequented by the outriding men or thieves of the Scottish border' (Chandler 1993: 342). Shakespeare had particular reason to be aware of the troubled nature of the Border because his fellow King's Man Laurence Fletcher had worked for James before his accession and had lived in Edinburgh, and his former patron Lord Hunsdon, father of Robert Carey, also had extensive Border experience. Shakespeare certainly shows knowledge of Border affairs in *2 Henry IV*, where Pistol says, 'Thrust him downstairs? Know we not Galloway nags?' (2.4.185–6). The Penguin editor's note glosses this as prostitutes, but Alistair Moffat notes the importance of Galloway nags for Reivers, and observes that 'when the era of reiving came to an end at the beginning of the seventeenth century, it was specifically forbidden to own a pony of a certain value – in other words a good Galloway nag' (Moffat 2010: 57). The Border area was, then, well known to be dangerous.

Once actually over the Border, some early moderns might have doubted that there were roads to be had at all, given that the road-building Romans had never ventured further north than the Antonine Wall. Saxton's maps of Northumberland and Westmorland (which includes Cumberland) stop at the Scottish Border, and the lack of any equivalent for Scotland leaves the reader with no idea how to proceed. Even Ortelius was not particularly helpful, for the 1570 map of Europe in the *Theatrum* shows almost no habitation in central Scotland except 'Badanck' (Badenoch); the one of the British Isles shows many more settlements, but also suggests that the middle of the country is so mountainous that the only safe and practicable routes are likely to be coastal ones (Binding 2003: 216, 223). Caxton's account (again quoted here in Marie Collins's modernisation) was even more bewildering:

> It is commonly said that the country now called Scotland is a projection of the northern part of Great Britain and is separated from Britain by inlets of the sea at its southern end (being surrounded by the sea everywhere else). It was formerly called Albany after its first settler Albanactus, son of King Brutus, or else after the province Albania, a region of Scythia, close to the country of the Amazons . . . Finally it was known as Hibernia, just like Ireland. (Collins 1978: 143)

Here Scotland is disconcertingly both strange and familiar, part of Britain and yet not part of it, possibly named after the quintessentially

British King Brutus and possibly named after Albania, and presenting itself as an uncanny double of Ireland yet without actually *being* Ireland. More significantly, it is not quite clear that it is actually attached to Britain at all, for Caxton declares that it is 'a projection of the northern part of Great Britain' but also says that it is 'separated from Britain by inlets of the sea at its southern end'. Only a map could confirm that what he is talking about are the indentations made by the Solway and the Tyne and that there is solid ground between which allows the traveller to pass from one country into the other, and even then the comparison with Ireland might well discourage potential visitors from attempting the journey.

However, even the wildest country, if regularly traversed, develops the signs of a path, and Caxton does concede that there are some possible ways of finding Scottish locations, even if they are unorthodox ones, when he tells how Ungus, King of the Picts, brought the body of Saint Andrew back from Constantinople:

> Since he was uncertain what city to assign to Saint Andrew he fasted for three days, and he and his men prayed to the saint to show them what place was his choice. One of the guardians who watched over the body of Saint Andrew in Constantinople was warned in a dream to go to a place to which an angel would lead him, and so he reached Scotland with seven companions, going to the top of a hill called Ragmund. At that very moment a light shone from heaven and surrounded the King of the Picts on his way to a place called Carcenan. (Collins 1978: 148)

Here there is no road (indeed much of this journey must have been accomplished by sea) but there is a way, which is picked out by a series of supernatural lighting effects.

There was also the evidence of more recent times that it was possible for those with knowledge of the terrain to find their way to and from Scotland: James VI and his retinue came down from it in 1603, and Ben Jonson and John Taylor the Water Poet were only two of various Renaissance adventurers to walk to Scotland, both in 1618. Such journeys demonstrated that the road out of England did not simply stop at the Scottish Border, leaving a pathless and unmapped waste in its place; indeed Taylor, who started his walk to Scotland six days after Jonson's, was surprised to notice no differences when he first crossed the Border, while Jonson and his unnamed companion were alerted to the event by a special ceremony. When they left Berwick,

> After dinner we took our journey, brought out of town with all the knights, gentlemen, mayor and aldermen; two miles out of town was wine ready, where Sir William had sent a company of musketeers who gave us a volley of

shot. Sir William could not contain himself of tears when he took his leave. (Loxley et al. 2015: 85)

This is exciting – a little bit like the crossing of the line ceremony on an ocean liner – but also potentially faintly ominous: as Jonson's party crosses into Scotland, his host of the night before begins to weep. Jonson and his companion were being guided at this point, a reminder that there were always routes between England and Scotland for those who knew the terrain. In some modern novelisations of *Macbeth*, the authors include explicit reference to a map of all or part of Scotland, even if it is a map that is only just being made (Hopkins 2018), but the play itself implies a world in which this is not necessary; Banquo knows the way to Forres, even if he does not know how far it is (1.3.39), and other characters have no doubt of their ability to find Scone, Dunsinane or St Colm's Inch. It is particularly instructive in this respect to consider the various journeys undertaken by Sir Robert Carey, youngest son of the aforementioned Border Warden (and patron of Shakespeare) Lord Hunsdon, who in 1592 became deputy to his brother-in-law Lord Scrope in Carlisle and was subsequently promoted to Warden of the East March, where he rather uncannily faced as his opposite number on the other side of the Border his near-namesake Sir Robert Ker. As Carey somewhat understatedly remarks of his time as a Border Warden, 'we had a stirring world, and few days passed over my head but I was on horseback, either to prevent mischief, or to take malefactors';[4] when he raided a Reivers' tower (possibly Netherby) he saw a boy riding away and was warned that 'he will be in Scotland within this half hour, and he is gone to let them know that you are here, and to what end you are come'. At the heart of Carey's difficulties lay the problem of local knowledge: 'the first care I took, was to cleanse the country of our inbred fears, the thieves within my March, for by them most mischief was done: for the Scotch riders were always guided by some of them in all the spoils they made' (Mares 1972: 48).

Before, during and after his time as a Warden, Carey made a number of trips to Scotland, which collectively show the dangers of the route. In his *Memoirs*, he notes that in summer 1583 'I went with Mr. Secretary Walsingham into Scotland, he being sent thither Ambassador from her Majesty; it pleased the King at that time to take such a liking of me, as he wrote earnestly to the Queen at our return to give me leave to come back to him again'; however, the queen countermanded this proposed second journey so Carey went to Ostend instead (Mares 1972: 5). After the execution of Mary, Queen of Scots,

> (few or none being willing to undertake that journey) her Majesty sent me to the King of Scots, to make known her innocence of her sister's death, with letters of credence from herself to assure all that I should affirm.
>
> I was waylaid in Scotland, if I had gone in, to have been murdered: but the King's Majesty, knowing the disposition of his people, and the fury they were in, sent me to Berwick, to let me know that no power of his could warrant my life at that time; therefore to prevent further mischief, he would send me no convoy, but would send two of his council to the bound-rode, to receive my letters, or what other message I had to deliver. (Mares 1972: 7–8)

In 1588, 'I should then have been sent ambassador to the King of Scots, but could not by reason of my sickness' (Mares 1972: 11), so instead in 1589 he made one of the 'wager journeys' of which early modern England was so fond (Parr 2015): 'having given out some money to go on foot in twelve days to Berwick, I performed it that summer, which was worth to me two thousand pounds, which bettered me to live at court a good while after' (Mares 1972: 12). Shortly afterwards Carey annoyed the queen by marrying without her consent, but seized the opportunity of another trip to Scotland to reinstate himself in her favour:

> My brother Sir John Carey, that was then Marshal of Berwick, was sent to by the King of Scots to desire him that he would meet his Majesty at the bound-rode at a day appointed; for that he had a matter of great importance to acquaint his sister the Queen of England withal ... My brother sent him word he would gladly wait on his Majesty, but durst not until he had acquainted the Queen therewith ... She was not willing that my brother should stir out of the town, but knowing ... that I was in court, she said, 'I hear your fine son that has lately married so worthily, is hereabouts; send him if you will to know the King's pleasure.' ... Sir, said I, If she be on such hard terms with me, I had need to be wary what I do. If I go to the King without her licence, it were in her power to hang me at my return. (Mares 1972: 29)

Luckily the queen seems to have thought this was funny; she granted him a safe-conduct and he went first to Carlisle, where he stayed the night with his wife, then to Berwick, and thence to Edinburgh.

Finally, when the queen died,

> I returned and took horse between nine and ten o'clock, and that night rode to Doncaster. The Friday night I came to my own house at Widdrington ... Very early on Saturday I took horse for Edinburgh, and came to Norham about twelve at noon, so that I might well have been with the King at supper time: but I got a great fall by the way, and my horse with one his heels gave me a great blow on the head that made me shed much blood. (Mares 1972: 62–3)

Catherine Loomis has suggested that Carey's bloodstained state on arrival is echoed in *Macbeth* by Duncan's question 'What bloody man is that?' (1.2.1), and there is certainly a faint suggestion of the uncanny about the encounter: Carey recalls that James 'asked what letters I had from the Council' (Mares 1972: 63), to which the answer was none because he had come on his own initiative, but he did have 'a blue ring' which he showed the king, who replied, 'it is enough: I know by this you are a true messenger' (Mares 1972: 64). The ring, which Carey's sister Philadelphia had apparently taken from the queen's dead finger and thrown out of the window to her waiting brother, had never before been seen by James, but seems almost to have spoken to him.

I want to build on Loomis's suggestion by arguing that there are in fact several suggestive points of similarity between Carey's journey and *Macbeth*'s representation of travel in Scotland. Carey brings news of death and of ascension to power; so too do the Weird Sisters. In both encounters there is also a suggestion of untrustworthiness: the king is not sure whether to believe Carey, and Carey certainly concludes afterwards that he was wrong to trust James, lamenting that after his accession James 'deceived my expectation' (Mares 1972: 65). It is also worth paying attention to Carey's complaint that Scots came into his March and cut wood (Mares 1972: 23–4, 55), because there is a sense in which this is an exact reversal of what the English army will do as they approach Dunsinane. Obviously the English want the wood for disguise rather than firing, and are unknowingly fulfilling the Weird Sisters' prophecy that Birnam will move, but reading Carey helps us to see that the episode also echoes a traditional format of cross-Border warfare.

A more general point worth remembering in the context of *Macbeth* is that travel along early modern roads, on horseback or on foot, was at a much slower pace than a twenty-first-century person can easily appreciate, allowing time to absorb details of the landscape and vicinity; Loxley et al. calculate Jonson's walking speed for at least some of the route as 3.2 mph (2015: 118–19), and suggest that 'to the walkers travelling through it, the landscape itself was in movement' (2015: 141). The idea of landscape as an active agent is found in a number of early modern contexts, including George Peele's play *Edward I*, where Queen Eleanor wishes that if she is telling lies the ground may open and swallow her (she is, and it does), and the doom paintings found in many churches (though sometimes whitewashed over by Shakespeare's time) in which rocks move and the dead rise from the ground.

Macbeth offers a series of sickening disjunctions between things which ought to be still but are in fact in movement, and things which ought to move but are in fact still. The 'travelling lamp' (2.4.7), logically a lamp for people who are travelling, is syntactically travelling itself; the earth bubbles as if it were water (1.3.79); the Captain figures the combatants as two men who should be swimming, but have rendered each other motionless (1.2.89). If we think of how a traveller would experience it, the wood *does* move, and as Macbeth watches it advance on him, he is placed in the position of a traveller, even though he is standing on the battlements. There is a temporal displacement here too: until this moment, he has been the one making the running towards the future; now, it is rushing upon him.

For all the play's interest in travel, the word 'road' does not appear in *Macbeth* (I will consider later why it does not), but the idea is recurrently implicit. In the first place, there are two references to ditches: the First Murderer says of Banquo 'safe in a ditch he bides, / With twenty trenchèd gashes on his head, / The least a death to nature' (3.4.26–8) and one of the ingredients of the Weird Sisters' cauldron is 'Finger of birth-strangled babe / Ditch-delivered by a drab' (4.1.30–1). Ditches are found only in conjunction with roads; like modern gutters, they are both parallel and antithetical to roads, there in order *not* to be walked on but rather to act as receptacles for the water, filth and debris that would otherwise impair the functioning of the road. In the second place, *Macbeth* is full of images of journeying, sometimes physical, sometimes spiritual, sometimes tinged with both, always fraught with peril. Travelling in the play is difficult and tiring – Lady Macbeth says 'When Duncan is asleep, / Whereto the rather shall his day's hard journey / Soundly invite him' (1.7.62–4) – but above all it is dangerous, and particularly so because physical journeys are so often also spiritual ones. Living bodies move from place to place; dead ones are carried, for kings of Scotland, as the play reminds us, were invariably buried at Iona (including Macbeth). On the road, people change from alive to dead and meet creatures whom they consider to be not of their world. On roads, people understand themselves to be travelling either towards heaven or towards hell.

Any road led to somewhere immediate, but always potentially to somewhere further too; the roads in *Macbeth*, like those in the story of Thomas the Rhymer, go further still, for they lead potentially clean out of the material world. The three witches, who collectively recall the Celtic triple goddess, have access to three different routes: the actual physical road on which Macbeth and Banquo are travelling; a network of sea and air lanes which connect them to places as far away as Aleppo; and, most troublingly of all, the future. Macbeth asks 'why / Upon this blasted heath you stop our way' (1.3.76–7), implying that he and Banquo are on a track or path rather than an actual road, but nevertheless when they meet the Weird Sisters Macbeth and Banquo stand poised at a metaphorical if not a literal crossroads. For Banquo, the road alongside the palace also leads beyond itself: to death for him, while for Fleance these are the first steps on a path that will lead him to Wales, and to a destined future as progenitor of the Stuarts. Macbeth tells the first two murderers that the killings 'must be done tonight, / And something from the palace' (3.1.131–2), and the murderers collectively give the audience a strong sense of the spot appointed as on a busy if potentially dangerous route. First Murderer says,

> Now spurs the lated traveller apace
> To gain the timely inn, and near approaches
> The subject of our watch. (3.3.5–7)

Although it need not be the case that Banquo and 'the lated traveller' are the same person, they are syntactically and imaginatively connected, creating an impression of Banquo as on a route appointed for travel, in that it is provided with inns, but where one would not want to linger after dark, for roads were particularly dangerous at night. In *A Midsummer Night's Dream*, Puck speaks of how

> Damnèd spirits all,
> That in cross-ways and flood have burial,
> Already to their wormy beds are gone,
> For fear lest day should look their shames upon. (3.2.380–3)

In explicitly declaring that the spirits have gone, Puck also implicitly reminds us that at one point they were there, but they can only come out in the dark. *Macbeth* too heightens our sense of the danger of travel at night. Loxley et al. note that 'if the way is one important vector in the experience of the walk as mapped out, performed and experienced, equally significant are the planned and happenstance stopping places enjoyed by the walkers, both the middle-ranking – the inns and postmasters' households ... and the elite, the estates of noble and gentry families' (Loxley et al. 2015: 137); Sanders also observes elsewhere that 'the locations that remain crucial on the spectrum of hospitality that is tested by the penniless pilgrim in general, and by Taylor's performance in particular, are those stopping places central to Yi-Fu Tuan's sense of how space makes place: inns, alehouses and households' (Sanders 2013: 18). The mention of an inn thus positions Banquo, like Duncan, as being 'in double trust', both as a guest in the palace and as a traveller who ought to be able to rely on an inn for refuge, and it reminds us too that even a road which was safe by day might be a very different place by night.

Banquo never reaches an inn. In fact, the spot appointed for the murders proves to be the end of the road in more senses than one:

> FIRST MURDERER His horses go about.
> THIRD MURDERER Almost a mile – but he does usually,
> So all men do, from hence to th'palace gate
> Make it their walk. (3.3.12–15)

This is a place where everyone dismounts, sending their horses off to the stable but themselves taking a shortcut direct to the palace. It is thus a place where journeys on horseback come to a halt and journeys on foot begin, but it is also a place which is, for Banquo at least, the beginning of a road of a different sort, as Macbeth says, 'Banquo, thy soul's flight, / If it find Heaven, must find it out tonight' (3.1.141–2). Like Macbeth on the battlements of Dunsinane, Banquo is standing still on a physical spot, but it is a spot which also has temporal and metaphysical dimensions, and in those terms he is travelling even at the moment at which his physical body permanently ceases to move.

Why are none of these roads actually called roads? On the first and most obvious level, the absence of the word 'road' gives us the impression of somewhere wild. The second reason is that in the context of the Border, 'roads' already meant something else: in his *Memoirs*, Robert Carey records that 'The winter being begun, there was roads made out of Scotland into the East March, and goods were taken three or four times a week' (Mares 1972: 33–4), and says of his opposite number Sir Robert Ker that 'to make open road upon the March would but show his malice' (Mares 1972: 37). Perhaps most importantly, it creates the impression of a moral as well as a literal tracklessness. The idea that a physical choice of path or route had spiritual and moral implications was well established on the early modern English stage. In *Macbeth*, 'as I descended' has an obvious symbolic significance as well as a spatial one, since Macbeth is not only coming down the stairs but engaged in murdering his king and guest, and he has earlier envisaged Malcolm as an obstacle lying across his path:

> The Prince of Cumberland: that is a step
> On which I must fall down, or else o'er-leap,
> For in my way it lies. (1.4.49–51)

Lady Macbeth implies a similar idea when she declares, 'Yet do I fear thy nature, / It is too full o'th'milk of human kindness, / To catch the nearest way' (1.5.15–17), and Macbeth is still worrying about whether routes are negotiable or not when he says, 'But here, upon this bank and shoal of time, / We'd jump the life to come' (1.7.6–7). Almost more alarming is his vision of a network of heavenly routes which know nothing of obstacles or bars:

And pity, like a naked new-born babe,
Striding the blast, or Heaven's cherubim, horsed
Upon the sightless couriers of the air,
Shall blow the horrid deed in every eye
That tears shall drown the wind. (1.7.21–5)

The personified pity and the heavenly messengers can go wherever they want, and have universal access. They thus present a striking contrast with Macbeth's final image of the journey he himself is on:

I am in blood
Stepped in so far, that should I wade no more,
Returning were as tedious as go o'er. (3.4.137–9)

Macbeth figures himself as having in effect no control at all: the tide of blood, too strong for him to fight against, has him in its power. Even though it is not termed so, this is a road on which one cannot turn back.

Perhaps the most surprising absence in the play, though, is not the lack of mentions of the word 'road', but the fact that there is no suggestion at all of travel to one particular place. In Macbeth's Scotland, there are roads to Forres, Scone, Inverness and St Colm's Inch, but there are none that are said to lead to Edinburgh. This is all the more striking because the city is explicitly mentioned in Greene's *James the Fourth* – 'I must to Edinburgh unto the king' (5.1.40) – which looks suspiciously like a source for *Macbeth* when we find in the Additional choruses, Chorus VIII, the stage direction 'Enter four kings carrying crowns' (132). In any case, Edinburgh was famous, and it also carried a potential symbolic charge. Loxley et al. note that 'Edinburgh was not only the Scottish capital . . . but also the birthplace of the king himself' and that 'at least one panegyrist had already suggested [the journey to Edinburgh] was a British Protestant alternative to the Camino de Santiago' (Loxley et al. 2015: 145–6). This refers to the anonymous 1604 *Northerne poems congratulating the Kings majesties entrance to the crowne*, which comments censoriously on how

The foolish Pilgrime oft to Spayne doth post,
O Sacred *Iames* to worship thy drye scull:
But he that's wise forhights the Spanish cost,
Iberus waters now are venim full.
If though [thou] thy conscience seeke or purse to fill,
Spaine can in neither satisfie thy will.
England (O Pilgrim) keepes Saint *Iames* aliue,
Whome thou maiest loue, long may it him preserue. (Anon 1604: sig. B4^r)

The year before *Macbeth*, Shakespeare had written *All's Well That Ends Well*, which gestures at the Camino de Santiago when Helena sends her mother-in-law the countess a letter informing her that '*I am Saint Jaques' pilgrim, thither gone*' (3.4.4, italics in original). In the event Helena turns away from the Camino and fetches up in Florence. For Richard Wilson, '*All's Well* turns away from the Pyrenees to disavow the ultramontanes' (Wilson 2004: n.p.). That cannot be the motive for Shakespeare's decision the next year to keep away from Edinburgh, and yet I think Edinburgh is a very noisy silence in *Macbeth*.

What is the reason for the play's apparent ignorance of James's capital? Shakespeare cannot possibly have failed to have heard of it. He might possibly have been aware that the oldest surviving part of the castle, St Margaret's Chapel, was founded by Malcolm's wife, and thus be observing chronological decorum by implying that at the time of *Macbeth* Edinburgh was not yet an important settlement, but the hats and clocks of the Roman plays are abundant evidence that he does not normally let such considerations trouble him. Does he shy away from it for a variant on the reason that Wilson suggests obtains in *All's Well*, that he does not want to be too political, or because to recall James's birth is also inevitably to recall James's mother, another pointed absence from *Macbeth*? Given how soon *Macbeth* follows on from *All's Well*, it seems to me that the studied avoidance of Saint James in one and the avoidance of Edinburgh in the other (not to mention the choice of the name 'Iago' for the villain of the 1604 *Othello*) might be connected, and meant with intent. There is a definite suggestion of miracle in *All's Well* when the apparently virgin Helena appears visibly pregnant, but the idea of miracle is kept well away from the idea of Compostela. There is also a clear suggestion of the numinous in *Macbeth*, even if only by implication as the expected opposite of the hellish, but it is kept well away from Edinburgh, and the locus of the play's real power is not male and royal but female and disorderly. The road into Scotland operates according to a logic of its own: it takes us not towards Edinburgh and James, but on a much stranger and more destiny-laden trajectory which implies that the physical landscape is always potentially a metaphysical one too, and that the ultimate destination will be not a Scottish city but either heaven or hell, besides which kings and their power dwindle into insignificance. For Shakespeare, the road into Scotland offers little safety and many risks. There is a faint chance that Pity might be riding above it, or that St Colm's Inch might stretch its protection along it, but it is equally possible that Weird Sisters will spring out of the ground. Either way, the king's writ does not run on it, as James had to warn Robert Carey that his would not in 1587, and indeed its very existence serves to suggest that there are powers in Scotland older and greater than that of the king.

Notes

1. Poley was later to be one of the three other men in the room in which Marlowe died, and I have speculated elsewhere that Marlowe might have been intending to visit Scotland at the time (Hopkins 2006).
2. Loxley, Groundwater and Sanders have a very helpful map showing both (Loxley et al. 2015: 117).
3. Although it was not published until 1655, M. Hope Dodds argues that Brewer's play was certainly written for one of James I's two visits to Newcastle in 1603 and 1617 and that the likelier is in 1617, since there would not have been time to prepare it in 1603, when he was there from 9 to 13 April on his way south after the death of Elizabeth (Dodds 1924: 164).
4. It is unclear whether Carey knew that he was quoting *Coriolanus*, where a Servingman says, 'Why, then we shall have a stirring world again' (4.5.221–2).

Works cited

Anon. (1604), *Northerne poems congratulating the Kings majesties entrance to the crowne*, London: J. Windet for E. Weaver.

Binding, Paul (2003), *Imagined Corners*, London: Headline.

Boyle, Nicola (2017), 'The Documentary History and Repertory of the Lady Elizabeth's Men', unpublished PhD thesis, De Montfort University.

Chandler, John (1993), *John Leland's Itinerary: Travels in Tudor England*, Stroud: Sutton.

Collins, Marie (1978), *Caxton: The Description of Britain*, New York: Weidenfeld & Nicolson.

Dodds, M. Hope (1924), '"Edmund Ironside" and "The Love-Sick King"', *The Modern Language Review* 19.2 (April), pp. 158–68.

Greene, Robert (1970), *James the Fourth*, ed. Norman Sanders, London: Methuen.

Hopkins, Lisa (2006), 'Was Marlowe Going to Scotland When He Died, and Does It Matter?', in J. R. Mulryne and Takashi Kozuka (eds), *Shakespeare, Marlowe, Jonson: New Directions in Biography*, London: Ashgate, pp. 167–82.

—— (2018), 'A Man with a Map: The Millennial Macbeth', in A. J. Hartley (ed.), *Shakespeare and Millennial Fiction*, Cambridge: Cambridge University Press, pp. 145–58.

Loomis, Catherine (2001), '"What Bloody Man Is That?": Sir Robert Carey and Shakespeare's Bloody Sergeant', *Notes and Queries* 246 (September), pp. 296–8.

Loxley, James, Anna Groundwater and Julie Sanders (2015), *Ben Jonson's Walk to Scotland: An Annotated Edition of the 'Foot Voyage'*, Cambridge: Cambridge University Press.

Mares, F. H. (ed.) (1972), *The Memoirs of Robert Carey*, Oxford: Clarendon Press.

Moffat, Alistair (2010), *The Reivers*, Edinburgh: Birlinn.
Nicholl, Charles (2002), *The Reckoning*, 2nd edn, London: Vintage.
Parr, Anthony (2015), *Renaissance Mad Voyages: Experiments in Early Modern English Travel*, London: Ashgate.
Ravenhill, William (ed.) (1992), *Christopher Saxton's 16th Century Maps*, Shrewsbury: Chatsworth Library.
Robb, Graham (2018), *The Debatable Land: The Lost World between Scotland and England*, London: Picador.
Sanders, Julie (2013), 'The *Pennyles Pilgrimage* of John Taylor: Poverty, Mobility and Performance in Seventeenth-Century Literary Circles', *Rural History* 24.1, pp. 9–24.
Shakespeare, William (1969), *Richard II*, ed. Stanley Wells, Harmondsworth: Penguin.
—— (1977), *Henry IV, Part 2*, ed. P. H. Davison, Harmondsworth: Penguin.
—— (1979), *A Midsummer Night's Dream*, ed. Harold F. Brooks, London: Methuen.
—— (1990), *Macbeth*, ed. Nicholas Brooke, Oxford: Oxford University Press.
—— (2007), *All's Well That Ends Well*, ed. G. K. Hunter, London: Cengage Learning.
—— (2013), *Coriolanus*, ed. Peter Holland, London: Bloomsbury.
Wilson, Richard (2004), 'To Great St Jaques Bound: *All's Well That Ends Well* in Shakespeare's Europe', in Yves Peyré and Pierre Kapitaniak (eds), *Shakespeare et l'Europe de la Renaissance*, Paris: Actes du Congrès de la Société Française Shakespeare, <http://www.societefrancaiseshakespeare.org/document.php?id=847> (last accessed 7 May 2019).

Chapter 2

Uncolting Falstaff: The Oats Complex and Energy Crisis in *1 Henry IV*

Todd Andrew Borlik

> The proper way to explore humanity's new mutual relationships is via the exploration of new subject-matter. The first thing is to comprehend the subject-matter; the second to shape new relations. The reason: art follows reality. An example: the extraction and refinement of petroleum represents a new complex of subjects, and when one studies these carefully one becomes struck by quite new forms of human relationship. A particular mode of behaviour can be observed both in the individual and in the mass, and it is clearly peculiar to the petroleum complex. But it wasn't the new mode of behaviour that created this particular way of refining petrol. The petroleum complex came first, and the new relationships are secondary. . . . *Petroleum resists the five-act structure*; today's catastrophes do not progress in a straight line but in cyclical crises.
>
> Bertolt Brecht, 'Über Stoffe und Formen'

In his bid to theorise an epic theatre, Brecht carves out an approach situated at a crossroads where ecomaterialism meets actor-network theory.[1] There is, Brecht posits, a dialectic between 'stuff' and 'form' in which seemingly inert matter radiates an agency as significant as that of humans, transforming society and hence socially engaged art (Brecht 1974: 29–30). Innovations in petroleum refinement, for example, produce new relationships or networks, the complexity of which poses a problem for the modern dramatist since 'petroleum resists the five-act structure'. *Prima facie*, Brecht's concerns seem remote from Shakespeare's era. For Brecht, it is the unprecedented nature of these technological and social changes wrought by the 'stuff' of modernity that renders conventional theatrical forms, modes and structures obsolete. Yet an ecomaterialist lens will detect the existence of something like an 'oats complex' in sixteenth-century England. The increasing mobility of Shakespeare's culture helped spur him in his Second Henriad not only to expand the five-act structure into a tetralogy and violate the Aristotelian unity of place, but also to introduce characters and settings omitted from the Tudor Chronicles.

By deploying centaurian imagery and hinting at the architectural parallels between playhouse and inn-yard, Shakespeare brings the mobility of early modern culture on to the stage. Even more importantly, he reveals how this mobility was powered by more-than-human networks (fodder-horse-rider-road) that were redefining both the body and the body politic. Composed in the midst of a dire energy crisis, Shakespeare's *1 Henry IV* in particular offers an appealing test-case for extending the purview of the 'energy humanities' (Szeman and Boyer 2017) back to the early modern era.

Imagine a Hollywood film about the Iraq War in which a scene at a clandestine Al-Qaeda compound featuring a cabal of insurgents abruptly cuts to a truck stop off the New Jersey Turnpike. A group of disgruntled truckers huddle around their rigs cursing the price of gas. An uncannily similar *coup de théâtre* occurs in an oft-overlooked episode in *1 Henry IV*. From the rebel camp where Hotspur has hatched his treasonous revolt, the action shifts to a roadside inn outside London, where we eavesdrop on a conversation between two carriers.

> SECOND CARRIER Peas and beans are as dank here as a dog, and that is the next way to give poor jades the bots. This house is turned upside down since Robin Ostler died.
> FIRST CARRIER Poor fellow never joyed since the price of oats rose; it was the death of him. (2.1.8–13)[2]

This curious exchange is more than just a tour-de-force display of Shakespeare's mastery of working-class argot. It is a phenomenal example of his ability to humanise history from the bottom up, from the perspective of carriers – the early modern equivalent of truckers. But the scene goes beyond merely humanising history. As the First Carrier barks at Tom Ostler to soften the saddle and place cotton padding beneath it to relieve the chafing on the ridge between the horse's shoulder-blades, one might go so far as to say that here, even if only briefly, Shakespeare imagines English history from the point of view of a horse, its neck rubbed raw from over-riding and its bowels ravaged by enteritis brought on by an inadequate diet. The First Carrier's concern for his steed, as this chapter will unfold, stands in stark contrast to the attitudes of several other characters in *1 Henry IV*. But what other hay, as it were, might an ecocritic make of this extraordinary scene? Why has this horse been ridden to death's door? Why has the price of oats skyrocketed? And why might this trigger a fatal coronary in an ostler?

Rather than an expendable interlude designed merely for comic relief, the carrier scene possesses a thematic significance that would be difficult to overstate. The increasing sophistication of early modern transportation networks paved the way for a more complex mercantile economy and indirectly led to the demise of the feudal demesnial system, a profound social transformation that is, after all, the central narrative arc of Shakespeare's history plays. Like the Romans, the Tudors understood the economic and military importance of roadways, and Parliament passed several acts for their upkeep and expansion.[3] Road-building played a crucial role in the formation of modern nationhood, as Andrew McRae and others have documented, and the chorographical scope of the Second Henriad reflects the growing sophistication of transportation networks in sixteenth-century Britain.[4] The bracing realism of the carriers scene in *1 Henry IV* may also owe something to the playwright's first-hand knowledge of this profession and its hardships. Alan Stewart has shown that Shakespeare himself was personally acquainted with carriers and carrier inns, and must have made frequent use of their services to communicate and commute between Stratford and London (Stewart 2007). Fittingly, Shakespeare's name appears on a list of supporters of a 1611 bill in Parliament for the repair of highways (Schoenbaum 1977: 279–80). While the 'story of Shakespeare's life is', to quote the opening line of Schoenbaum's magisterial biography, 'a tale of two towns' (1977: 1), the road linking those two towns deserves ecocritical scrutiny. After all, the development of England's transportation grid had profound environmental consequences as well. This chapter will attempt to measure the ecological hoofprint of these transportation networks as depicted in the Elizabethan history play. Not only did the need to make the roads safe from thieves like Falstaff and his companions lead to deforestation, but the boom in personal transit caused a voracious drain on the nation's biomass resources. In this respect, the Second Henriad anticipates Henri Lefebvre's understanding of the 'fundamental triadic unity of space-time-energy' (1991: 13; Schmid 2008: 34) by reminding us that the movement of goods and persons was literally fuelled by oats and other crops, the availability of which was subject to the vagaries of the English climate. When Shakespeare composed *1 Henry IV* during the nadir of the Great Dearth, oats soared to their highest price ever recorded in early modern England. It should not, therefore, come as a surprise that Shakespeare would view the overconsumption of fodder and its displacement of crops for human sustenance as subjects of moral concern. In addition to undermining the chivalric heroism of the past, the *Henry IV* plays conduct a timely interrogation of the horse's role in a post-chivalric society as a means of personal transport. Specifically, the horse imagery that clusters around Hotspur and Falstaff betrays a lack of restraint or stewardship that marks them as unfit for either rule or friendship, whereas Shakespeare associates Prince Henry's equestrian management with the green virtue of temperance. In the context of a late Elizabethan energy crisis exacerbated by surging demand for fuel, the jabs at Falstaff's belly and Poins's stealing of Falstaff's horse pack an ecocritical punch.

While the gradual transition to the horse-drawn plough in early modern England improved agricultural efficiency, its biggest impact, John Landon argues, may have been in facilitating the most important transportation revolution prior to the advent of the automobile (2002: 270–2). Whereas oxen had been employed mainly in field-work, horses would be increasingly used for hauling and personal transit. In the sixteenth century, members of the 'middling orders' were also acquiring saddle horses, specifically for riding, at a growing rate (Edwards 2007: 2–3). In a related trend, transportation historians have noted a decline throughout the Tudor period in two-wheeled waggons and a corresponding rise in four-wheeled vehicles, a change indicative of swelling demand for 'passenger traffic'. In 1557 a foreign visitor observed that the English would never walk if they could ride (Thomas 1983: 29; Gerhold 1996: 157). As horse-drawn waggons and coaches became more commonplace, the pace and frequency of travel escalated. Shakespeare's awareness of his culture's reliance on horses can be gauged by the number of centaurs that gallop through his verse. Typically, as Eric C. Brown has remarked, the centaur in Renaissance culture signifies a half-repressed inner animality. For those interested in charting cross-species networks in early modern England, however, the centaur presents a sterling example of Shakespeare's capacity to think in terms of beast-human hybrids. While the Aztecs were reportedly flummoxed by the sight of Cortez's cavalry, Shakespeare's characters often revel in the ontological confusion created by a human on horseback. Claudius, for instance, praises a Norman rider who manages his steed with such grace he seems to be 'demi-natured' (4.7.73) with it. In *The Taming of the Shrew*, Biondello spouts some doggerel about the mounted rider confounding the distinction between singular and plural:

> I hold you a penny,
> A horse and a man
> Is more than one
> And yet not many. (3.2.81–4)

Few critics today would take Biondello's wager. From the perspective of actor-network theory, such banter primes the mind to perceive assemblages that cut across the species divide and defy the ordinary grammatical constructs that shape how we see the world. But such assemblages extend beyond the easily discernible fusion of horse and rider. They would also encompass the roads and carrier inns that sustained England's growing transportation infrastructure. It thus seems highly fitting that Shakespeare regarded the centaur as an apt namesake for a roadside inn. In *The Comedy of Errors* Antipholus spends the night at 'the Centaur' (2.2.2) and Othello, in his play, elopes with Desdemona to the 'Sagittary' (1.1.160). While these allusions foreshadow the characters' ensuing lapses of reason, it is not only befuddled foreigners or racial outsiders who become suspended in a state of incomplete metamorphosis. The names of these roadside inns reflect Shakespeare's understanding that the intensified mobility of his culture was forging new relationships between humans and other animals, as well as between province and metropolis.

Recent work in Animal Studies by the likes of Peter Edwards, Karen Raber and Bruce Boehrer has affirmed the titanic importance of the human-equine bond in early modern culture.[5] Yet far less attention has been given to the humble crops that helped cement this bond. The resources devoted to fuelling England's fleet of horses were considerable. According to a 1562 calculation, horses were fed fourteen pounds of hay, seven pounds of straw, a half-peck of peas, and a peck of oats per day.[6] As a key ingredient in fodder, oats were in effect the petrol of the early modern world, and a horse's prescribed ration of a peck per day was roughly equivalent to nine litres. As demand for travel grew, an increasing proportion of the nation's arable land had to be diverted for oats cultivation. Oats grow well in dank soil, and were thus the major crop in places such as the Peak District, the Staffordshire moorlands, the Yorkshire Dales, parts of Wales, Westmorland, Northumberland and Scotland (Thirsk 1967: 19, 50, 171). Though a few areas in the south such as Dartmoor and the Kentish Weald also raised oats, the bulk of it was grown in the very counties in revolt against the king in Shakespeare's Second Henriad. A northern rebellion would tend to catapult the price of oats skyward.

The affordability of oats was also subject to the vicissitudes of the British climate. During Henry IV's reign England had suffered a series of cool, damp summers that recurred on and off throughout the 'Little Ice Age' (Lamb 1982: 84–5, 195–8; Fagan 2000). Although one should not ignore the rifts between the medieval and early modern, this period of climatic turbulence creates a continuum between the medieval past depicted in these history plays and Shakespeare's early modern present. Citizens of both eras knew that agricultural prices could jump dramatically when harvests failed. During the lean years of 1555–6, the cost of oats vaulted to more than double what it had been the decade before. The years 1586 and 1590 also witnessed massive hikes due to inclement weather, but the worst spike occurred during the streak of wet summers between 1594 and 1596. In 1596 the already exorbitant price of oats doubled again, skyrocketing to a rate eleven times what it had fetched at the start of the century, a staggering 82 per cent above the norm. In fact in 1596 it hit the highest price ever recorded for oats in England in a two-hundred-year span between 1450 and 1649 (Hoskins 1964: 46; Thirsk 1967: 819–20, 602, 627; Fischer 1996: 91–5). The cost of peas and beans – two other fodder ingredients mentioned by Shakespeare's carriers – also soared to unprecedented levels at this time. *1 Henry IV* was written in late 1596 or early 1597, in the midst of what might be considered the greatest fuel crisis in early modern English history. Under these conditions, public awareness of an oats complex and the environmental toll of horse-powered mobility would have sharpened, particularly among those Londoners who commuted (as Shakespeare may have) to the provinces.

In response to this economic volatility, towns throughout England sought to regulate the market to prevent price-gouging. One Elizabethan law book prescribes 'hostelers do not sell hay, nor oats, but at reasonable prices' (Adames 1599: B4^v). Since oats were a major expense, early modern fuel merchants also seem to have devised various swindles for short-changing their customers. Beaumont's *The Knight of the Burning Pestle* mentions a few, praising the ostler at the Bell in Waltham as an exception to the rule:

> [Ostlero] will our palfreys slick with wisps of straw,
> And in the manger put them oats enough
> And never grease their teeth with candle-snuff. (Beaumont 1969: 2.368–70)[7]

Unlike cars, horses have no fuel gauge; there was no way to tell how much they had been fed or if their fodder had been sophisticated. When prices were high, workhorses might be allotted only grass pasturage, while cash-strapped farmers would reduce the amount of oats or, like the proprietor of the carriers' inn in *1 Henry IV*, substitute fetid ingredients. In Shakespeare's day, the task of monitoring the price and quality of horse fodder at inns like that depicted in *1 Henry IV* fell to the Ale-Taster. As he climbed his way up the hierarchy of civic government, Shakespeare's father occupied this post in the mid-1550s – not long after a streak of poor harvests had triggered a spike in the price of grains. These harsh conditions returned with a vengeance in the mid-1590s when his son William was writing the Second Henriad. Hamlet's proverb 'while the grass grows, [the horse starves]' (3.2.330) may have been already musty in 1600, but such sayings also reflect the hard economic circumstances of the time in which owners could not afford to feed their steeds properly. Shakespeare makes frequent allusions to horses suffering from galled 'withers' (a form of bursitis), a condition exacerbated by malnourishment. Emaciated horses would have been a common sight in the 1590s. In *The Taming of the Shrew*, Biondello describes Petruccio's mount as 'begnawn with the bots' (3.2.54) – an intestinal parasite whose presence the carriers in *1 Henry IV* blame on rotten fodder. This helps explain Gremio's bizarre quip: 'the oats have eaten the horses' (3.3.79). Such jests would have resonated with Shakespeare's audience precisely because they vent some of the growing discontent with the soaring cost of horse fodder.

As part of the 'vagrant economy', Elizabethan players would have kept a wary eye on the fluctuating price of oats.[8] Theatre historians have noted the decline in provincial touring in the late sixteenth century, and William Ingram has demonstrated that a major factor must have been the sheer economics of travel: the steep cost of fodder simply did not allow companies to turn a profit (1993). As companies invested money in permanent playhouses they would instead have sought to profit from this demand. When Oliver Woodliffe undertook in 1594 to retrofit the inn-yard at the Boar's Head – coincidentally the exact same name as the inn in *1 Henry IV* – as a playhouse, he specified that the builders construct not only a tiring house and stage but also 'an oat loft' (Berry 1986: 24). The oft-forgotten Boar's Head points to the correspondence between inns and playhouses, and its 'oat loft' is a useful reminder of the energy demands required to bring an audience to a performance.

Besides affecting commerce and the entertainment industry, the late Elizabethan fuel crisis had troubling implications for national defence. A striking illustration of this comes from a desperate letter, dated 31 December 1594, addressed to Lord Burghley from the head of the Berwick garrison:

> On St. Stephen's Day the whole horse garrison came to my house, saying they must either sell their horses or let them starve, for they could neither get in the 'palace' oats, peas, beans for money – which last they have always hitherto had on a dearth to shift with. But where there is nothing, it is hard shifting. (Bain 1894–6: 2.554)

The purpose of the Berwick garrison was to deter and repel invaders from Scotland. This same threat of a Scottish invasion, spearheaded by the fearsome Douglas, also dogs Shakespeare's Second Henriad. As Kevin De Ornellas remarks in his astute study of equine hunger in early modern England, 'anxieties of healthy consumption and healthy nationhood become inextricably linked within a cross-species vacuum of food supply' (2005: 114). It was proverbial in Shakespeare's day that 'a famine in England begins at the horse-manger' (Fuller 1662: 85).⁹ This was particularly true in the northern counties and in Scotland, where oats – notoriously defined by Samuel Johnson as 'a grain which in England is generally given to horses, but in Scotland supports the people' (1755: 18Kʳ) – were a staple of the peasant diet. Since food acts as a marker of both species and cultural identity, dearth threatens to corrode the boundaries not only between human and horse but also between England and Scotland.

In its broad outlines, the Second Henriad can be taken as dramatising England's transition from a feudal society of semi-autonomous regions to a centralised nation-state with imperial ambitions. This transition was abetted by affordable transportation and the shrinking of the distance between the periphery and the centre, between Northumberland and London. In other words, the consolidation of monarchial power in the metropolis was made possible by horse travel and an intensified level of agricultural development capable of sustaining a sophisticated transportation grid. *1 Henry IV* repeatedly calls attention to the emergence of such a grid. More to the point, it suggests that the efficient use of this grid in times of scarcity translates into political power over the realm.

Paul Frazer has cogently argued that Prince Hal's victory 'relies upon his recognition and appropriation of the mobile energies of the nation's lower orders' (2013: 1) who walked rather than rode. But for the swelling number of middling classes who preferred to travel by horse or coach, this mobility came at a steep price in ecological terms. With his knack for expressive metaphors that leap across the species barrier, Shakespeare conveys how political disorder and immoderate consumption harm both humans and non-humans alike. In an odd stage direction in *Richard II*, the King touches the ground as if exercising the monarch's reputed power to cure through the laying on of royal hands: 'Dear earth, I do salute thee with my hand / Though rebels wound thee with their horses' hoofs' (3.2.6–7). In the opening scene of *1 Henry IV*, Bolingbroke has stolen not only Richard's crown but also his imagery, proclaiming that with the recent truce cavalry will no longer trample roughshod over England and 'bruise her flow'rets with the armèd hoofs / Of hostile paces' (1.1.8–9). Both speeches imagine the hoofprints of rebel horses harming a sentient earth. These images convey a sense of the ecological violence perpetrated by war. As the preceding pages have illustrated, horses did wound England's natural economy but with their stomachs rather than their hooves. Given the play's abiding interest in horse-power, it is significant that Henry immediately draws a contrast between the hoof-scarred roads of England and the Holy Land 'over whose acres walked those blessèd feet' (1.1.25) of Christ. Shakespeare evokes a sense of the holiness of the Holy Land by picturing it as free from the tramp of cavalry. As Henry's ensuing pun on 'bootless' (1.1.29) suggests, he wishes not simply to launch a crusade but to undertake a barefoot pilgrimage to Jerusalem. The speech revives a medieval regard for walking as a devotional act that imitates the humility of Christ. In contrast, the over-reliance on horses (and later carriages) for transport becomes a symptom of the degeneracy of the early modern world.

King Henry's dream of a cavalry-less Britain is abruptly punctured by news of a 'post from Wales, loaded with heavy news' (1.1.37). Soon afterwards Walter Blunt arrives, 'new lighted from his horse, / Stained with the variation of each soil' (1.1.63–4). Riding furiously, Blunt has travelled all the way from Northumberland and the dirt of each shire between Holmedon and London now clings to his armour. The line could be an encrypted stage direction, calling for the actor to besmear himself with soil. This dirt serves as a visual emblem of the materiality of the earth. Like the blood on the wounded Captain in *Macbeth*, the soil on Blunt acts as a marker of offstage violence and exertion that cannot be crammed within the Wooden O. Like stage directions calling for a character to enter in 'riding boots', it is a visual synecdoche for the network of roads that criss-cross England upon which so much of the plot of *1 Henry IV* depends. Just as Brecht observed that 'petroleum resists the five-act structure', Shakespeare understood that the new transportation networks defied the mimetic limitations of the Elizabethan stage. In his history plays, Shakespeare disregards the Aristotelian unity of place to better convey the vast geographical dimensions of the realm. Shakespeare would have found a precedent for Brecht's epic approach in Renaissance chorography – a genre that Michael Drayton was already versifying while composing history plays for the Admiral's Men, including his *1 Henry IV* spin-off *Sir John Oldcastle*. In dramatising chorography, Shakespeare manages to underscore not only the regional divisions within the realm that threaten its stability but also the profound ecological costs of seeking to conquer and govern an immense expanse of territory.

The Carriers and Blunt are not the only characters in the play reliant on horse-power. In fact so much travelling occurs in *1 Henry IV* that one critic has dubbed it a Shakespearean 'road movie' (Hertel 2010: 56). The aptly named Hotspur is an indefatigable traveller and rabid equiphile. In the latter respect he resembles his Elizabethan descendant, the ninth Earl of Northumberland, who employed no fewer than fifty-seven stable-hands between 1585 and 1632 (Edwards 2007: 38). In the two plus hours' 'traffic' of the play, Hotspur travels from the Scottish border to Windsor to Northumberland to Wales to Shrewsbury

– a journey of over 1,000 miles. Ralf Hertel has recently accounted for Hotspur's 'super-human speed' as duplicating the 'logic of cartography' (2010: 56). But on a literal level his speed is really super-human because it exploits the vehicular power of the horse. Given the mileage he racks up, small wonder Hotspur 'speak[s] terms of manège to [his] bounding steed' (2.4.44) in his sleep. Like the French Dauphin in *Henry V* who composes a sonnet in praise of his horse (3.7.36), Hotspur rambles on incessantly about its beauty, and perversely fetishises it as an object of erotic desire in preferring it to his wife. When he prophesies 'that roan shall be my throne' (2.4.65) the rhyme underscores the connection between horse-power and political power. By the end of the sixteenth century, however, the art of equestrian manège was already becoming an anachronism, as the nobility gradually transformed itself from a warrior class into a leisure class. Throughout the early modern period the horse underwent a corresponding transformation from a weapon of war to a means of personal transport.

The character in *1 Henry IV* who most obviously reflects this transformation is the fat knight Falstaff. Rather than bridling his horse, Falstaff's inability to control his appetites renders him horse-like, and an 'unyoked' (1.1.193) one at that. Whereas Hotspur dreams of riding whilst asleep, Falstaff is discovered during a booze-induced doze 'snorting like a horse' (2.5.534). Falstaff invites Hal to 'call [him] horse' (2.5.195) if he tells a lie – when he is of course lying. Paradoxically, he later imagines himself as a 'brewer's horse' (3.3.9), that is, a workhorse, when he has been forced to walk on foot. Even his celebrated 'honour prick[s] me on' (5.1.129) speech, despite its critique of Hotspurian chivalry, exposes his transhuman merger with his steed, which he regards more or less as a superior set of prosthetic legs. While much ink has been spilled over Shakespeare's changing of Oldcastle's name to Falstaff, less attention has been paid to the fact that the Oldcastle character in *The Famous Victories of Henry V* had the revealing name of Jockey.

During the Gad's Hill robbery, Poins plays a practical joke on Falstaff, the thrust of which has not been fully appreciated by Shakespeare scholars: he steals his horse. It is sadly fitting that Falstaff's gut protrudes out so far that he cannot see his own feet. Accustomed to riding everywhere, he can now scarcely walk up an incline unaided: 'Eight yards of uneven ground is threescore and ten miles afoot with me' (2.2.25–6). The 'uncolted' Falstaff seems to parody Richard III's outburst in a line that should be equally notorious: 'Give me my horse, you rogues, give me my horse, and be hanged!' (2.2.29–30). Falstaff then underscores his distress at having to walk by punningly protesting that the robbery was 'so forward and afoot too' (2.2.46–7). The play also comments on how

Falstaff's massive girth increases the burden of his mount. Among the colourful insults hurled at Falstaff, 'horse-back-breaker' (2.5.246) serves as a retrospective justification of Poins's gag. Whereas the travellers he robs decide to walk to 'ease' their horses' legs (2.2.79), Falstaff thinks only of his own discomfort: 'I'll not bear my own flesh so far afoot again for all the coin in thy father's exchequer' (2.2.35–6). The verb 'bear' here is highly suggestive. It bespeaks Falstaff's centaurian consciousness of his own body as not only vehicle but also rider. In a culture where vehicular travel has become the norm, walking comes to be perceived as onerous. Falstaff, the play insinuates, has not grown fat on sack alone.

Just as sociologists today link obesity and car culture, some early modern social critics feared that increased reliance on horse-transportation was promoting both moral and physical lassitude. The Elizabethan satirist Thomas Nashe advocated reviving a draconian cure:

> The Roman censors, if they lighted upon a fat corpulent man, they straight away took away his horse, and constrained him to go afoot; positively concluding his carcase was so puffed up with gluttony or idleness. If we had such horse-takers amongst us, and that surefeit-swollen churls who now ride on their foot-cloths might be constrained to cary their flesh budgets from place to place on foot, the price of velvet and cloth would fall with their bellies. (Nashe 1592: E2^v)

So, too, would the price of oats. Whether or not this passage supplied Shakespeare with a source for the uncolting of Falstaff, it reveals a moral impetus behind Poins's prank. Its purpose is not simply to avoid staging horses or to comment on the obsolescence of chivalry (Levin 1976: 121–30). It is a theatre of punishment directed at environmentally irresponsible behaviour that was aggravating an Elizabethan energy crisis.

Hal follows Nashe's prescription again when he deliberately procures 'the fat rogue a charge of foot' (2.5.548). When he breaks the news to Falstaff, the knight sighs, 'would it had been of horse' (3.3.189). Shakespeare then envisions the offstage spectacle of the overweight knight sweating profusely as he is forced to march on his own two feet. In a memorable image, Hal describes Falstaff as 'lard[ing] the lean earth as he walks along' (2.3.17). The line brilliantly imagines the dissolution of Falstaff's fat – that is, his surplus of accumulated energy – returning back to the earth from which it has been hoarded. Since Jockey – the Falstaff/Oldcastle character in *The Famous Victories* – does appear on horseback, Shakespeare's artistic decision to remove horses from stage mirrors Poins's uncolting. In forcing his audience to 'think, when we talk of horses, that you see them' (Prol. 26), the playwright replaces crude visual spectacle with a verbal poetry that provokes a more complex understanding of the material networks that undergird the mobility of early modern culture.

There is an important caveat, however, with this jab at Falstaff's belly. As Robert Shaughnessy has noted, contemporary audiences might misconstrue the significance of the knight's girth. Today, obesity is associated with poor health, low socio-economic status, a fast-food diet, or low self-esteem, not a carnivalesque *joie de vivre*. Mikhail Bakhtin spoke of the carnivalesque as celebrating the 'organic unity' between the porous body and the earth, and in certain situations feasting can be an expression of environmental attachment (McDowell 1996). When Falstaff contrasts himself with 'pharaoh's lean kine' (2.5.478) the allusion to a biblical famine associates his fatness with enviable conditions of plenty. Nevertheless, critics who uphold Falstaff as the real hero of the play often fail to consider how the Great Dearth would have predisposed the audience to view the fat knight askance.[10] Falstaff's bacchanals would consume bushels of what agricultural writers called 'drink-corn' that could have been used to feed the populace or at least bring down the price of bread. In the context of widespread food shortages and soaring fuel costs, Falstaff's obesity and refusal to walk would have incited resentment as much as amusement; his uncolting may have inspired something like *Schadenfreude*.[11]

Nashe's comments serve as a reminder that the Renaissance viewed the obese body on horseback not as carnivalesque but as an object of medical and moral concern. Hippocrates had advised the corpulent to walk more often and at a faster pace than the slim, and Graeco-Roman ethics about moderation and temperance were absorbed by Christianity in Pauline denunciations of the belly god. Gluttony, however, is not Falstaff's only shortcoming. In early modern iconography of the seven deadly sins, the equally heinous sin of sloth is often shown as both overweight and on horseback. In Bruegel the Elder's painting of Sloth, a personification of the sin rides half asleep on the back of an ass. Similarly, in Spenser's *Faerie Queene*, Idleness rides upon an ass (1.4.18). Depicting Sloth upon an ass enables early modern artists to further associate it with lassitude, a point Spenser underscores with his punning spelling of the sin as 'Slowth'. *1 Henry IV* implicitly links Falstaff with sloth for his diurnal sleeping and his reluctance to walk on foot. When Hal labels Falstaff 'that reverend Vice' (2.5.458) and imagines him wielding a 'dagger of lath' (2.5.137), the play makes its debts to the early Tudor morality tradition explicit: Shakespeare models part of his parody of Falstaff on the condemnation of vices such as sloth in morality plays like *Seven Deadly Sins*.

A long-lost theatrical cousin of Falstaff can be found in the neglected morality play *The Contention of Liberality and Prodigality*, first published in 1602. Like *1 Henry IV*, the play features scenes at a roadside inn, a highway robbery, and a gang of dissipated, slothful Vice characters – one of them grotesquely overweight – who moan about walking. In the opening scene, Prodigality claims he is too weary to walk the final six miles of his journey and must rest at the inn. Tenacity (Stinginess) soon shows up at the same inn riding upon an emaciated ass and complains, 'these old stumps are stark tired' (Anon. 1913: B2^v). These two are joined by an obese personification of Money, who by Act 5 has grown 'fat as a hog' to the point where he cannot budge a single step or even lift himself up off the ground: 'For if I should stir me one inch from the ground / I think I shall die, sure, or fall in a [swound]. . . . I cannot stir me, my breath is clean gone' (E3^v). The short-winded Falstaff imagines himself in the same predicament; when Hal asks him to put his ear to the ground to listen for hoofbeats he snaps, 'Have you any levers to lift me up again being down?' (2.2.35). Money's tavern companions also run him through a gauntlet of fat jokes – 'bull-kine', 'fat ox' – that echo Hal's mockery of Falstaff as a 'bull calf' (2.5.264) and 'Manningtree ox' (2.5.457). To the extent that *1 Henry IV* draws on the morality tradition to satirise Falstaff's slothful dependence on vehicular transport, it offers an early modern forerunner of attacks on car culture as a source of personal and ecological ill health.

While it is a critical commonplace that Hal embodies a golden mean in between two extremes represented by Hotspur and Falstaff (Watson 1983), modern readers may fail to appreciate how Shakespeare inscribes this in terms of equestrian management. When Hal concedes he will temporarily bear 'the unyoked humour' (1.2.193) of his companions, he likens them and himself to horses. By Act 4, however, the play envisions Henry on horseback as a nimble Mercury upon Pegasus, poised to 'witch the world with noble horsemanship' (4.1.111). Although Hal is clad in armour, Shakespeare emphasises the lightness with which he sits in his saddle in contrast to the 'horse-back-breaker' Falstaff. Significantly, Henry's victory over Hotspur results from his more efficient use of England's mobile energies. The Battle of Shrewsbury hinges on the arrival of fresh cavalry. But Worcester's horses are exhausted from a hard day's ride, so that 'not a horse is half the half himself' (4.3.26). In *1 Henry IV* Hotspur commits the tactical error of engaging in battle with 'journey-bated horses' (4.3.28). His rebellion fails because he is oblivious to the physical suffering he causes and the energy he consumes by over-exerting his horses. The modern equivalent of his name would be something like Leadfoot. Although in the symbolic calculus of the Henriad, medieval chivalry dies with Hotspur, we are, nonetheless, committing the same mistake in the post-chivalric era of the automobile. We are all Hotspur now.

Although it might seem anachronistic to imply that Shakespeare's contemporaries concerned themselves with the ethics of transportation, anti-coach satire is surprisingly commonplace in early modern literature. When the coach was imported to England shortly before Shakespeare's birth, many sniffed at it as a wasteful extravagance. The Elizabethan historian John Stow grumbled that what was once a royal luxury was now regarded as necessity among the merchant classes so that 'the world runnes on wheels with many, whose Parents were glad to goe on foot' (1603: 85). With his fondness for parison, the dramatist John Lyly noted, 'they that were accustomed on trotting horses to charge the enemy with a lance now in easy coaches ride up and down to court ladies' (4.3.10–11). The fad for expensive coaches draws scorn in Jacobean city comedies such as Ben Jonson and John Marston's *Eastward Ho!*, Thomas Middleton's *The Puritan*, and George Chapman's *All Fools*, which may originally have been entitled *The World Runs on Wheels* (Gurr 2009: 242). This proverb also supplies the title for John Taylor's 1623 attack on coaches, the title page of which depicts the vehicle as yoked not to a horse but to a devil (Figure 2.1).[12] A similar contempt radiates from Michael Drayton's sonnet, 'How many paltry, foolish painted things / That now in coaches trouble ev'ry street' (2:313). Tellingly, when residents of Blackfriars petitioned to have the local theatre shuttered in 1619, their argument was not that it was a licentious or idle pastime. Their chief grievance was that it created too much traffic congestion from coaches (Gurr 1996: 35).[13] In 1601, four years after Shakespeare uncolted his fat knight, a bill was debated in Parliament 'to restrain the excessive use of coaches within this realm' (Markham 1824: 465).

Following in the tradition of Renaissance historiography, in which readers are invited to take *nunc pro tunc*, this chapter has nudged readers to consider the resemblance between transportation problems in the early modern period and those today. Of course such a reading risks putting the car, as it were, before the horse. To state the obvious, early moderns did not worry about greenhouse gas emissions. If this chapter were simply to metamorphose horses into cars it would risk perpetuating some of the worst excesses of presentist criticism. Yet as Hugh Grady and Cary DiPietro propose, the split between historicism and presentism is a misleading dichotomy. The best New Historicist scholarship always had a presentist subtext, and present-oriented criticism only grows more compelling when it anchors a text in its historical milieu. In carving out a middle way, this chapter has sought to follow Robert Watson's witty prescription to 'Tell Inconvenient Truths but Tell Them Slant'

Figure 2.1 John Taylor, *The World Runs on Wheels*, 1623. © The British Library Board. General Reference Collection C.30.d.29.

(2015). Shakespeare's own somewhat cavalier treatment of English history, evident in his glaring anachronisms, provides a warrant for this Janus-faced approach. Moreover, the historical distinction between the medieval and early modern is far less pronounced from a meteorological perspective: both were under the sway of the 'Little Ice Age'. As Brecht recognised, energy crises are cyclical rather than linear. Since England also suffered a spate of anomalously wet summers in the early decades of the fifteenth century, the conditions in the roadside inn resemble those of the reigns of both Henry IV and Elizabeth I. Nevertheless, the scepticism with which Shakespeare treats the archaic medieval cult of chivalry reflects not only his social status but also his historical vantage point. Extrapolating on Bruce Boehrer's claim that Shakespeare's history plays 'enact the downward displacement of the horse's character as a social signifier' (Boehrer 2005: 91) in a post-chivalric era, an ecocritic might uphold the Second Henriad as a historical precedent for the denigration of the car in a post-carbon economy.

In Sonnet 44 Shakespeare voices a wistful fantasy that humans possessed the power of teleportation – a capacity to leap through space instantaneously with no other fuel than thought. The inability of our body to do this is a source of melancholy for Shakespeare as it is for the environmentally conscious today. The remorse Shakespeare expresses in Sonnet 50 for causing his horse to groan may not be exactly similar to that which prompts academics to purchase carbon offsets for travelling to professional conferences, but his work reminds us – with its homophonic pun on travail – that travel was not and should not be easy. In an era when transportation took place on the back of sentient creatures – what if our cars moaned in pain each time we stepped on the accelerator? – and was fuelled by the sweat of animals and local farmers who grew their food, the energy required to generate such horse-power could not be hidden under the hood.

Notes

An early version of this chapter was presented at the ASLE conference in Bloomington in 2011, and appeared in the *Shakespeare Jahrbuch* 153 (2017), pp. 81–99. I am grateful to the editors of the *Shakespeare Jahrbuch* for permission to reprint it.

1. See the influential works by Latour 2005; Bennett 2010; Iovino and Opperman 2014.
2. All quotations from Shakespeare in this chapter are taken from *The Oxford Shakespeare* (2005).

3. The first Highways Act was passed in 1555 and strengthened seven years later. In 1597, around the time Shakespeare composed *1 Henry IV*, Parliament passed another act for the creation of new highways (39 Eliz. c. 17).
4. See McRae 2009; Sanders 2014: 133–77; Brayshay 2014. On water transport, see Gurr 2010; for a big-picture study of the topic, see Cresswell 2006.
5. Edwards 2007; Raber and Tucker 2005; Boehrer 2010.
6. Edwards calls this a 'generous' ration (2007: 4), but even if it were halved it would still be considerable. Gervase Markham also prescribes each horse a 'peck of oats' per day (1607: 3.21).
7. Candle snuff presumably functioned as an appetite suppressant.
8. I have borrowed the term 'vagrant economy' from Fumerton 2010: 194.
9. Camden [1605] (1636) records a slight variant: 'No dearth but breeds in the horse-manger' (303).
10. Levy-Navarro contends that the Henriad conducts a 'critique of thin privilege', celebrating Falstaff's corpulence as 'an obstacle to [Hal's] imperialist aims' (2008: 8). While there is some merit to this argument, it is debatable whether Falstaff makes a respectable poster child for Fat Studies; when Falstaff attacks the travellers, he ridicules them for being overweight, calling them 'gorbellied', 'fat chuffs' and 'bacons' (2.2.81–2).
11. For a recent discussion of the play in the context of the dearth, see Mukherjee 2014: 45–9.
12. See also Taylor's ballad 'The Coaches Overthrow' (1636).
13. One critic has dubbed the coach an 'environmental nuisance' (Hogarth 2014: 1).

Works cited

Adames, Jonas (1599), *The Order of Keeping a Court Leete*, London.
Anon. [1602] (1913), *The Contention of Liberality and Prodigality*, ed. W. W. Greg, London: Malone Society.
Bain, John (ed.) (1894–6), *The Border Papers: Calendar of Letters and Papers Relating to the Affairs of the Border of England and Scotland*, 2 vols, Edinburgh.
Beaumont, Francis [1607] (1969), *The Knight of the Burning Pestle*, ed. Michael Hattaway, New York: W. W. Norton.
Bennett, Jane (2010), *Vibrant Matter: A Political Ecology of Things*, Durham, NC: Duke University Press.
Berry, Herbert (1986), *The Boar's Head Playhouse*, Amherst: Folger.
Boehrer, Bruce (2005), 'Shakespeare and the Social Devaluation of the Horse', in Karen Raber and Treva J. Tucker (eds), *The Culture of the Horse: Status, Discipline, and Identity in Early Modern England*, Basingstoke: Palgrave Macmillan, pp. 91–111.
—— (2010), *Animal Characters*, Philadelphia: University of Pennsylvania Press.
Brayshay, Mark (2014), *Land Travel and Communications in Tudor and Stuart England: Achieving a Joined-up Realm*, Liverpool: Liverpool University Press.

Brecht, Bertolt (1974), 'Über Stoffe und Formen', in *Brecht on Theatre*, trans. John Willet, London: Methuen, pp. 29–30.
Brown, Eric C. (1998), '"Many a Civil Monster": Shakespeare's Idea of the Centaur', *Shakespeare Survey* 51, pp. 175–91.
Camden, William [1605] (1636), *Remains Concerning Britain*, London.
Cresswell, Tim (2006), *On the Move: Mobility in the Modern Western World*, New York: Routledge.
De Ornellas, Kevin (2005), '"Faith, Say a Man Should Steal Ye and Feed Ye Fatter": Equine Hunger and Theft in *Woodstock*', in Karen Raber and Treva J. Tucker (eds), *The Culture of the Horse: Status, Discipline, and Identity in Early Modern England*, Basingstoke: Palgrave Macmillan, pp. 113–37.
Drayton, Michael (1932), *The Works of Michael Drayton*, 5 vols, ed. J. W. Hebel, Oxford: Shakespeare's Head.
Edwards, Peter (2007), *Horse and Man in Early Modern England*, London: Continuum.
Fagan, Brian (2000), *The Little Ice Age: How Climate Made History, 1300–1850*, New York: Basic.
Fischer, David (1996), *The Great Wave: Price Revolutions and the Rhythm of History*, Oxford: Oxford University Press.
Frazer, Paul (2013), 'Itinerant Identities: Walking Low in *Henry IV*', *Shakespeare* 9.1, pp. 1–20.
Fuller, Thomas (1662), *The History of the Worthies of England*, London.
Fumerton, Patricia (2010), 'Making Vagrancy (In)visible', in Craig Dionne and Steve Mentz (eds), *Rogues and Early Modern English Culture*, Ann Arbor: University of Michigan Press, pp. 193–212.
Gerhold, Dorian (1996), 'Packhorses and Wheeled Vehicles in England 1550–1800', in Dorian Gerhold (ed.), *Road Transport in the Horse-Drawn Era*, Aldershot: Scolar Press, pp. 139–64.
Grady, Hugh, and Cary DiPietro (eds) (2013), *Shakespeare and the Urgency of Now*, New York: Palgrave Macmillan.
Gurr, Andrew (1996), *Playgoing in Shakespeare's London*, Cambridge: Cambridge University Press.
—— (2009), *Shakespeare's Opposites: The Admiral's Company*, Cambridge: Cambridge University Press.
—— (2010), 'Baubles on the Water: Sea Travel in Shakespeare's Time', *SEDERI* 20, pp. 57–70.
Hertel, Ralf (2010), 'Mapping the Globe: The Cartographic Gaze in Shakespeare's *1 Henry IV*', *Shakespeare Survey* 63, pp. 49–62.
Hogarth, Alan James (2014), '"Hide, and Be Hidden, Ride and Be Ridden": The Coach as Transgressive Space in the Literature of Early Modern London', *Early Modern Literary Studies* 17.2, pp. 1–20.
Hoskins, W. G. (1964), 'Harvest Fluctuations and English Economic History 1480–1619', *Agricultural History Review* 12, pp. 28–46.
Ingram, William (1993), 'The Cost of Touring', *Medieval and Renaissance Drama in England* 6, pp. 57–62.
Iovino, Serenella, and Serpil Opperman (eds) (2014), *Material Ecocriticism*, Bloomington: Indiana University Press.
Johnson, Samuel (1755), *A Dictionary of the English Language*, London.

Lamb, H. H. (1982), *Climate, History, and the Modern World*, London: Methuen.
Langdon, John (2002), *Horses, Oxen and Technological Innovation*, Cambridge: Cambridge University Press.
Latour, Bruno (2005), *Re-assembling the Social: An Introduction to Actor-Network Theory*, Oxford: Oxford University Press.
Lefebvre, Henri (1991), *The Production of Space*, trans. Donald Nicholson Smith, Oxford: Blackwell.
Levin, Harry (1976), *Shakespeare and the Revolution of the Times*, New York: Oxford University Press.
Levy-Navarro, Elena (2008), *The Culture of Obesity in Early and Late Modernity: Body Image in Shakespeare, Jonson, Middleton, and Skelton*, New York: Palgrave.
Lyly, John (1584), *Campaspe*, London.
McDowell, Michael (1996), 'The Bakhtinian Road to Ecological Insight', in Cheryll Glotfelty and Harold Fromm (eds), *The Ecocriticism Reader*, Athens, GA: University of Georgia Press, pp. 371–91.
McRae, Andrew (2009), *Literature and Domestic Travel in Early Modern England*, Cambridge: Cambridge University Press.
Markham, Gervase (1607), *Cavelarice, or the English Horseman*, London.
Markham, James (1824), *Some Remarks on the Early Use of Carriages in England*, London.
Mukherjee, Ayeshee (2014), *Penury into Plenty: Dearth and the Making of Knowledge in Early Modern England*, London: Routledge.
Nashe, Thomas (1592), *Pierce Penniless, His Supplication to the Devil*, London.
Raber, Karen, and Treva J. Tucker (eds) (2005), *The Culture of the Horse: Status, Discipline, and Identity in Early Modern England*, Basingstoke: Palgrave Macmillan.
Sanders, Julie (2014), *The Cultural Geography of Early Modern Drama, 1620–1650*, Cambridge: Cambridge University Press.
Schmid, Christian (2008), 'Henri Lefebvre's Theory of the Production of Space: Towards a Three-Dimensional Dialectic', in Kanishka Goonewardena, Stefan Kipfer, Richard Milgrom and Christian Schmid (eds), *Space, Difference, Everyday Life: Reading Henri Lefebvre*, New York: Routledge, pp. 26–45.
Schoenbaum, Samuel (1977), *William Shakespeare: A Compact Documentary Life*, New York: Oxford University Press.
Shakespeare, William (2005), *The Oxford Shakespeare*, ed. Stanley Wells and Gary Taylor, Oxford: Clarendon.
Shaughnessy, Robert (2010), 'Falstaff's Belly: Pathos, Prosthetics, and Performance', *Shakespeare Survey* 63, pp. 65–74.
Stewart, Alan (2007), 'Shakespeare and the Carriers', *Shakespeare Quarterly* 58.4, pp. 431–64.
Stow, John (1603), *Survey of London*, London.
Szeman, Imre, and Dominic Boyer (eds) (2017), *Energy Humanities: An Anthology*, Baltimore: Johns Hopkins University Press.
Taylor, John (1636), *The Coaches Overthrow*, London.
Thirsk, Joan (1967), *The Agrarian History of England and Wales 1500–1640*, Cambridge: Cambridge University Press.
Thomas, Keith (1983), *Man and the Natural World*, London: Penguin.

Watson, Robert N. (1983), 'Horsemanship in Shakespeare's Second Tetralogy', *English Literary Renaissance* 13.3, pp. 274–300.
—— (2015), 'Tell Inconvenient Truths but Tell Them Slant', in Jennifer Munroe and Edward J. Geisweidt (eds), *Ecological Approaches to Early Modern English Texts*, Farnham: Ashgate, pp. 17–28.

Chapter 3

The Night, the Crossroads and the Stake: Shakespeare and the Outcast Dead

Bill Angus

In Shakespeare's lifetime and long after, to live or to die in certain proscribed ways – as a traitor or a suicide, for instance – meant, *post extremis*, to be treated as public refuse and buried in or by a roadway, the detritus of a social and religious construction of the world which could admit no incoherence in death. When Thomas Nashe suggested in 1589 that the rebellious authors of the Martin Marprelate tracts, once dead, 'should not be buried in any church . . . chapel, nor churchyard . . . but in some barn, outhouse . . . field [or] . . . dunghill', the sentiment expressed this commonly held belief about the rightful interment of the remains of those who troubled fundamental social or religious norms (Gittings 1984: 49). This was not the case for the majority of the victims of execution, who were typically buried in the churchyard of the parish where the gaol or gallows stood: Clare Gittings notes the parish register for St Mary's, Reading, for 26 March 1679, which records four men 'hanged and buried' there on that same day (Gittings 1984: 67). Even after the notoriously draconian 'Black Act' of 1723, Christian burial rites were denied only to the most serious offenders (Gittings 1984: 67; Rogers 1974). But throughout the period, there were quite a number of people who were considered to be in this category and it is probable that, like many in his community, Shakespeare was familiar with some.

Indeed, it is highly likely that in the five years between 1582 and 1586 – that is, between the formative ages of eighteen and twenty-two – Shakespeare knew of at least five people, either related to his family or close local contemporaries, regarded by many as the direst of society's delinquents: Thomas Cottam, Edward Arden, John Somerville, Francis Throckmorton and Robert Dibdale.[1] Their final resting places are unlikely to have been proximate to the consecrated ground of church, chapel or churchyard. Rather than a barn or dunghill, their graves would most likely have been beside or beneath some sort of public road. Although the specific treatment of these unfortunate persons' remains varied with the circumstances of crime, and places of execution, their ceremony would be one designed to arrest an unquiet spirit, its most common traditional elements being the night, the crossroads and the stake.

The first of these, Thomas Cottam, was the brother of one of Shakespeare's schoolmasters at King's New School in Stratford. Having been trained in the Catholic priesthood at Douai and ordained in 1580, Cottam was arrested upon his return to England as a missioner and eventually executed as a traitor at Tyburn on 15 May 1582. The fact that, soon after this, his schoolmaster brother John Cottam left both the school and the Stratford area points to local knowledge of the facts surrounding his execution (Honigmann 1985: 5).

In the following year, the second, Edward Arden, a possible kinsman of Shakespeare on his mother Mary Arden's side, was arrested after being implicated in his son-in-law John Somerville's mad plot to assassinate Elizabeth I. He was hanged, drawn and quartered, at Smithfield on 20 December 1583 (Brownlow 1993: 109).[2] Some years later, in 1599, Shakespeare applied to the official herald for the authority to 'quarter his arms with those of Arden', indicating a continuing relationship with the family over the intervening period (Brownlow 1993: 109).

Opinion differs on whether the third troubling person, the would-be assassin John Somerville, either 'hanged himself in Newgate' or was otherwise found suspiciously strangled in his cell (Ackroyd 2006: 94; Cooper 2011: 255). Either way, if Somerville were not known to Shakespeare it would be a very curious coincidence that the name 'John Somerville' appears in *3 Henry VI*, one of Shakespeare's earliest plays and written only a few years after Somerville's death in 1583 (Ackroyd 2006: 95; Shakespeare 2001: 110).

Edward Arden's wife, Mary Throckmorton, meanwhile, was a probable kinswoman of the fourth of these locals, Francis Throckmorton, who was arrested in November 1583 as an agent for a conspiracy in which England was to be invaded by a French army under Henri, Duc de Guise, a plot which was aimed at freeing Mary, Queen of Scots and restoring the authority of the Pope.[3] Shakespeare's local acquaintance with this family is also very likely, and Throckmorton's execution as a traitor at Tyburn on 10 July 1584 would have certainly been 'common talk in Stratford-upon-Avon' that year, as Charlotte Carmichael Stopes suggested (Stopes 1907: 160).

Fifthly, and perhaps most significantly, in October 1586 another Catholic missionary priest, Robert Dibdale, also ended his days at the Tyburn Tree as a traitor. Dibdale was not only an associate of the schoolmaster's renegade brother Thomas Cottam but also an exact local contemporary of Anne Hathaway. Anne must certainly have known Dibdale and his family, and Frank Walsh Brownlow cites the fact that his brother-in-law had witnessed Anne's father's will, of which she was a beneficiary (Brownlow 1993: 108). By extension it is extremely likely that Shakespeare would also have known, or at the very least known of, Dibdale, and his fate at the time. Edgar Fripp speculates about an even closer possible relation between the two through their respective maternal lines (Fripp 1929: 30–1). This connection is of particular interest since Dibdale had also been involved in the notorious case of the Denham exorcisms, an episode of deeply spurious priestly practice and Catholic propagandising, later the subject of Samuel Harsnett's 1603 text *A Declaration of Egregious Popish Impostures*.[4] Harsnett's *Declaration* is a book that Shakespeare is known to have read sometime before 1605, after which it seems to influence his writing of *King Lear* and other plays (Muir 1951; Brownlow 1993: 107; Bate 2009: 154).[5] It also offers some conceptual and geographical associations that we will come back to.

However, despite the various possible connections between the fate of these contemporaries and the author's own background, in the main Shakespeare's drama tends to skirt around the issues of imprisonment, and execution, and what happens at crossroads is largely unacknowledged in his imaginative world. Richard Wilson has pointed out his relative 'effacement of contemporary violence' and others have noted that Shakespeare's project seems to 'occlude the barbarity of Tyburn and the Tower', especially where this is connected to any hint of religious controversy (Wilson 2004: 116). This may have been a self-protective measure and was perhaps a symptom of the unmentionable nature of his early connections with the conspiratorial Catholicism of such outcast dead. But nevertheless, despite Shakespeare's relatively light handling of these weighty contemporary issues, the specific question of the burial of such dubious subjects emerges in various hints and allusions found in his plays, occasionally wandering on to the stage themselves like the shadowy revenants of unquiet thoughts.

One such intimation is found in the phrase Hamlet uses to reply to his father's ghost, '*hic et ubique*' (1.5.156), or 'here and everywhere', which is an extract from a church liturgy that may have been used to refer to those buried in unconsecrated ground, as John Klause notes (2008: 290, n. 41). This would be an important usage because it functions to express Hamlet's uncertainty about the ghost at this point in the play, since an uncertain burial would imply that it might indeed be merely a typical wandering spirit rather than the authentic ghost of his murdered father. Another allusion, in *All's Well That Ends Well*, has Parolles refer to the same trope of unconsecrated burial among the sophistry of his comedic discourse on the nature of virginity: 'He that hangs himself is a virgin. Virginity murders itself and should be buried in highways out of all sanctified limit, as a desperate offendress against nature' (1.1.131–3).[6] This appears to be delivered with some irony – the hanging of virgins possibly alluding to the perceived innocence of the Catholic priests who may be hanged, and afterwards buried 'out of all sanctified limit', in the 'highways' he mentions. Biron, of *Love's Labour's Lost*, also refers obliquely to the hanging of innocents in Shakespeare's only direct reference to Tyburn, specifically its triangular construction, as the scene's three watching lovers make up what he describes as 'the triumviry, the corner-cap of society, / The shape of love's Tyburn that hangs up simplicity' (4.3.43–4). 'Simplicity' was again synonymous with innocence at the time, and thus this may again refer to the innocence of the religious victims of Tyburn.

Highway burial outside a 'sanctified limit' is also described in *Richard II*, where the deposed king offers to exchange his large kingdom for an obscure and trivial grave, or even worse, as he petulantly complains,

> I'll be buried in the king's highway,
> Some way of common trade, where subjects' feet
> May hourly trample on their sovereign's head;
> For on my heart they tread now whilst I live;
> And buried once, why not upon my head? (3.3.155–9)

Richard's concern here with the public nature of the putative grave indicates partly the form of punishment such burial is intended to perform. As Lisa Hopkins discusses above, this is very much the 'low road' for a monarch's interment. Shakespeare's understanding of the dishonour of such a burial is shown when Henry V, begging a blessing before Agincourt, feels the need to assure God, 'I Richard's body have interrèd new / . . . and I have built / Two chantries where the sad and solemn priests / Sing still for Richard's soul' (4.1.288, 293–5), though the fact that God appears so far to have missed this might suggest a certain level of irony.

Typically, the bodies of those executed for treason, or their recoverable pieces, would be laid to rest 'near or under the gallows', and the public gallows, Tyburn included, were most often sited at a common crossroads (Gittings 1984: 69). The gallows known as 'Tyburn' was actually situated at various locations on the crossroads of Tyburn Road and Watling Street (now Marble Arch and Edgeware Road).[7] Richard Challoner describes such gallows burials of both Catholic priests and laymen, including those of Robert Grissold, a layman executed in 1604 at Warwick, and Fathers Thomas Maxfield, in 1616 at Tyburn itself, and Hugh Green, in 1642 at Dorchester gallows, another scaffold sited at a road junction (Challoner 1839: 12, 64, 125). The remains of one Father Philip Powell, executed at Tyburn in 1646, were allowed to be buried in a cemetery, but only by express permission of Parliament (Challoner 1839: 167). A further, and very prominent, example serves to show the continuity of these burial practices throughout the early modern period: on 30 January 1661, the anniversary of Charles I's execution, 'the bodies of [regicides] Cromwell, Ireton and Bradshaw, having been disinterred from Westminster Abbey, were solemnly hanged at Tyburn and then buried beneath the gallows', as Gittings recounts (1984: 71). Burial at such places implies utter rejection, the ousting of the unclean spirit from the community's bosom and from rest with the revered dead. It also suggests the permanent outing of private space, placing the ultimate privacy, the grave, by that most public of passing places, the confluence of common roadways. Such crossroads burials were no doubt a signal of the differential values associated with public and private spaces, but also of an association with a particular kind of publicness: one denoting a suspect liminality and a lack of Christian oversight.

In a society used to performing the 'beating of the bounds' over the days of 'rogation' in the church festival calendar in which the party walked the parochial boundaries on three successive days 'to drive away the devil ... [in] an annual exorcism of the parish', the roads which lay between these boundaries might be the only neutral space (Cox 2000: 167). If the most neutral between-spaces of early modern Britain are highways and roads lying between boundaries of estates, parishes or other geographical authorities of oversight, then the ultraliminal place, the place between the edges, would be where such highways crossed, the 'transitional gaps between defined, bounded areas, that is, between roads or between the areas of land that roads define' (Johnston 1991: 217). The name 'Tyburn', for instance, derives from 'Teo Bourne' meaning 'boundary stream' (Gover et al. 1942: 6). Such places may be suitable for the things no one wishes to claim, for dishonourable graves and gibbets. Burial at the public crossroads, then, implies both an exorcism and an enforced liminality that no doubt adds to the troubling ambiguity of the status of the corpse. The crossroads thus operates as a kind of public caging area for the netherworld beyond, in comparison with which even a marketplace has a certain privacy, delineated by its boundaries.

Aside from the function of social exorcism actioned by its very public nature, as Richard II's complaint implies, a question may remain over why many societies specifically chose the 'crossways' as an appropriate place for the burial of outcasts. In fact, early modern graveyards were also notoriously public places, and so much so that concerned bishops issued injunctions, one against the 'feeding of cattle ... the playing of games, depositing dung, the emptying of chamber-pots or "easing of nature", fighting, performing plays and hanging out washing', all of which were apparently taking place in early modern churchyards (Gittings 1984: 140). Some greater privacy was promised with burial inside the church itself, but this became so prevalent that churches were often overcrowded with underfloor corpses, and thus strong discouragement was offered to this preference (Gittings 1984: 140–1).[8] A crossroads, therefore, offered some deeper level of public disgrace, connected with its particular geographical nature, or its historical associations.

Equally as disruptive of the natural order of things and likewise considered the direst of offenders, the corpses of traitors and suicides were often similarly punished and dishonourably buried in roadways. In fact, the self-destructive act itself was portrayed as another species of treasonous revolt. In dealing with the estate of Sir James Hales, who drowned himself in 1554, Lord Dyer described suicide as 'an offence against nature, against God, and against the King' (Gittings 1984: 72). As A. Van Gennep has outlined, 'mortuary rites ... proceed through three phases: separation, transition, and integration'; suicides were perceived as disrupting this process and therefore not making this transition into integration (Van Gennep 1960: ch. 8). It was thought that they could not 'fully enter the realm of the dead, since they did not await Death's summons ... [and so] their ghosts are dangerous and intrusive' (MacDonald and Murphy 1990: 46). They were 'transitional beings ... particularly polluting' (Turner 1969: 97). By burying the body by a road, in a highway, or at a crossroads at night, the community was able to remove the 'spiritual pollution' that the suicide attracted and to protect itself against the unfortunate person's malevolent revenant (MacDonald 1986: 314).[9] The clearly insane Somerville, for instance, if suicide was indeed considered to be the cause of death, would in all likelihood have been barred from having his remains interred in consecrated ground even if he were found innocent of his treasonous assassination plot. Sixteenth- and seventeenth-century courts were very rarely in favour of returning the *non compos mentis* verdict that would have excused the act as the result of madness rather than badness and allowed the full rites of burial in sanctified earth (MacDonald 1986: 310).[10] Although the ban on consecrated burial for the *felo de se* might be clear, in Shakespeare's lifetime the burial of suicides was unregulated and chiefly guided by convention. Both highway burial and the rites of desecration that were visited upon self-murderers were, as MacDonald has argued,

Figure 3.1 Roads outside London 3, Janelle Jenstad (ed.) (c. 1562), The Agas Map, University of Victoria, <http://mapoflondon.uvic.ca/map.htm> (last accessed 24 June 2019).

merely 'relics of the pagan past, customs based on popular superstitions' and tolerated by the church rather than specifically authorised by it (MacDonald 1986: 314).

The pre-eminent discussion of these issues in Shakespeare studies is of course that surrounding the case of Ophelia in *Hamlet*, a play entirely premised on the idea of a troubled, walking spirit, though its gravity is somewhat lightened in the play by its introduction through the misprision of clowns. The Gravedigger asks, 'Is she to be buried in Christian burial, when she wilfully seeks her own salvation?' and the Second Man replies, 'I tell thee she is. Therefore make her grave straight. The crowner hath sat on her and finds it Christian burial' (5.1.1–5). However, he concedes 'if this had not been a gentlewoman she should have been buried out o'Christian burial' (5.1.22–5). Social rank was indeed a factor in these matters. For example, when Francis Norris, 1st Earl of Berkshire, shot himself with his crossbow in 1622, as MacDonald shows, 'the court directed letters to the coroner ordering that "the evidence touching the earle of Berkshires manner of death must not be urged, but the matter made as fair as possible."' 'Fair' in this context, of course, means a whitewash, and the Earl was ruled *non compos mentis*, a verdict five times more likely for the wealthy than for commoners at this time (MacDonald 1986: 312).[11]

In terms of contemporary understanding of received wisdom on the matter, although both Luther and Calvin had argued that suicide was caused by demonic attack or possession, other influential theologians Augustine and Aquinas had not (Smith 2008: 101–3, n. 5). Luther in particular asserted that this circumstance freed the cleric from worries about punitive burial. In *Hamlet*, Shakespeare does not imply Ophelia's suicide is demonic in origin and thereby leaves the question of legitimate burial open. Her right to 'Christian burial' in consecrated ground, rather than in or by a road, therefore, is uncertain, although the Priest accompanying her burial party concludes the matter by declaring,

> Her death was doubtful;
> And but that great command o'ersways the order
> She should in ground unsanctified been lodged
> Till the last trumpet: for charitable prayers,
> Flints and pebbles should be thrown on her.
> Yet here she is allowed her virgin crants
> Her maiden strewments, and the bringing home
> Of bell and burial. (5.1.216–23)

Gittings gives a contemporary report of the burial of one lacking Ophelia's wealth and influence who 'wilfully' sought his own 'salvation' in Pleasley, Derbyshire, in 1573: 'Tho[mas] Maule f[oun]d hung on a tree by the wayside after a drunken fit April 3. Coroner's inquest in church porch April 5. Same night at midnight buried at the highest crossroads with a stake in him, many people from Mansfield' (Gittings 1984: 72). Thomas R. Forbes notes another case from the coroner Thomas Wilbraham's report in 1590 of Amy Stokes who, not 'having the fear of God before her eyes ... hanged herself from a beam in a bedroom' with a ha'penny cord. Since the jury called her a *felo de se*, Forbes notes, 'according to the harsh law and custom of the time, the body of the suicide was buried at night at a crossroads with a stake driven through the chest' (Forbes 1973: 378; 1971: 165–9, n. 7). Another instance, in this case of a renegade priest who died falling from a rooftop in 1614 while fleeing his pursuers, as Peter Marshall recounts, resulted in its victim being 'buried at a cross-roads, with a stake driven through his stomach, the persecutors representing his death as a suicide' (Marshall 2012: 68). A later and more prominent example, with some similarity to the case of John Somerville, is of the body of one Miles Sindercombe, who was indicted and sentenced to death for treason for trying to kill Oliver Cromwell but somehow contrived to poison himself in prison. His corpse was ordered by the coroner on 17 February 1656 to be buried 'according to Law, in the next Common High-way' and according to the anonymous author was, thus,

> drawn to the open place upon Tower Hill ... and there under the Scaffold of Common execution a Hole being digg'd, he was turned in stark naked, and a stake, spiked with Iron, was driven through him into the earth; That part of the stake which remaines above ground, being all plated with Iron; which may stand as an example of terror to all Traytors for the time to come. (Anon. 1657: n.p.)

The scaffold on Tower Hill was on a rise overlooking what was at the time a crossing of obscure roads leading to Chick Lane and Tower Street, just outside the Tower of London's Postern Gate, where passers-by would have had ample opportunity to consider the iron-plated butt of the stake which pinned the corpse below. Perhaps local children would dare each other to kick it. Failing the privilege of wealth and influence, Ophelia's 'ground unsanctified' would most likely, or at least conventionally, have been at such a crossroads, where the body would be roughly and unceremoniously dumped into its hole at night, and possibly staked with a long enough piece of wood that its end might be left protruding above ground. This intention that the stake might serve as a warning to the living persists through time; John Weever could still report in 1767 that suicides were buried 'in or near to the highways, with a stake thrust through their bodies, to terrify all passengers, by that so infamous and reproachful a burial, not to make such their final passage out of this present world' (Weever 1767: xxii). Such a protruding stake, possibly with its butt bound in iron, must in fact have been a fairly common thing to have seen at various crossroads throughout the land during this period and may therefore be threateningly implicit in the priest's invocation of Ophelia's own burial arrangements.[12]

But the provocation to terror, however socially useful it may have been, was not the stake's only purpose. Besides its evidently cautionary role, there is another function of the stake that is also important to early modern societies, which accords with the location of a burial at a crossroads and which relates to the commonly accepted and persistent element within European ghost-lore, that the spirits, or even corpses, of criminals, suicides and murder victims walked the earth after death (Moorman 1906: 193, 197). Since spirits were thought itinerant in general, the likelihood of roaming for troubled spirits seemed fairly strong. *A Midsummer Night Dream*'s Puck declares:

> Now it is the time of night
> That the graves, all gaping wide,
> Every one lets forth his sprite
> In the churchway paths to glide;
> And we fairies . . . do run
> By the triple Hecate's team
> From the presence of the sun. (5.1.365–71)

A 'churchway path' is the often very ancient route by which a dead body would be carried from an outlying parish to one which had burial rights. As might be imagined, such paths were invested with some superstition regarding the walking of spirits, and especially those who might return along the road from the place of burial. This superstition was not restricted to the fanciful imaginings of dramatists but was rather one which many funeral rituals and traditions of the day, and of long afterwards, were designed to guard against. As late as the nineteenth century in Lincolnshire, for instance, it was common practice to tie a coarse thread called an 'incle' around the corpse's ankles to stop the ghost of even an entirely innocent deceased from roaming and finding its way back to the home from which the corpse was carried; the preparation of the corpse by spreading it with salt was also supposed to prevent the same thing (Gittings 1984: 111–12). In his poem 'To Perilla' (1648) Robert Herrick, whose father's own suicide clearly exercised continued influence over his poetry, writes, 'Dead when I am, first cast in salt . . . / Then shall my ghost not walk about, but keep / Still in the cool and silent shades of sleep' (Herrick 1891: 8). Prevention of a corpse's 'walking' could also be effected by employing a person known as a 'sin-eater'. As John Aubrey explained in 1686, these were 'poor people, who were to take upon them all the sinnes of the party deceased', and when the corpse was brought out of the house and 'layd on the Biere', a loaf and a maple bowl full of beer were delivered to the sin-eater, plus 'sixpence in money, in consideration whereof he tooke upon him . . . all the Sinnes of the Defunct, and freed him (or her) from walking after they were dead' (Aubrey 1881: 35). These various ways of stopping a ghost from returning to trouble the community help to explain the necessity for the stake in cases of particularly troubled revenants, who might want to 'rise again . . . / And push us from our stools' (*Macbeth*, 3.4.82, 84).

Probably written shortly after Shakespeare read Harsnett, *Macbeth* plays around with these issues of superstitious fear, spiritual credulity and the walking of the unquiet dead. When Lady Macbeth dreams and herself walks like one dead, she talks to reassure her disturbed self, saying, 'look not so pale. I tell you yet again, Banquo's buried; he cannot come out on 's grave' (5.1.56–7). But it is dawning on this sceptic, at least in her unquiet dreams, that Banquo has already done so. Macbeth's own concern is with the disturbance of the natural order that this implies, as he complains, 'If charnel houses and our graves must send / Those that we bury back, our monuments / Shall be the maws of kites' (3.4.72–4). The strong imagery of these spewing sepulchres seems to follow strong sentiment on these matters. In terms of his depiction of the returning ghost, rather than reproducing the typical Senecan gibberers of a classical underworld, Shakespeare offers something closer to 'superstition drawn from native ghost-lore' as F. W. Moorman shows, and this is linked syncretically to both pagan deities and the satanic cloak that Christianity threw over them (Moorman 1906: 193, 197). Not only is Puck himself a restless, metamorphic, musical wanderer, like *The Tempest*'s Ariel, as he says 'Over hill, over dale . . . / Over park, over pale . . . / I do wander everywhere' (2.1.2, 4, 6), but he is also Robin Goodfellow – a euphemism for the Christian Devil, and the Devil is himself a wanderer. The 1611 version of the Bible describes how 'the LORD said unto Satan, From whence comest thou? And Satan answered the LORD, and said, From going to and fro in the earth, and from walking up and down in it' (Job 2: 2). Coleridge will later speak of Milton's Satan as representing 'the Molochs of human nature', whose success is due to their 'outward restlessness' (1816: 34–5). Shakespeare does not exactly celebrate this spiritual itinerancy, but neither is it entirely satanic; its danger tends rather towards creative chaos than simple malice.

In early modern minds, a ubiquitously wandering Satan is also an inspirer of artists, as Nancy Rosenfeld suggests (2008: 46). On 15 May

1611, Dr Simon Forman saw a production of *The Winter's Tale* and spent a full third of his report on the play warning his reader about Autolycus, firstly associating him with a folk monster of the Hampshire countryside, calling him 'the rogue that came in all tattered like colt pixie', and describing his transformative character: 'how he changed apparel with the king of Bohemia his son, and then how he turned courtier', before concluding, 'Beware of trusting feigned beggars or fawning felons' (Forman 1611: 202). Such a dangerously transformative wandering figure may be linked with jesters and jig-dancers, as a survival of what Robert Weimann has called the 'lower' aspects of pagan worship, 'seasonal rites and vegetation magic' (Weimann 1987: 23). As a masterless man wandering the roads of early modern Britain (via Bohemia) he is simultaneously exotic and threatening, embodying the fear of, and desire for, the unknown. Inasmuch as he is an itinerant musician (which is to say, a musician) and seller of bawdy and disturbing ballads, one concerning 'a monstrous birth' and another 'a monstrous transformation', even such an apparently human figure as Autolycus resonates with the suspicion of devilry (Cox 1969: 285). A vagrant in fear of a lynching, he confesses that 'Gallows and knock are too powerful on the highway. Beating and hanging are terrors to me' (4.3.27–9). In Ovid, Autolycus is the grandfather of Odysseus, another notable wanderer, but more pertinently he is the son of Mercury, and shrines to Mercury are found at the crossroads as well as that other mediator between this world and the next: the gallows that he fears.

The causes of wandering in general are issues of social concern at the time, but the wandering propensities of ghosts in particular are also pertinent to post-Reformation debates on the precise mechanisms of the afterlife, acting for the Catholics as manifest proof of the doctrine of purgatory, and for Protestants of the apparition of demons in human form (Moorman 1906: 198–9). The ghost of old Hamlet, for instance, is quite the equivocator in this and displays characteristics of both, reeking of purgatorial fire while carrying the suspicion of being satanic in origin rather than human. A belief in the walking of unquiet spirits was not universal, however. Harsnett's *Declaration* ridicules this widespread conviction as part of his critique of the credulity of the Denham exorcists' audience and victims, using the story of Creüsa, Aeneas' wife, who, after simply becoming lost, returned as a spirit to announce that she had become 'one of the walking night-ghosts' (Harsnett 1603: 133). But even in excoriating this superstitious belief, Harsnett of course records its very currency, and the idea persists in his choice of metaphor as he discusses walking ghosts, including the spectral appearance of Caesar to Brutus. Here he exclaims, 'out of this, and such like Heathenish dreams, what a world of hel-work, deuil-work, and Elue-work, had we walking amongst vs heere in England' (Harsnett 1603: 134). In this he primarily laments the general spiritual credulity that resulted in the exorcisms and subsequent conversions achieved by Dibdale and the renegade Catholics, but it is nevertheless interesting that he feels the metaphor best suited to communicate this is of another kind of walking ghost.

In the case of roadside burials, not only were the crimes or traumas of these outcast dead enough to disturb their eternal repose, but because a proper funeral was required 'to assist the passage of the soul to the hereafter', as Gittings says, merely withholding this ceremony alone might cause the soul to walk (Gittings 1984: 60). Denying these literal rites of passage, refusing the dead integration, compounded the potential spiritual predicament in a way which needed rectifying in its own turn. Thus, the stake comes to seem like a reasonable insurance policy against the almost inevitable return of the dead. In other words, without the stake to hold her troubled spirit in place, an Ophelia bereft of rites might well have become as one of Puck's feared 'ghosts wandering here and there, / ... Damned spirits all' who must 'Troop home' in this case to the 'cross-ways and floods' where they 'have burial'; one of those who, since they 'wilfully themselves exil'd from light ... must for aye consort with black-brow'd night' (*A Midsummer Night's Dream*, 3.2.381–4, 386–7).

In early modern culture, and in some places still, the crossroads is not only a liminal place but also a nexus where paths, movement and points of decision simultaneously converge and part, its very geography somehow rendering the boundaries between past, present and future negotiable, subject to certain artifice. For many, crossroads were haunted places, echoing with folk memory of forbidden religious and magical rituals of transformation and binding. Puck's crossways-buried spirits reference this history of the crossroads as a place with an apotropaic function, to guard against evil. Since the geographical confluence of roadways itself was supposed to confuse the restless spirit, 'to diffuse the evil influence of the body in several different directions', as Gittings describes, its own effective power was to arrest the movement of turbulent ghosts who might otherwise walk the roads of the night home to the scenes of their particular traumas (Gittings 1984: 73). Here at the crossroads, besides being sometimes literally staked, they may be fixed, their movement arrested, paradoxically, in a place of permanent transit and transition.

Such an inherent arresting quality of the crossroads may be related to the idea, as Russian, Irish, French, German and Albanian myths seem to agree, that spirits have the tendency to walk in straight lines (Devereux 2003: 28, 45–7). The 1611 Bible also describes the movement of spirits in this way, describing how 'they went every one straight forward:

whither the spirit was to go, they went; and they turned not when they went' (Ezekiel 1: 12; see also 1: 9, 10: 22). Thus the parting of ways at the crossroads could in itself potentially be a means of confusing the restless but unidirectional spirit and preventing its wandering. In fact even the gods could be bound at a crossroads. In the Germanic tradition, if one was being pursued by Woden's wild hunt, the 'riders on the storm' or 'ghost riders in the sky' of popular legend, one only needed to get to a crossroads for them to be bound there while you, the hunted, sped on.

But the crossroads was not regarded merely as a place where worldly problems might be contained in the well-trodden earth, it was also a geographical trysting place, in many cultures the abode of various gods. Religions that include crossroads mythology and conjuration practices are many and varied. Divine dwellers at the crossroads include Odin, Diana, Hermes/Mercury, Eshu Elegba of the African tradition, and Puck's 'triple Hecate'. In the early modern period this is noted: Francis Rous (1654) describes a classical past in which 'Hecate was worshipped by [the Athenians], where three wayes met' (Rous 1654: n.p.), and Robert Stapylton's Virgil exclaims, 'O Hecate howl'd-for in crosse wayes!' (Stapylton 1634: n.p.). Because of her connections with the underworld, Hecate is later connected with Christian hell. There is also at least one Christian saint who is revered at the crossroads: Saint Theodore of Cyprus (Marianthi 2006). Since at least early classical times, crossroads were therefore places of magical or semi-divine transaction, giving access to transformative powers beyond the earthly, and requiring special rituals. Johnston gives examples: 'at the time of the new moon, suppers were taken to the images of Hekate found at crossroads. The corpses of those polluted by certain crimes were thrown onto the cross roads and stoned or burned. $Οξυθύμια$, polluted household refuse, was left at crossroads. Magic was performed there' (Johnston 1991: 217). Crossroads were also significant sites in the practice of European witchcraft and were thus the subject of bans from church authorities from early times (Kors and Peters 2001: 63–4).

These instances might explain why, when Harsnett warns of 'helwork, deuil-work, and Elue-work' walking the roads of England, he emphasises this by lamenting how 'our children, old women and maides [are] afraid to crosse . . . a three-way leet' (Harsnett 1603: 134). A 'three-way leet' is a Y-shaped crossroads, of the kind that has been particularly associated with 'triple' Hecate. Harsnett equates the fear of crossing this space with the necessity, if for instance one's church tithes are unpaid, to 'ware where you walke' for fear of a menagerie of monsters:

> bull-beggers, spirits, witches, urchins, Elves, hags, fairies, Satyrs, Pans, Faunes, Syluans, Kit with the candlesticke, Tritons, Centaurs, Dwarffs, Giants, impes, Calcars, coniurers, Nymphs, changlings, scritchowles, Incubus the spurne, the mare, the man in the oake, helwayne, the fire-drake, the puckle, Tom thumbe, hobgoblin, Tom-tumbler, Boneles, and the rest. (Harsnett 1603: 134)

One can only wonder at Shakespeare's reading of this as Harsnett connects the credulity of believers in folk religion and even a basic paganism with Catholic sympathies. Shakespeare himself must have been well aware of the superstitious nature of attitudes to the physical crossroads and must have made the connection between these superstitions and those buried there. The felt necessity to beware where one might walk that Harsnett describes speaks of places clearly haunted by the presence of the unknown, and in a period when place was tightly connected to a sense of belonging and spiritual oversight, to consign a corpse to such a place, the crossroads, was to abandon it to a kind of primal chaos.

These traditions and beliefs are not merely coterminous with the early modern period, however, but have also been surprisingly persistent. Writing in 1754, William Borlase could still report that the 'common people' of Cornwall were fully persuaded even then that there was 'something more than ordinary at such places', explaining that

> their stories of apparitions gain greater credit, if the Spirit, Demon, or Hobgoblin is said to have appear'd where four Lanes meet; there they think apparitions are most frequent, and at such places it is common for these people travelling in the dark to be most afraid. (Borlase 1754: 117–18)

Even into the early twentieth century these ideas had social resonance. When the biographers of the short-lived blues legend Robert Johnson rehearsed the claim that he had been down to the Dockery Plantation crossroads at midnight to exchange his soul for guitar skills, they were referencing this very long history of myth and ritual connected with the liminal space of the crossroads (Wardlow 1998: 91–4). Johnson's death at twenty-seven did nothing to dispel this. In his case, the god imagined was most probably the god of the crossroads, of generative transformations and, ominously, of death itself, Eshu Elegba, of the Yorùbá religion from Nigeria and Benin – the origins of the plantation's slave community. In invoking this god for the sake of his personal artistic mythology, Johnson's biographers perpetuated a mythology that still lingers inside some of the cultural forms of the twenty-first century. One reviewer of the mercurial London soul singer Amy Winehouse, also twenty-seven when she died, asks of the album *Back to Black* (2006): 'It's almost too good . . . did she sell her soul to the devil at the Golders Green and Finchley Road crossroads?' (Morgan 2007: n.p.).

Such persistent beliefs have an interesting social effect. Just as the nature of truck with forbidden gods produces a useful myth of danger for the purveyors of roots blues and rock music throughout the twentieth century and beyond, the burial conventions of the past, though intended to symbolise extreme posthumous rejection, displacement, deracination, and excommunication by the community, could have a similar long-term effect. Paradoxically, anyone excluded in this primal way from the company of the righteous dead was by implication forced into the company of pagan deities or other unknown spiritual forces, and thus were often empowered to make a lasting mark, their memories enshrined in local tradition and in place names sometimes to this day. The place name 'Oram's Grave' in Maddington, Wiltshire, one of many such places, records the suicide who was buried at the crossroads there in 1849, twenty-six years after the practice was banned by an Act of Parliament (Reynolds 2009: 216). It is, as Jeremy Harte has said, the paradox of suicide burials 'that rituals which were focused, above all, on exclusion should have so perversely preserved the memory of the dead' (Harte 2011: 267). What begins as shock and awe perhaps simply ends in awe. Although bound and obstructed by the crossroads and the stake, then, the outcast dead who linger on the outskirts of Shakespeare's imagination by their very persistent nature troop home to us as spirits not merely 'doomed for a certain term to walk the night' but walking well beyond their terms. Despite the urge to exorcise such delinquents, they are often obstinately incarnate, and being inscribed into popular cultural forms, or even more so into the fabric of the landscape, they may outlast monuments.

Notes

1. It is also possible that oblique references in *The Tempest* and *Cymbeline* refer to the martyred Anne Line, who was also killed and initially buried at Tyburn; see Dodwell 2013.
2. The earlier date of October 1583 has been suggested, though sources seem to agree on the December date; see entry for 'Edward Arden' in Harrison 1885–1900: 74.
3. She was also the aunt of the gunpowder conspirator Robert Catesby.
4. Various scholars have also suggested further connections of this kind between Shakespeare and the Catholic missionaries Edmund Campion, executed on 1 December 1581, and Robert Southwell, another distant relation, who was put to death on 21 February 1595. Both of these were also dispatched at Tyburn; see, respectively, Wilson 2004: 127; Kilroy 2015: 355–6.
5. Jonathan Bate suggests personal connections between Shakespeare and Dibdale; see Bate 2009: 154.

6. For all quotations from Shakespeare's plays, please see the list of works cited for the particular edition consulted.
7. From 1196 this was the site of the 'King's Gallows', an elm tree. When the tree died, a two-legged structure with a six-person capacity was erected in its place and in 1571 this was upgraded to a three-legged, triangular structure, each side with an eight-person capacity, that inherited the title of the 'Tyburn Tree'. See also Eddy 2015.
8. Gittings records one church where, between 1580 and 1640, 118 people were buried inside the church itself.
9. See also Moore 1790: 310–11 and Thomas 1971: 594–5.
10. 'Prior to about 1660, the *non compos mentis* verdict was very seldom used. Among the coroners' inquisitions filed in the central courts between 1487 and 1660, only 1.6% of suicides were returned *non compos mentis*. Almost all the rest were declared *felo de se*.' MacDonald is citing Public Record Office, London, KB 9, 10, 11; PL 26; HCA 1/83.
11. Barbara Smith notes connections with the contemporary Hales v. Petit case; see Smith 2008: 105.
12. Incidentally, the last official crossroads burial in England occurred in June 1823 when Abel Griffiths, a twenty-two-year-old law student who had killed himself after murdering his father, was buried at the crossroads of Eaton Street, Grosvenor Place and the Kings Road, London. Since the crowd attending held up George IV's carriage, pressure from the king led to the 1823 Burial of Suicide Act, banning such interments.

Works cited

Ackroyd, Peter (2006), *Shakespeare: The Biography*, London: Vintage.

Anon. (1657), *The Whole business of Sindercome, from first to last, it being a perfect narrative of his carriage, during the time of his imprisonment in the Tower of London*, <http://gateway.proquest.com/openurl?ctx_ver=Z39.88-2003&res_id=xri:eebo&rft_id=xri:eebo:citation:99863809> (last accessed 14 March 2019).

Aubrey, John [1686–7] (1881), *Remaines of Gentilisme and Judaisme*, ed. James Brittan, London: W. Satchell, Peyton, & Co.

Bate, Jonathan (2009), *Soul of the Age: The Life, Mind, and World of William Shakespeare*, London: Penguin.

Borlase, William (1754), *Observations on the antiquities historical and monumental, of the county of Cornwall*, London: W. Bowyer and J. Nichols.

Brownlow, Frank Walsh (1993), *Shakespeare, Harsnett, and the Devils of Denham*, London and Toronto: Associated University Presses.

Challoner, Richard (1839), *Memoirs of Missionary Priests: And Other Catholics of Both Sexes, that Have Suffered Death in England on Religious Accounts, from the Year 1577 to 1684*, Philadelphia: John T. Green.

Coleridge, Samuel Taylor (1816), *The Statesman's Manual*, London: Gale and Fenner.

Cooper, John (2011), *The Queen's Agent: Francis Walsingham at the Court of Elizabeth I*, London: Faber & Faber.

Cox, John D. (2000), *The Devil and the Sacred in English Drama, 1350–1642*, Cambridge: Cambridge University Press.
Cox, Lee Sheridan (1969), 'The Role of Autolycus in The Winter's Tale', *Studies in English Literature, 1500–1900* 9.2 (Spring), Elizabethan and Jacobean Drama, pp. 283–301.
Devereux, Paul (2003), *Spirit Roads*, London: Collins & Brown.
Dodwell, Martin (2013), *Anne Line: Shakespeare's Tragic Muse*, Brighton: Book Guild.
Eddy, Margita (2015), 'Mapping Shakespeare's London', <http://map.shakespeare.kcl.ac.uk/blogs/map-articles/tyburn-deadly-tree-to-tree-of-life/> (last accessed 9 May 2019).
Forbes, Thomas R. (1971), *Chronicle from Aldgate: Life and Death in Shakespeare's London*, New Haven: Yale University Press.
—— (1973), 'London Coroners Inquests for 1590', *Journal of the History of Medicine and Allied Sciences* 28.4, pp. 376–86.
Forman, Simon (1611), *The Bocke of Plaies and Notes therof per forman for Common Pollicie*, London.
Fripp, Edgar (1929), *Shakespeare's Haunts near Stratford*, Oxford: Oxford University Press.
Gittings, Clare (1984), *Death, Burial and the Individual in Early Modern England*, London: Croom Helm.
Gover, J. E. B., Allen Mawer and F. M. Stenton (eds) (1942), *The Place-Names of Middlesex*, Nottingham: English Place-Name Society.
Harrison, Robert (1885–1900), 'Edward Arden', *Dictionary of National Biography*, vol. 2, London: Smith, Elder and Co., p. 74.
Harsnett, Samuel (1603), *A Declaration of Egregious Popish Impostures*, London: Iames Roberts.
Harte, Jeremy (2011), 'Maimed Rites: Suicide Burials in the English Landscape', *Time and Mind: The Journal of Archaeology, Consciousness and Culture* 4.3 (November), pp. 263–82.
Herrick, Robert (1891), *Works of Robert Herrick*, vol. 1, ed. Alfred Pollard, London: Lawrence & Bullen.
Honigmann, E. A. J. (1985), *Shakespeare: The 'Lost Years'*, Manchester: Manchester University Press.
Johnston, S. I. (1991), 'Crossroads', *Zeitschrift für Papyrologie und Epigraphik* 88, pp. 217–24.
Kilroy, Gerard (2015), *Edmund Campion: A Scholarly Life*, London: Ashgate.
Klause, John (2008), *Shakespeare, the Earl, and the Jesuit*, Madison: Fairleigh Dickinson University Press.
Kors, Alan Charles, and Edward Peters (2001), *Witchcraft in Europe, 400–1700: A Documentary History*, Philadelphia: University of Pennsylvania Press.
MacDonald, Michael (1986), 'Ophelia's Maimèd Rites', *Shakespeare Quarterly* 37.3 (Autumn), pp. 309–17.
—— and Terence R. Murphy (1990), *Sleepless Souls: Suicide in Early Modern England*, Oxford: Clarendon.
Marianthi, Kaplanoglou (2006), 'The Folk Cult of St Phanourios in Greece and Cyprus, and its Relationship with the International Tale Type 804', *Folklore* 117.1, pp. 54–74.

Marshall, Peter (2012), 'Confessionalisation and Community in the Burial of English Catholics, c.1570–1700', in Nadine Lewycky and Adam David Morton (eds), *Getting Along? Religious Identities and Confessional Relations in Early Modern England*, Farnham: Ashgate, pp. 57–75.
Moore, Charles (1790), *A Full Inquiry into the Subject of Suicide*, 2 vols, London.
Moorman, F. W. (1906), 'Shakespeare's Ghosts', *The Modern Language Review* 1.3 (April), pp. 192–201.
Morgan, Nick (2007), 'Amy Winehouse, Shepherd's Bush Empire, London, ~~February 2nd, March 9th~~, May 29th 2007', <http://www.whiskyfun.com/Gigs/Amy-Winehouse.html> (last accessed 9 May 2019).
Muir, Kenneth (1951), 'Samuel Harsnett and King Lear', *The Review of English Studies* 2.5 (January), pp. 11–21.
Nashe, Thomas (1589), *Martin's Month's Mind*, London.
Reynolds, Andrew (2009), *Anglo Saxon Deviant Burial Customs*, Oxford: Oxford University Press.
Rogers, Pat (1974), 'The Waltham Blacks and the Black Act', *The Historical Journal* 17, pp. 465–86.
Rosenfeld, Nancy (2008), *The Human Satan in Seventeenth-Century Literature: From Milton to Rochester*, Aldershot: Ashgate.
Rous, Francis (1654), *Archaeologiae Atticae libri septem: Seaven books of the Attick antiquities*, <http://gateway.proquest.com/openurl?ctx_ver=Z39.88-2003&res_id=xri:eebo&rft_id=xri:eebo:citation:13530852> (last accessed 25 March 2019).
Shakespeare, William (1994), *Macbeth*, ed. Nicholas Brooke, Oxford: Oxford University Press.
—— (2001), *King Henry VI, Part 3*, ed. John D. Cox and Eric Rasmussen, London: Arden.
—— (2002), *A Midsummer Night's Dream*, ed. Harold F. Brooks, London: Arden.
—— (2016), *All's Well That Ends Well*, ed. Stephen Greenblatt, New York and London: W. W. Norton.
—— (2016), *Love's Labour's Lost*, ed. Stephen Greenblatt, New York and London: W. W. Norton.
—— (2016), *The Winter's Tale*, ed. Stephen Greenblatt, New York and London: W. W. Norton.
Smith, Barbara (2008), 'Neither Accident nor Intent: Contextualizing the Suicide of Ophelia', *South Atlantic Review* 73.2 (Spring), pp. 96–112.
Stapylton, Robert (1634), *Virgil, Dido and Aeneas*, <http://gateway.proquest.com/openurl?ctx_ver=Z39.88-2003&res_id=xri:eebo&rft_id=xri:eebo:citation:99854581> (last accessed 28 March 2019).
Stopes, Charlotte Carmichael (1907), *Shakespeare's Warwickshire Contemporaries*, Stratford-upon-Avon: Shakespeare Head Press.
Thomas, Keith (1971), *Religion and the Decline of Magic*, New York: Charles Scribner's Sons.
Turner, Victor (1969), *The Ritual Process*, Ithaca: Cornell University Press.
Van Gennep, A. (1960), *The Rites of Passage*, trans. M. B. Vizedom and G. L. Caffee, Chicago: University of Chicago Press.

Wardlow, Gayle Dean (1998), *Chasin' That Devil Music: Searching for the Blues*, San Francisco: Miller Freeman Books.
Weever, John (1767), *Antient Funeral Monuments of Great-Britain, Ireland, and the Islands*, London: W. Tooke.
Weimann, Robert (1987), *Shakespeare and the Popular Tradition in the Theater*, ed. Robert Schwarz, London: Johns Hopkins.
Wilson, Richard (2004), *Secret Shakespeare: Studies in Theatre, Religion and Resistance*, Manchester: Manchester University Press.

Chapter 4

Gender, Vagrancy and the Culture of the Early Modern Road in *As You Like It*

Karalyn Dokurno

In *Literature and Domestic Travel in Early Modern England*, Andrew McRae argues not only that roads 'were not considered poetic' in the early modern period, but that 'they have little place on the stage either' (McRae 2009: 69). Indeed, the word 'road' appears only once within *As You Like It*, a brief, denigrating reference by Orlando to the vagaries of 'the common road' as he contemplates his impending homelessness (2.3.33),[1] and even a broadening of the term to include cognates such as 'path' and 'way' yields hardly better results. Nonetheless, as I will argue here, although roads, paths and ways occupy very little physical or verbal space upon the stage of *As You Like It*, their presence looms conceptually large throughout the play. Given the play's investment in themes of social and political order and disorder,[2] this is perhaps fitting when considered in light of the fact that, as McRae further remarks, 'roads had always coupled a promise of connection with a threat of disorder' (2009: 90).

In this chapter I will examine some of the ways in which Celia and Rosalind, by taking to the road in their flight from Frederick's court to the Forest of Arden, embody this double nature. On the one hand, their class-crossing disguises evoke the complicated issue of vagrancy in early modern Britain, foregrounding the period's excessive anxieties concerning the increasing prevalence of common mobility – particularly that which, like vagrancy, was often centred on roads. However, while Celia and Rosalind's recourse to Orlando's aforementioned 'common road' is disruptive in numerous ways, allowing them to veer dangerously from their socially prescribed gender, class and/or domestic roles, it is simultaneously indispensable to the realisation of a comedic ending, one complete with a set of marriages that effectively repair the inherently patriarchal structures of the play's society. This paradoxical presentation of roads is alluded to as early as Act 1, for Celia's declaration to Rosalind that 'if we walk not in the trodden paths, our very petticoats will catch [burs]' (1.3.13–15) becomes intensely ironic in retrospect: in linguistic and conceptual terms, a 'common road', Orlando's appellation for vagrancy, is in many ways a very well-trodden path, and Celia and Rosalind's habitation of it is anything but easy or conventional. In fact, as I will show, the double nature of Celia and Rosalind's road travel is even further amplified by the way in which their vagrant-like mobility intersects with another paradox, the early modern female traveller, for despite early modern British censure of women's travel as culturally, politically and religiously disruptive, there is nonetheless an enduring fascination with the supposedly constructive or reparative potential of the exceptional travelling woman in literature of the era.[3]

I will take up an examination of the double function of both roads (primarily represented on stage through references to vagrant mobility) and female travel within *As You Like It* in three sections. I will begin by examining how Shakespeare explicitly foregrounds Celia and Rosalind's physical travel to the Forest of Arden, a journey that is often considered by critics to be largely absent from the play, through his careful construction of their vagrant-like disguises. In the following section, I will consider the multiple ways in which Celia and Rosalind's travel is cast as dangerously or disruptively vagrant by various characters who alternately criminalise and romanticise it. Finally, I will turn to the patriarchally reparative function of their vagrant female travel. Despite my use of categorical terms such as 'disruptive' and 'reparative', which I use partly as a structuring mechanism, I will throughout be concerned with addressing the tensions that arise between them on different levels. That is, what is 'disruptive' or 'reparative' of various patriarchal structures can of course be quite the opposite for the individual woman, as well as for the work of dismantling those very structures.

The 'common road' to Arden

In a 1975 article entitled 'The Way to Arden: Attitudes toward Time in *As You Like It*', Rawdon Wilson counters an assumption he finds to be implicit within much previous criticism of the play: that it 'contains no mention of the journey from Duke Frederick's court to the Forest of Arden' (1975: 16). Although he maintains, alongside earlier critics, that there is no description of a journey 'marked by dusty highroads, worn boots, and all the common perils of travel' (1975: 23), he nonetheless suggests that Shakespeare does not, in fact, set up a stark 'structure of contrast and juxtaposition in which a bare minimum of casual and sequential development is present' between the court and Arden (1975:

16). There is, Wilson maintains, indeed a 'way to Arden', which can be found in the slow shift from objective to subjective understandings of time experienced by characters such as Orlando, a shift which constitutes 'a mental voyage of discovery which leads to the recognition of self and the importance of feelings' (1975: 23).

While Wilson sees the play's various journeys to Arden within metaphysical terms, I wish to argue that Shakespeare, while admittedly confining Celia and Rosalind's actual physical travel off stage, does not neglect it; the image of 'dusty highroads' is called to mind systematically throughout the play and is, in fact, integral to both Shakespeare's construction of the women's dissenting behaviour and the play's comedic ending. In his essay 'Where Are the Woods in *As You Like It?*', Stuart Daley calls for a 'thorough study of the settings' of the play, one which resists 'exaggerating [its] sylvan settings' (1983: 180, 172). Daley is primarily interested in re-examining assumptions surrounding the term 'forest', which to early modern audiences would have 'denoted a largely untilled district composed of pastures, wastes, and usually but not necessarily woods', as well as in calling attention to the ways in which 'the sunny fields' inhabited by Celia and Rosalind comprise a neglected setting that is distinct from the 'dark, perilous woods' haunted by Duke Senior (1983: 174, 180). I suggest that the road or roads from Frederick's court to Arden comprise another oft-neglected, non-sylvan backdrop to the events which follow Celia and Rosalind's departure from home, one which also deserves further critical discussion than it has received to date. Julie Sanders writes of 'the world of the early modern roads and highways that forms a kind of spectral geography to [plays like Ben Jonson's] *The New Inn*, shaping, shadowing, and standing behind its onstage events and actions' (2011: 155). Similarly, the road to Arden, like a ghost, appears to linger persistently behind many other elements of the play, spectrally ubiquitous through the constant presence of Celia and Rosalind's vagrant-like disguises.

The association between vagrancy and roads was an enduring commonplace in early modern Britain, and reflects the production of the early modern road as what Henri Lefebvre (1991) would term a socially constructed space.[4] As Robert Jutte puts it, although 'the beggar on the road is a figure as old as the phenomenon of poverty itself', in the sixteenth century 'the problem of vagrancy had progressed beyond the narrow confines of towns which were hostile towards idlers and itinerant poor, reaching nation-wide European dimensions' (1994: 191). William Carroll writes that, in England,

> Vagrants were . . . considered a physical threat as well as a philosophical one, because their very nature was to cross boundaries, to transgress categories of all kinds. Their actual wandering over the rural roads and urban streets of the kingdom is the external figure of their equally radical slippage between other conceptual and political categories. (Carroll 1996: 6)

Accordingly, there is an abundance of early modern texts that depict beggars and vagrants committing criminal activities on the road. Take, for instance, S. R.'s 'Martin Markall', which avidly describes figures who 'stand in highways to ask alms, whom men are afraid to say Nay unto honestly, lest it be taken away from them violently' and cautions that 'men cannot safely ride in the highway, unless they ride strong' ([1610] 2002: 394). Critics such as Linda Woodbridge (2011) and Patricia Fumerton (2003) warn of the danger in assuming that such texts reveal historical facts about the lived experience of vagrancy in the early modern period. Woodbridge, for instance, shows how texts such as Thomas Harman's *A Caveat or Warning for Common Cursetors, Vulgarly Called Vagabonds* (1566), from which many contemporary authors drew their so-called facts, actually 'influenced statutes' on vagrancy and homelessness (2011: 4). Meanwhile, Fumerton shows in particular how drama, with its emphasis on acting and role playing, 'reinforces the illusion promoted by rogue pamphlets that vagrants were rogues in disguise'; thus, dramatisations of vagrancy often characterise the abject poverty of the vagrant poor as a mask to be donned at will for profit (Fumerton 2003: 226). Nonetheless, rogue pamphlets and drama alike can reveal important information, if not on the facts of vagrancy then on the cultural significance of its false or exaggerated representation.

In addition to this physical correlation between roads and vagrant or vagrant-like figures within early modern texts, the link between roads and attributes considered to be innately vagrant appears in more abstract formulations as well. In a 1568 letter to Elizabeth I concerning Mary, Queen of Scots, for instance, Lord Scrope and Sir Francis Knollys stress that 'surely to have hyr [Mary] caryed furr into the realme is the high waye to a dangerous sedition' ([1568] 1825: 243). In her 1570 'Declaration of the Queen's Proceedings since her Reign', issued following the Northern Rebellion, Elizabeth similarly refers to those who have 'enticed the vulgar and common sort to fancy some novelties and changes of laws and rulers, as the ordinary high way to all sensual and unruly liberty' ([1570] 1899: 37). 'Unruly liberty', as I will discuss later, is a particularly important concept both for *As You Like It* and for early modern representations of vagrancy in general.

Although critics of *As You Like It* have frequently focused on Rosalind's gender-crossing disguise, 'a swashing and a martial outside' (1.3.116) that is meant to help ward off potential 'assailants' (1.3.110) on the road, Celia's initial plan when Rosalind laments 'what danger will it be to us, / Maids as we are, to travel forth so far?' (1.3.104–5) involves not a gender-crossing disguise but a class-crossing one. Rather than deterring 'assailants' through the appearance of brute, masculine strength, Celia means to do so by imitating them:

> I'll put myself in poor and mean attire,
> And with a kind of umber smirch my face;
> The like do you. So shall we pass along
> And never stir assailants. (1.3.107–10)

Janna Segal has called attention to the fact that not only has Celia's class-crossing disguise been largely neglected by critics, but so has the fact that 'as Ganymede, Rosalind denaturalizes not only gender but social-class structures to become the brother to Celia as Aliena' (Segal 2008: 4).[5] It must be noted, of course, that the mobile or itinerant poor were not automatically and exactly equivalent to the vagrant poor – that is, Celia and Rosalind's class-crossing disguises do not necessarily, in and of themselves, disguise the women as vagrants. As Fumerton has shown, however, the line between 'itinerant poor workers' who moved frequently to find employment and those considered to be legally vagrant was thin; 'as a result', she writes, 'the "legitimate" destitute traveller not only rubbed elbows with the "illegitimate" vagrant, but also risked at any moment being identified as such' (2006: xi–xii). As I hope to show in the next section, the repeated association of Celia and Rosalind's 'common' travel with characteristics that were attributed (however wrongly or stereotypically) to the vagrant poor reflects the blurring of these two categories.

First, however, I would like to briefly outline some of the ways in which Shakespeare explicitly constructs the onstage presence of Celia and Rosalind's class-crossing disguises; present throughout four acts of the play, these disguises would appear to abide on stage as a perpetual reminder of the link between roads and vagrant mobility, and therefore of the physical journey that Shakespeare supposedly so neglects. In particular, Shakespeare takes pains to emphasise Celia and Rosalind's class-crossing by departing in a number of ways from Lodge's prose romance *Rosalynde*, which was first published in 1590 and from which Shakespeare draws the basis for many (though certainly not all) of the play's characters. There are three divergences that I wish to highlight. First, Shakespeare magnifies the degree of Celia's adopted poverty. Whereas Lodge's Alinda is only described as putting off 'her royall weedes' in favour of 'more homelie attire' (Lodge 1590: 34), Shakespeare's Celia specifies distinctly that she will take on 'poor and mean attire' (2.3.107). This disparity is exemplified by the very names of the characters, for Celia tells Rosalind that as part of her disguise she will use a new name 'that hath a reference to my state, / No longer Celia, but Aliena' (1.3.124); both her name and her assumed character are further removed from her former identity as princess than are those of Alinda, who takes on the same appellation (Aliena) as her literary antecessor.

Second, and related to the first, changes to the status of Rosalind's Ganymede disguise also throw into relief the greater impoverishment of Celia's Aliena. Lodge's Rosalynde assures her cousin that 'I will buy mee a suite, and haue my rapier very handsomely at my side, and if any knaue offer wrong, your page wil shew him the point of his weapon' (Lodge 1590: 34). By effectively positioning herself as Alinda/Aliena's servant, Rosalynde/Ganymede upholds a measure of Alinda's former status. Although Shakespeare's Rosalind states that 'I'll have no worse a name than Jove's own page, / And therefore look you call me Ganymede' (1.3.120–1), she is never otherwise explicitly described as Aliena's page; indeed, in all references afterwards, Ganymede is Aliena's brother.

Finally, although Lodge's Alinda expresses discomfort with the fact that they 'haue no man in their companie' and suggests that 'it would be their greatest preiudice in that two women went wandring without either guide or attendant' (Lodge 1590: 34), in *As You Like It* it is Rosalind who voices dismay over the idea of two women travelling alone; Celia appears to be perfectly confident that simply 'pass[ing] along' (1.3.109) as denizens of the road will be enough to protect them. In an even greater departure from Lodge's romance, Shakespeare then has Rosalind propose that they convince Duke Frederick's fool, Touchstone, to accompany them. Although her reasoning is that Touchstone will 'be a comfort to our travel' (1.3.127), his presence also presumably, based on Rosalind's own professed misgivings, makes unnecessary not only her own gender-crossing disguise but also both women's class-crossing disguises. As has been suggested by critics such as Robert Kimbrough (1982: 23–4), Rosalind's decision to disguise herself despite Touchstone's presence – not to mention her refusal to discard her male attire upon encountering both her father and Orlando in the Forest of Arden – suggests reasons for her gender-crossing disguise that go deeper than the need for protection. However, I would argue that the same can be said for Celia's disguise. Despite her uncle's nearby presence and her purchase of a cottage, Celia remains 'browner than her brother' (4.3.88) and the 'poverty of her' (5.2.5–6) is so blatant as to be immediately noticeable even to a man (Oliver) who has been dispossessed of everything he owns, almost up to and including his life.

'These foolish runaways': disrupting the social order

If Celia ostensibly presents these class-crossing disguises as a guarantor of personal safety, protecting against assault, her strategy of donning 'poor and mean attire' has a major flaw, in early modern British terms, that I wish to highlight: to travel as a commoner without a passport – that is, without permission – would have been to open oneself to the very real possibility of punishment and arrest as a vagrant.[6] From the very start, then, the play invites awareness of the criminal and socially disruptive nature of the two women's travel. At multiple points throughout the sixteenth and seventeenth centuries, legislation was passed criminalising vagrancy and detailing appropriate discipline for those individuals who were apprehended. The effect was, in some ways, to essentially render poverty a crime; such legislation was aimed not at those who had committed serious offences in their travels, such as murder or assault, but rather at those who simply begged or wandered unchecked. Were this not the case, Paul Slack notes, there would have been no need for vagrancy legislation at all, for those guilty of more egregious crimes 'would have been indicted and convicted for the more serious offense' (1988: 92). The 1597 'Acte for Punyshment of Rogues, Vagabondes and Sturdy Beggars' was aimed at, among others, 'all persons calling themselves Schollers going about begging'; 'all idle persons going about in any Cuntry eyther begging or using any subtile Crafte or unlawfull Games and Playes'; 'Juglers Tynkers Peddlers and Petty Chapmen wandring abroade'; and 'all such persons not being Fellons wandering and pretending themselves to be Egipcyans, or wandering in the Habbite Forme or Attyre of counterfayte Egipcians'. Such people, the act determined, should be

> stripped naked from the middle upwardes and . . . openly whipped untill his or her body be bloudye, and shalbe forthwith sent from Parish to Parish by the Officers of every the same the nexte streighte way to the Parish where he was borne, if the same may be knowen by the Partyes Confession or otherwise; and yf the same be not knowen, then to the Parish where he or she last dwelte before the same Punyshment by the space of one whole yeare, there to put him or her selfe to labour as a true Subject ought to do. (Tawney and Power 1924: 355–6)[7]

These and other typical punishments, such as the use of pillories and stocks, point towards what Woodbridge calls 'the period's desperate need to pin down any kind of slipperiness with punishments producing immobility' (2011: 56).

Although all vagrant mobility was seen as an ongoing crisis throughout the early modern period, there appears to have been a special unease over the threat posed by vagrant women. While records reveal that the vagrant population was predominantly male, with poor women much more likely to remain close to their home towns or villages and men more likely to take to the road (Woodbridge 2011: 253), texts such as Harman's *Caveat* insist that 'for one man that goeth abroad there are at the least two women' ([1567] 1990: 123). Given both the essential criminalisation of poverty and the deep concern over female vagrants, the frequency with which Celia and Rosalind's class-crossing, vagrant-like travel is cast in criminal terms is unsurprising. Even in the planning stages, the cousins themselves conceive of their journey within the parameters of criminal activity. In addition to her identification of Celia's 'umber smirch[ed] ... face' (1.3.108), which recalls the 1597 Acte's condemnation of anyone 'wandering in the Habbite Forme or Attyre of counterfayte Egipcians' (Tawney and Power 1924: 355), Segal highlights Celia and Rosalind's other criminal acts: their 'plot "to steal" (1.3.128) Touchstone from the court'; 'Celia's offer to "woo" Touchstone (1.3.123) into agreeing to accompany them', which 'invokes ... sexually licentious behaviour'; Celia's suggestion that she and Rosalind make off with their jewels and wealth; Celia's decision to become a 'fugitive' from her father; and their choice of new names, an act that references what was seen to be a distinct element of criminal culture – the practice of 'adopting names identifying one's status or occupation' (Segal 2008: 12). Although Segal is more specifically focused on the racial aspect of Celia's disguise and her use of the gypsy sign, all of these 'criminal' acts Segal lists above have links to early modern representations of vagrancy more generally as well.

Perhaps less immediately overt than the manner in which Celia and Rosalind depict their own travel as criminal – but significant nonetheless – are the ways in which Frederick characterises both their travel and their physical mobility in general. Notably, this is something that he does even without knowledge of their vagrant-like disguises; the implication appears to be that, even without the framework of vagrancy to magnify the criminal aspects of their travel, there is a criminal aspect to their female mobility in and of itself. His first lines to Celia and Rosalind set the stage:

DUKE FREDERICK How now, daughter and cousin! are you crept hither to
see the wrestling?
ROSALIND Ay, my liege, so please you give us leave. (1.2.144–6)

Not only does Frederick's use of the word 'crept' (which the *OED* notes was 'Formerly said of snakes, worms, and other creatures without limbs' [1.a]) associate Celia and Rosalind's physical movement with deceit and treachery, but Rosalind's response can be read as an echo of Charles's comment to Oliver in the first scene of the play that, because their 'lands and revenues enrich' Frederick, he has given Duke Senior and his lords 'good leave to wander' (1.1.103–4) within the Forest of Arden.

The repetition, in subsequent scenes, of Frederick's 'leave' to move or to travel foregrounds the absence of 'leave' that accompanies Celia's departure from her father's court. In Frederick's very next scene on stage, this issue of 'leave' or permission for physical mobility rises again. Having learned that both Celia and Rosalind are missing despite the fact that only Rosalind has been banished, Frederick instructs his lords to 'let not search and inquisition quail / To bring again these foolish runaways' (2.2.20–1). Although Frederick does not know of Celia's disguise, it is notable that vagrants were essentially treated as runaways, often duly returned to their home parishes upon apprehension. This is a link that Shakespeare makes elsewhere as well: his Richard III refers to his enemies as 'A sort of vagabonds, rascals and runaways, / A scum of Bretons, and base lackey peasants' (5.5.45–6).[8]

Aside from the attendant connotations of 'fugitive, deserter, or escapee' (*OED*, A.1.a), Frederick's use of the term 'runaways' is important not only for the way in which it criminalises Celia's travel, but also for the way in which her travel potentially criminalises the movements of others. Having been exiled from remaining 'So near our public court as twenty miles' (1.3.40), Rosalind has technically been given leave to depart; however, in Frederick's assumption that her travel is connected to Celia's escape, Rosalind's previously sanctioned flight becomes criminal as well. She is presumably one of the 'runaways' to which Frederick refers, given that, for the entirety of this scene (as well as his next scene, following which he never returns to the stage), he never once refers to Celia and Rosalind as separate people. The scene commences with his incredulous query, 'Can it be possible that no man saw *them*?' (2.2.1, emphasis added), and ends with his reference to 'runaways', plural. The two lords who go on to respond to Frederick's opening inquiry switch from singular to plural pronouns; the first, presumably expecting that Frederick is only concerned about the whereabouts of his daughter, states that

> I cannot hear of any that did see her [Celia]
> The ladies her attendants of her chamber
> Saw her abed, and in the morning early,
> They found the bed untreasur'd of their mistress. (2.2.4–7)

The second lord, however, follows Frederick's lead and reinforces the conflation of Celia and Rosalind; he tells Frederick that Hisperia 'believes wherever *they* are gone / That youth [Orlando] is surely in *their* company' (2.3.15–16, emphasis added).[9]

If Celia's flight turns Rosalind's previously acceptable travel into a matter for Frederick's concern, it similarly transforms the movements of various male characters as well. In this way, although Frederick exhibits concern with the mobility of both men and women within his realm, there appears to be a special emphasis on the criminality of his daughter's travel. Outside of his connection to Celia, Frederick has little cause for interest in Orlando's whereabouts: Le Beau 'counsel[s]' Orlando 'To leave this place' in order to avoid Frederick's displeasure (1.2.251–2), and once Orlando has done so, Frederick does not consider him again until one of his lords, as quoted above, suggests that Orlando has departed in the company of Celia and Rosalind. Likewise, Jacques de Boys announces a sudden reversal of Frederick's 'good leave to wander' in the final scene of the play, declaring that

> Duke Frederick, hearing how that every day
> Men of great worth resorted to this forest,
> Address'd a mighty power; which were on foot,
> In his own conduct, purposely to take
> His brother here and put him to the sword. (5.4.153–7)

It remains a fact that Frederick is content to let Duke Senior freely roam Arden not until more *men* have joined him, but until Frederick's daughter and niece have entered the confines of the forest as well. Aside from Touchstone, Orlando, Adam and Oliver, all of whom Frederick sees as connected to Celia's travel,[10] we see no 'men' enter Arden who were not already there – unless, of course, we are to include Rosalind's Ganymede, who is described as a 'boy' rather than a 'man' on multiple occasions.

In addition to the many criminal nuances of Celia and Rosalind's class-inflected travel, their journey to Arden also draws on early modern representations of vagrancy in one other very important way: it idealises freedom from the restraints of society. Celia's declaration that 'Now go we in content / To liberty, and not to banishment' (1.3.133–4), which closes the scene in which she and Rosalind plan their flight from court, has been read by critics such as Chris Fitter (2010) and Will

Fisher (2010) as a reference to the liberties of London, 'where the city authorities lack jurisdiction' (Fitter 2010: 136); this becomes particularly significant given both the Globe's situation in such a liberty and the fact that players often ran the risk of being labelled 'vagrant'. Celia's use of the term 'liberty', however, also evokes the prevalence of outlandish tales that, as outlined by Fumerton, were 'repeatedly cited by authorities of the period about respectable persons willfully "going over" to the "sweet" "liberty" of vagrancy' (2003: 255).[11]

Woodbridge addresses in detail the presence of this phenomenon in early modern rogue literature, suggesting

> that vagrants became associated with the freedom that ordinary citizens felt they lacked, that romanticizing their free-wheeling life was a vicarious escape from a world of religious strictness, moral probity, humanistic moderation, civil manners, homekeeping domesticity – all of which a citizen could assent to in theory but which in practice must often have felt confining. (2011: 21)

Although Celia and Rosalind do set up a household in Arden, and thus in a sense maintain a type of 'homekeeping domesticity', it is not a strictly patriarchal one. As Segal points out, readings that view Celia and Rosalind as approximating a heterosexual relationship through their Aliena and Ganymede disguises do 'not take into account the sibling relationship they adopt when in disguise' (2008: 17, n. 10). Further, critics such as Allison Grant and Will Fisher have examined the homoerotic possibilities offered by Celia and Rosalind's joint purchase of a cottage. Grant considers 'the nature of Celia's affection for Rosalind' and the place of female-female desire in the play (2011: 54), while Fisher (2010) explores the ways in which Celia and Rosalind challenge patriarchal ideals of the household. Ultimately, Shakespeare's specific placement of this alternative household within the 'skirts' (3.2.329) of the Forest of Arden is telling of its troublesome status, for this single word simultaneously genders their household as feminine and implies marginality and trespass. If Celia's class- and race-crossing disguise and her journey to Arden are an 'extenuat[ion]' rather than an inauguration of her 'dissident acts at court', as Segal argues (2008: 8), there are certain transgressive endeavours that can only easily take place once she and Rosalind have taken to the road.

'The measure of their states': the reparative 'value' of travel

His rightful rule abruptly restored by the abdication of his brother Frederick, Duke Senior addresses the inhabitants of the Forest of Arden who have gathered to witness the four weddings that close the final act of the play:

> First, in this forest, let us do those ends
> That here were well begun and well begot:
> And after, every of this happy number
> That have endured shrewd days and nights with us
> Shall share the good of our returned fortune,
> According to the measure of their states. (5.4.169–74)

For all of the transgressive potential of Celia and Rosalind's travel, Duke Senior's insistence that their marriages within the Forest of Arden 'were well begun and well begot' implies that their travel also holds an implicit patriarchal value, for such 'ends' would have been unthinkable without it. The same can be said for a number of the play's other events as well, for Celia and Rosalind's flight from Frederick's court precipitates Oliver's banishment, and thus his redemption and reconciliation with Orlando. It also, as discussed above, spurs Frederick's advance on the Forest of Arden, which in turn instigates not only his religious conversion but also the restitution of the crown to his elder brother.

The revelation that all will be rewarded 'according to the measure of their states' is ambiguous: it can alternately (or simultaneously) be read as constructing a system in which each individual is honoured based on merit, or as reinstituting a hierarchical system based on ranks of state at court. Celia and Rosalind's positions in either system seem clear: once they reappear on stage with Hymen, Celia is directly spoken to once but never speaks herself, and Rosalind communicates her own possession first by father and then by husband. However, this line also recalls in interesting ways Celia's determination to take the name 'Aliena' because it 'hath a reference to my *state*' (1.3.123, emphasis added) – that is, to her position as alien, outsider and transgressor, all designations that can be associated in some way with vagrancy. This recollection throws into relief the complicated relationship between Celia and Rosalind's criminal 'state[s]' and the comedic 'ends' of *As You Like It*, the first of which, as we have seen, must precede the latter.

As Woodbridge shows in impressive detail, there are deeply seated links between vagrancy and certain types of comedy. Not only was the figure of the vagrant often idealised, as discussed above; it was also comedised in adverse ways. Drawing a link between rogue literature and jestbooks in particular, Woodbridge emphasises 'The weirdly comic nature of much Renaissance writing about vagrancy and the poor' (2011: 18–19). She comments further that 'what happened to women through antifeminist jesting happened to vagrants and other powerless groups – they were laughed into corners from which they could not escape' in order to make them appear less threatening (2011: 50). This is not exactly what happens in *As You Like It*, and certainly there are differences between the comedic structure of a jestbook and that of a comedy play. But there is, I think, a kind of connection. Woodbridge continues by arguing that 'to position a book about homeless people as a jestbook was to identify the poor as funny, worthy of contemptuous laughter rather than social concern – the same impulse that relegated the lowborn to comic subplots in the drama' (2011: 51). There is a certain insidiousness to the way in which the play's ending co-opts the travel of two women, in vagrant-like disguises, to repair the patriarchal structures of a society that will ultimately confine them.

And yet, I would argue that the road does not necessarily end here. In many ways Susan Carlson's observation holds true – 'the conventions of the comic genre that Shakespeare adapted to his drama' ultimately cannot resist 'accord[ing] [Celia and Rosalind] a loss of freedom, a loss of choice'. Carlson entertains the hope, however, that *As You Like It*, 'with its surprising lack of a definition for marriage, leaves ample room for producers (and scholars) to posit their own definitions' (1987: 167). Indeed, work by a number of critics in the past decade does just that. Allison Grant, for instance, suggests that Celia's sudden marriage to Oliver might be read not as adherence to convention, but 'as a way for her to subvert the very system which is pressuring her yet again' (2011: 65). While Celia and Rosalind are supposedly folded back into the patriarchal structure of society through their marriages, Celia's decision to marry Oliver, as Grant points out, also allows her to 'maintain her intimacy with Rosalind' (2011: 65). In the end, the double nature of Celia and Rosalind's road becomes circular. Even at the supposed end of their journey, they push at the boundaries.

Notes

With many thanks to Glenn Clark and Judith Owens for reading drafts of this chapter.

1. Shakespeare (2005), *As You Like It*, ed. Agnes Latham. All further

quotations from the play will be taken from this edition and reference will be given in the text.
2. See, for instance, Barnaby 1996, Fitter 2010, McDonald 1995, Montrose 1981 and Wilson 1992.
3. Consider, for example, the importance of Britomart's travel to Faerie Land in Merlin's prophecy of Britain, the role of Imogen's travel in *Cymbeline*, or the role played by Portia's travel to Venice in achieving a (supposedly) comedic ending in *The Merchant of Venice*. While gender-crossing is here a repeated theme, as it is with Rosalind (although not, significantly, with Celia), these women's travel and gender-crossings are inherently tied to their positions as marriageable women or wives.
4. For the spaces inhabited by the unsettled, the vagrant and the itinerant poor in early modern England, see Fumerton 2006, especially pp. 53–6.
5. Throughout her article, Segal also argues that in 'smirch[ing] [her] face' with 'umber' (*As You Like It*, 1.3.108) Celia partakes in the early modern practice referred to by Brian Reynolds (2002) as 'becoming gypsy', another criminal act and one related to vagrancy.
6. Other potential problems are also raised by their disguises. For instance, women associated with roads were often interpreted by others as sexually licentious. For more on the perceived link between women, roads and licentiousness, see Sharon Emmerichs's chapter in this volume.
7. The 1597 act, 39 Elizabeth, c. 4, is reprinted in Tawney and Power 1924.
8. Shakespeare 2000.
9. Such twinning of Celia and Rosalind is in keeping with the way in which Celia describes herself and her cousin, telling Frederick that she and Rosalind 'still have slept together, / Rose at an instant, learn'd, play'd, eat together, / And whereso'er we went, like Juno's swans, / Still we went coupled and inseparable' (1.3.69–72).
10. Or would see, if Frederick were ever to acknowledge Adam.
11. Fumerton here quotes from Edward Hext's 1596 'Letter to Burghley on the increase of Rogues and Vagabonds'; see also Kim Durban's chapter on *A Jovial Crew*, in this volume.

Works cited

Barnaby, Andrew (1996), 'The Political Conscious of Shakespeare's *As You Like It*', *Studies in English Literature, 1500–1900* 36.2, pp. 373–95.
Carlson, Susan (1987), 'Women in *As You Like It*: Community, Change, and Choice', *Essays in Literature* 14.2, pp. 151–69.
Carroll, William C. (1996), *Fat King, Lean Beggar: Representations of Poverty in the Age of Shakespeare*, Ithaca and London: Cornell University Press.
Daley, Stuart (1983), 'Where Are the Woods in *As You Like It*?', *Shakespeare Quarterly* 34.2, pp. 172–80.
Elizabeth I [1570] (1899), 'A Declaration of the Queen's Proceedings since her Reign', in William Edward Collins, *Queen Elizabeth's Defence of her Proceedings in Church and State*, London: Society for Promoting Christian Knowledge, pp. 35–47.

Fisher, Will (2010), 'Home Alone: The Place of Women's Homoerotic Desire in Shakespeare's *As You Like It*', in Rebecca Bach and Gwynne A. Kennedy (eds), *Feminisms and Early Modern Texts: Essays for Phyllis Rackin*, Selinsgrove: Susquehanna University Press, pp. 99–118.

Fitter, Chris (2010), 'Reading Orlando Historically: Vagrancy, Forest, and Vestry Values in Shakespeare's *As You Like It*', *Medieval and Renaissance Drama in England* 23, pp. 114–41.

Fumerton, Patricia (2003), 'Making Vagrancy (In)visible: The Economics of Disguise in Early Modern Rogue Pamphlets', *English Literary Renaissance* 33.2, pp. 211–27.

—— (2006), *Unsettled: The Culture of Mobility and the Working Poor in Early Modern England*, Chicago: University of Chicago Press.

Grant, Allison (2011), 'The Dangers of Playing House: Celia's Subversive Role in *As You Like It*', *Selected Papers of the Ohio Valley Shakespeare Conference* 4, pp. 53–67.

Harman, Thomas [1567] (1990), *A Caveat for Common Cursitors, Vulgarly Called Vagabonds*, in Arthur F. Kinney (ed.), *Rogues, Vagabonds, & Sturdy Beggars: A New Gallery of Tudor and Early Stuart Rogue Literature*, Amherst: University of Massachusetts Press, pp. 109–53.

Jutte, Robert (1994), *Poverty and Deviance in Early Modern Europe*, Cambridge: Cambridge University Press.

Kimbrough, Robert (1982), 'Androgyny Seen through Shakespeare's Disguise', *Shakespeare Quarterly* 33.1, pp. 17–33.

Lefebvre, Henri (1991), *The Production of Space*, trans. Donald Nicholson-Smith, Oxford: Blackwell.

Lodge, Thomas (1590), *Rosalynde*, <http://gateway.proquest.com./openurl?ctx_ver=Z39.88-2003&res_id=xri:eebo&rft_id=xri:eebo:citation:99845219> (last accessed 15 May 2019).

McDonald, Marcia A. (1995), 'Elizabethan Poor Laws and the Stage in the Late 1590s', *Medieval and Renaissance Drama in England* 7, pp. 121–44.

McRae, Andrew (2009), *Literature and Domestic Travel in Early Modern England*, Cambridge: Cambridge University Press.

Montrose, Louis (1981), '"The Place of a Brother" in *As You Like It*: Social Process and Comic Form', *Shakespeare Quarterly* 31.1, pp. 28–54.

Reynolds, Brian (2002), *Becoming Criminal: Transversal Performance and Cultural Dissidence in Early Modern England*, Baltimore: Johns Hopkins University Press.

S. R. [1610] (2002), 'Martin Markall, Beadle of Bridewell', in A. V. Judges (ed.), *Key Writings on Subcultures, 1535–1727: Classics from the Underworld*, vol. 1, London and New York: Routledge, pp. 383–433.

Sanders, Julie (2011), *The Cultural Geography of Early Modern Drama, 1620–1650*, Cambridge: Cambridge University Press.

Scrope, Henry, and Francis Knollys [1568] (1825), 'The Lord Scrope and Sir Francis Knollys to Queen Elizabeth, reporting their first Interview with the Queen of Scots', in Henry Ellis (ed.), *Original Letters, Illustrative of English History*, vol. 2, London: Harding, Triphook and Lepard, pp. 238–43.

Segal, Janna (2008), '"And Browner than Her Brother": "Misprized" Celia's Racial Identity and Transversality in *As You Like It*', *Shakespeare* 4.1, pp. 1–21.

Shakespeare, William (2000), *Richard III*, ed. John Jowett, Oxford: Oxford University Press.
—— (2005), *As You Like It*, ed. Agnes Latham, London: Arden Shakespeare.
Slack, Paul (1988), *Poverty and Policy in Tudor and Stuart England*, London and New York: Longman.
Tawney, R. H., and Eileen Power (eds) (1924), *Tudor Economic Documents*, vol. 2, London: Longmans.
Wilson, Rawdon (1975), 'The Way to Arden: Attitudes toward Time in *As You Like It*', *Shakespeare Quarterly* 26.1, pp. 16–24.
Wilson, Richard (1992), '*As You Like It* and the Enclosure Riots', *Shakespeare Quarterly* 43.1, pp. 1–19.
Woodbridge, Linda (2011), *Vagrancy, Homelessness, and English Renaissance Literature*, Urbana: University of Illinois Press.

Chapter 5

Traversing Monstrosity: Perilous Women and Powerful Men upon Shakespeare's Roads

Sharon Emmerichs

Roads and women

At first thought, a mundane and utilitarian object such as a road or a street may not conjure cultural associations with gendered behaviours, dubious morality, or transformation and loss of self, though it takes a very short journey to get there. We soon remember that the word 'streetwalker' became a common word for a prostitute in the early 1590s, that warnings against the dangers of 'street people' have existed for centuries, and that in Shakespeare's time – as well as our own – the road was a common location for various violent crimes, such as rape, theft and bodily assault. Roads are essential for a working civilisation, as they make travel, trade and commerce possible, but they have also become irrevocably connected to notions of bodily, spiritual and sexual danger – especially for women. This dichotomic identity of the road did not originate in the early modern period; in ancient Greek, the word for 'road' is *hê hodos*, which has a masculine ending (*-os*) but uses a feminine article (*hê* instead of *ho*). The road itself, therefore, is masculine, but speakers express it as feminine to create a dual gendered identity. Granted, this happens within the context of linguistic 'grammatical gender', which does not predict gender based on the characteristics of the object, but this unusual construction does prompt us to consider the value – and effect – of ascribing both a masculine and a feminine modifier to the object. This idea of a dual-gendered tension of the road survives in many of Shakespeare's works where the road (street, avenue, highway, path, etc.) signifies variable and often oppositional meanings for his male and female characters, and for many characters it becomes a conduit for various forms of transformation and change. As such, Shakespeare portrays the road as a place of moral, spiritual, sexual, religious and cultural danger for his characters, particularly for the women. This is partially due to roads acting as public areas aligned with the concept that women belong primarily to private or domestic spaces, but in many instances Shakespeare translates the literal concept of the road – that is, a manufactured object that starts in one place, ends in another, and facilitates movement between these locations – into the movement of characters who travel upon them from one state of being to another. Specifically, in the case of his European Christian female characters, interaction with roads causes a transformation from innocence to corruption[1] and represents potentially malignant spaces that ultimately produce monstrosities by the end of the journey.[2] According to Peter Swirski, Henri Lefebvre contends that urban spaces are themselves transformative objects that 'must be seen in the context of what preceded [them]' (Swirski 2007: 83), and this is certainly true of the circulatory system of any urban centre – the roads. It therefore stands to reason that those who traverse them are changed by them as well. Within Shakespeare's plays, however, the road diverts women from their 'natural' or intended paths, usually defined by their masculine protectors (fathers, brothers, husbands, etc.), and turns them into the Aristotelian concept of a monster. They transform into something unnatural that leads them away from their original, intended purpose. In comedies such as *As You Like It*, which is the main focus of this chapter, such characters can often escape the subversive power of the road and find their intended purposes once more. In his tragedies, such as *Titus Andronicus*, they cannot, and these women end up degraded, mutilated and dead.[3]

Roads and men

This is not to say that portrayals of men completely escape the dangerous and corruptive forces associated with public roads in early modern history and literature, but Elizabethan texts often show that such corruption originates from a female influence. In Robert Greene's famous pamphlet 'A Notable Discouery of Coosinage: Now daily practised by sundry lewd persons, called Connie-Catchers, and Crosse-Biters', for example, Greene discusses the practice of 'crossbiting' wherein women stand idly in the road and lure innocent men into sexual encounters and then steal their money and goods. He sets the scene by describing how,

> In summer euenings, and in the winter nightes, these trafickes, these common truls I meane, walke abroad either in the fields or streetes that are commonly hanted, as stales to drawe men into hell ... Some vnruly mates that place their content in lust, letting slippe the libertie of their eies on their painted faces, feede vpon their vnchaste beauties till their hearts be set on fire: then

come they to these minions, and court them with many sweet words. (Greene 1591: 14)

Greene makes it clear that the danger originates with 'such damnable stales as drawes men on to inordinate desires' (17) who frequent the public roads rather than with the characters of the victims themselves. His language emphasises the corrupt nature of the women, calling them 'truls',[4] 'stales'[5] and 'vnchaste beauties', which implies that their transformation to the monstrous caused by their association with the 'streetes' they frequent has already occurred. Only then can the women transfer that corruption to men, and though it is the female body that enacts their transformations from innocent to corrupt rather than the street itself, the street presents a danger as a locus of that corruption. Greene's description of the women drawing 'men into hell' makes this claim rather pointedly, especially when we remember that in the early modern era 'hell' was a euphemism for female genitalia. If the street can make monsters out of women, such women can destroy men with their monstrous bodies, and Greene warns all

> gentlemen, marchents, yeomen and farmers, let this to you all, and to euery degree else, be a caueat to warn you from lust, that your inordinate desire not be a meane to impouerish your purses, discredit your good names, [or] condemn your soules. (Greene 1591: 15)

So, while streets and roads can certainly pose a threat to masculine morality, the danger is first distilled from feminine monstrosity.

In Shakespeare, the road and feminine licentiousness are so closely connected that they can become one and the same thing. In *2 Henry IV*, Prince Hal, upon hearing of a woman with whom Falstaff keeps company, states, 'This Doll Tearsheet should be some road,' to which Poins replies, 'I warrant you, as common as the way between Saint / Albans and London' (2.2.158–60).[6] Doll Tearsheet, a prostitute, becomes synonymous with a well-travelled road; she is common, used by many men, and obliquely poses a great danger to England and to Hal himself – or at least his future family and lineage. St Albans, a city just to the north and west of London, was the site of the start of the War of the Roses in 1455, the English civil war that presaged the fall of the House of Lancaster, Henry's family house. The road between St Albans and London became a strategic one in the Battle of St Albans in 1461 (Davis and Frankforter 1995: 432) that determined the Yorkist victory, and Poins's invocation of this particular road alludes to the downfall of Prince Hal's future son, Henry VI, and the beginning of the Tudor reign. Doll Tearsheet is not just a road; she's the road that helped bring down an empire and destroy Prince Hal's legacy. In two sentences, Hal and

Poins manage to describe Doll Tearsheet as powerful enough to destroy both the country of England and the men who live there, sexually and violently, simply by conflating her character with a road.[7]

The direct violence men faced from other men on the road, however, tended to be represented as physical and monetary, rather than moral. Indeed, Ivor Brown states that 'if Shakespeare carried home his London gains for the support of his family in Stratford, he must have seen to it that he had stout companions and have tried to avoid night-travel, gaining shelter from the highwaymen before dark' (Brown 1960: 88). The roads out of London were notoriously dangerous as prime locations for violence and theft, but the streets within London also represented perilous spaces, especially for outsiders coming into the city carrying cash or goods. Once again, Greene explains the dangers regarding the entrapment of these 'conies' (victims of theft and pickpocketing), but he does so with very different language than he employed for the female 'crossbiters'. Greene defines a player of a coneycatching con as a 'Setter' and labels this particular criminal only as male – 'the nature of the Setter, is to draw any person familiarly to drinke with him, which person they call the Conie' (Greene 1591: 5) – and elaborates how

> Conny-Catchers, apparalled like honest ciuil gentlemen, or good fellowes, with a smooth face, as if butter would not melt in their mouthes, after dinner when the clients are come up from Westminster hal and are at leasure to walke vp and down Paules, Fleet-street, Holborne, the sttronde, and such common hanted places. (6)

Greene neglects to employ the stinging insults and accusations of moral degradation in these descriptions. These con men are not 'common' or 'vnchaste' or 'damnable'; instead he paints them as 'ciuil gentlemen' and 'good fellowes'. Greene in no way attempts to argue that coneycatchers are in fact good men, but it becomes clear that the thievery women perform on the roads comes with a heaped helping of moral degradation, whereas the male criminals that work on the 'sttrondes' of London are depicted as smart, savvy and cool enough that butter 'would not melt in their mouthes'. Elsewhere in the pamphlet, Greene lambasts the coney-catchers for preying upon innocent victims, but still describes them as being able to 'imploy all their wits to overthrow such as with their handy thrifte satisfy their harty thirst: they preferring cosenage before labour, and chusing an idle practise before any honest form of good liuing' (6). Several pages later, he refers to the victimisation of a Welshman as a 'merry iest' (10) rather than as an actual crime, which invokes an image of a gentleman rogue or friendly prankster. Such violence upon the road would certainly create victims, but not necessarily monsters. So while both coneycatchers and crossbiters practise their trades in the street, the men are described as idle, witty, clever and merry while the women are scripted as monstrous.

Roads and placelessness

One source of this negative depiction of streets and roads is the problem of public vagrancy that had plagued English cities and outlying areas since the medieval era, as Karalyn Dokurno describes in her chapter. Roads were sites for visible homelessness, civil disorder and disobedience, drunkenness and idle behaviours, and came to be associated with a type of citizen who actively works against the public good. According to Richard Kaeuper, 'medieval agrarian society had undoubtedly long generated a floating population of vagabonds who attracted the suspicions of those in authority' that resulted from overpopulation (1988: 172–3), and Andrew McRae states that,

> Like social mobility, geographical mobility was widely condemned. Placelessness was generally equated with the crime of vagrancy: a category which, as Patricia Fumerton has recognised, was wielded in an effort to comprehend a condition actually experienced by a significant proportion of the population. . . . Such people functioned within a society which simply did not have adequate mechanisms to comprehend them – in a sense, to place them. (McRae 2008: 86)

Trustworthiness, then, was contingent on having a single, identifiable space – a home or a brick-and-mortar business – into which one could step off the road. Migrant workers, itinerant merchants, tinkers and gypsies[8] have long been associated with lawlessness and civil disorder due to the inherent placelessness of their professions.[9] Orlando, a noble gentleman, voices this anxiety in *As You Like It* when he learns that his brother Oliver means to kill him, to 'burn the lodging where you used to lie / And you within it' (2.4.24–5). Orlando laments:

> What, wouldst thou have me go and beg my food?
> Or with a base and boisterous sword enforce
> A thievish living on the common road?
> This I must do, or know not what to do:
> Yet this I will not do, do how I can;
> I rather will subject me to the malice
> Of a diverted blood and bloody brother. (2.3.31–7)

Orlando, facing either death by his brother's hand or a life of vagrancy and crime on the public road, voices his choice for death. His faithful servant, Adam, saves him with the offer of five hundred crowns, which is enough money to establish a respectable existence and avoid a life on the road. Orlando's fears are not entirely unfounded; according to A. L. Beier, 'just over half [of the vagrants in Elizabethan England] were single males' and 'frequent references in official records to "whole", "mighty", "sturdy", and "lusty" rogues suggest a fear of the physical violence a gang of men could use against individuals' (Beier 1974: 6). The description in these records reflects the language found in Greene's account as well, and scripts those men who live a life of criminality on the road using positive adjectives, and they are given signifiers of approbation. We can understand why Orlando might choose a quick death at his brother's hands over the unknown violence and pain at the hands of 'mighty', 'sturdy' and 'lusty' strangers.[10]

Orlando also fears how the road will change him from a productive citizen to an idle one, as vagrancy was considered the purview of those who actively refused to look for or perform honest work. Orlando tells Adam:

> O good old man, how well in thee appears
> The constant service of the antique world,
> When service sweat for duty, not for meed!
> Thou art not for the fashion of these times,
> Where none will sweat but for promotion,
> And having that, do choke their service up
> Even with the having: it is not so with thee.
> But, poor old man, thou prunest a rotten tree,
> That cannot so much as a blossom yield
> In lieu of all thy pains and husbandry. (2.3.56–65)

Orlando praises Adam's work ethic, as only a hard and assiduous worker could have managed to save such a sum of money by being in service, while defining himself as a 'rotten tree' that cannot produce anything worthwhile. In leaving his home and taking to the road, Orlando fears a fall into idleness, especially since 'by this time idleness was considered a voluntary act and a form of disobedience, rebellion and sin to be punished' in Elizabethan England (Beier 1974: 10). While modern historians understand that most vagrants were 'classed as migrants in search of subsistence' (11), the popular view of placeless men in Shakespeare's time corresponded more with Greene's perception of those who make their living in the road as having nefarious and idle agendas. In truth, the majority of the masculine vagrants on Elizabethan roads most likely came from a troubled history of discharged military troops left without any form of financial support, farmers displaced by the practice of enclosure, and the dissolution of the monasteries – practices that had absolutely nothing to do with laziness or idleness.[11] According to Gāmini Salgādo, 'many of the men and women who had been ousted from their livings turned to a life of vagrancy and a large army of them were to be found thronging the Elizabethan highways, making travel an event not to be undertaken lightly' (Salgādo 1977: 120). Orlando would not be alone in his anxiety regarding his loss of position, status, employment and household. His fears make perfect sense considering the ease with which a man could transform from an established, productive and respectable citizen to a vagrant who must scratch out a living through charity and violence on the roads. Orlando considers no other options for himself, as he has most likely witnessed this story played out time and again in his own society. However, Shakespeare inserts the implied argument that while men could certainly fall to immoral behaviours on the road, those behaviours are considered the *natural* outcome of difficult circumstances. Orlando does not fear becoming someone monstrous – something *unnatural*. Instead, he defines his sword, through which he would enact his violence, as 'base' and 'boisterous' – words that imply anxiety about the low-class implications of those actions rather than the moral or spiritual outcomes they could produce. Orlando does not fear for his soul; he does not fear hell. His language is, in fact, quite Greene-like in its gentle use of benign adjectives, lacking vitriol and implications of moral degradation. It is clear, however, that Orlando has no desire to become another Falstaff, losing himself to the depravity of highway robbery and low-class associations with the criminal underworld.[12]

Women who take to the road, however, risk much more. There are many reasons women would have need and cause to travel: for pleasure; for pilgrimage; with an army to tend to the soldiers;[13] to give birth at a desired location, such as a particular abbey or relative's home;[14] to escape contagion or plague; or, as with men, because of a loss of home, position or livelihood. In fact, women were such a common sight on the roads that Thomas Platter, a Swiss gentleman and diarist, wrote in 1599 that women in England

> have far more liberty than in other lands and know just how to make good use of it for they often stroll out or drive by coach in very gorgeous clothes and the men must put up with such ways and may not punish them for it. (Qtd in Hogarth 2014: 5)

Platter's complaint implies a recognition of male powerlessness at odds with his vision of masculine sovereignty over women, which also fits the narrative of roads – and women on those roads – having a transformative power over men. Ivor Brown, also writing about Platter, attests that one thing which immediately surprised the Swiss visitor must also have impressed Shakespeare when he came from the country to the capital. That was the freedom enjoyed by women. They could go about the town, watch its spectacles, and sample its various forms of gaiety and conviviality in a way little known at that time on the mainland of Europe. This liberty was not restricted to the rich and titled ladies on the exalted fringe of society or to those on the lowest level, the types whom Shakespeare said should be set down as 'the sluttish spoils of opportunity / And daughters of the game.' (Brown 1968: 124)

Women, then, were a common sight on the roads of London, but this freedom did not come without a cost. According to Caroline S. Dunn, most women in medieval and early modern London who suffered from sexual assault were 'taken from the street outside into indoor locations' (Dunn 2007: 107), which means they suffered from increased vulnerability via increased visibility. Shakespeare alludes to this in *Titus Andronicus* when Aaron devises a plot to enact revenge upon Titus through his daughter, Lavinia:

> Take this of me: Lucrece was not more chaste
> Than this Lavinia, Bassianus' love.
> A speedier course than lingering languishment
> Must we pursue, and I have found the path.
> My lords, a solemn hunting is in hand;
> There will the lovely Roman ladies troop:
> The forest walks are wide and spacious;
> And many unfrequented plots there are
> Fitted by kind for rape and villany:
> Single you thither then this dainty doe,
> And strike her home by force, if not by words. (2.1.109–19)

A masculine protector is not enough to save Lavinia in this case, as the villains kill her husband, Bassianus, and snatch her directly off the road. As a result, Lavinia transforms into one of the most visible monsters of Shakespeare's canon of women, with her hands 'lopp'd and hew'd' (2.4.17) from her body and her tongue cut from her mouth. After the rape she can no longer fulfil her natural purpose, since 'Lavinia's archetypally Roman womb is polluted and forever disabled as a source of true Roman issue' (Gillies 1994: 107), and as a result Titus kills her with his own hands. She went from being the idealised Roman woman and daughter – obedient, full of filial piety, loyal and chaste – to an abomination of nature that must be destroyed, and all because she walked down a specific road and fell prey to its dangers. The sexual nature of her assault reinforces the peril women faced on the roads, despite the freedoms they enjoyed to traverse them. Even Queen Elizabeth, who set quite an example of a woman's ability to travel with her many progresses, moved from estate to estate around England with an enormous retinue of court nobles and soldiers to ensure her safety because of such dangers to her person and her life.[15] As such, Elizabeth's progresses were a source of great anxiety to the court, not only for the staggering amount of money and resources she and her entourage consumed during her travels, but also for how open and vulnerable she made herself by being outside, in public, and travelling upon the roads. It was much too easy for her advisors to envision her falling to Lavinia's fate.

However, a startling number of early modern women struggled with placelessness and made up a significant portion of the vagrant population in Shakespeare's age. Women were often more at risk of displacement due to their inability to engage in highly paid and skilled professions. As J. M. Bennett states, 'women tended to work in low-skilled, low-status, low-paid jobs, and they also tended to be intermittent workers, jumping from job to job or juggling several tasks at once. This was true in 1300, and it remained true in 1700' (Bennett 1992: 158). This lack of job security and opportunity made women particularly vulnerable to vagrancy, but nowhere in the writings and descriptions of these women do we see them described as 'whole', 'sturdy' or 'mighty' in their activities or physical bodies. Instead, they are once again linked to sexual licentiousness and leading men into moral decay. Beier describes a body of Elizabethan work he calls 'rogue literature' written by the likes of Robert Greene, Thomas Dekker and Thomas Harman in which female vagrants 'were supposed to attach themselves to male rogues as concubines' (Beier 1974: 7). Women also acted as beggars, decoys and hucksters, but they could rarely escape the moral condemnation that came with the intersection of women's bodies and the public road. To turn again to *As You Like It*, Celia alludes to the problems women experience when their bodies occupy roads in response to Rosalind's plaintive lament:

> ROSALIND O, how full of briers is this working-day world!
> CELIA They are but burs, cousin, thrown upon thee in holiday foolery: if we walk not in the trodden paths our very petticoats will catch them.
> (1.2.8–12)

Rosalind describes the world as riddled with briers, which are sharp, thorny branches that will scratch and snag skin and clothing, and prevent her from moving forward. To her mind, the world is full of obstacles that stop her from reaching her goals, specifically resolving her father's exile and her own thwarted desire to marry Orlando. Celia, however, turns the metaphor around; to her, a woman's experience on the less-travelled (i.e. rural) road is full of burs that are thrown at women when they dare to deviate from their expected path, when they leave the protection of the familiar and (implied) safer main road.[16] These burs can represent permanent blemishes on their reputations, stuck fast to their bodies and difficult to remove, but ultimately the burs become part of women's physical bodies, as Rosalind describes when she says, 'I could shake them off my coat: these burs are in my heart' (1.2.13). There is no way to remove the blemishes of the road from women's bodies or experiences once they have been acquired. They become internalised and indistinguishable from the woman herself.

Rosalind and Celia's stories are in many ways defined by their relationship with roads. When Duke Frederick exiles Rosalind upon pain of death, she and Celia decide to run away together. They devise a plan for Rosalind to dress as a man and name herself Ganymede, for Rosalind states that, 'Alas, what danger will it be to us / Maids as we are, to travel forth so far! / Beauty provoketh thieves sooner than gold' (1.3.107–9). Even though English women were 'allowed' freedoms of travel that startled foreign visitors, Rosalind demonstrates a keen awareness of the dangers the road poses for women, especially as they are forced to travel out of the city and into the forest of Arden. Once beyond the protective and civilised walls of the city, they would be easy victims for all kinds of masculine assault, from the theft of their purses to the loss of their virtue. According to Dunn, 'in rural parts of the country outdoor areas – fields, forests, and parks – generally afforded the rapist the isolation required to commit the deed' and in such spaces 'a woman was likely to be found alone and outside in an isolated area, with no one close by to protest if she was merely dragged from the road or taken behind a tree' (Dunn 2007: 109–10). The crossdressing ruse is necessary, then, to protect themselves from such violence, for Rosalind's masculine identity would at least help to defend both her and Celia, who dresses as a poor woman under 'Ganymede's' protection. Both women are more willing to be mistaken for vagrants than they are to present as noble women on the road. This is perhaps one of the best examples of Aristotelian monstrosity in Shakespeare, as Rosalind's journey upon the road visibly turns her into a person acting against her own nature – her womanhood. She deliberately chooses a name that represents both masculine and feminine identities, as Ganymede 'embodies the androgynous beauty celebrated in descriptions of the mythological figure' (Carter 2011: 101) to retain at least some control of her own nature. However, like the dual-gendered linguistic rendering of the ancient Greek *hê hodos*, Rosalind now embodies a dual-gendered identity as she prepares to step on to the road to begin her journey to Arden. Now the burs in her heart that come from following the roads less travelled are the only things she can link to her natural femininity:

> Were it not better,
> Because that I am more than common tall,
> That I did suit me all points like a man?
> A gallant curtle-axe upon my thigh,
> A boar-spear in my hand; and – in my heart
> Lie there what hidden woman's fear there will –
> We'll have a swashing and a martial outside,
> As many other mannish cowards have
> That do outface it with their semblances. (1.3.13–21)

While her exteriority reflects her new masculine identity, her heart – her inner self – remains true to her original nature. However, she earlier described her heart as filled with the burs picked up on the road, which Celia visualises as obstacles women face in society. They could also represent the dangers of such unfrequented roads, such as loss of reputation, virtue, virginity and value. Either way, Rosalind becomes monstrous in her androgyny; she simply chooses the form of monster that protects her moral and physical self while attempting to retain at least part of her natural identity. It is rather ironic that Rosalind chooses this method to retain her sexual virtue, considering that crossdressing and androgyny in the early modern period in England were considered a cultural problem often associated with prostitution and led to a controversy regarding appropriate female dress that raged through London from about 1580 to 1620. Jean E. Howard states that,

> At the simplest level, the polemical, monarchical, and theatrical preoccupation with crossdressing ... signaled a gender system under pressure. As fact and as idea, crossdressing threatened a normative social order based upon strict principles of hierarchy and subordination, of which woman's subordination to man was a chief instance, trumpeted from pulpit, instantiated in law, and acted upon by monarch and commoner alike ... Nonetheless, there *are* records of women, in particular, who did so, and were punished for offenses, such as prostitution, associated with crossdressing. (Howard 1994: 95–6, her emphasis)

Howard also alludes to how crossdressing intersects with monstrosity in her description of 'mannishly attired women' viewed as 'unnatural' by early modern people, and argues that even in theatre 'it was this confounding of sexual "kinds" on the actor's part that particularly roused the fury of a Northbrooke, a Stubbes, a Prynne' (94).

Shakespeare takes this representation of the crossdressing woman as monstrous one step further and employs the literal language for it. In *Twelfth Night*, Viola finds herself in a situation similar to that of

Rosalind and Celia.[17] She is alone in a foreign land without any masculine protection, and so dresses up as Cesario and travels to the court of Duke Orsino to find employment. Knowing that her virtue would be suspect if she simply showed up on her own having traversed the public roads without supervision, she risks the danger to her body by presenting herself as male[18] rather than gamble with the dangers to her virtue by remaining a woman. As such, she self-identifies as monstrous after Olivia makes known her interest in Cesario:

> I am the man: if it be so, as 'tis,
> Poor lady, she were better love a dream.
> Disguise, I see, thou art a wickedness,
> Wherein the pregnant enemy does much.
> How easy is it for the proper-false
> In women's waxen hearts to set their forms!
> Alas, our frailty is the cause, not we!
> For such as we are made of, such we be.
> How will this fadge? my master loves her dearly;
> And I, poor monster, fond as much on him;
> And she, mistaken, seems to dote on me. (2.2.25–35)

Both Rosalind and Cesario must choose between two forms of social deviance when they take to the road, both of which result in a form of monstrosity that endangers their bodies and souls, as well as those of the people around them.[19] Because these plays are comedies, however, Shakespeare allows both women to revert to their natural selves, unlike Lavinia, who fulfils the tragic trope of the loyal and innocent woman permanently corrupted by agents beyond her control. The influence of their time on the road is not permanent, which allows for a traditionally happy ending. During their respective plays, they experience another type of placelessness, a vagrancy of self in which they remain constantly in motion between two fixed points of natural and unnatural behaviour. Therefore, they stay under suspicion until the play's resolution allows them to shed the title of 'monster' and settle back into their natural selves, ready to perform their expected functions and purposes for their societies. Orsino in *Twelfth Night* makes a point of remarking on how Viola spent their entire association 'So much against the mettle of your sex' (5.1.319), yet Viola is quick to reclaim her original identity once it is safe for her to do so:

> If nothing lets to make us happy both
> But this my masculine usurp'd attire,
> Do not embrace me till each circumstance
> Of place, time, fortune, do cohere and jump
> That I am Viola. (5.1.247–51)

Rosalind likewise rejects her masculine disguise so that she can lawfully marry Orlando, and both women find permanence and a home in the resolution of their conflicts. They have a place, sanctioned by law and society and away from the lawless dangers of the roads they have travelled.

It becomes clear, then, that in his works Shakespeare demonstrates an easy familiarity with the many definitions and cultural meanings of the road; roads are places of power, places of peril, and places where these two elements of early modern life come together. Roads have helped to define nations and characterise cities, from the 'stynking streets' and 'lothsome lanes' (Wilcox 2010: 21) of London to the high roads lined with inns, coach houses and shops to attract weary travellers and eager tourists. Roads were sites for perpetrating crimes as well as administering punishments.[20] They are contradictions, paradoxes and juxtapositions. For a seemingly simple manufactured and maintained object, the road carries with it a multitude of meanings of seemingly infinite variety, to conscript one of Shakespeare's own terms of character.

The intersection of roads, gender and Shakespeare, then, merges to create a snapshot of early modern attitudes regarding not just the physical dangers of travelling the roads, but the moral and spiritual concerns as well. Roads had a profound impact on every aspect of life, and it is not surprising that they would come to be associated with England's triumphs as well as its anxieties and shame. It is essential to remember, however, that these characteristics, both positive and negative, change their meanings – in essence, transform – when viewed through the lenses of different genders. An association of gender, whether overt and physical or metaphorical and figurative, changes everything it touches – and roads touch nearly every element of early modern society. Shakespeare's works reflect this, and whether that attention is deliberate or simply a product of cultural indoctrination is not particularly important; we can still read the road in Shakespeare's dramas and tease meaning from his plays and characters via this examination.

Notes

I would like to thank my research assistants for their invaluable help and contributions to this project: Nancy Strahan and Charlee Laurie, students of the University of Alaska, Anchorage Department of English Internship Program, headed by Dr Trish Jenkins.

1. For characters who do not naturally represent the Renaissance idealised, and therefore traditionally desirable, Caucasian English woman, however,

either the transformation from 'natural' to 'unnatural' is reversed, as we see in comedies, such as with Jessica in *The Merchant of Venice*, or a woman's inherent monstrousness intensifies and becomes permanent, as happens in tragedies, for instance with Tamora in *Titus Andronicus*.

2. For the purposes of this chapter, I am using Aristotle's definition that depicts a monster as a mistake that occurs in nature and fails to achieve its designed purpose. In his *Physics* Aristotle defines monstrosity thus:

> Now surely as in intelligent action, so in nature; and as in nature, so it is in each action, if nothing interferes. Now intelligent action is for the sake of an end; therefore, the nature of things also is so . . . Now mistakes come to pass even in the operations of art: the grammarian makes a mistake in writing and the doctor pours out the wrong dose. Hence clearly mistakes are possible in the operations of nature also. If then in art there are cases in which what is rightly produced serves a purpose, and if where mistakes occur there was a purpose in what was attempted, only it was not attained, so must it be also in natural products, and monstrosities will be failures in the purposive effort. (Aristotle 1941: 250)

Shakespeare himself uses the word 'monster' to express a multitude of meanings for both masculine and feminine characters.

3. Clearly roads are not the only factor in such fates, but I argue that their contributions to the transformative elements of the plays are noteworthy and significant.

4. According to the *OED*, the word 'trul[l]' means first 'A female prostitute' and second simply 'A girl'.

5. The *OED* also defines this word as both 'a person who acts as a decoy; esp. the accomplice of a thief or sharper' and 'a prostitute of the lowest class, employed as a decoy by thieves. Often used as a term of contempt for an unchaste woman.'

6. All quotations from Shakespeare come from *The Oxford Shakespeare* (2005).

7. Her name could also be explicitly connected to the concept of streets and roads. While Eric Partridge argues that the name 'Tearsheet' is reflective of Doll's profession because 'she tore the bed-sheets in her amorous tossings or because her partners did so while consorting with her' (Partridge 1967: 258), René Weis claims that Tearsheet could be read 'as a misprint of 'Tearstreet' (i.e. streetwalker) in the light of Hal's anticipating meeting 'some road'' (Shakespeare 1997: 166).

8. Interestingly, David Cressy tells us that,

> Fragmentary as it is, the evidence leaves the impression that Gypsies could travel around England with little risk of molestation, despite the intent of the law. Interceptions and arrests were rare. Notably distinct from ordinary vagrants and beggars, the Gypsies moved on foot, or with small strings of horses, following the geography and calendar of markets and fairs. Banded in groups of a dozen or so members, and occasionally gathering in companies of a hundred or more, they must have seemed intimidating as well as strange. (Cressy 2016: 58)

9. Shakespeare recognised the problematic definitions of such folk, especially as pertains to women and sexuality, as we can see in Mercutio's speech in *Romeo and Juliet*:

> Now is he for the numbers
> that Petrarch flowed in: Laura to his lady was but a

    kitchen-wench; marry, she had a better love to
    be-rhyme her; Dido a dowdy; Cleopatra a gipsy;
    Helen and Hero hildings and harlots. (2.3.36–40)

10. To be fair, some contemporary people objected to this language as well. John Northbrooke (*fl.* 1568–79), a Protestant clergyman who often spoke out against plays and the theatre, lamented that 'If a man be a roister, and knowing how to fight his fight, then he is called by the name of honesty. If he can kill a man, and dare rob upon the highway, he is called a tall man, and a valiant man of his hands' (Northbrooke 1582: n.p.).
11. Nor was all vagrant and violent behaviour on the roads confined to the lower classes. According to Keith Thomas, 'the upper classes had their "roisters", "hectors", and duellists' as well (Thomas 2009: 51).
12. Falstaff himself laments the difficulties that roads pose for him when Poins steals his horse on the highway, forcing him to walk rather than ride. He states, 'Eight yards of uneven / ground is threescore and ten miles afoot with me' (2.2.25–6).
13. According to Elizabeth Anne Gross, '[Barton] Hacker cites compelling statistical evidence for the presence of women accompanying armies as non-combatants throughout Renaissance Europe' (Gross 2006: 100).
14. For an interesting examination of this subject, see McPherson 1998.
15. For more information on Elizabeth's progresses, see Leslie 1998 and Kapelle 2011.
16. Joseph Papp and Elizabeth Kirkland write that 'There are only four or five major roads in all of England. The roads connecting smaller towns and villages are just dirt tracks, frequented by bands of robbers' (Papp and Kirkland 1988: 12).
17. It is important to remember, also, that the actors playing these characters would be adolescent boys, which adds some extra layers of complex social gendered confusion to the mix.
18. As is demonstrated when she is challenged to a duel while walking the road alone on her way from visiting Olivia back to Duke Orsino's house.
19. A person harbouring someone engaged in criminal activity would fall under suspicion almost as strongly as the guilty party.
20. Gustav Ungerer discusses the civil punishment of 'carting' in early modern England and makes the point that carting 'was not a gender-specific punishment' but was 'inflicted on both Englishmen and women throughout the sixteenth century irrespective of their social status' (Ungerer 2003: 176).

Works cited

Aristotle (1941), *Physics*, trans. R. P. Hardie and R. K. Gaye, in Richard McKeon (ed.), *The Basic Works of Aristotle*, New York: Random House.

Beier, A. L. (1974), 'Vagrants and the Social Order in Elizabethan England', *Past & Present* 64, pp. 2–24.

Bennett, J. M. (1992), 'Medieval Women, Modern Women: Across the Great Divide', in David Aers (ed.), *Culture and History 1350–1600: Essays on English Communities, Identities, and Writing*, London: Harvester Wheatsheaf, pp. 147–75.

Brown, Ivor (1960), *Shakespeare in his Time*, London: Thomas Nelson and Sons.

—— (1968), *The Women in Shakespeare's Life*, New York: Coward-McCann.

Carter, Sarah (2011), *Ovidian Myth and Sexual Deviance in Early Modern English Literature*, New York: Palgrave Macmillan.

Cressy, David (2016), 'Trouble with Gypsies in Early Modern England', *The Historical Journal* 59.1, pp. 45–70.

Davis, J. Madison, and A. Daniel Frankforter (1995), *The Shakespeare Name and Place Dictionary*, New York: Routledge.

Dunn, Caroline S. (2007), 'Damsels in Distress or Partners in Crime? The Abductions of Women in Medieval England', dissertation, Fordham University, New York.

Gillies, John (1994), *Shakespeare and the Geography of Difference*, London: Cambridge University Press.

Greene, Robert (1591), *A notable discouerie of coosinage*, <http://gateway.proquest.com./openurl?ctx_ver=Z39.88-2003&res_id=xri:eebo&rft_id=xri:eebo:citation:99841559> (last accessed 15 May 2019).

Gross, Elizabeth Anne (2006), 'Domestic Agents: Women, War, and Literature in Early Modern England', dissertation, Pennsylvania State University.

Hogarth, Alan James (2014), '"Hide, and Be Hidden, Ride and Be Ridden": The Coach as Transgressive Space in the Literature of Early Modern London', *Early Modern Literary Studies* 17.2, pp. 1–20.

Howard, Jean E. (1994), *The Stage and Social Struggle in Early Modern England*, London: Routledge.

Kaeuper, Richard (1988), *War, Justice and Public Order: England and France in the Later Middle Ages*, Oxford: Clarendon Press.

Kapelle, Rachel (2011), 'Predicting Elizabeth: Prophecy on Progress', *Medieval and Renaissance Drama in England* 24, pp. 83–105.

Leslie, Michael (1998), '"Something Nasty in the Wilderness": Entertaining Queen Elizabeth on her Progresses', *Medieval and Renaissance Drama in England* 10, pp. 47–72.

McPherson, Kathryn Read (1998), 'Great-Bellied Women: Religion and Maternity in Seventeenth-Century England', dissertation, Emery University, Atlanta.

McRae, Andrew (2008), 'The Literature of Domestic Travel in Early Modern England: The Journeys of John Taylor', *Studies in Travel Writing* 12.1, pp. 85–100.

Northbrooke, John (1582), *Spiritus est Vicarius Christi in Terra*, <http://gateway.proquest.com./openurl?ctx_ver=Z39.88-2003&res_id=xri:eebo&rft_id=xri:eebo:citation:99848529> (last accessed 15 May 2019).

Papp, Joseph, and Elizabeth Kirkland (1988), *Shakespeare Alive!*, New York: Bantam Books.

Partridge, Eric (1967), *Shakespeare's Bawdy*, New York: Routledge.

Salgādo, Gāmini (1977), *The Elizabethan Underworld*, Totowa, NJ: Rowman & Littlefield.

Shakespeare, William (1997), *Henry IV, Part 2*, ed. René Weis, Oxford: Oxford University Press.

—— (2005), *The Oxford Shakespeare: The Complete Works*, 2nd edn, ed. Stanley Wells and Gary Taylor, Oxford: Oxford University Press.
'stale, n.', *OED Online* (2017), <http://www.oed.com/view/Entry/206916?p=emailAwCa9fQY8mtkw&d=206916> (last accessed 27 November 2018).
Swirski, Peter (2007), *All Roads Lead to the American City*, Hong Kong: Hong Kong University Press.
Thomas, Keith (2009), *The Ends of Life: Roads to Fulfilment in Early Modern England*, Oxford: Oxford University Press.
'trull, n.', *OED Online* (2017), <http://www.oed.com/view/Entry/206916?p=emailAwCa9fQY8mtkw&d=206916> (last accessed 27 November 2018).
Ungerer, Gustav (2003), 'Prostitution in Late Elizabethan London: The Case of Mary Newborough', *Medieval and Renaissance Drama in England* 15, pp. 138–223.
Wilcox, Helen (2010), '"Ah, Famous Citie": Women, Writing, and Early Modern London', *Feminist Review* 96, pp. 20–40.

II. The Embodied Road

Chapter 6

Not So Tedious Ways to Think about the Locations of the Early Playhouses

Laurie Johnson

In 1590, having been ordered to vacate the Rose playhouse and perform instead at the smaller venue at Newington Butts, Lord Strange's Men petitioned the Privy Council to allow them to return to their Bankside venue.[1] The Councillors relented, claiming they were 'satisfied ... by reason of the tediousness of the way' to the alternative venue (Foakes 2002: 285). This notion that Newington Butts was too remote to be viable remains widely accepted, with many scholars reiterating the Councillors' claim (see, for example, Jolly 2014: 161; Schoenbaum 1987: 136; Thomson 1999: 67; Wickham 1972: 60). Such a view props up an abiding logic that oscillates between what Henri Lefebvre calls the 'paradigmatic' and 'symbolic' approaches to the history of space, but it crucially ignores the 'syntagmatic' approach (Lefebvre 2009: 230). The paradigmatic distinction between travelling players and those who settled in London playhouses supports the symbolic focus given to playhouses in descriptions of the golden age of the London theatre. A key feature of this distinction is the relative absence of roads from one side of the binary: a London-centric bias at the symbolic core of these histories positions roads as a focus for travelling players, but roads disappear from narratives of the rise of the purpose-built 'permanent' playhouses around London. A syntagmatic approach allows us to put the London playhouses back on the roads, so to speak, by understanding how the mobility of prospective audiences, rather than simply the push for permanence by travelling players, contributed to the rise of the early modern playhouses. By mandating the practice of archery, Elizabeth and her predecessors ensured a steady stream of Londoners to the fields surrounding the city, making the roads to these fields profitable sites for the establishment of the playhouses.

'London companies' and strolling players

In 'Space and the State', Lefebvre explains that a history of space should decipher how it has been represented. One way to do this is to 'compare space to a language and study its dimensions: the *paradigmatic* (relevant oppositions . . .) – the *syntagmatic* (sequences and linkages: roads, avenues and boulevards, routes, etc.) – the *symbolic*' (Lefebvre 2009: 229–30). Space in and around Elizabethan London has long been construed in Shakespeare studies principally on the basis of only the first and third of these dimensions. Shakespeare, of course, is symbolically positioned at the epicentre of the Shakespearean theatre. By the end of the eighteenth century, it was established that Shakespeare had been a key member of a company of players and that his plays were performed at the Globe and the Blackfriars. Accordingly, Edmond Malone's monumental 'Historical Account of the English Stage' was principally confined to the study of these two venues, with only cursory treatment of others. Regarding the Theatre, Malone supposed that it was the 'first building erected in or near the metropolis purposely for scenick exhibitions' (Malone 1799: 52), but he knew only that it was '*erected in the fields*' (Malone 1799: 53, nn. 8–9, italics original). His focus thus turned inward toward the symbolic centre of the 'English' stage as the sites that housed Shakespeare's company, which at the time was believed to include only the Blackfriars within the City of London and the Globe on the Bankside.

This Shakespeare-centric focus contributed to a paradigmatic opposition in Malone's work between the 'Companies of London' and the 'strolling players' (Malone 1799: 48–9, n. 3), with his interest directed exclusively toward the former. While theatre historians have for over a hundred years been more interested than Malone in studying provincial playing, their studies of the period tend invariably to be shaped by this paradigm. John Tucker Murray's *English Dramatic Companies 1558–1642* gave readers in 1910 records of known performances by all playing companies in the period from the start of Elizabeth's reign to the Interregnum, but he organised the study into two volumes: the first for the 'London Companies' and the second for 'Provincial Companies'. His first volume runs to 370 pages, without appendices – lists of both court and provincial performances are included with the scholarly commentaries offered on each of the companies – but his second volume devotes just 117 pages to documenting the known dates of performance of 159 different companies, with almost no commentary save for the occasional biographical note on a patron. Edmund Kerchever Chambers could have been expected to expand this model in his four-volume study, *The Elizabethan Stage*, in 1923, but the 352 pages he devotes to 'The Companies' (Volume II, Book III) focus almost exclusively on those London companies to which Murray lent only his first volume.

More recently, Andrew Gurr's influential *Shakespearian Playing Companies* follows in the same vein by focusing mainly on companies that fill out Murray's first volume. His first two substantive chapters explain Gurr's reasoning: in 'The First London Companies', he explains that the attraction of performing in the theatres in and around London, together with proximity to the court, was the biggest influence on the development of playing companies from 1574 to 1642 (Gurr 1996: 19); in 'Travelling', he describes the 1572 Act for the Punishment of Vagabonds as the precipitating cause for companies to bind themselves to patrons, which saw companies deployed in London to fulfil each patron's goal of providing entertainment for the Queen (Gurr 1996: 37, 55–7). Gurr's argument is that players quickly came to think of London as their 'home' (21). This argument is replicated by Simon Blatherwick in the 'London' entry for *The Oxford Companion to Shakespeare* (Gurr 1996: 256–9), pointing out how the repressive poor laws drove players to permanently locate their businesses in London (Gurr 1996: 257). Similarly, *The Cambridge Introduction to Early Modern Drama, 1576–1642* begins by asking why London by the early seventeenth century became 'the epicentre of an unparalleled theatre industry' (Sanders 2014: 1). Although it is an introductory volume on 'early modern drama', the focus rarely shifts beyond this epicentre.

The paradigmatic distinction between London companies and touring companies is maintained even when the same group of players is known to have been ostensibly involved in both – it has become customary to view the touring cohort as a lesser offshoot, reduced in size, limited in resources, performing the 'bad' quartos, and only one poor return away from 'breaking'. At the heart of this distinction is thus not necessarily the players themselves, who from one moment to the next could readily be identified either as 'at home' in London or as 'on tour' in the provinces. A language of proximity to London defines the representation of space in which the players conduct their business and is, as such, characterised by the presence or absence of movement: the touring player is *on the road*, strolling from one playing stop to the next; the London player is well established *in a permanent playhouse*. It is perhaps ironic that a syntagmatic view is most often apparent in studies of individual companies (McMillin and MacLean 1998; Manley and MacLean 2014; Ostovich et al. 2016), where having the scholarly gaze fixed on a single object allows opportunities to map touring routes, trace networks of connections, and so on. Yet when an individual company is studied in connection with one or another playhouse, or when the playhouse itself is the object of study, a syntagmatic approach gives way again to a paradigmatic one – understandable when the playhouse is understood as a fixed object.

Tediousness of the way

When Glynne Wickham describes the decision by Philip Henslowe to purchase the land at the Little Rose in 1585, he notes that the earlier playhouse at Newington Butts was 'badly sited', and supposes that Henslowe 'knew he could reduce "the tediousness of the way" to Newington by perhaps as much as 50 per cent' (Wickham 1972: 60). By using the Privy Council's wording to differentiate between a badly sited venue and Henslowe's Rose, Wickham reinforces the old paradigmatic opposition by configuring a fixed object (the Playhouse at Newington Butts[2]) as an object *on the road*. While I want to suggest that putting playhouses on the road is the right way to proceed, I will do so by reinforcing the syntagmatic dimension of the spatial language through which we may understand their locations rather than, as Wickham does, reinforcing a problematic paradigm that has enabled Newington Butts to be dismissed on the basis that it was sited too far away from London to have been viable. To this end, I shall first examine how and why the phrase 'tediousness of the way' was used by the Privy Council in their response to the players in 1590.

The phrase in question was by 1590 already in common use, but what is perhaps most striking is how recently it had done so. The earliest example found using the EEBO-TCP Key Words in Context search facility via Early Modern Print (Washington University in St Louis) is in Matteo Bandello's *Certaine tragicall discourses written out of Frenche and Latin*, translated in 1567 by Geffray Fenton. Writing of the travels of Dom Diego and Geniuera, Bandello notes that 'they toke away the tediousnes of the way with the pleasaunt deuises, whych passed between the two louers' (Bandello 2007: 304). The word 'tediousness' only dates in English to around half a century earlier,[3] almost exclusively to refer to an unpleasant length of time in one place or state. Of the 133 appearances of the word from 1520 to Fenton's translation of Bandello, only one ties tediousness to a 'longe iourney' – Edward Hall uses this wording in his 1548 chronicle of the houses of Lancaster and York in the context of explaining what circumstances would prevent certain Christians from travelling to Rome for the Jubilee of 1500, with comparable obstacles including being 'letted by warre, enemyes, infirmitie, weaknes' (Hall 2003: lii). Not until Bandello, then, is there tediousness 'of the way', and even here tediousness is of the inability of the lovers to 'consommat the rest of their desiers' rather than of the journey itself (Bandello 2007: 304).

As a translation, of course, Fenton's text presents the prospect that the phrase derives directly from its Italian source. A cursory glance at Bandello's tale proves the opposite: in the source text, the passage from the hermit's cave to Roderico's castle is parsed without mention of the difficulty of the journey and there is no 'tediousness' (*tediosità*) or any term based on the adjectival *tedioso* (Bandello 2007: 143). While the young don is certainly treated to his share of '*miseria*' and '*tormento*' in this brief episode, the cause of his anguish is attributed solely to being in the presence of the woman he loves without being able to act upon his feelings, and even then it is '*le forze dell'amore*' (the power of love) that makes this trial easy (Bandello 2007: 143). Thus, Fenton's 'tediousness of the way' is in no respect conveying either a metaphrastic (word-for-word) or a paraphrastic (sense-oriented) equivalence with its original. These two approaches had been the focus of translation method since antiquity (Goodwin 2013: 109), but Fenton seems to be more inclined to add new flavour to the tale by linking Diego's misery to the distance being travelled. Fenton may have been adhering to the approach to translation adopted by Martin Luther, whereupon the focus is on neither metaphrase nor paraphrase but shifts instead to the distinct form and spirit of the target language (Nida 1964: 14). William Tyndale's translation of the Bible (1525–6) had adopted this approach and, by doing the same, Fenton altered the source text to suit 'the spoken language of the people' (Nida 1964: 14).

The phrase 'tediousness of the way' may therefore have already circulated in English in common parlance. Philip Sidney's *An Apology for Poetry*, most likely written around 1580,[4] uses the phrase in comparing the inability of the philosopher to move a reader as well as the poet:

> The philosopher showeth you the way, he informeth you of the particularities, as well of the tediousness of the way, as of the pleasant lodging you shall have when your journey is ended, as of the many by-turnings that may divert you from your way. But this is to no man but to him that will read him, and read him with attentive studious painfulness. (Sidney 2002: 94)

Sidney's work was not published until 1595, so it cannot be considered a source from which others acquired the phrase. Sidney's use of it merely indicates its availability to writers by the start of the 1580s, but throughout this decade it appears to have been exclusively deployed by translators of foreign texts, suggesting common use in speech. Jeannette Fellheimer pointed out twenty-one unusual words in Fenton's translation of Bandello, from 'biggined' to 'tosspot', and observed that several were 'not represented in the *New English Dictionary*, and a number he uses earlier than the other instances noted' (Fellheimer 1946: 539). It seems reasonable to assume that these unusual words are present in his work because they exist previously in common speech. His use of 'tediousness of the way' fits into a pattern of translation toward the target language by adopting common phrases. Fenton used the phrase again in his 1579 translation of Francesco Guicciardini's *Historia d'Italia* (1130), and three other translators followed his initial example between 1576 and 1587,[5] before Anthony Munday also used the phrase in his translation of the first book of *Amadis of Gaule* circa 1590 (Munday 2003–5: 17). By the time the Privy Council used the phrase in their response to the players, then, 'tediousness of the way' appears to have been adopted as a peculiarly English expression of the difficulties of travel; it is worth asking whether this is an accurate description of the journey from London or Bankside to Newington Butts.

Clearing the King's Highway

In all of the examples of the use of the phrase 'tediousness of the way' considered above, the implied distance was substantial. What makes the way tedious is the length of the journey. In the case of Newington Butts, the distance from the river to the junction is just one mile, so it is unlikely that the Privy Council seriously considered Strange's Men endured any hardship. For the players, the distance from the Rose to Newington Butts, heading south from Maiden Lane via one of several streets on to Borough Street and then directly to the turnpike, would have been considerably less than the mile from the river to the Playhouse. Indeed, any player who performed at both the Rose and the Theatre knew that the distance between these two venues significantly exceeded that between Bankside and Newington Butts – a player would wind his way through the streets of the Clink to travel the 400 yards to the main thoroughfare, cross the river, and then travel the further mile from the north bank to the site of the Theatre in Shoreditch, or else cross the river 100 yards to the north of the Rose via ferry, then traverse crooked streets to make the journey that covers a further mile and a half.

With distance not being a valid basis for associating the trip to Newington Butts with tediousness, Gurr imagines conditions that must have contributed to the difficulty. He points out that the location 'must have been less advantageous than the Theatre's in Shoreditch on the northern side, being a good mile, or rather a muddy and difficult mile' from the bridge and adds that the 'mud on the route' was a 'serious drawback' for the venue, guaranteeing its failure (Gurr 1996: 171). There is no evidence provided to support the claim that the mile in question was any more muddy or difficult than any other stretch of road in or near London at the time. Where does Gurr's mud come from? The image may have come from Samuel Schoenbaum, whose description of the passage to Newington Butts reckons on it being 'reachable by foot on the road which, continuing Southwark High Street, cut across St. George's Fields' (Schoenbaum 1987: 136). Schoenbaum expresses relief for those who 'no longer had to cross the fields to see a play' after the venue was closed (Schoenbaum 1987: 136). It is true that St George's Fields were established on what was marshland on a tidal flood plain and were frequently wet, yet nobody ever had to cross one of these fields to get to Newington Butts. It is instead ironic that in 1618, Edward Alleyn and other residents of Bankside were sued by the innkeepers of Borough High Street for loss of business because a path through St George's Fields (later dubbed 'Dirty Lane') was being used by the people of Surrey as a shortcut to reach the Bankside attractions (Darlington 1955: 40; Roberts and Godfrey 1950: 133–5). Here the potentially muddy route was the one used to cross the fields from the south to Bankside, not the other way around, and it was to *bypass* the main thoroughfare (Figure 6.1).

Regarding Gurr's comparison, the reality of both the Newington Butts and Shoreditch playhouses is that they were situated along the same road: the King's Highway. The Theatre was closer to the City, just over half a mile to the north of Bishopsgate, but to anybody who lived inside the City, the distance could be a mile or more, depending on which streets they traversed to get to Bishopsgate. On either the north or south of London, the condition of the road was comparable not simply due to them being opposite stretches of the same highway. Both Shoreditch Street to the north of the city and the Newington Causeway to the south were established atop sections of the ancient Roman road network. The road leading north from Bishopsgate was what the Anglo-Saxon inhabitants called 'Earningas' (later Ermine) Street (Blair 2003: 256–7), and formed the basis of the modern A10 into Hertfordshire. The southern stretch of the highway is not as easy to identify with the road that the Anglo-Saxons named 'Sten' (later Stane) Street, but archaeological surveys of London have long confirmed that the Newington Causeway was one section of the road which lasted from Roman through to modern times.

Figure 6.1 Detail showing Newington Butts juncture and the highway adjacent to St George's Fields, from *A Plan of the Cities of London and Westminster, and Borough of Southwark*, 1746, John Rocque, Sheet D3, reproduced courtesy of MOTCO Enterprises Limited. © MOTCO 2001.

The Roman city of Londinium consisted of settlements on both sides of the river, with the southern settlements making up about one-quarter of the city but scattered across islands dotting the south side of the river (Cowan et al. 2009: 10–11). The earliest bridge here connected the central thoroughfare on the north settlements to Stane Street, which then connected two islands on the site of modern Southwark and continued on through the mainland to modern Chichester. As the banks of the Thames took shape in later centuries, and the site of the bridge shifted, the stretch of Roman road that extended through these islands faded into disuse, and it was presumed even by the great historian of Roman roads Ivan Margary that some remnants of Stane Street align with Borough High Street in the direction of Kennington but that the curvature of the Newington Causeway took a sharp deviation from the alignment of the Roman way from Londinium to Noviomagus Reginorum (Margary 1948: 76). Yet in 1952, roadworks 300 yards north of the Newington Butts juncture unearthed a section of metalled road on top of the gravel subsoil, some four feet below the surface, and consistent with Roman road construction (Darlington 1955: 1–2). The deviation could be explained by the topography, with the Elephant and Castle (at the northern point of the Newington Butts juncture) and St George's Church (halfway toward the juncture) being the two highest points in that area to the south of the river (Darlington 1955: 1).

The Roman preference for straight lines was superseded in the construction of Stane Street by the issue of having to cross the flood plain. As Ida Darlington explains, evidence can be found throughout the region that it was liable to flooding even in Roman times, so it was probable that 'the line of the Newington Causeway was the only route through St. George's Fields that could have been made into a firm road without the use of piles' (Darlington 1955: 2).[6] Darlington adds that in the great tidal flood of 29 September 1555, as described in John Stow's *Annales*, the waters reached inland from Lambeth as far as the causeway but the elevation of the road acted as a barrier preventing the water from spreading any further to the west (Darlington 1955: 2). Stow adds some harrowing but pertinent detail:

> That morning ye kings palace at Westminster, & Westminster hal was ouerflowne unto the staire foot going to the Chancerie and Kings bench, so that when the lord maior of London should come to present the sherifes to the barons of the exchequer, all Westminster hall was full of water, and by report there that morning, a whirrie man rowed with his boat ouer Westminster bridge into the pallace court, and so through the Staple gate ... and all the marshes on Lambeth side were so ouerflowne, that the people from Newington church could not passe on foote, but were caried by boate from

the said church to the pinfold, neare to Saint Georges in Southwarke. (Stow 1631: 627)

This day in 1555 being the Sabbath, the parishioners attended church but were stranded by the inundation, so boats conveyed them safely to the north of the turnpike.

Based on the available evidence, then, rather than the muddy and difficult mile across the fields as imagined by Gurr and Schoenbaum, the passage to Newington Butts would have been a relatively high and dry stretch of highway. Darlington notes also that in Tudor times the road was paved from London Bridge to Stones End, which is about two-thirds of the way to Newington Butts (Darlington 1955: 2–3). Instead of a muddy mile, the walk south from London would have normally consisted of a trek on paved roads for two-thirds of a mile, followed by a little over 550 yards on an elevated dirt or gravel road that even during periods of rain would drain quicker than the surrounding fields. Against the persistent fantasy of mud and drudgery, I therefore posit a reality of paving stones and high ground offered by the highway to anybody seeking to make the trek south of London.

Following the arrows

The Red Lion was erected as a temporary performance space in Whitechapel in 1567, but its exact location has remained a mystery. Only from the lawsuit by the proprietor John Brayne against the builder of some of the scaffolds have scholars been able to piece together clues to the building's location, as William Ingram does in *The Business of Playing*: 'it was built a fair distance from the City – as far to the east as the later Newington Butts playhouse would be to the south – and on a site near, though not on, the main eastern highway out of the City' (Ingram 1992: 110). Speculating on the choice of location, Ingram notes that the Red Lion Farm was just off the main road to the famous green in Mile End, which was used each May for the drill and muster of the City militia, so it would have provided occasion for the locals to be able to profit from providing ale and entertainment to both the militia and the many who gathered to witness the spectacle (Ingram 1992: 110–11). Suppose however that Brayne had more permanent goals in mind and that the poor quality of the scaffolding (which gave rise to his suit) merely cut these goals short – in this case, the annual muster would not be sufficient to support such a venture, but the expense of building the stage seems excessive for only a short-term enterprise. What else could justify Brayne's choice of location? One answer can be found, I suggest, by seeing the choice in terms of the syntagmatic dimension of the space, understanding its location as a prominent node along a path to somewhere else.

The green at Mile End was of course used for more than the annual muster. Scanning the less busy sections of the so-called 'Agas Map' which purports to depict London circa 1560,[7] a careful eye might catch the two small stick figures in the open field to the north of Whitechapel: one has a drawn bow in preparation to shoot and the other is leaning against what we might assume, given the activity of his companion, to be a longbow – the artist has clearly intended to convey the presence of archers. Mile End had been since at least the reign of Henry VII the site of the range used by the Society of London Bowmen, with whom both princes, Arthur and Henry (the later Henry VIII), regularly participated (Harewood 1835: 20). The importance of archery in Tudor society cannot be overstated – since 1363, when Richard II sought to ban all amusements on Sundays and holidays excepting archery (12 Rich. II c. 6), there was a succession of statutes and ordinances to maintain the practice, and Henry VIII alone made no fewer than eight separate statutes ultimately intended to mandate possession of bows in every household and commanding every adult male to use them regularly (Gunn 2010: 53). As recently as 1565, Elizabeth handed down three statutes to update those of her father and predecessors with respect to the price and construction of bows, and ordered that every bowyer within the city and suburbs of London, Southwark and Westminster must stock at all times a minimum of fifty bows for sale (8 Eliz. c. 11). In 1567, the green at Mile End would thus have been a frequent destination for many in and around eastern London to practise at shooting, making the road at Whitechapel a popular site for any additional pastimes.

Mile End was not the only option available to Londoners seeking to practise at the butts. A further glance at the top line of plates on the 'Civitas Londinum' ('Agas Map') reveals a number of similar representations of archers in various fields to the north and west of the city walls. Again, the artist is representing a well-known activity associated with the fields – on 20 January 1561, a bill was recorded in the Middlesex Session Rolls reinforcing existing statutes ensuring the availability of practice ranges for archers:

> whereas the citizens and other inhabitants of London have been accustomed from time beyond the memory of man to shoot with bows in all the open fields in the parish of Stebbynhith co. Midd. and elsewhere near the said city, viz. in the common lands called Stebbynhyth feyldes, Ratclyff feyldes, Mylende feyldes, Blethnall grene, Spyttlefeildes, Morefeldes, Fynnesbury

feyldes, Hoggesdon feyldes, co. Midd. without hindrance from any person, so that all archers have been able to go out in the same open fields to shoot with the bow. (Jeaffreson 1886: 37)

In accordance with the bill, one John Draney, 'citizen and clothier', was fined at the Session of the Peace at Westminster on 21 May for trenching deep ditches and planting green hedges to prevent archers from practising on Stepney ('Stebbynhith') Close (Jeaffreson 1886: 37). In addition to Mile End ('Mylende'), then, the bill refers to the long-standing freedoms given to archers within the vicinity of London in Middlesex. After the failure of the Red Lion venture, Brayne tried again to establish a playhouse space in 1576, when he and James Burbage leased land in Shoreditch to build the Theatre, and it is noteworthy that the highway passing by this location could be used by Londoners to make their way to the northern stretches of Finsbury Fields (to the west of the highway) as well as to Bethnal Green (to the north-east).

Could it be that proximity along a main road to archery butts was a determining factor in the selection of sites for the early playhouses? This was unlikely to be a factor in the rise of the Bankside venues, where proximity to the baiting arenas – or indeed the double use of the same spaces – was the more significant determinant (Mackinder et al. 2013). Yet even as late as 1604, Aaron Holland's decision to convert the yard at the Red Bull inn into a playhouse might easily be seen to fit the pattern of the Red Lion and the Theatre. It is more commonly thought that the location of the Red Bull was chosen for its proximity to Smithfield markets, but because the markets were located more than 400 yards south of the playhouse location, this theory relies on the assumption that the site was chosen to capture the traffic along St John's Street by those who were bringing their stock to market from outside London (Griffith 2013: 1–3). Apart from the fact that stock was more likely to have been brought to market on the western side of Clerkenwell Priory via Turnmill (colloquially known as Turnbull) Street, leading into the aptly named Cow Cross,[8] one problem with this theory is that a marketplace relies on more customers than there are vendors. A venue built 400 yards from such a lucrative customer base seems ill-advised if it is designed only to draw money from the purses of the vendors. It seems more reasonable to suppose that St John's Street was chosen because it was on the way to some other destination that draws the market customers further north again. At the time of its construction, the Red Bull playhouse was at the upper end of St John's Street with not much more to the north that might attract potential playgoers except for the open fields of Islington; these fields, as William Howitt confirmed in his antiquarian history of *The Northern Heights of London*, were all being used for archery 'from time immemorial' (Howitt 1869: 444).

In the case of the Red Bull, of course, the location was first adopted for the inn, and the name given to it suggests that proximity to the stock route was clearly a factor – any sense that 'Red Bull' references an archer's bullseye is quickly dispelled by confirming that 'bull' was not used as a term for the centre of a target until the late eighteenth century.[9] One venue that leaves no doubt about the link to archery is the Playhouse at Newington Butts. Despite claims from several scholars during the last sixty-five years that the 'butts' in the name of the location was not a reference to archery butts (Darlington 1955: 84–5; Ingram 1992: 155; Wickham et al. 2000: 320), it has recently been confirmed from evidence in the Acts of the Privy Council that there was indeed an archery range on the southern side of the location, which the Council noted in 1577 'hathe of long tyme ben mainetayned' there (APC, 1577–8: 272; Johnson 2018: 60–2). In choosing the site at Newington Butts, Jerome Savage was no doubt keen to draw custom from among the people who regularly made their way across the river to enjoy Southwark Fair or to use the fields for bowling, ball sports, horse riding and duck baiting (Darlington 1955: 39–40). Yet just as the Red Bull needed crowds to have a reason to continue beyond the nearby markets, the Playhouse needed its audiences to continue south beyond the fairs and fields – and that reason could very well have been the mandatory practice of their archery skills.

Redefining the field

Evelyn Tribble asks where the archers are in Shakespeare, observing that in only one play is there a direction for arrows to be shot on stage: in *Titus Andronicus*, a group of archers enters at the beginning of Act 4, Scene 3, and at the request of Titus that their arrows be shot to the gods, Marcus orders them to 'Shoot all your shafts into the Court' (Tribble 2015: 803). Pointing out the inherent risks of shooting inside a theatre in any era, but also of shooting blindly into a residential district from an open-air theatre, Tribble concludes that 'early modern actors would have shot as "feebly" as modern actors, and for similar reasons' (Tribble 2015: 803). Yet if the stage was located adjacent to or very near an archery range, such an exercise becomes viable. *Titus* was performed twice by the Lord Chamberlain's Men (possibly together with the Admiral's Men) when they stayed for a short time at the Playhouse in Newington Butts in June 1594, and this venue was separated from the archery range potentially by as short a distance as the dwelling on the southern end of the playhouse property and a sewer (see Johnson 2018: 67–8). Earlier that year, the same play (or a version of it) debuted at the Rose with Sussex's Men; Henslowe's Bankside venue would have required the feeble display described by Tribble, prompting me to ask whether the archery scene in *Titus* was added for the Newington performance and was retained due to the success of the spectacle?

The play was also likely to have been performed at the Theatre in Shoreditch by the Chamberlain's Men or, earlier, by Pembroke's Men (both of which are credited with having performed the play on the title pages of the quartos of 1594 and 1600). John Stockwood had written in 1578 that the Theatre was '*erected in the fields*' (Malone 1799: 53, n. 8), indicating that there were no residences to the north of the location at that time, so it was also viable for the play to have included the archery spectacle when performed in Shoreditch. One other play that may have included an archery spectacle, when occasion and location allowed, is *Hamlet*, the Second Quarto of which ends with the relevant order given by Fortinbras:

> Take vp the bodies. Such a sight as this
> Becomes the field, but heere showes much amisse.
>   Goe bid the souldiers shoote. *Exeunt.* (TLN 3902–4)

The Folio adds the direction '*Exeunt Marching, after the which a Peal of Ordenance are shot off*', which clearly requires the 'peal' of gunshots off stage (and which can be made by using gunpowder without discharging a firearm), but without this requirement the quarto could be interpreted as calling for a salvo of arrows to be shot into 'the field' and, perhaps, due to the lack of visible targets, 'much amiss'. A version of *Hamlet* was certainly staged at the Theatre in 1596, when Thomas Lodge reported having watched it, and a play called *Hamlet* was also staged at Newington Butts during the short run there by the Chamberlain's Men; the closing lines may record a key element of these performances.

While I am suggesting here that being next to a range could allow the stage archers to avoid deploying their arrows in feeble form, Tribble's broader point about the rarity of such spectacles is undeniable. It could indeed be that *Titus* and the early versions of *Hamlet* were test cases for the shooting of arrows from stage to nearby fields, but the practice was short-lived, and so the ending of *Hamlet* was changed to suit. Both plays contain demonstrations of another martial skill that would remain far more prevalent in early modern drama: fencing. As Mary McElroy and Kent Cartwright have argued in relation to the English fascination with public fencing throughout the sixteenth century, the makeshift stages on which bouts could be held evolved to accommodate drama as well, so the rise of the popular theatre went hand in glove with the popularity of fencing contests: between 1578 and 1585, numerous bouts were recorded to have been hosted at the Theatre and Curtain in particular (McElroy and Cartwright 1986: 207). In the case of early modern drama and fencing, then, the capacity to share the same stage space was always going to lead to dramatists using the dynamic action of a fencing contest to heighten the conflict and entertainment value of their plays. For those who frequented the archery butts around London to meet their civic duty, the spectacle of fencers crossing weapons was surely an attractive way to round out a day on the outskirts of the city.

By viewing the locations of the playhouses in terms of existing routes that drew their potential audiences to a mandated pastime, we add the syntagmatic dimension that Lefebvre adds to the paradigmatic and symbolic approaches to the history of space. The conventional narrative of the rise of the playhouses has for too long pursued the tedious line about their permanence, and these buildings have been fixed in the landscape of London as timber beacons of this golden age. By casting an eye to the roads that passed by them, though, we may remind ourselves that their placement along these roads was every bit as purposeful as their 'purpose-built' construction. It thus becomes possible to imagine a mobile audience making their way to the playhouses through the gates and out into the fields around the city, particularly for a mandated activity like archery. It was too big a risk for Brayne, Burbage, Savage and the others who followed to simply construct their purpose-built playhouses in the fields, assuming the populace would be drawn toward these beacons. The more likely scenario from a business perspective is to picture them being placed in the path of an existing and reliable flow of people. The roads on which these people made their routine trek to the outskirts of the city were paved, well maintained and well drained, protected at times by royal proclamation. This is equally as true for the 'tediousness of the way' to Newington Butts as it was for the pathway to Bethnal Green or Mile End. By casting our minds to the roads on which the early modern playgoers went about their other routine activities, we might finally arrive at a point from which the tired old binary of the London playhouses versus the strolling players might be allowed to dissipate. Are we there yet?

Notes

1. While the Privy Council warrant and the petitions by the players and the watermen to which it responds are undated, they have often been assumed to be linked to the 1592 Southwark 'riots' or the plague closures of 1593 to 1594. I accept instead the dating evidence provided by Alan H. Nelson – chiefly, that two signatories on the watermen's petition were buried in 1591, the first of them on 5 January. See Nelson 2012; also see Manley and MacLean 2014: 51–2, 302.
2. On the evidence for adopting this name for 'the Playhouse', see Johnson 2018: 77–9.
3. OED, 'tedious, *adj.*' and 'tediousness, *n.*'. While 'tedious' is dated to as early as John Lydgate's 'Troy Book' (c. 1412–20), the long gap until the next examples suggests that Lydgate might merely be using a transliteration from the Latin used in Colonne's *Historia Troiana*. A couple of examples are offered from around 1475, but 'tedious' only appears more regularly after about 1520, at which time the noun form 'tediousness' also begins to appear with greater frequency in English texts.
4. In his 1965 edition of the *Apology*, Geoffrey Shepherd considered the date to be between 1581 and 1583, but R. W. Maslen's 2002 update to the edition opts for a date closer to the 1579 release of Stephen Gosson's *School of Abuses*, to which Sidney is clearly responding with the *Apology* (Sidney 2002: 2–4). If we accept that Sidney was writing in response to Gosson, we can at least confirm a *terminus a quo* of 1579.
5. The Early Modern Print search reveals use of the phrase in Abraham Fleming's translation of Claudius Aelian (1576), William Goodyear's translation of Jean de Cartigny (1581), and Edward Aggas's translation of François de La Noue (1587). The search also reveals, inter alia, two examples of the phrase being used in the sermons of John Prime (1583 and 1585), which may constitute the earliest examples in English that was not written as a translation.
6. For a summary of more recent archaeological evidence of flood events during Roman occupation, reinforcing the claims made by Darlington, see Cowan et al. 2009: 32.
7. See the cover to this book. The provenance of the 'Civitas Londinum' is disputed, but the attribution to Ralph Agas is almost certainly erroneous: the map is most likely based on the earlier 'copperplate map' which has been dated to no later than 1559, and as late as 1588 Agas claimed to still be wanting to produce his first survey of London – see Marks 1964; Mitton 1908: 8–11.
8. Eva Griffith notes that travellers from Islington would know by the street names that they were approaching a region in which a venue called the Red Bull would not be out of place. Yet the 1682 map on the previous page of her book demonstrates that the streets with these bovine names are *not* in the path of the traveller approaching London from Islington; rather, they run convergent to St John's Street, meeting at Smithfield (see Griffith 2013: 2–3).
9. OED, '*bull's-eye*, n. 7a' – the earliest reference given in this entry is 1833. Hargrove's *Anecdotes of Archery* contains an earlier reference, with the collection published in 1792 and a report on the matches at Blackheath on 27

May 1791 noting that the 'Loyal Archers shot once into the Bull's Eye of the Target' (Hargrove 1792: 101). I have found no evidence to suggest the term was in use two centuries earlier.

Works cited

Bandello, Matteo [1554] (1832), *Novelle di Matteo Bandello*, Florence: Tipografia Borghie Companie.

—— [1567] (2007), *Certaine tragicall discourses written out of Frenche and Latin, by Geffraie Fenton, no less profitable then pleasaunt, and of like necessitye to all degrees that take pleasure in antiquiyes or forreine reapportes*, London: Thomas Marshe; repr. Ann Arbor; Oxford: Text Creation Partnership, EEBO-TCP Phase 1.

Blair, Peter Hunter (2003), *An Introduction to Anglo-Saxon England*, Cambridge: Cambridge University Press.

Blatherwick, Simon (2001), 'London', in Michael Dobson and Stanley Wells (eds), *The Oxford Companion to Shakespeare*, Oxford: Oxford University Press, pp. 256–9.

Chambers, Edmund Kerchever (1923), *The Elizabethan Stage*, 4 vols, Oxford: Clarendon Press.

Cowan, Carrie, Fiona Seeley, Angela Wardle, Andrew Westman and Lucy Wheeler (2009), *Roman Southwark, Settlement, and Economy: Excavations in Southwark, 1973–91*, MOLAS Monograph 42, London: Museum of London Archaeology.

Darlington, Ida (1955), *Survey of London, Vol. 25: St. George's Fields, the Parishes of St. George the Martyr, Southwark and St. Mary, Newington*, London: London County Council.

Desant, John Roche (ed.) (1890–1901), *Acts of the Privy Council of England*, vols 1–25, London: Her Majesty's Stationery Office.

Fellheimer, Jeannette (1946), 'Some Words in Geoffrey Fenton's *Certaine Tragicall Discourses*', *Modern Language Notes* 61.8, pp. 538–40.

Foakes, R. A. (ed.) (2002), *Henslowe's Diary*, Cambridge: Cambridge University Press.

Goodwin, Phillip (2013), *Translating the English Bible: From Relevance to Deconstruction*, Cambridge: James Clark.

Griffith, Eva (2013), *A Jacobean Company and its Playhouse: The Queen's Servants at the Red Bull Theatre (c. 1605–1619)*, Cambridge: Cambridge University Press.

Guicciardini, Francesco [1579] (2007), *The historie of Guicciardin conteining the warres of Italie and other partes, continued for many yeares vnder sundry kings and princes, together with the variations and accidents of the same, deuided into twenty bookes: and also the argumentes, with a table at large expressing the principall matters through the vvhole historie. Reduced into English by Geffray Fenton* (London: Thomas Vautrouillier; repr. Ann Arbor; Oxford: Text Creation Partnership, EEBO-TCP Phase 1.

Gunn, Steven (2010), 'Archery Practice in Tudor England', *Past & Present* 209, pp. 53–81.

Gurr, Andrew (1996), *The Shakespearian Playing Companies*, Oxford: Clarendon Press.

Hall, Edward [1548] (2003), *The vnion of the two noble and illustre famelies of Lancastre [and] Yorke, beeyng long in continual discension for the croune of this noble realme*, London: Richard Grafton; repr. Ann Arbor; Oxford: Text Creation Partnership, EEBO-TCP Phase 1.

Harewood, Harry (1835), *A Dictionary of Sports: Or, Companion to the Field, the Forest, and the River Side*, London: Thomas Tegg and Son.

Hargrove, E. (1792), *Anecdotes of Archery, from the Earliest Ages to the Year 1791*, York.

Howitt, William (1869), *The Northern Heights of London: Or, Historical Associations of Hampstead, Highgate, Muswell Hill, Hornsey, and Islington*, London: Longmans, Green and Co.

Ingram, William (1992), *The Business of Playing: The Beginnings of the Adult Professional Theater in Elizabethan London*, Ithaca and London: Cornell University Press.

Jeaffreson, John Cordy (ed.) (1886), *Middlesex County Records, Volume 1: 1550–1603*, London: Middlesex County Record Society.

Johnson, Laurie (2018), *Shakespeare's Lost Playhouse: Eleven Days at Newington Butts*, New York and Abingdon: Routledge.

Jolly, Margrethe (2014), *The First Two Quartos of Hamlet: A New View of the Origins and Relationship of the Texts*, Jefferson, NC: McFarland & Company.

Lefebvre, Henri (2009), 'Space and the State', in Neil Brenner and Stuart Elden (eds), *State, Space, World: Selected Essays*, trans. Gerald Moore, Neil Brenner and Stuart Elden, Minneapolis and London: University of Minnesota Press, pp. 223–53.

McElroy, Mary, and Kent Cartwright (1986), 'Public Fencing Contests on the Elizabethan Stage', *Journal of Sport History* 13.3, pp. 193–211.

Mackinder, Anthony, Lyn Blackmore, Julian Bowsher and Christopher Phillpotts (2013), *The Hope Playhouse, Animal Baiting and Later Industrial Activity at Bear Gardens on Bankside: Excavations at Riverside House and New Globe Walk, Southwark, 1999–2000*, MOLA Archaeology Studies Series 25, London: Museum of London Archaeology.

McMillin, Scott, and Sally-Beth MacLean (1998), *The Queen's Men and their Plays*, Cambridge: Cambridge University Press.

Malone, Edmond (1799), *The Plays of William Shakespeare*, vol. 3, Basel: J. J. Tourneisen.

Manley, Laurence, and Sally-Beth MacLean (2014), *Lord Strange's Men and their Plays*, New Haven: Yale University Press.

Margary, Ivan Donald (1948), *Roman Ways in the Weald*, London: Phoenix House.

Marks, Stephen Powys (1964), *The Map of Mid Sixteenth Century London: An Investigation into the Relationship between a Copper-Engraved Map and its Derivatives*, London: London Topographical Society.

Mitton, G. E. (1908), *Maps of Old London*, London: Adam and Charles Black.

Munday, Anthony [c. 1590] (2003–5), *The first book of Amadis of Gaule*, repr. Ann Arbor; Oxford: Text Creation Partnership, EEBO-TCP Phase 1.

Murray, John Tucker [1910] (1963), *English Dramatic Companies, 1558–1642*, 2 vols, New York: Russell and Russell.
Nelson, Alan H. (2012), 'Philip Henslowe and the Bankside Watermen: A Fresh Look at Three Familiar Documents', from conference 'Who Invented the "Shakespearean Theatre"?', Grace Ioppolo, Convenor, University of Reading, 24 November 2012, cited with permission.
Nida, Eugene Albert (1964), *Toward a Science of Translating: With Special Reference to Principles and Procedures Involved in Bible Translating*, Leiden: E. J. Brill.
Ostovich, Helen, Holger Schott Syme and Andrew Griffin (eds) (2016), *Locating the Queen's Men, 1583–1603: Material Practices and the Conditions of Playing*, London and New York: Routledge.
Roberts, Howard, and Walter H. Godfrey (1950), *Survey of London, Volume 22: Bankside. The Parishes of St. Saviour and Christchurch, Southwark*, London: London County Council.
Sanders, Julie (2014), *The Cambridge Introduction to Early Modern Drama, 1576–1642*, Cambridge: Cambridge University Press.
Schoenbaum, Samuel (1987), *William Shakespeare: A Compact Documentary Life*, New York and Oxford: Oxford University Press.
Shakespeare, William (1601), *Hamlet*, ed. David Bevington, Internet Shakespeare Editions, <https://internetshakespeare.uvic.ca/doc/Ham_EM/index.html> (last accessed 6 June 2019).
Sidney, Philip [1595] (2002), *An Apology for Poetry (or The Defence of Poesy)*, ed. R. W. Maslen and Geoffrey Shepherd, Manchester: Manchester University Press.
Stow, John [1603] (1631), *Annales, or a Generall Chronicle of England*, ed. Edmond Howes, London: Richard Meighen.
Thomson, Peter (1999), *Shakespeare's Professional Career*, Cambridge: Cambridge University Press.
Tribble, Evelyn (2015), 'Where Are the Archers in Shakespeare?', *ELH* 82.3, pp. 789–814.
Wickham, Glynne (1972), *Early English Stages 1300 to 1660, Volume 2: 1576 to 1660, Part II*, London: Routledge & Kegan Paul.
Wickham, Glynne, Herbert Berry and William Ingram (eds) (2000), *English Professional Theatre, 1530–1660*, Cambridge: Cambridge University Press.

Chapter 7

Wandering Fools and Foolish Vagrants: Folly on the Road in Early Modern English Culture
Alice Equestri

In the early modern period fools were not only luxury entertainers in rich households or acclaimed professional performers on London stages. On the contrary, the road was a privileged space for historical and literary negotiations of folly. Cultural historians of Renaissance folly[1] have occasionally noted how fools were linked to itinerancy, but they have rarely acknowledged how numerous and diversified such intersections really were. Because the different manifestations of 'road folly' have apparently been perceived as discrete cultural phenomena, very few attempts have been made to put them into closer dialogue with each other.[2] Critical mentions of folly on the road have focused almost exclusively on clowns at seasonal festivals or at public open-air performances:[3] this has determined a lopsided approach towards a specific type of 'artificial' folly – or the simulation of witlessness aimed at entertaining an audience – and its itinerant presentation. Much less attention has been devoted to other forms of 'folly', in particular 'natural' folly – what we would call 'intellectual disability' – with its links to mobility as homelessness. This chapter makes up for this neglect by describing the multiple ways in which folly interacts with both mobility and vagrancy. By identifying analogies and divergences among them, it will show how the road becomes a productive space for connected yet nuanced forms of folly.

Spatial theorists have suggested that space should be seen as a multi-level construction. Joël Bonnemaison, for example, argues that the objective, geographic, structured space as the creation of a society that moulds nature according to its aims and needs is only the first level. The second level is the lived space: it is about how people experience that space daily and how they shape it through their own subjectivity. Finally, the third level, the 'cultural' one, transcends the other two, because it has to do with how the cultural products of a society give a symbolic meaning to space:

> Cultural space is a geosymbolic space laden with emotions and meanings: in its strongest expression, it becomes a sanctuary-like territory, that is to say, a space of communion with an ensemble of signs and values. (Bonnemaison 2005: 46–7)

The discussion that follows, about the early modern intersections between the road and folly, exemplifies how these three levels coexist: they are revealed, respectively, in the materiality of the road; in the ways impaired vagrants experienced it; and in the ways literature and art fashioned it. The connections between the levels will simultaneously emerge: the subjective space of the road, occupied by impaired vagrants, feeds into the cultural space created by the diverse literary or artistic figurations of those people. Further, the material road, when occupied by fooling professionals, acquires a symbolic, idealising quality.

In Tudor and Stuart everyday reality, individuals born with intellectual deficiencies – those which early modern legislation termed 'idiots' or 'natural fools' (McDonagh 2009: 6, 85) – wandered the roads: they were rarely locked up in hospitals, unless they became violent (Zijderveld 1982: 35). When 'idiots' were not a danger to themselves or others, they were actually excluded from charitable institutions for the care of the sick and infirm poor, because their condition was considered incurable (Stainton 2001: 24). On a 1624 visit to Bethlem, Governors of the renowned London psychiatric institution ordered eleven patients to be discharged because, being 'Idiot', 'simple' or 'something idle headed', they were 'not fit to bee kepte'. A little later the hospital is recorded to have started more formal entry examinations to reject 'idiots' (Andrews et al. 1997: 326). 'Idiots' therefore lived in the community, to the point that, as Zijderveld remarks, 'fools were seen as vagabonds, literally or metaphorically' (1982: 38). Unsupported destitutes were left wandering and sleeping in the streets, at the risk of being verbally or physically assaulted and even, in the case of female innocents, sexually abused (Metzler 2016: 83). Even in the few cases where the presence of idiot inmates in medieval and Renaissance charitable institutions is recorded, their assimilation to vagrants is apparent. Tim Stainton has clarified how in these cases poverty – whether or not it was a consequence of intellectual deficiency – was the main reason for residence, and not faulty wits. These 'idiots' also enjoyed some freedom, as they paid for their own maintenance by leaving the house and begging for alms in the streets (Stainton 2001: 25). This would have reinforced the public perception of them as beggars. In *Jack of Dover* (1604), for instance, the Fool of Hampshire is a 'begger-woman' (Wright 1842: 30) who takes a monkey for a child; then the Fool of Gloucester begs for money, giving a warning in return: 'take heed . . . when you see a fool or a knave . . . let him not come near by you, by the length of this thread' (27). Shakespeare himself might have wanted to ironise this social issue by having Feste, the artificial fool, wander around the roads of Illyria asking for tips, or by having Lear term the Fool 'houseless poverty' (3.4.26)[4] after the banishment from the royal palace, thus involving him in a sympathetic speech on the wider community of the unsheltered poor.

Also the reverse was true: vagabond beggars would have been seen as fools via their correlation with physical disability. In 1577 William Harrison listed the 'blind and lame' among the 'poore by impotencie' and 'the wounded souldier' among the 'poor by casualtie' – these 'by begging here and there annoy both town and countrie' (1877: 213–14). The cripples were the category of people who, because of their unemployability, most ran the risk of becoming street beggars (Jütte 1994: 24–5; Salamon 2004: 262), but were also those most readily associated with intellectual disability. The intersection between foolishness and bodily defectiveness had informed cultural representations of the fool since antiquity (Welsford 1968: 58), and in literature it was famously exploited by, among others, Shakespeare and Robert Armin,[5] but it was also commented on in more scientific discourses on folly. Paracelsus argued that 'all goitrous people are more likely to be foolish than skillful' (Cranefield and Federn 1963: 465) and in *De generatione stultorum* (1567) he equated 'crooked children, ... there blind ones, there deaf ones, there mutes, there cripples ..., there fools, there monsters, there misgrowths and the like', linking fools' malproportion to their being 'marred statue[s]' (Cranefield and Federn 1967: 63). The Paduan doctor Gianbattista da Monte (1498–1551) wrote that the Cardinal of Ferrara's fool had a 'crippled hand and large head resembling a vegetable', judging him 'foul and deformed' (Goodey 2011: 232).

In short, the relation between the two categories of fools and beggars was all the more strong for being multi-layered and multifaceted; yet, the wealth of correspondences that has emerged so far from a consideration of the early modern socio-historical reality is only a small part of the larger discourse encompassing folly and life on the road. The arguably unfortunate reality of vagrant innocents in England was symbolically reworked in more universal conceptualisations of folly, namely those offered by humanist thinkers. Indeed, the Renaissance saw a substantial change in attitudes towards poverty, which started to lose its Franciscan significance as a gift of God, a test of one's humility, and the chance for the rich man to be redeemed through acts of Christian charity. In sixteenth-century England, poverty was instead the leading cause of vagrancy, crime and social disorders, so that beggars and vagabonds were demonised rather than pitied (Beier 1987: 4–7).

As prominent examples of sin – especially sloth – their deeds entered humanist discourses of moral folly, so when Alexander Barclay adapted Sebastian Brant's *Ship of Fools* in 1509 he contributed to the general desacralisation of vagabonds by reporting his Tudor experience of them. 'Of folysshe beggers and of theyr vanytees' is the sixty-third chapter in his poem. False beggars, rather than needy ones, are targeted, though it is unclear how a passer-by could have told the difference when coming across one in the streets. Barclay turns the trust in Christian charity on its head as he denounces 'the clerke, the frere, or monke', 'the abbot, the Pryor, and also theyr convent' who

> oft complayne the charge of pouerte
> In garmentis goynge raggyd and to rent
> But yet haue they of ryches great plente. (Brant 1874: 302)

Some of them 'fayne miracles', 'pardon' and carry about 'relyques newes', wandering through 'alehows', 'stretis tauernes townes and vyllagys' (Brant 1874: 303). Similarly, Erasmus's *Praise of Folly* attacks such practices for causing 'the great loss of all the other beggars' (Erasmus 1993: 96). The other type of beggars that Barclay criticises are those called 'sturdy' in the period (see Jütte 1994: ch. 9).

> Other beynge stronge and full of lustynes
> And yonge ynoughe to labour for theyr fode
> Gyuyth theyr bodyes fully to slewthfulnes
> The beggers craft thynkynge to them moost good
> Some ray theyr legges and armys ouer with blood
> With leuys and plasters though they be hole and sounde
> Some halt as crypyls, theyr legge falsely vp bounde. (Brant 1874: 303)

A look at early modern art gives an idea of how prominent this association between vagrancy and folly really was. The English engraver Renold Elstrack illustrated a verse satire on the folly of the world with a depiction of a beggar pulling the ass of folly with its burden of doomed men-fools along a road, while a fool in cap and bells holds its tail. The company is portrayed while on the move and the beggar invites people he encounters on the road to join the other passengers. The scene thus highlights his power as a leader of folly at the expense of the actual fool at the back of the procession. Also, the Flemish engraver Dirk van Hoogstraten depicted the bust of a fool in the frontispiece to a series of beggars' scenes (van Hoogstraten 1613). Sometimes the beggar was even a stand-in for the fool. In tarots, for instance, a beggar on a shabby street corner could appear on the card with the functions of the 'fool', as in the Tarocchi Cards of Mantegna or the tarots by the Ferrara Master of Sola-Busca ('Misero'; Nicola). Such depictions were partly an evolution of medieval representations of the allegorical naked or ragged fool standing in an outdoor environment, to hint at his lack of fixed abode (Laharie 1991: 61; Billington 1984: 4–5), related to his ignorance of God.

Barclay's and Erasmus's insistence on false beggars rather than on all vagabonds reveals their concern with folly as imitation just as much as sin. This prompts a larger reflection on the meaning of folly. In fact, within the broad range of significations of the term 'folly' in the period, mystification and performance of inauthentic actions in more or less wilful imitation of someone else's behaviour were substantially equivalent accomplishments. Both natural folly as idiocy and artificial folly as the professional ability to entertain an audience relied on a sophisticated show of mimicry. The congenital idiot was a mimic because he aped the actions of intelligent people. Yet he had no hope of making those actions really 'his': in C. F. Goodey's wording, his being 'a mere mimic' who just copies 'surface behaviours' was actually evidence of his disability (2011: 65). Conversely, the professional fool built his performances on the mimicry of real idiots' ways: his success was actually determined by his skill at concealing wit or dexterity under the pretence of folly. But before such a show became more confined to static playhouse stages, professional fools and clowns had often obtained expertise and popularity by joining companies of players travelling around the country. And, ironically, it is also in this form that comedians, like minstrels, jugglers, bearwards, street jesters and acrobats, were not so dissimilar from vagabonds. In fact, the Tudor Laws, with a 1545 proclamation by Henry VIII and the 1572 Act for the Punishment of Vagabonds, prosecuted unlicensed strolling performers (Salgãdo 1977: 138).[6]

The three star clowns of the Elizabethan era – Richard Tarlton, Will Kemp and Robert Armin – had all been itinerant players in their early days. When Tarlton first arrived in London from the provinces, he started building his fame as a comedian by improvising his way across taverns, alehouses and banquets; later, in the 1580s, he toured the country with the Queen's Men (Thomson 2004; Wiles 1987: 14–15). More broadly, it was his mobility as a provincial man migrating to the capital that helped him attract his first audiences, principally made of visitors and immigrants who would have found in Tarlton the rustic clown a familiar individual sharing their anxiety about city life (Wiles 1987: 23). Tarlton's clown persona projected an appearance of poverty and drunkenness. In the famous Harley MS drawing he is portrayed playing pipe and tabor in the garments of a peasant, and *Tarlton's Jests* (1600) reports anecdotes of how, for instance, Tarlton 'plaid the

Drunkard before the Queene', fell down in Fleet Street 'as though he had been drunke' or in Salisbury was 'as mad angry, as he was mad drunk' (Halliwell 1844: 5, 31). Will Kemp toured across England with Leicester's Men and he even reached the continent. In December 1585 he travelled from Flushing to The Hague in the Netherlands, as a member of the prospective governor's entourage (Wiles 1987: 31). Later, he improvised for the Prince Elector on a walking trip to Amersfoort. In 1586 he travelled to Denmark and Saxony with a group of English musicians. But his fortunes as an itinerant clown shone even more once his career in Shakespeare's company ended. In 1600 he took up a nine-day Morris dance from London to Norwich, a famed enterprise which anticipated a (potentially) greater one: dancing from England to Rome. Day, Rowley and Wilkins were perhaps thinking of Kemp's Italian experience when in a scene of *The Travailes of the Three English Brothers* (1607) they had him agree to act in an extemporary performance with a Harlequin (E4^r–F14; Wright 1926). In late 1601 Kemp was back in the Netherlands, touring the country in a company of English actors who then led him to Münster, Germany, where he became popular for his jigs. Back in London he hired younger actors and took them to the continent (Wiles 1987: 36–8). Robert Armin also started his clowning career as a player in a touring company, Lord Chandos's Men, with whom he probably remained until 1599. There are records of the company's presence in the West Midlands, York and East Anglia, besides Gloucestershire, in the years between 1595 and 1597 (Wiles 1987: 137). The routes of travelling companies in provincial England were shaped within a relatively dense network of highly efficient roads, which guaranteed easy communications. A regular traffic of entertainers could then be witnessed on Britain's roads (Palmer 2005: 261), so that itinerant players would have been visible – to country people and people embarking on road journeys alike (Brayshay 2005) – while heading to their next venue: a town hall or a private house, but also a roadside inn or inn-yard, a church, an open-air theatre or even a marketplace held in high streets or squares. But players were also to be seen on roads when they walked around the city to advertise their upcoming show with drums and trumpets (Keenan 2002: 15–17, 136–7).

So, like his predecessors in medieval pageants – the Vices or Devils who cavorted their way from station to station across the city streets – and similarly to the Fools of the Feasts of Fools, of Christmas and Easter seasons, or of May games,[7] the stage fool was not only a comedian but also a travelling player, who made of showmanship and flamboyancy his greatest strengths. Because of their skills in engaging spectators, the Vice and the clown were, as Preiss argues, 'the play's built-in audience manager[s]' (Preiss 2014: 66–7). Itinerant performing was inherently different from acting in a domestic playhouse: its effectiveness was potentially jeopardised by the need to employ simple, provisional stages, and by the language or culture barrier. Hence the need to boost the audience's comprehension through a universal language: action. Facial mimicry, body movements, contextuality and energetic interaction with the audience were therefore assets for these actors: the clown was naturally the company member whose agility and improvisation skills were counted on the most (Bosman 2013: 498–9). Clownish tricks had such a major part in itinerant performances that they easily ran the risk of becoming immoral, so that English companies travelling abroad, while creating memorable stock clown figures such as Pickle Herring, Hans von Stockfisch and John Posset (Welsford 1968: 285; Schrickx 1983), might also get into trouble with foreign authorities (Limon 1985: 13).

Details about the importance of itinerancy for the major Elizabethan stage clowns are given by their own works. *Nine Daies Wonder* (1600), Kemp's report of his jig to Norwich, clarifies how itinerancy was part of a precise market strategy. After abandoning every advance to patronage and the financial stability of a theatrical company, Kemp saw the jigging project as a way to further his fame in the long term and as a juicy opportunity for a quick monetary capitalisation of his already established popularity (Thomas 1992). His introductory statement, 'I began frolickly to foote it, from the right Honourable the Lord Mayors of London, towards the right worshipfull . . . Master Mayors of Norwich' (Kemp 1985: 3–4), shapes the travel experience as a road not only to success but also to social fulfilment, a step forward into Kemp's symbolical admission into the power structures of society.

Kemp's narration, however, is anything but focused on the dance. On the contrary, numerous details are given about the route, the towns he visited, and the landmarks he came across. For example, he writes how 'being past White Chappell, and having left faire London, with all that North-east Suburb before named, multitudes of Londoners left not me' (4), how 'the multitudes were so great at my coming to Burntwood, that I had much a doe . . . to get passage to my Inne' (7), or 'I left Hingham, not staying till I came to Barford-bridge' (19). The meticulous localisation of performance sites, at the expense of details on the performance itself, is insistently accompanied by an enthusiastic evaluation of the size and excitement of his audience. Comments like 'many good fellows being there met . . . had prepared a Beare-bayting' (5), 'I come to Witfordbridge where a number of country people, and many Gentlemen and Gentlewomen, were gathered together to see me' and 'so much a doe I had to pass by the people at Chelmsford, that it was more than an hour ere I could recover my Inne' (8) point at geographical mobility as an effective way to be seen by ever-changing spectators, to attract large crowds where members of different classes mixed, and to promote his identity outside the boundaries of London. Kemp's strategy combines hope for success with the chance to earn money – not by begging, but by betting on his own performance and leading onlookers to wager. Some even offered to jig with or race against him, but Kemp systematically comments on the unsuitability of his opponents. For example, in Chelmsford a 'Mayde not passing fourteen years of age' followed him and 'a whole houre she held out: but then being ready to lye downe I left her off' (9); or in Sudbury, 'a lusty tall fellow', a butcher, 'gave me over in the plain field protesting, that if he might get a 100 pound, he would not hold out with me; for indeed my pace in dancing is not ordinary' (12). In Kemp's view, therefore, the road stands for a continual challenge, a field of competition, encapsulating the performer's self-assertion in his unfailing superiority to ordinary people, a journey into the self-fashioning of the actor as a myth. Though the journey takes place in the earthy reality of the road and the province – so initially appears to be meant to take the famous London actor back among the people of the English country – it ultimately has the effect of distancing him from his 'ordinary' audience, the common Englishmen and peasants that he strove to look like on stage.[8]

A comedian who normally did not even pretend to empathise with rural or city audiences was Robert Armin, whose witty fool persona was as pungent as it could be.[9] Yet travelling, other than an opportunity to achieve popularity, represented for him a chance to study village idiots (Wiles 1987: 137) and use this knowledge to improve his professional fooling and affirm himself both as a player and as an author. One such encounter is documented in Armin's *Foole upon Foole* (1600):

> In the town of Esom in Worcestersh[ire] Jacke Miller being there borne, was much made of in every place: it hapned that the Lord Shandoyes Players came to towne, and used their pastimes there, which Jacke not a little loved, especially the clown whose he would imbrace with a joyfull spirit, and call him *grumball* (for so he called himself in Gentlemens houses, where he would imitate playes dooing all himself, King Clowne, Gentleman and all: having spoke for one, he would soddenly goe in, and againe returne for the other, and stambring, so beastly as he did, made mighty mirth: to conclude he was a right innocent without villainy at all). When these Players as I speak of, had done in the towne they went to Partiar, and Jacke swore he would got all the world over with Grumball, that he would: it was then a great frost new begun and the Haven was frozen over thinly . . . but [He] sayde I come to thee Grumball: . . . he got down very daugerously, and makes no more a doe but boldly ventures over the Haven, which is by the long bridge as I gesse

some forty yards over: yet hee made nothing of it, but *my heart ached to see it*, and my ears heard the Ize cracked all the way: when he was come unto me, I was amazed, and tooke up a brickbat ... and threwe it, which no sooner fell upon the Ize but it burst; was not this strange that a foole of thirty years was borne of that Ize which would not endure the fall of a brickbat? (Armin 1973: 112–14)

The story of Jack Miller includes the only reference in the text to the narrator's presence at the events: the mention of Lord Chandos's players then indicates Armin himself as the clown whom Jack loved. The episode shapes mobility as the quintessential prerogative of the comedian's search for fools. Just as Armin met Jack personally on the road and took careful note of his quirks, he might equally have known some of the other five fools in his account. Jack Miller's story, however, maximises the importance of mobility, in that the alliance between artificial and natural fool is successfully brought about both by the comedian's itinerancy and by the idiot's freely wandering the roads from his city of birth to Partiar (Pershore). While on their first meeting Armin sees Jack only as 'a right innocent without villainy', it is on their second encounter, physically shifted a few miles southward, that the idiot touches the comedian's heart with his foolish bravery. It might appear extraordinary of the witty stage clown to be this sympathetic toward a member of his audience, when all his career revolved around quipping about those who watched him, yet it is thanks to episodes of this type that the comedian was able to enact his activity as a symbolical 'fool hunter', as Nora Johnson has wittily commented (2009: 35): not to take fools away with him physically, as many household lords would do when finding an interesting country fool potentially suitable for entertainment, but to rob them of their peculiarities and seize their performative identity. This would let the comedian rise as a legend both on stage and in print.

Real or fictional kidnappings of natural fools were not the only types of 'fool-takings' that took place on Renaissance English roads. 'Fool-taking' was in fact the late sixteenth-century underworld cant name for an older widespread practice: the 'Figging law' or 'pickpurse craft' (Walker 1973: 72). Gulls had customarily been called 'fool', 'foolish' or 'ignorant', 'sots' in rogue or cony-catching pamphlets by, for instance, Thomas Harman or Robert Greene,[10] but the craft became even more notorious in the latter's *The Third and Last Part of Cony-Catching* (1592), whose subtitle anticipates that the text will give more details about 'the new-devised knavish art of fool-taking' (Greene 2002b: 180). It is an art where the road is shaped as a space of transformation, because that is where the gull is turned into a fool, or where the dullness of the victim gets fully revealed. A cozener, for example, works his way to a respectable London house by first hooking the victims on a stroll from 'a garden in Finsbury Fields' to 'St Laurence Lane'. He crosses their way 'near unto the conduit in Aldermanbury' (Greene 2002b: 182), and there persuades them that he is a kinsman of theirs, a performance that the victims receive by 'thinking *simply* that all he said was true' (183, italics mine). Or another 'subtle fellow' chooses 'Gracious' (Gracechurch) Street and a 'stall singing of ballads' as the ideal setting for his 'villainous prank', which entails 'taking a great many of fools with one train' (189). The road is therefore a porous setting which attracts cozeners and foolish victims alike, and their meeting – essential for the rogues' purposes – invites a comparison between the moral and intellectual capacities of the two categories. In Greene's world, 'fool' and 'cony' are equivalent terms. Both are associated with an idea of folly which signifies credulousness and lack of sophisticated reasoning: it is 'honest simplicity beguiled' (181). The 'fools' Greene's cozeners deceive generally lack any psychological depth and are rarely granted anything more than a sketchy description. They are all variants of the same stock character, identified by recurring epithets: 'citizen', 'gentleman', 'goodman', 'simple', 'honest', or also 'poor', despite their wealth and status. These last three adjectives set the victims of the tricks diametrically apart from the fool-takers, who are defined instead as 'wicked' (186), 'villain' or 'knave' (192–3). Even more significant is the insistence on the rogues' relative superiority in terms of brain skills: cony-catchers are indeed termed 'subtile' (180), 'crafty' (190, 201, 203), 'sly' (179, 182, 189), 'wily' (183, 191), 'cunning' (202), 'professor[s]' (191, 195) and 'scholars' (188), and express surprise that 'men are so simple to be so beguiled' (182) by tricks which, in fact, do not always need to be so cunning. Some are indeed uncomplex and direct, such as that of the rogue picking a cutler's purse while saying to him 'With this knife . . . mean I to cut a purse' (12), or that of the gull who cannot recognise his own trunk.

Thomas Dekker in *The Gull's Hornbook* (1609) took upon himself the task of educating the crowd of 'gulls' that swarmed the city streets and playhouses against the threat of 'fencers and cony-catchers' (Dekker 1904: 21). His students get a distinctly more varied set of epithets than in Greene's pamphlet: 'fools', 'antics', 'dry-brained polypragmonists' (9), 'loggerheads', 'loon[s]', 'Cockneys and Coxcombs' (10), 'ninnyhammers', 'graduates in these rare sciences of barbarism and idiotism', 'sots' (11), 'woodcocks' (12). Like a novel helmsman of the ship of fools, the narrator conceives of his pedagogical mission as an attempt to 'sail boldly and desperately alongst the shore of the Isle of Gulls' (9) and the 'shores of Barbaria' (39), for whose inhabitants he has bought the iconic 'motley . . . and a coat with four elbows' (7). However, Dekker's maritime image contrasts with the urban setting of the following chapters, where the gull is portrayed – much like rogues and beggars – as a mobile individual who idly walks around the city streets and public spaces. Dekker's view of the road is overtly sarcastic; it is not only a potentially dangerous place but also a runway where the gull foolishly struts and makes himself more visible: 'In the streets [he] walk[s] like a braggart' (10). After heavily drinking and smoking in the tavern he 'pass[es] through the goodliest streets in the city' (77) and attracts the watch's attention. Sometimes the road is enclosed in wide inner spaces, as is the case of Paul's walk and Paul's churchyard, and offers great opportunities to be admired. The typical gull here is a gentleman, heir to his father's fortune, who walks down the aisle to 'pour himself into all fashions'; he is 'various in his salads, curious in his tobacco' and proud of his 'new Scotch hose' (39). As Dekker writes that the gentleman's head shall be 'fit . . . for an excellent block' (40), he satirises the early modern noble society's presumptuous belief that intelligence is predetermined by status and that wit is innate in the gentry (Goodey 2011: 77–8).

A similar rhetoric of folly was obviously employed by playwrights, who drew from rogue pamphlets for many crime scenes. Jonson's *Bartholomew Fair*, for instance, is a play where most of the action takes place on thoroughfares between stalls at the famous Smithfield fair, a place dramatised as a den of mystifiers preying on naive fellows. Wasp mocks Cokes for being twice robbed of his purse: 'cry yourself an ass through the Fair afore your time' (Jonson 1989: 3.5.204), he suggests, and begs him to 'seek some other gamester, to play the fool with' (3.5.207–8); the cutpurse Edgworth, on his part, says 'away, ass, away . . . Dost thou think the gentleman is foolish?' (3.5.220–2), mocking the noble classes' anxiety about a fool being born to what Goodey calls the in-group (2011: 63). Yet perhaps the most memorable convergence of the road and folly is dramatised in Shakespeare's *The Winter's Tale*. Named after Odysseus' thieving grandfather and also sharing the name of a mythical character who joined the Argonauts' journey, Autolycus is a character constantly on the move and who never appears in enclosed spaces. The road is a home to him, but also his main worry, because 'gallows and knock are too powerful on the highway' (4.3.27–8). Yet it is the same place that earns him a living, at the expense of those he bumps into, people whom he laughs at by calling them synonyms of 'fool': 'good-faced' (4.3.114), 'cock' (4.3.34), 'simple men' (4.4.745) or 'puppies' (4.4.706). His distorted view of morality produces the axiom 'what a fool honesty is, and trust – his sworn brother – a very simple gentleman' (4.4.596–7), which echoes Greene's cony-catchers' idea that honest naivety turns a man into a fool.

Rogue literature also fashioned vagabonds themselves as fools, first because their quasi-theatrical function as deceivers links them to the tricksters and mocking fools of drama. Autolycus is again the obvious example of the dramatic intersection between vagabondage and foolery. The road for him is a stage where he can meta-theatrically don multiple identities: this is best represented in his first scene, where he 'grovel[s] on the ground' (4.3.49) to simulate convulsions. As Paola Pugliatti notes, cheaters and cozeners were fixed types who owed much to the ancient theatrical figure of the *parasite*, whose characteristics were later to be found in the rogue, the fool and the clown (Pugliatti 2003: 153–4). These, according to Bakhtin, all have 'a vital connection with the theatrical trappings of the public square' and their appearance, as well as 'everything they do and say, cannot be understood in a direct and unmediated way but must be grasped metaphorically' (Bakhtin 1981: 159). Yet sometimes the connection between the fool and rogue types is less symbolical, as in texts belonging to the tradition of the legendary English rogue Cock Lorel, who might have lived in Henry VIII's era. His deeds were first narrated in the anonymous fragmentary poem *Cock Lorell's Bote* (first extant edition 1518), where the title character is an anti-hero who recruits people to sail with him around England. His crew is knavish in character. Members of all crafts request a place on the boat, both ordinary workers and rogues, but even individuals belonging to apparently legal trades often display moral ambiguities. For example the tanner, the butcher and the raker are included in the 'slovenly sorte', a 'myller dustypoll' stole 'floure and put chauke' in his sacks, 'towlers' are 'false' (Rimbault 1843: 3), the 'pye baker' is 'lusty' (5), a cobbler, a currier and a shoemaker fight over a piece of leather. Among the lowlife characters are 'theues hores & baudes w' mortherers ... / Spyes / lyers and grete sclaunderers, ... Sluttes drabbes and counseyll whystelers' (11). If these characters' connection to the road on the one hand is implicit in the underworldly quality of their professions, on the other it is stressed by Cock Lorel's perception of his would-be followers as a mass that 'sprede' 'the stretes all ouer' (10), and by the degree of detail the narrator gives on the provenance of many of them. The road thus pictures not only a communication route with the hero but also, much as in Will Kemp's case, a measure of the hero's projected popularity. Cock Lorel's own standing at the intersection between life on the road and folly is displayed foremost by his name, the juxtaposition between a symbol of stupidity (*cock*) and a synonym for 'scoundrel' (*lorel*) (*OED*). The text itself, then, seems to owe much to the narrative frame of Brant's *Ship of Fools*, though it focuses on sin and leaves the discourse on folly in the background. Still, we perceive it is there, first of all visually, as the woodcuts of the early edition depict men in fool's caps located on country roads or sea ships. The lowlife characters in Cock Lorel's crew are not only very English, but also very similar to the members of the orders of fools described by Brant or Lydgate (Baumgartner 1963: 74). Besides, Cock Lorel's folly is implied not just by his name, but also by his identification as a 'knyght / and symkyn' (Rimbault 1843: 4), and by his function as a jocular Lord of Misrule. This comes to full view when he interrupts the crew's busy working by blowing his whistle. The captain's action has the effect of changing the mood of the 'lusty company', who from then onwards 'thought all to play' and 'banysshed prayer peas and sadnes' (13).

Even more compelling is the reception of the Cock Lorel myth in the rogue literature of the mid to late sixteenth century. John Awdeley's *The Fraternity of Vagabonds* (1561), which provides the most detailed taxonomy of road dwellers, mentions Cock Lorel on the title page. Notwithstanding the legendary nature of the rogue-fool, Awdeley sets him as supreme guarantor of truth, promising that the 'xxv orders of knaues' are 'confirmed forever by Cocke Lorel' (1973: 98). The customary discourse of the all-encompassing moral folly of sinful humanity is, as in *Cock Lorell's Bote*, implicit but simultaneously very perceivable. Its pervasiveness is visually tied to the action of roaming: the company is a 'brotherhood of vagabonds' lodging in 'Gravesend barge', a dwelling that 'never stands', and the reader may see them anywhere, just by 'walking' (87–8) in the streets. The allegorical deformity of human morals becomes intellectual disability as Awdeley describes some of the brotherhood members. All of his subjects are portrayed as fools in some way, with a tendency to slothfulness, but Troll Hazard of Tritrace's foolishness gets the most effective physiognomical and behavioural description:

> Troll Hazard of Tritrace is he that goeth gaping after his Master, looking to and fro til he have lost him. This knave goeth gazing about like a fool at every toy, and then seeketh in every house like a Masterless dog, and when his Master needeth him, he is to seek. (98–9)

The verb 'goeth', stressing vagabondage, recurs here twice in correspondence with both 'gaping' and 'gazing' at toys, two actions that would have been regarded as symptoms of intellectual impairment. The attraction to toys illustrates the conception of the fool as a perpetual child, someone lingering in the early phase of human development (McDonagh 2009: 85), one who likes to play because, as Bartholomeus Anglicus had explained, children 'think only on things that be, and reck not of things that shall be' (Steele 1924: 'Mediaeval Manners'). Awdeley stresses the importance of the here and now for the fool, at the expense of the effects of his actions, by satirising also the lack of orientation in the adult individual and the inclination towards getting lost. The image of the gaping mouth, then, is not only one of the central manifestations of the grotesque body as famously described by Bakhtin (Bakhtin 2009: 317, 325), but it was also seen as a sign of more recognisable disability. The influential Italian physiognomist Giambattista Della Porta, for instance, described the wide-open mouth as a chief sign of great 'stolidity' and 'ignorance', and linked that characteristic with the mouth of male sheep or dogs (1586: 113). In art, Pieter Bruegel's painting *The Cripples* (1568), which famously depicts a group of gaping beggar-fools on crutches seeking to attract attention on the streets outside the town walls, evokes a similar connection between life on the road and disability as Awdeley's description of Troll Hazard.

Other members of the roguish team are foolish: Troll With, who wears a 'cap on his head like Capon hardy' (Awdeley 1973: 98), gets one of the most recurring animal epithets and head accessories for fools; Troll and Troll By, 'who would bear rule in a place and hath no authority nor thanks, and at last is thrust out of the door like a knave' (98), exposes the early modern definition of legally declared 'idiot' as someone deprived of authority, responsibility, honour, and also property (Neugebauer 1997). As such, his description also revolves around the view of the fool as, more generally, any member of the masses who did not have any social or economic power and was usually stigmatised by nobles as intellectually inferior. The sarcastic portrayal of this particular rogue-fool targets society at large via the image of the masterless man who takes to the road after being dismissed from his workplace. Finally, Chase Litter seems unable to look after himself, lacks everyday intelligence, and finds it hard to perform even the simplest tasks correctly, an ability that was inquired into at incompetency examinations by the Court of Wards (Rushton 1988: 37):

> he . . . will pluck up the Featherbed or Mattress, and piss in the bedstraw, and will never rise uncalled. This knave berayeth many times in the corners of his Master's chamber, or other places inconvenient, and maketh clean his shoes with the coverlet or curtains. (Awdeley 1973: 99)

Embarrassing feats of this type would fill later fools' jestbooks. Yet they also testify to a transformation of the view of folly from a universal attribute of man in the middle ages to a direct conflation between disability and depravity (Stainton 2004).

This chapter has gathered instances of folly's convergence with mobility and the road in early modern English culture. It turns out that they are numerous and diverse. In its interaction with the material, subjective or symbolic level of the road, folly acquires many different, sometimes contrasting, significations. It is artificial in the configuration of the professional travelling clown, but also of the false beggar and the cony-catching rogue in disguise, as their symbolical witlessness consists in the sinful ignorance of God's precepts. Besides, for all these figures the road acts as a medium through which their folly can become lucrative, enabling a quick monetisation of their efforts. Folly is natural in the case of wandering 'idiots', of depersonalised cozened gulls, and of the foolish members of roguish fraternities. Yet sometimes the distinction between artificial and natural is not clear cut either: the gulls' stupidity is fully revealed by the duping actions of the cozeners; the wise clown simulates idiocy; the foolish rogue straddles instead real disability, the impersonation skills proper of the professional fool and moral folly. The physical location of the road thus not only offers a common ground for all these cultural forms, even perhaps infusing all of them with some shadiness, but also, by allowing real and metaphorical witlessness to variously combine, produces original personifications of folly.

Notes

1. For example Welsford 1968; Swain 1978; Billington 1984; Janik 1998; Otto 2001.
2. Though Woodbridge (2001) pays passing attention to fools as sinners and household jesters.
3. For example Welsford 1968: 69 ff.; Janik 1998: 275; Billington 1984: 6, 112; Swain 1978: 73, 120.
4. All references to Shakespeare in this chapter are to the 2005 *Complete Works*, ed. Stanley Wells and Gary Taylor.
5. That is, in Shakespeare, Thersites is deformed and Caliban is stigmatised as a stupid monster; in Armin's *Foole upon Foole* all the fools have bodily defects; see also Welsford 1968: 55–9, 123, 135.
6. See also Pugliatti 2003: 2–4.
7. See Billington 1984: 1–15; Preiss 2014: 67–70.
8. For Kemp as plain Englishman, see Wiles 1987: 24–5.
9. For a recent discussion on Armin, see Van Es 2015: 163–94.
10. See, for example, Harman 2002: 75, 97; Greene 2002a: 123, 124.

Works cited

Andrews, Jonathan, Asa Briggs, Roy Porter, Penny Tucker and Keir Waddington (1997), *The History of Bethlem*, London: Routledge.

Anon., 'Misero' from the so-called Tarocchi Cards of Mantegna (1530–61), engraving, London: British Museum.

Armin, Robert [1600] (1973), *A Shakespeare Jestbook, Robert Armin's 'Foole upon Foole': A Critical, Old-Spelling Edition*, ed. Henry Frederick Lippincott, Salzburg: Institute of English Language and Literature, Salzburg University.

Awdeley, John (1973), 'The Fraternity of Vagabonds', in Arthur F. Kinney (ed.), *Rogues, Vagabonds, and Sturdy Beggars: A New Gallery of Tudor and Early Stuart Rogue Literature*, Amherst: University of Massachusetts Press, pp. 85–101.

Aydelotte, Frank (1967), *Elizabethan Rogues and Vagabonds*, London: Routledge.

Bakhtin, M. M. (1981), *The Dialogic Imagination: Four Essays*, trans. Michael Holquist, Austin: University of Texas Press.

—— (2009), *Rabelais and His World*, Bloomington: Indiana University Press.

Baumgartner, Paul R. (1963), 'From Medieval Fool to Renaissance Rogue: Cocke Lorelles Bote and the Literary Tradition', *Annuale Mediaevale* 4, pp. 57–91.

Beier, A. L. (1987), *Masterless Men: The Vagrancy Problem in England, 1560–1640*, London: Methuen.

Billington, Sandra (1984), *A Social History of the Fool*, London: Faber & Faber.

Bonnemaison, Joël (2005), *Culture and Space: Conceiving a New Cultural Geography*, ed. Chantal Blanc-Pamard, Maud Lasseur and Christel Thibault, London and New York: I. B. Tauris.

Bosman, Anston (2013), 'Mobility', in Henry S. Turner (ed.), *Early Modern Theatricality*, Oxford: Oxford University Press, pp. 493–515.

Brant, Sebastian (1874), *The Ship of Fools*, ed. Thomas Hill Jamieson, trans. Alexander Barclay, Edinburgh: W. Paterson.

Brayshay, Mark (2005), 'Waits, Musicians, Bearwards and Players: The Inter-Urban Road Travel and Performances of Itinerant Entertainers in Sixteenth and Seventeenth Century England', *Journal of Historical Geography* 31, pp. 430–58.

Cranefield, Paul F. and Walter Federn (1963), 'Paracelsus on Goiter and Cretinism: A Translation and Discussion of "De Struma, Vulgo Der Kropf"', *Bulletin of the History of Medicine* 37.5, pp. 463–71.

—— (1967), 'The Begetting of Fools: An Annotated Translation of Paracelsus' "De generatione stultorum"', *Bulletin of the History of Medicine* 41, pp. 56–74.

Dekker, Thomas [1609] (1904), *The Gull's Hornbook*, ed. Ronald Brunlees McKerrow, London: De La More Press.

Della Porta, Giambattista (1586), *De humana physiognomonia*, Vico Equense: G. Cacchi.

Elstrack, Renold (1607), *While Maskinge in Their Folleis All Doe Passe*,

Though All Say Nay yet All Doe Ride the Asse, engraving, London: British Museum.

Erasmus, Desiderius [1511] (1993), *In Praise of Folly*, ed. Betty Radice, London: Penguin Books.

Goodey, C. F. (2011), *A History of Intelligence and 'Intellectual Disability': The Shaping of Psychology in Early Modern Europe*, Farnham: Ashgate.

Greene, Robert [1591] (2002a), 'A Notable Discovery of Cozenage', in A. V. Judges (ed.), *The Elizabethan Underworld*, London: Routledge, pp. 119–48.

—— [1592] (2002b), 'The Third and Last Part of Cony-Catching', in A. V. Judges (ed.), *The Elizabethan Underworld*, London: Routledge, pp. 179–205.

Halliwell, James O. (ed.) (1844), *Tarlton's Jests, and News Out of Purgatory*, London: Shakespeare Society.

Harman, Thomas [1567] (2002), 'A Caveat for Common Cursetors', in A. V. Judges (ed.), *The Elizabethan Underworld*, London: Routledge, pp. 61–118.

Harrison, William (1877), *Harrison's Description of England in Shakspere's Youth*, ed. Frederick James Furnivall, London: New Shakespeare Society.

Janik, Vicki K. (ed.) (1998), *Fools and Jesters in Literature, Art, and History*, Westport: Greenwood Press.

Johnson, Nora (2009), *The Actor as Playwright in Early Modern Drama*, Cambridge: Cambridge University Press.

Jonson, Ben (1989), *The Selected Plays of Ben Jonson*, vol. 2, ed. Martin Butler and Johanna Procter, Cambridge: Cambridge University Press.

Jütte, Robert (1994), *Poverty and Deviance in Early Modern Europe*, Cambridge: Cambridge University Press.

Keenan, Siobhan (2002), *Travelling Players in Shakespeare's England*, Basingstoke: Palgrave Macmillan.

Kemp, William (1985), *Kemps Nine Daies Wonder: Performed in a Daunce from London to Norwich*, ed. Susan Yaxley, Dereham: Larks Press.

Laharie, Muriel (1991), *La Folie au Moyen Age XI–XIII Siècles*, Paris: Le Léopard d'Or.

Limon, Jerzy (1985), *Gentlemen of a Company: English Players in Central and Eastern Europe, 1590–1660*, Cambridge: Cambridge University Press.

McDonagh, Patrick (2009), *Idiocy: A Cultural History*, Chicago: University of Chicago Press.

Metzler, Irina (2016), *Fools and Idiots? Intellectual Disability in the Middle Ages*, Oxford: Oxford University Press.

Middleton, Thomas (2007), *Thomas Middleton: The Collected Works*, ed. Gary Taylor and John Lavagnino, Oxford: Oxford University Press.

Neugebauer, Richard (1997), 'Mental Handicap in Medieval and Early Modern England: Criteria, Measurement and Care', in Anne Digby and David Wright (eds), *From Idiocy to Mental Deficiency: Historical Perspectives on People with Learning Disabilities*, London: Routledge, pp. 22–43.

Nicola di Maestro Antonio (15th century), 'Mato' from the Tarots of Sola Busca, engraving, Milan: Pinacoteca di Brera.

Otto, Beatrice K. (2001), *Fools Are Everywhere: The Court Jester around the World*, Chicago: University of Chicago Press.

Palmer, Barbara D. (2005), 'Early Modern Mobility: Players, Payments, and Patrons', *Shakespeare Quarterly* 56, pp. 259–305.

Preiss, Richard (2014), *Clowning and Authorship in Early Modern Theatre*, Cambridge: Cambridge University Press.
Pugliatti, Paola (2003), *Beggary and Theatre in Early Modern England*, Aldershot: Ashgate.
Rimbault, Edward F. (ed.) (1843), *Cock Lorell's Bote: A Satirical Poem*, London: Percy Society.
Rushton, Peter (1988), 'Lunatics and Idiots: Mental Disability, the Community, and the Poor Law in North-East England, 1600–1800', *Medical History* 32, pp. 34–50.
Salamon, Linda Bradley (2004), 'Vagabond Veterans: The Roguish Company of Martin Guerre and Henry V', in Craig Dionne (ed.), *Rogues and Early Modern English Culture*, Ann Arbor: University of Michigan Press, pp. 261–93.
Salgādo, Gāmini (1977), *The Elizabethan Underworld*, London: J. M. Dent.
Schrickx, Willem (1983), '"Pickleherring" and English Actors in Germany', *Shakespeare Survey* 36, pp. 135–47.
Shakespeare, William (2005), *William Shakespeare: The Complete Works*, ed. Stanley Wells and Gary Taylor, Oxford: Oxford University Press.
Stainton, Tim (2001), 'Medieval Charitable Institutions and Intellectual Impairment c. 1066–1600', *Journal on Developmental Disabilities* 8, pp. 10–29.
—— (2004), 'Reason's Other: The Emergence of the Disabled Subject in the Northern Renaissance', *Disability & Society* 19, pp. 225–43.
Steele, Robert (1924), *Mediaeval Lore from Bartholomew Angelicus*, London: Chatto & Windus.
Swain, Barbara (1978), *Fools and Folly during the Middle Ages and the Renaissance*, Norwood: Norwood Library Editions.
Thomas, Max W. (1992), '*Kemps Nine Daies Wonder*: Dancing Carnival into Market', *PMLA* 107, pp. 511–23.
Thomson, Peter (2004), 'Tarlton, Richard (d. 1588)', *Oxford Dictionary of National Biography*, <http://www.oxforddnb.com/view/10.1093/ref:odnb/9780198614128.001.0001/odnb-9780198614128-e-26971> (last accessed 16 May 2019).
Van Es, Bart (2015), *Shakespeare in Company*, Oxford: Oxford University Press.
van Hoogstraten, Dirk (1613), Frontispiece to a series of beggars' scenes, engraving, London: British Museum.
Walker, Gilbert (1973), 'A Manifest Detection of Diceplay', in Arthur F. Kinney (ed.), *Rogues, Vagabonds, and Sturdy Beggars: A New Gallery of Tudor and Early Stuart Rogue Literature*, Amherst: University of Massachusetts Press, pp. 59–83.
Welsford, Enid (1968), *The Fool: His Social and Literary History*, London: Faber & Faber.
Wiles, David (1987), *Shakespeare's Clown: Actor and Text in the Elizabethan Playhouse*, Cambridge: Cambridge University Press.
Woodbridge, Linda (2001), *Vagrancy, Homelessness, and English Renaissance Literature*, Urbana: University of Illinois Press.
Wright, Louis B. (1926), 'Will Kemp and the Commedia Dell' Arte', *Modern Language Notes* 41, pp. 516–20.

Wright, Thomas (ed.) (1842), *Jack of Dover, His Quest of Inquirie, Or, His Privy Search for the Veriest Foole in England*, London: Percy Society.

Zijderveld, Anton C. (1982), *Reality in a Looking-Glass: Rationality through an Analysis of Traditional Folly*, London: Routledge.

Chapter 8

'Fallen Am I in Dark Uneven Way': Wandering from the Road in Early Modern Folklore and Drama

Jennifer Allport Reid

This chapter has a dual focus, asking what the relationship between theatrical and folkloric will-o'-the-wisps and hobgoblins reveals about the social practices and experiences of travelling on the early modern highway. Figuring forth the lived experience of getting lost, these supernatural tricksters embody everyday anxieties about wayfinding, recasting the state of disorientation as resulting from a purposefully deceptive external force. Meanwhile, the passivity associated with aimless movement and journeying gone wrong finds its corollary on the early modern stage in a number of comedies concerning magic and the supernatural. In plays such as Anthony Munday's *John a Kent and John a Cumber* (early 1590s) and Shakespeare's *A Midsummer Night's Dream* (c. 1594–6) and *The Tempest* (1611), the romantic plot is directed by a sorcerous or non-human figure who orchestrates the protagonists' wanderings.[1] This chapter will begin by asking whether the space of the lonely, pixie-haunted road as it appears in early modern folklore can fruitfully be read in terms of Henri Lefebvre's spatial theory: as 'representational' or 'lived space', 'embodying complex symbolisms, sometimes coded, sometimes not, linked to the clandestine or underground side of social life'. In this reading, supernatural beings which haunt the road would be seen as emblematic of how the rural highway was experienced in the period; as reflecting and personifying the 'close association . . . between daily reality (daily routine) and . . . the routes and networks which link up the places set aside for work, "private" life and leisure' (Lefebvre 1991: 33, 38). The chapter will then turn to the plays themselves, exploring how the effectively absent space of the road (not only hidden from the audiences' sightline, but also lost from the characters themselves) nevertheless shapes the dramatic action, staging both the actors' physical movement and the narrative movement of the plot, in terms of searching for the road.

'Led of Robyn Goodfelowe': the haunted highway

The experience of the nocturnal pedestrian encountering and following a mysterious wandering light, only to be led out of their way and into a perilous or disorientating landscape, is frequently attested to throughout the early modern period. From the early eighteenth century onwards the precise nature of this strange light was much discussed by natural philosophers, particularly once Isaac Newton had provided 'the first scientific report' of the *ignis fatuus*, describing it as 'a vapour shining without heat' possessing 'the same difference between this vapour and flame, as between rotten Wood shining without heat and burning Coals of fire' (Edwards 2014: 3; Newton 1704: 2s3v). The density of allusions to the will-o'-the-wisp evidences the anxieties about road travel that it both generated and reflected, for travelling around the local roads of sixteenth-century England could certainly be a trial. The road network was not at this time constructed according to any national plan or scheme; rather, as Garrett A. Sullivan has shown, the precarious state of the highways meant that when, as was not infrequent, the road became impassable, travellers could exercise their right of way across private land, leading to 'ongoing struggles over highway maintenance' (Sullivan 1998: 169; McRae 2009: 67–121). The highway was vulnerable to tensions, conflicts and tangible physical discomfort even before the interference of the misleading *ignis fatuus*.

Moreover, while the literal existence of these wandering fires is hard to establish with any certainty, neither can it be dismissed out of hand. Although after the nineteenth century eyewitness accounts of the will-o'-the-wisp cease, a number of modern scientists have taken the numerous earlier recorded sightings seriously, attributing these to a 'manifestly real and widely observed [phenomenon] ... associated with stagnant water in marshy terrain and ... seen on dark, warm nights' (Edwards 2014: 4; see also Mills 2000). As Alison Shell notes, the 'misleading resemblance' of these dancing lights to lanterns made them 'a real danger for the early modern traveler', and one can surmise that their tendency to appear in treacherous landscapes could make such encounters potentially fatal (Shell 2015: 92). The Laudian clergyman John Swan summarised the learned consensus on the occurrence in his encyclopaedia of 1635, characterising the '*Ignis fatuus*, or *foolish Fire*' as 'a fat and oily Exhalation hot and drie' that 'feareth or scareth fools'. Demonstrating an assumption implicit in many learned sources, Swan takes pains to characterise those afraid of the *ignis fatuus* as foolish, but conspicuously does not cast doubt on its literal existence. Such fears he attributes to a supernatural interpretation of a scientific manifestation, and an interpretation, moreover, with a confessional subtext:

> the much terrified, ignorant, and superstitious people ... have deemed these lights to be walking spirits; or (as the silly ones amongst the Papists beleeve) they can be nothing else but the souls of such as go to Purgatorie. (Swan 1635: sig. M3)

That contemporaries took seriously the perilousness of being led astray is made evident in Swan's definition. Despite his derisive insistence that 'these lights be not walking spirits', he nevertheless feels it necessary to explain 'why is it that they leade men out of their way':

> those who see them are amazed, and look so earnestly after them that they forget their way; and then being once out, they wander to and fro ... [to] dangerous places; whereupon the next day they will undoubtedly tell you strange tales ... how they were led up and down by ... some devil or spirit in the likenesse of fire which fain would have hurt them. (Swan 1635: sig. M4ʳ)

These lights, then, have an almost mesmeric effect upon passers-by, and significantly provoke reactions of amazement, an etymologically laden word which will be discussed further below. Amazement here is disorientating, dislocating, evidenced not only in the traveller's immediate confusion, but also in the subsequent compulsion to communicate the experience, to transform it into a tall tale.

Equally, however, Swan's clear concern to counter the related errors made by 'superstitious people' and 'Papists' reflects a discourse well established by the seventeenth century which mapped educational and confessional difference on to the figure of the will-o'-the-wisp. Given their readymade associations with errancy, it is perhaps unsurprising that Robin Goodfellow and his 'crew' became a potent metaphor for Protestant writers in the long century after the Reformation. As historians including Peter Marshall, Jesse Lander, Darren Oldridge and Ronald Hutton have noted, a persistent polemical discourse developed over the period which figured the hobgoblin both as a superstitious remnant of an antiquated, specifically Catholic, corpus of beliefs, and more allegorically as an abstract illustration of the misleading darkness of popery in which, as William Tyndale wrote in the 1530s, the ignorant 'wandre as in a myst / or (as we saye) led of Robyn Goodfelowe' (Tyndale 1531: Prol. n.p.). A rhetorical association abounds throughout the period between false belief, unreliable narrative, and being both physically and spiritually misled. The usefulness to religious writers of depicting Catholicism itself as tale-spinning is readily apparent: drawing on the established, trivialising connection between 'old wives' tales and old papists' tales', this discourse fed into both the virulent anti-popery of the late Elizabethan and Jacobean period and the already decades-old accusation that Catholicism relied for its false authority on tradition, orality and populism rather than on the revealed word of God (Dolan 1999: 28). At the same time, it lent the fey being a peculiar symbolic weight, a suggestive profundity and richness that made being pixie-led away from the right road an ideal image for literary and dramatic writers.

'Shaping fantasies' and 'airy nothing': the false light of reason in *A Midsummer Night's Dream*

The most famous literary incarnation of the mischievous hobgoblin, of course, is Shakespeare's Puck. Rather than focusing on Shakespeare's faithfulness or otherwise in his use of English folklore as a source, this chapter will instead suggest that being led enchantedly astray from the road in this play functions synecdochally to represent conflict both internal and external. Puck's role as the 'merry wanderer of the night' (2.1.43), deceiving hapless travellers, is established at his first introduction when one of the tricks explicitly attributed to him by the hostile Fairy is 'Mislead[ing] night-wanderers, laughing at their harm' (2.1.39), and this characteristic behaviour is later made explicit in his promise to appear as 'sometimes a fire' (3.1.105) and 'lead you about a round, / Through bog, through bush, through brake, through brier' (3.1.102–3).[2] While Puck is its chief 'wanderer', losing the way is central to the action of this comedy. The vocabulary of travel, of terrain and of movement, whether aimless or purposeful, saturates the play. The word 'way' recurs throughout the text (including 'church-way' and 'crossway'), on eight occasions carrying its original, primary meaning of 'A track, a road, a path', with perhaps the suggestion of another meaning current in the sixteenth century, 'A path, track, or trail through a wood or across country'.[3] Forms of 'lead' or 'mislead' appear ten times, implying how emphatically the fairy lore of this play is bound up with the risk of getting lost, losing one's bearings. Finally, there are nine instances of 'wander' or 'wanderer': while 'The course of true love never did run smooth' (1.1.134), this is only exacerbated by the lovers' crucially directionless movement through the forest.[4]

Supernatural intervention is hardly necessary to lose one's way in the forest, of course, and even before Puck's meddling Lysander has sheepishly admitted as much: 'Fair love, you faint with wandering in the wood / And to speak troth, I have forgot our way' (2.2.39–40). In the previous scene, Demetrius had hinted at a more sinister disordering of his senses, proclaiming 'here am I, and wood within this wood' (2.1.192). The pun on wood (forest/insane) presages the psychological, as well as physical, disorientation experienced by the lovers over the course of the night.[5] On the most immediate level, Puck is ostensibly chiefly responsible for their chaotic 'wandering', metaphorically as well as physically leading the lovers astray through his mistaken application of love-in-idleness to Lysander's eyes. Even the solution to the initial mistake of accidentally drugging the wrong Athenian is depicted in mobile terms: Oberon instructs Puck first to 'lead these testy rivals so astray / As one come not within another's way' (3.2.358–9) and, once they have collapsed with weariness, 'fallen ... in dark uneven way' (417), to 'crush this herb into Lysander's eye ... / To take from thence all error' (366–8). The choice of noun is highly significant, evoking as it does the Latin-derived residual connotation of 'the action of roaming or wandering; hence a devious or winding course, a roving, winding'.[6] The charged choice of word allows for entirely contradictory interpretations: the 'error' is that of the misleading fairies, and yet Lysander himself is the one erroneous, roving. Despite Helena's statement that 'Love looks not with the eyes but with the mind' (1.1.234), Lysander has a literally wandering eye, and the proximity between passion and madness is made uncomfortably apparent, suggesting another cause of the lovers' straying in the forest. Lysander's speech to Helena under the influence of the love potion deludedly attributes his love for her to reason, rather than to the bewitchment to which we know he has been subjected:

> The will of man is by his reason swayed, . . .
> Reason becomes the marshal to my will
> And leads me to your eyes (2.2.119, 124–5)

Tellingly, the metaphor depicts reason as 'leading' him, 'sway[ing]' his will and 'marshal[ling]' his love for Helena. Shell notes the network of references to 'misdirected worship', conversion and 'idolatrous perception' in *A Midsummer Night's Dream*, 'echo[ing] the play's wider, Reformation-inflected anxieties about misdirection and delusion' (2015: 82). Relatedly, the above discussion also reveals that the play's saturation with folkloric references to being pixie-led from the road adds to its thematic destabilisation of reason, implying that it is at best a 'foolish fire', at worst a more actively false guide. In the final act of the play, Theseus famously draws a connection between the 'shaping fantasies' of 'Lovers and madmen' (5.1.4–5); significantly, there is an echo of the nocturnal trickster spirit in Theseus's oft-quoted description of the poetic process by which

> as imagination bodies forth
> The forms of things unknown, the poet's pen
> Turns them to shapes, and gives to airy nothing
> A local habitation and a name. (5.1.14–17)

Theseus appears to offer an alternative, retrospective reading of the forest scenes, as the promptings of the imagination working upon 'shapes' and 'airy nothing'. Tellingly, the speech ends upon an example which recalls exactly the kind of pranks which Puck played upon the mechanicals: 'in the night, imagining some fear, / How easy is a bush supposed a bear!' (21–2). Theseus's interpretative comments appear to conform to Protestant polemic that connects fear of 'airy nothing[s]' with the unreason of 'much terrified, ignorant, and superstitious people' (Swan 1635: sig. M3). More profoundly, *A Midsummer Night's Dream* presents internal disturbance as both reflective of and impactful upon the natural world, and as connected in turn to the playworld's interrelation of festive culture and fairy lore. The symbolic interpretation of the misleading supernatural being as rooted in division – whether external conflicts or internal struggles between the false light of faulty reason, one's wayward desire, or lingering cultural memory of purportedly erroneous belief – is literalised in the quarrel between the Fairy Queen and King, whose disagreement has caused the natural landscape to become disordered in turn. This, too, is figured in spatial terms; due to the discord between Oberon and Titania, we learn, the distempered seasons so 'change / Their wonted liveries [that] the mazed world . . . now knows not which is which' (2.1.112–14). The 'mazed world' reverberates with the 'quaint mazes in the wanton green' mentioned fourteen lines later which, 'For lack of tread, are indistinguishable' (2.1.99–100). The echo between 'mazes' and 'mazed' reinforces the etymological connection between physical and emotional disorientation, with the world amazed that the seasons are suddenly topsy-turvy ('delirious or bewildered; distraught; unsettled or incoherent in one's mind') and, picking up on the 'quaint mazes', 'mov[ing] in a winding course; wander[ing] as if in a maze'.[7] We are reminded of Swan's description of travellers encountering wandering fires who 'are amazed, and look so earnestly after them that they forget their way; and . . . wander to and fro' (1635: sig. M4r). In both texts, the figure of the will-o'-the-wisp or hobgoblin encodes within it a sense in which spatial experience is a reflection of emotional state; to be pixie-led is to be 'unsettled or incoherent in one's mind'.

'Auncient Englishe guyse': competing customs in *John a Kent and John a Cumber*

If Oberon is a disinterested observer of the foolish mortals' 'fond pageant' (3.2.114–15), he finds a more partial counterpart in the stage-managing magician who recurs in comic drama of the late Elizabethan period, as in Robert Greene's *Friar Bacon and Friar Bungay* (c. 1589), the anonymous and wildly popular *The Merry Devil of Edmonton*, and Anthony Munday's *John a Kent and John a Cumber*.[8] This last is sometimes identified as the play listed by Philip Henslowe under the title *The Wise Man of West Chester*, first staged by the Admiral's Men in December 1594 and then intermittently until July 1597, and it too takes a folkloric figure as its protagonist; John a Kent is thought to be an anglicisation of the fifteenth-century Welsh poet Siôn Cent, who became the subject of the folklore of the Welsh Marches and, later on, a recurring figure in nineteenth- and twentieth-century folklore collections (Foakes 2002: 26–34, 36, 47, 59, 60).[9] While critics such as Nevill Coghill have argued that Munday's comedy might have suggested various details to Shakespeare when he was writing *A Midsummer Night's Dream*, there has been little discussion of the specific shared importance to both comedies of being pixie-led.

In contrast to Shakespeare's (eventually) neat pairings, *John a Kent* presents a conflict between four young men competing for the love of two women: Marian and Sidanen are secretly affianced to Lord Geoffrey Powis and Sir Griffin Meriddock respectively, but their fathers prefer the Earls of Pembroke and Morton. Powis and Meriddock enlist the aid of the Welsh magician John a Kent in winning back the ladies, but the apparent success of his intervention is overturned by the immediate arrival of the Scottish magician John a Cumber, who joins with Pembroke, Morton, and their prospective fathers-in-law the Earl of Chester and Prince Llwellen. The ensuing scenes see a dizzying succession of ploy and counter-ploy in which the two magicians switch identities back and forth in their attempts not only to bring success to their selected suitors, but to cause as much humiliation as possible to their rival, and utmost chaos in general. Even having agreed to help the lovers, John a Kent gleefully plans to

> help, hinder, giue, take back, turne, ouerturne,
> deceiue, bestowe, breed pleasure, discontent
> yet comickly conclude. (134–6)[10]

Indeed, the disorder that he evokes here accurately summarises the back and forth movement of the play, suggesting the twists and turns of the contest between the two magicians and consequently the backtracking and circular wandering of the lovers themselves. The play is filled with literal wandering back and forth, with most of the action appearing to take place en route to somewhere else.

Most obviously redolent of the hobgoblin is John a Kent's mischievous spirit Shrimp who, in a particularly suggestive episode, rescues Sidanen and Marian by leading astray their guardians, Chester's son Oswen and his friend Amery. Following the sound of the invisible Shrimp's music, Oswen optimistically declares that the sound 'questionlesse... guydes vs, least we mistake our way' (1103–4). The fear of getting lost is ironically at the forefront of Oswen's mind, yet he 'mistake[s]' not the route, but the trustworthiness of the mysterious being that 'haunt[s]' them. Finally appearing to the hapless young men face to face and claiming to be John a Cumber's assistant, Shrimp tells them, 'If ... youle speed, follow me presently' (1182). In a play so full of punning references to movement and travel, his deceptive promise could stand for the role of magic in *John a Kent* more generally: given the dizzying rapidity of many of the changes of fortune which take place, speed of movement is certainly no guarantee of the word's older denotation of achieving success. With comically belated insight, poor Amery finally realises 'This villayne boy is out of doubt some spirit' (1395), and by the time they rejoin the other lords, Oswen has relabelled him again as 'questionlesse some fiend' (1425). The misleading wanderer, then, is once again crucial to the happy resolution of the romantic comedy: tellingly, Sidanen describes being happily reunited with Meriddock as 'bringing her where she desyre to be' (1323).

More broadly, this is again a comedy permeated with movement, figuring both parental and filial experience as different forms of pedestrianism. The interchangeability of Shakespeare's Athenian lovers is often remarked upon, and we learn similarly little about the suitors in Munday's comedy; indeed, even the scribe appears to have lost track of which was which, as the manuscript shows the speech heading 'S Griffin' entered before being deleted and replaced with his rival's name, 'Morton' (1243).[11] The swiftness with which Marian and Sidanen are moved from one party to the other, in addition to the eponymous rivals' dizzying role-swapping, ensures that the love-matches and the arranged marriages alike appear as little more than a series of exchanges or, more fittingly, rounds in the game being played by the two magicians. As in Shakespeare's play, the key dichotomy in terms of marital choice is that between romantic preference and paternal direction; in *John a Kent*, this dichotomy is symbolised in surprisingly itinerant terms and is, further, given a particularly nationalistic and political edge. The action is set in the historically tense Welsh Marches, the border between England and

Wales, and there is a noticeable division between the Welsh Powis and Meriddock beloved of the young women, and the English Pembroke and Scottish Morton selected by their fathers (the latter's nationality is mentioned twice, at lines 96 and 180). The Earl of Chester's first speech on stage celebrates the upcoming nuptials of his daughter and niece in terms of customary processing:

> sith it is our aunciennt Englishe guyse,
> the Bridegroomes should vppon the wedding day,
> come from some distant place to fetch their Brydes,
> my house at *Plessye* is for you preparde.
> Thence to the Castell shall walke along
> And at St Iohns shall be solemnized,
> the nuptialles of your honors. (156–62)

Like Theseus, Chester imagines the 'solemnities' of the 'nuptial hour' in terms of a triumphal procession, conducted 'With pomp, with triumph and with revelling' (*MND*, 1.1.11, 1, 19). This ceremonial progress incorporates ancestral house, castle and church, bringing into the fold the new family members from 'some distant place', and tracing in footsteps an officially sanctioned, parentally approved, dynastically motivated ideal of marriage. At the same time, his reference to this apparently old custom, an 'aunciennt Englishe guyse', betrays an unconscious prescience as to the tricks and disguises which will unfold on the road between his home and the castle.[12]

This paternal vision is specifically opposed to unruly nocturnal wandering, as well as to a specifically female form of customary observance. After Chester and the lords have exited, John a Kent appears to the ladies disguised as a hermit, and pretends to read their fortune, insisting that their marriages will be blighted, if 'you washe not at Saint winifrides fayre spring, your lilly handes, and list the holy voyce' (260–1). Although unaware that the apparent hermit is working on the behalf of their beloveds, they are able to convince Marian's mother the Countess to allow a visit to Winifred's spring that night, despite her concern about Chester's disapproval. Chester apparently has less reverence than does his wife for this local 'guyse': 'my Lord condemnes these aunciennt rules, / religiously obserued in these partes' (270–1). Crucially, however, the main reservation that the Countess expresses is that they might get lost: she would agree 'had we some trusty freend to be our guyde' (280). The hermit's reassurance stresses both his familiarity with the route and its visibility by moonlight:

> vse hath made me perfect in the way.
> And if your honors deigne so olde a guyde:

So speed my soule as shall to you betyde . . .
The siluer shyning horned lamp . . .
by whose cleere light we may discerne the pathe,
wherin . . .
will I guyde ye safely to the spring. (283–94)

Two different forms of custom are here opposed, one associated with an 'aunciente', specifically English, aristocratic (male) processing which figures nuptial celebration as a display of seigneurial and clerical prestige and unity, the other evoking Welsh local belief, popular 'vse', and nocturnal observance associated with the aged and the female. It is significant to note that Chester remarks on the specifically ambulatory form of his daughter's transgression, casting himself as an 'aged father' and complaining of his 'peeuish' wife having encouraged Marian, 'agaynst bothe course and kynde', to go 'gadding foorth without my leaue' (803–8). The 'course' to which he here refers is, of course, the course he has defined for her, not that of true love, while their visit to the holy spring is labelled as 'gadding'. Indeed, Chester explicitly redefines the women's nocturnal pilgrimage as subtlety, seduction and hypocrisy: he confronts (as he thinks) John a Kent with the accusation of

Thy subtill wandring in an Hermits weede,
wherby thou didst seduce my aged wife,
to let her daughter, and my loouely Niece,
walke wth her to Saint vvinifrydes fayre spring
to offer vp theyr latest mayden vowes,
and thou, like to an hippocrite, their guyde. (1257–62)

The proliferation of swaps, doubling, exchanged disguises, and changes of fortune, in its chaotic confusion, comes to represent as visual stage business the miscommunication between generations, for indeed, despite their presence on stage together at a number of points, the fathers and daughters never once address each other. In *The Tempest*, the reverse is notoriously the case: far from presenting the distant and ultimately disappointed father figure of the two earlier plays, this play stages a father whose parental control is mirrored and symbolised by his supernatural control of the other protagonists' physical movement. Nevertheless, the connections between these plays suggest an influence not often critically remarked upon. Much as Munday's play appears to suggest the folkloric intertext and dramatic dynamic of magical director and mischievous assistant which is amplified and expanded in *A Midsummer Night's Dream*, the ambivalence of John a Kent's control of the action and the other characters' socio-religious interpretation of events can also be detected in Shakespeare's later play, to which this chapter will now turn.[13]

'Ling'ring perdition': spiritual loss in *The Tempest*

More so than any of the other plays under discussion, Shakespeare's late play presents a magical stage manager who directs the feet and the futures of the other protagonists. The urgency attached to movement is reflected in, and reinforced by, the play's verbal register: of the nine scenes, seven conclude with a reference to movement or instruction to 'Come, follow', 'lead the way' or 'draw near'. Prospero's commands to those around him (chiefly Ariel, Miranda, Caliban and Ferdinand) repetitively emphasise movement: he issues the order 'come' eighteen times, with ten instances of instructions to 'go' and an additional five to 'follow'. This ability to direct others reflects the dual aspects of Prospero's magic: not only the capacity to (mis)lead that has been the focus of this chapter, but also the more critically noted, and considerably more controversial, power that Prospero holds to conjure spirits of markedly indeterminate provenance to do his bidding. At the same time, Prospero's unusually total control over the action is accentuated by his role as matchmaking parent. In stark contrast to John a Kent, Prospero is deeply emotionally invested in the outcomes of his spatial trickery. Prospero is a practically unique figure in comedy, a father whose daughter does ultimately marry the man whom he chooses, 'although a basic dramatic law ... dictates that any suitor favored by a young woman's parents will never suit her', a law borne out by the other comedies discussed above (Levin 2009: 214). In a sense, Prospero combines the roles of Oberon, Egeus and Theseus: he coordinates the action, is its chief onlooker, yet is ultimately the most invested in the comedic outcome.

Accounts of the will-o'-the-wisp, and the ambivalence with which the being was regarded by Shakespeare's contemporaries, therefore provide an important lens through which to view Prospero's complex and fluid characterisation. Much like Munday's play, *The Tempest* participates in a literary tradition of all-powerful magicians which, as Barbara Traister has established, was drawn both from medieval romance and from learned treatises, and was 'associated with role-playing; in many ways the magician is an actor. Even more, however, he is a director, a presenter of spectacular shows for the discomfort, edification, or entertainment of spectators' (Traister 1984: 23–4). Whether Prospero's powers should be viewed as neutral, positive or problematic remains the topic of much critical debate, yet less often noted is the markedly folkloric, rather than solely literary, tradition in which the play's enchantments participate, and the potential light that this can shed on understanding the nature of Prospero's magic.[14] There is little doubt that the misleading powers of Prospero's supernatural servants are of the same category as those of Robin Goodfellow. Caliban, concerned that the spirits have heard his curses, reflects upon the punishments which they would administer on Prospero's instruction:

> they'll nor pinch,
> Fright me with urchin-shows, pitch me i' th' mire,
> Nor lead me, like a firebrand in the dark,
> Out of my way unless he bid 'em. (2.2.4–7)

As Caliban's trepidation suggests, to a far greater degree than the other comedies considered here *The Tempest* vividly evinces the genuine fears and traumas associated with being led from the road, an experience to which island-dweller Caliban and courtly visitors alike are subjected. This is rendered in the most physical terms in the scenes in which Stephano, Trinculo and Caliban plot to take over the island. The possibility of being 'pitch[ed] . . . i' th' mire' is clearly no exaggeration or rhetorical flourish on Caliban's part: Ariel later assures Prospero that he has subjected Stephano, Trinculo and Caliban to just this experience, having

> charmed their ears
> That calf-like they my lowing followed, through
> Toothed briars, sharp furzes, pricking gorse and thorns,
> Which entered their frail shins. At last I left them
> I'th' filthy-mantled pool beyond your cell,
> There dancing up to th' chins, that the foul lake
> O'erstunk their feet. (4.1.178–84)

Despite his role as guide rather than guided, Ariel's description powerfully evokes the sensations of wandering from the path, the scratches and scrapes of the thorns and the malodorous water in which the unfortunate clowns find themselves immersed. While his description is undoubtedly comical, the glimmer of sympathy towards their 'frail shins' and 'calf-like' credulity provides a note of ambivalence which is reinforced by a persistent undercurrent throughout the play. Upon his first appearance to the hapless clowns in Act 3, Scene 2, visible only to the audience and highly reminiscent of John a Kent's assistant Shrimp, Ariel uses music to lead them after him, invisibly piping back to them 'the tune of [their] catch, played by the picture of Nobody' (3.2.126–7). In contrast to Oswen's optimism, their first thought is that they are in the presence of the diabolical. Stephano challenges the invisible musician, 'If thou be'st a devil, take't as thou list' (129), prompting Trinculo to exclaim, 'O, forgive me my sins!' (130).[15] Although Caliban reassures them, 'Be not afeard. The isle is full of noises, / Sounds and sweet airs that give delight and hurt not' (135–6), his own earlier description of being led 'like a firebrand in the dark' (2.2.6), as much as their subsequent experience of being pixie-led, suggests the greater likelihood of the invisible musician being a false guise rather than merely 'sweet airs'. Nor are these admittedly untrustworthy witnesses the only commentators who connect their bewildering experiences on the island with devilish activity: even Ferdinand, we learn, makes this association, responding to Ariel's appearance as St Elmo's fire on board the ship with the cry 'Hell is empty, / And all the devils are here' (1.2.214–15). Significantly, Ariel's own description of his magical activities on the ship is that he 'flamed amazement' (198), a phrase that connects the wandering fire once again with the emotional and spatial resonances of being amazed.

Such references to demonic intervention return us to the reformed polemicists' association between directional and spiritual errancy. In addition to connecting narrative traditions surrounding hobgoblins with popish superstition, these writers often added the further gloss that, if such a being existed at all, it must be a devil. Scholars have argued that, faced with widespread popular belief, reformed theologians had the choice of either 'dismiss[ing] [fairies] as delusions or idle tales, or reinterpret[ing] [them] as demons' (Oldridge 2016: 2). This conflation is found, for example, in an entry in the antiquarian Abraham Pryme's diary from the end of the seventeenth century, describing how a member of his acquaintance encountered an *ignis fatuus* and, having unsuccessfully tried to run away, managed to 'beat it all in pieces. And he told it all over that he had killed the divel that would needs have carry'd him away ith' lane, if he could but have gotten hold on him' (Pryme 1870: 63–4). Pryme's tone wavers between wry scepticism at the man 'attesting seriously and soberly that he had kill'd the divel, which he did realy believe for a great while after', and willingness to credit particular details of the account. Apparently eager to absolve himself from accusations of credulity, he adds that

> He that told me this story affirm'd that he saw the stick that this fellow kill'd the divel with, and says that it was stained all black within towards the end with its strokes over this *Ignis fatuus*. (Pryme 1870: 64)

Pryme's anecdote is significant for our purposes because it attests to continuing belief in, and uncertainty over how to classify, the will-o'-the-wisp even towards the end of the period; indeed, his account agrees markedly well with Swan's comment that travellers will 'undoubtedly tell you strange tales . . . how they were led up and down by . . . nothing else but some devil . . . which fain would have hurt them' (1635: sig. M4^r). Moreover, it is telling that both Pryme and his acquaintances are comfortable with leaving this distinction unclear: the difference between devil and spirit is evidently one of degree, not kind. Given this frequent slippage in early modern thought between fairies or hobgoblins and devils, it is notable that the comic subplot repeatedly foregrounds the reminder that a similarly demonic interpretation could be applied to Prospero and his spirits.

In keeping, then, with Prospero's initially vengeful motivations, and with the marked ambivalence attached to his powers, the pixie-leading that he orchestrates is explicitly depicted here as vindictive and physically unpleasant.[16] It is given a further theological interpretation by the terminology with which Prospero himself frames his plans to reform the corrupt courtiers. In the scene following Stephano's misrecognition of Ariel as a devil, Prospero's spirit helper appears in the form of a harpy to Alonso and the other courtiers, the overt objects of Prospero's revenge. Ariel announces to the 'three men of sin' (3.3.53) that he and his 'fellows' come as 'ministers of Fate' (60–1), in order to 'pronounce' (76) divine punishment for their treatment of Prospero:

> Ling'ring perdition, worse than any death
> Can be at once, shall step by step attend
> You and your ways. (3.3.77–9)

Not only is their punishment expressed in ambulatory terms, but the term 'perdition' suggests yet another etymological conflation between eschatology and loss tracing back to the Latin root *'perdit-*, past participial stem of *perdere* to make away with, destroy, lose'[17] (a resonance Shakespeare had already exploited in *The Winter's Tale* in the aptly named character Perdita). Its penal use in this scene picks up and modifies Prospero's earlier and more equivocal use of the word, reassuring his compassionate daughter that there have been no casualties in the storm: 'not so much perdition as an hair, / Betid to any creature in the vessel' (1.2.30–1). The repetition of 'perdition', then, suggests a symbolic correlation between, firstly, being physically lost; secondly 'The fact or condition of being destroyed or ruined'; and finally 'The state of final spiritual ruin or damnation'.[18] This last denotation in particular recalls the polemical commonplace that 'the much terrified, ignorant, and superstitious people' believe wandering lights to 'be nothing else but the souls of such as go to Purgatorie', a connection which gives support to Corfield's suggestion that Prospero intends to subject his enemies to a form of purgatory (Swan 1635: sig. M3; Corfield 1985: 41).

A theological interpretation of the travails that they undergo through Prospero's disturbingly convergent processes of revenge and recuperation also evidently suggests itself to the courtiers themselves. In an echo of the 'mazed world' of *A Midsummer Night's Dream*, the lost nobles themselves view the island as 'a maze ... / Through forthrights and meanders' (3.3.2–3). The concluding scene develops the thematic connections between spatial disorientation, psychological disturbance, and unnatural or supernatural oversight, as in Alonso's wondering remark that

> This is as strange a maze as e'er men trod,
> And there is in this business more than nature
> Was ever conduct of. (5.1.242–4)

As in the earlier comedy, this reference to a maze points up the unconsciously punning resonance of Gonzalo's earlier association of the island with 'torment, trouble, wonder and amazement'; he, too, identifies a force 'more than nature' as the only means of escaping 'this fearful country', although the audience might recognise a misguided optimism in his call for 'Some heavenly power [to] guide us' (5.1.104–6). Indeed, even after the revelation of Prospero's intervention, Gonzalo attributes the stage-management of the scene to a divine rather than human director:

> Look down, you gods, ...
> For it is you that have chalked forth the way
> Which brought us hither. (5.1.201, 203–4)

Here, as in the anti-Catholic polemic, the path becomes allegorical of eschatological wayfinding, the misleading trickster spirit metonymic of larger guiding powers with the potential to be either providential or pernicious. Yet from the audience's privileged perspective, it is evident that no higher power has controlled their footsteps, but rather the all-powerful magician figure at the centre of the action. The spatial disorientation to which the courtiers are subjected both mirrors and highlights the emotional losses of their apparent bereavements at the play's outset, and the tensions and intrigues with which the court was already riven: in effect, Prospero visits upon his foes his own experience of being lost before the action of the play began. Ultimately, pixie-leading in *The Tempest* relates less to divine workings than to the machinations of the all-too-human protagonist, whose control of the other characters' footsteps drives the play's twin impulses of romantic resolution and revenge plot.

This chapter has suggested that the folklore of getting lost or being misled by supernatural, unknowable forces presented itself as a useful means by which dramatists could represent the pitfalls and circumlocutions of romantic love or of courtly intrigue. In the two Elizabethan comedies discussed, both Shakespeare and Munday draw upon and literalise a resonant linguistic connection between errancy and unfaithfulness; writing about these plays, it is in fact hard to find a language which does not draw on metaphors of lovers straying, eyes roving, desires wandering. Making physical this linguistic significance, one can imagine how the actors' aimless wanderings on stage could be ripe for physical comedy. For the purposes of this discussion, it is also striking to note the difficulty of literally staging the road, a space that limns the action of these plays and yet is invisible and unremarked upon except by its absence. The elusive route to safety, happiness and civilisation, represented only by the bare boards of the stage, becomes a staged absence, a spatial blank: the human protagonists' true path in these comedies is as obscure to the audience as to the characters themselves. At the same time, in their literalisation of the lived experience of getting lost, these theatrical will-o'-the-wisps and hobgoblins embody everyday anxieties about wayfinding, recasting the state of disorientation as resulting from a purposefully deceptive external force. Despite the overall benevolence of the magical figures and trickster spirits discussed in this chapter, the stage-management of the lovers' journeying tellingly removes their agency, suggesting the equivalent passivity of the misled traveller. As the opening of this chapter outlined, travel by foot was by no means a pleasant experience in the period, and the *ignis fatuus* of folktale and theatre allows an insight into how such experiences were processed by the early modern subject. In Lefebvre's terms, the 'perceived space' of the rural highway appears to have been experienced by those traversing it primarily as a place of insecurity from which one could all too easily be misled into error or injury, and this experience is, one might say, 'supernaturalised' in the figure of the will-o'-the-wisp as actively disruptive agent and false guide.

This chapter has also argued that the space of the road in early modern folklore became a vessel for more allegorical meanings which were projected on to this 'supernaturalisation' of the experience of road travel. Depictions of trickster spirits and fairies tempting travellers from the path brought a host of complicating associations for early modern writers, not least the reinterpretations imposed by Reformed thinkers who used the wandering spirit simultaneously as an example of superstition, as a metaphor for Catholic belief itself, and as a figurative depiction of the dangers of being misled by false belief. In Munday's comedy, this is manifested in terms of the tensions experienced between regional and gendered religious observances, with 'superstitious' custom being coded as both feminine and Welsh, and the processions of officialdom defined in terms of authority, Englishness and masculinity. Perhaps taking his cue from Munday, Shakespeare also develops this socio-religious reverberation with being pixie-led. In *A Midsummer Night's Dream*, he allegorises internal errancy, echoing Protestant accusations against the superstitious of being literally misguided and self-deluding. Finally, in *The Tempest* an equivalence is posited between pixie-leading and perdition which allows Shakespeare to exploit and explore this religious discursive subtext, in the process complicating the moral certainties of Prospero's magic and his ambivalent commixture of reformative and retributive motivations. As these various theatrical engagements suggest, although polemicists evinced clear disapproval of 'superstitious' readings of the *ignis fatuus*, nevertheless their reliance on examples drawn from folklore in fact worked to ensure the continued presence of these beings in public discourse.

While in religious and dramatic writings alike the metaphor's basis in either folkloric belief or genuine experiences of traversing the road can appear to slip from view, this chapter has nevertheless excavated some of the ways in which, in the early modern imagination, the will-o'-the-wisp could reflect the representational space of the highway, the 'images and symbols . . . overlay[ing] physical space, making symbolic use of its objects' (Lefebvre 1991: 39). While many of the chapters in this volume have pointed to early modern fears of the dangerously populated road, occupied by vagrants and thieves amongst other threats, pixie-leading is above all a solitary experience. Nevertheless, despite taking place at a remove from society in the spaces between home and the road away from home, these plays express movement and travel in terms which are as much to do with social as with geographical constraints, reproducing and reflecting upon the unique and individual pitfalls and false turns to which the solitary traveller is subject, in life as upon the highway.

Notes

1. Munday's play exists only in a manuscript, the date on which has been variously read as 1590, 1595 and 1596; see Munday 1923. For a discussion of dating Shakespeare's comedies, see Shakespeare 2017: 283–94; Shakespeare 2011: 6. All quotations from the plays will be from these editions.
2. Also see 2.1.2–5 and 3.2.396–9.
3. *OED*, 'way, n.1 and int.1.', <www.oed.com/view/Entry/226469> (last accessed 25 September 2018), esp. 1a and 2b.
4. *OED*, 'course, n.', 2a: 'Onward movement in a particular path, as of the heavenly bodies, a ship, etc.', <www.oed.com/view/Entry/43183> (last accessed 25 September 2018).
5. A similar point is also made by Shell 2015: 92.

6. *OED*, 'error, n.', <www.oed.com/view/Entry/64126> (last accessed 25 September 2018).
7. *OED*, 'maze, v.', <www.oed.com/view/Entry/115348> (last accessed 14 November 2018).
8. For the dating of the first two plays, see Greene 1963: xii; Anon. 1942: 28–35. The latter, *The Merry Devil of Edmonton*, was sufficiently popular that it went through six editions between 1608 and 1655.
9. This is not universally accepted, however; for further discussion, see Shapiro 1955; Rutter 2017: 77–9. For John a Kent, see Westwood and Simpson 2005: 184–5, 324.
10. Deletions and scribal errors from the original manuscript are silently omitted in order to maintain clarity.
11. For the interchangeability of the Athenian lovers, see Marshall 1982: 568; Holland 1994.
12. Compare two meanings given by the *OED* for 'guise, n.': 'Appointed, usual, or characteristic manner; custom, habit, practice; the "ways" (of a country)'; 'A disguise, a mask. Also, a dance or performance in disguises or masks; a masquerade, a show', <www.oed.com/view/Entry/82400> (last accessed 25 September 2017).
13. I have elsewhere argued for Munday's influence on Shakespearean depictions of folk culture; see Reid (forthcoming).
14. On the nature and moral status of the spirits who serve Prospero, see Corfield 1985; Harris 1980: 129–48; Lamb 1998: 543–8; Latham 1975; Levin 2009; Mowat 2001; Sisson 1958, esp. 75–6. On the Master Magician in English folklore, see Westwood and Simpson 2005: 184–5. An interesting discussion of the folkloric aspects of the play is offered by Johnson 1951, but this focuses more on the intertext of witchcraft than on spirits such as the hobgoblin.
15. Also see Act 2, Scene 2 in which the three meet. Tellingly, Caliban's first thought is that Trinculo is one of Prospero's spirits, while Trinculo and Stephano initially take Caliban and each other to be devils.
16. On Prospero's project being initially a vengeful rather than a restorative one, see Corfield 1985: 38–40.
17. See *OED*, 'perdition, n.', <www.oed.com/view/Entry/140642> (last accessed 25 September 2018).
18. Ibid.

Works cited

Anon. (1942), *The Merry Devil of Edmonton*, ed. William Amos Abrams, Durham, NC: Duke University Press.
Coghill, Neville (1964), *Shakespeare's Professional Skills*, Cambridge: Cambridge University Press.
Corfield, Cosmo (1985), 'Why Does Prospero Abjure his "Rough Magic"?', *Shakespeare Quarterly* 36, pp. 31–48.
Dolan, Frances Elizabeth (1999), *Whores of Babylon: Catholicism, Gender, and Seventeenth-Century Print Culture*, Ithaca: Cornell University Press.
Edwards, Howell G. M. (2014), '*Will-o'-the-Wisp*: An Ancient Mystery with

Extremophile Origins?', *Philosophical Transactions of the Royal Society A* 372, pp. 1–7.
Foakes, R. A. (ed.) (2002), *Henslowe's Diary*, Cambridge: Cambridge University Press.
Greene, Robert (1963), *Friar Bacon and Friar Bungay*, ed. Daniel Seltzer, Lincoln: University of Nebraska Press.
Harris, Anthony (1980), *Night's Black Agents: Witchcraft and Magic in Seventeenth-Century English Drama*, Manchester: Manchester University Press.
Holland, Peter (1994), 'Theseus' Shadows in *A Midsummer Night's Dream*', *Shakespeare Survey* 47, pp. 139–51.
Hutton, Ronald (2014), 'The Making of the Early Modern British Fairy Tradition', *The Historical Journal* 57, pp. 1135–56.
Johnson, W. Stacy (1951), 'Folklore Elements in *The Tempest*', *Midwest Folklore* 1, pp. 223–8.
Lamb, Mary Ellen (1998), 'Engendering the Narrative Act: Old Wives' Tales in *The Winter's Tale*, *Macbeth*, and *The Tempest*', *Criticism* 40, pp. 529–53.
Lander, Jesse M. (2013), 'Thinking with Fairies: *A Midsummer Night's Dream* and the Problem of Belief', *Shakespeare Survey* 65, pp. 42–57.
Latham, Jacqueline E. M. (1975), '*The Tempest* and King James's *Daemonologie*', *Shakespeare Survey* 28, pp. 117–23.
Lefebvre, Henri (1991), *The Production of Space*, trans. Donald Nicholson-Smith, Oxford: Blackwell.
Levin, Richard (2009), 'My Magic Can Lick Your Magic', *Medieval and Renaissance Drama in England* 22, pp. 201–28.
McRae, Andrew (2009), *Literature and Domestic Travel in Early Modern England*, Cambridge: Cambridge University Press.
Marshall, David (1982), 'Exchanging Visions: Reading *A Midsummer Night's Dream*', *ELH* 49, pp. 543–75.
Marshall, Peter (2009), 'Protestants and Fairies in Early-Modern England', in C. Scott Dixon, Dagmar Freist and Mark Greengrass (eds), *Living with Religious Diversity in Early-Modern Europe*, Farnham: Ashgate, pp. 139–59.
Mills, A. A. (2000), 'Will-o'-the-Wisp Revisited', *Weather* 55, pp. 239–41.
Mowat, Barbara A. (2001), 'Prospero's Book', *Shakespeare Quarterly* 52, pp. 1–33.
Munday, Anthony (1923), *John a Kent and John a Cumber*, ed. Muriel St Clare Byrne, Oxford: Malone Society Reprints.
Newton, Isaac (1704), *Opticks, or A Treatise of the Reflexions, Refractions, Inflexions and Colours of Light*, London.
Oldridge, Darren (2016), 'Fairies and the Devil in Early Modern England', *The Seventeenth Century* 31, pp. 1–15.
Pryme, Abraham (1870), *The Diary of Abraham de la Pryme, the Yorkshire Antiquary*, ed. Charles Jackson, Durham, London and Edinburgh: Andrews.
Reid, Jennifer Allport (forthcoming), '"Wearing the Horn": Class and Community in the Shakespearean Hunt', in Karen Raber and Holly Dugan (eds), *The Routledge Handbook of Shakespeare and Animals*, London and New York: Routledge.
Rutter, Tom (2017), *Shakespeare and the Admiral's Men: Reading Repertories on the London Stage, 1594–1600*, Cambridge: Cambridge University Press.

Shakespeare, William (2011), *The Tempest*, ed. Virginia Mason Vaughan and Alden T. Vaughan, London: Arden Shakespeare.
—— (2017), *A Midsummer Night's Dream*, ed. Sukanta Chaudhuri, London: Arden Shakespeare.
Shapiro, I. A. (1955), 'The Significance of a Date', *Shakespeare Survey* 8, pp. 100–5.
Shell, Alison (2015), 'Delusion in *A Midsummer Night's Dream*', in David Loewenstein and Michael Witmore (eds), *Shakespeare and Early Modern Religion*, Cambridge: Cambridge University Press, pp. 81–95.
Sisson, C. J. (1958), 'The Magic of Prospero', *Shakespeare Survey* 11, pp. 70–7.
Sullivan, Garrett A., Jr (1998), *The Drama of Landscape: Land, Property, and Social Relations on the Early Modern Stage*, Stanford: Stanford University Press.
Swan, John (1635), *Speculum mundi*, Cambridge.
Traister, Barbara Howard (1984), *Heavenly Necromancers: The Magician in English Renaissance Drama*, Columbia: University of Missouri Press.
Tyndale, William (1531), *The Exposition of the Fyrst Epistle of Seynt Jhon*, Antwerp.
Westwood, Jennifer, and Jacqueline Simpson (2005), *The Lore of the Land: A Guide to England's Legends, from Spring-Heeled Jack to the Witches of Warboys*, London: Penguin.

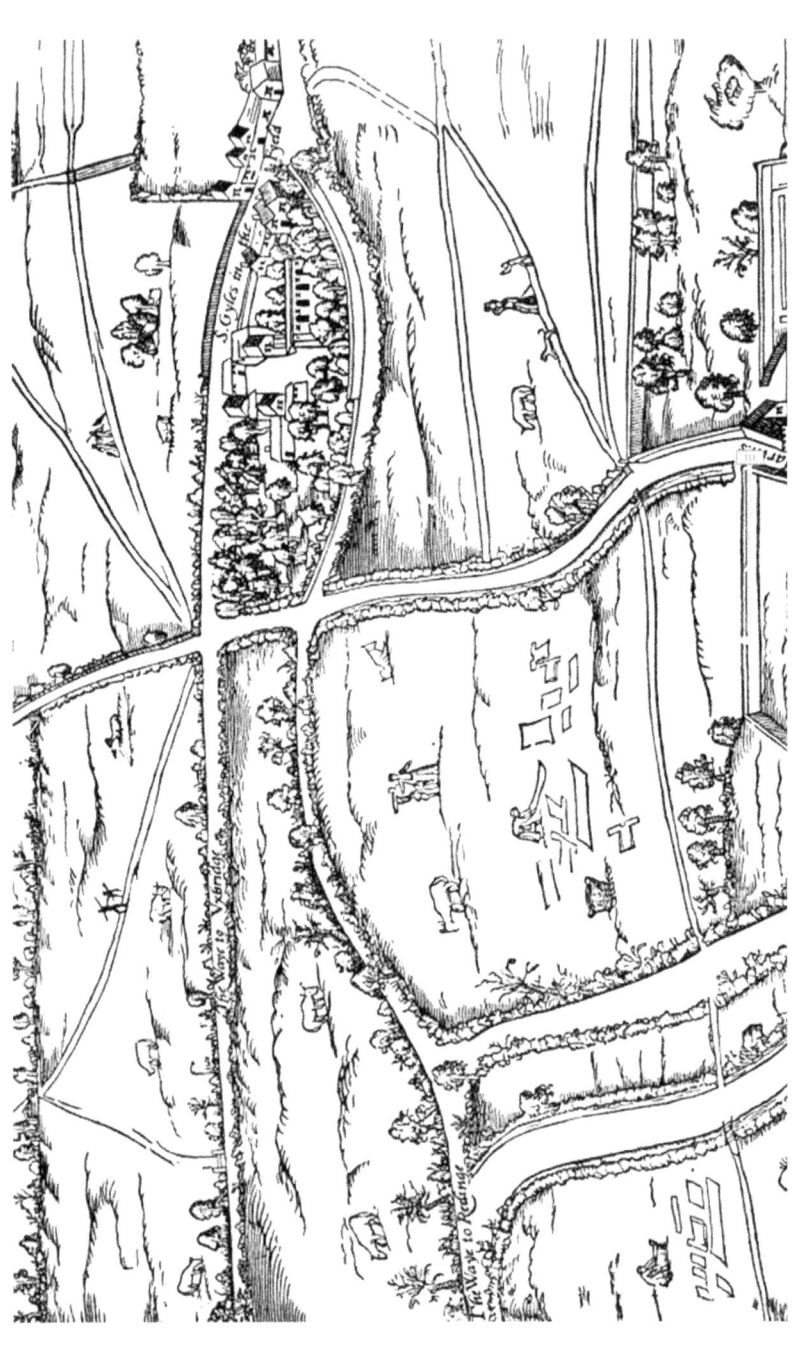

Figure 9.1 Roads outside London 2, Janelle Jenstad (ed.) (c. 1562), The Agas Map, University of Victoria, <http://mapoflondon.uvic.ca/map.htm> (last accessed 24 June 2019).

Chapter 9

'I Must Abroad or Perish!': The Meta-theatre of the Road in Brome's *A Jovial Crew*

Kim Durban

> ALL Come away! Why do we stay?
> We have no debt or rent to pay.
> No bargains or accounts to make;
> Nor land or lease to let or take;
> Or, if we had, should that reward us,
> When all the world's our own before us,
> And where we pass, and make resort,
> It is our kingdom and our court? (*A Jovial Crew*, 2.1.118)[1]

These words valorising freedom are sung by the cheerful beggars who form an on-road community in *A Jovial Crew* by Richard Brome, and their attitude defines the spine of this play from 1641. It was the most popular of Richard Brome's repertoire, yet, as late as 1992, the script was pronounced 'unperformable' by Stephen Jeffreys, the writer who adapted the play by removing 45 per cent of the original text for the first contemporary revival of the work for the Royal Shakespeare Company, in Stratford-upon-Avon.[2] But this chapter will argue and provide evidence for a contrasting view, namely that Richard Brome's road play in its original completeness can be seen to offer a unique 'downstairs dramaturgy' on meta-theatrical terms and one that is well suited to revival. Brome tells the story of a young steward, Springlove, who is compelled to run away from his duties and join the beggars on the road every spring. 'Democratised dramaturgy' is a term I have adopted to reflect upon the dramaturgical tropes that Brome uses in his plays, especially this one, for 'downstairs' characters such as servants and women (and, in this play, beggars) as his agents in the drama. They are the people pushing the plot along, and by their actions creating the narrative glue that holds the world of the drama together. If Shakespeare is 'upstairs', then Brome is 'downstairs'. But the open road has neither up nor down and offers a level playing field. Nowhere is democratised dramaturgy more possible, likely or evident than on the road. Indeed, the phrase 'the open road' speaks to the notion of democratisation. Alexandra Walsham has traced how the religious struggles of the time 'had a spatial as well as temporal and moral dimension':

> village greens, market places, commons, meadows and fields – could hardly avoid becoming sites of contention themselves . . . Depending on one's perspective, these were arenas in which the common people relaxed and refreshed themselves from their labours or places in which they profaned the Lord's day and scandalized their neighbours. (Walsham 2011: 260–1)

Richard Brome is not dealing with religion but his comedy touches on these concerns, especially in the creation of the fortune-teller Patrico and his apparently damaging astrological predictions. As the pursuer Sentwell describes the beggars, they have identities and personalities ascribed by living at large:

> Hedge–birds, said you? Hedge–ladybirds, hedge–cavaliers, hedge–soldier, hedge–lawyer, hedge–fiddlers, hedge–poet, hedge–players, and a hedge–priest among 'em. (*AJC*, 5.1.877)

These once respectable and now fallen-from-grace travellers form the community for Brome's meditation on movement within his own society and demonstrate the potential freedom to be found at the bottom of the stairs. Ania Loomba, in analysing another Brome play, *The Antipodes*, suggests his even-handedness by describing how in her view he 'considers the interrelation of social and psychic space by locating the production of male and female fantasies in the different spaces occupied by men and women' (Loomba 1989: 135).

Brome's road is a democratic space used by and common to all, and the perspective of *A Jovial Crew* flips between the privileged and enclosed space of Master Oldrents's house and events on the ramble. Anyone can use the road – see Oedipus and his natural and soon-to-be-dead father.[3] But I have no claim to mythologise the road as a democratised space; it is also, of course, a place for the demonstration and exercise of power. Characters in Brome's play taking to the road are soon disorientated. The democratising space of *A Jovial Crew* is the journey that entices its characters to emerge into the open air and take their chances in life. In Michel de Certeau's terms, they must learn to operate as 'poachers' whose playful tactics ensure their survival:

> A practice of the order constructed by others redistributes its space: it creates at least a certain play in that order, a space for manoeuvres of unequal forces and for utopian points of reference . . . People have to make do with what they have. (De Certeau 1988: 18)

This 'making-do' forms the substance of *A Jovial Crew*'s plot. As Joël Bonnemaison suggests, 'there is nothing more cultural than the ways in which human beings endeavour to survive, for the methods they use always go beyond the sheer satisfaction of surviving *stricto sensu*' (2005: 79). Brome's interest in the early modern road is dramaturgically constructed to investigate more issues than mere survival, with a key focus on family, as I will discuss later in this chapter. Brome's 'downstairs dramaturgy' can be characterised by several key theatrical tropes, including an interest in presenting the wealthy and the not-so-wealthy in proximity and engagement with one another (for example, the beggars supported by the wealthy in *A Jovial Crew*). The politics of staging this situation are interesting, as the laws against begging at the time reveal a stern intolerance for both begging and poverty, essentially enshrining into law a disapproval of free movement.[4]

Seeing the 1992 adaptation of *A Jovial Crew* inspired Christopher Hill's bracketing together (once again, as so often in their critical history) of *A Jovial Crew* and *The Beggar's Opera*, through his consideration of expressions of seventeenth-century liberty: 'it is worth asking ourselves seriously what late seventeenth- and eighteenth-century society looked like when seen from below' (Hill 1996: 4). Hill's summation of *A Jovial Crew* focuses on the difficulty of the beggars' lives. He astutely recognises the link that Brome continually makes in this play between the relative freedoms and limitations of both courtiers and beggars as they travel on the roads of early modern England. His invitation to invert the perspective traditional to analysis of a play such as *A Jovial Crew* frames my experience of directing the beggar scenes in a theatrical context, as these are the ultimate in 'downstairs' characters, even lower than servants.

I am the Program Coordinator of a Bachelor of Acting for Stage and Screen undergraduate degree at Federation University Australia in the regional city of Ballarat.[5] As an experienced director, it has been part of my role to direct classical plays with third-year actors, and in the past I have always programmed Shakespeare. Having been introduced to the plays in the Brome repertoire and finding them both individual and appealing, I have been staging Brome's work, including *The City Wit* (2007), *The Antipodes* (2008), *A Jovial Crew* (2013) and *Covent Garden Weeded* (2017, retitled for the local audience *Garden City Weeded*). At the time of writing, I am the director who has staged the largest repertoire of Brome plays, both in Australia and elsewhere. The important resource Richard Brome Online contains videoed rehearsal sequences with script in hand that have been selected to illustrate editorial issues in the online edition. My fully staged productions in Australia provide, therefore, a unique opportunity to engage with the complete dramaturgy of these works on stage, performed with the text largely uncut, by a complete cast. For my 2013 production of *A Jovial Crew* with third-year graduating actors, in interpreting my early modern beggars as contemporary musicians and photographers living cheap on the road, I wished to connect their issues to my local audience.

A Brome project taking place in a regional Australian city may seem to some in the northern hemisphere a surprising location for such a revival. Brome and Ballarat have become entwined ever since Elizabeth Schafer and I first stood by Lake Wendouree in 2006 and discussed the mystery of the black swans appearing in Brome's 1638 play *The Antipodes*. As we watched the same birds floating around in the Australian springtime, she captured my imagination by describing the research and practice that was going into the project that would become Richard Brome Online and invited me to read the plays. I consider Brome's *The Antipodes* a perfect play to reference Australia, and this the perfect place to stage Brome, given our white colonial beginnings, our fruity vernacular, our tendency to vote for the underdog and our appreciation of a 'fair go'. Only the democratically inclined Brome could have written *The Antipodes*, since he inverts the whole world to a 'downstairs' location. Like *A Jovial Crew*, *The Antipodes* is also a road play, but the journey is fictional, the road created by actor-servants of Lord Letoy inside his house. In this play, Lord Letoy takes his visitor/patient Peregrine to a fictional anti-London. Thus, Brome is the first playwright to imagine Australia, so for me there is a logic in reproducing his work here. My vast practice-led research project at the Arts Academy in Ballarat has mounted four Brome plays across ten years.

Brome's democratised dramaturgy is revealed in characteristic ways, such as the many examples in the text of open, playful, extemporised action, where the playwright leaves room for a characteristic flourish from his actors. For example, some of the songs seem unfinished, and the text is peppered with vague directions such as '*[Singing] Hey down, hey down a down, etc*' (AJC, 2.2) that leave scope for extemporised musical improvisation. R. W. Ingram is impressed by Brome's skill and suggests that *A Jovial Crew* 'is not a play with songs and music so much as a musical play' (Ingram 1976: 238). Also open in style is the detailed psychological portrayal of servants, who provide plot development and revelation, especially in this play the steward Springlove, who wants to go on the road, and the groom Randall, who prefers his home. Brome's tendency is to portray the inner freedom and sexual character of women with relish and detail; for example, in the play there is a quartet of sisters and lovers, yet it is never specified which daughter belongs to which suitor, and they themselves suggest that their virtue may be suspect:

> RACHEL Does he think us whores, trow, because sometimes we talk as lightly as great ladies? I can swear safely for the virginity of one of us, so far as word and deed goes. Marry, thought's free.
> MERIEL Which is that one of us, I pray? You or me? (*AJC*, 2.1.128–9)

Women can go out on the road, and although they are preyed upon, they are also protected, and survive. Brome's women in *A Jovial Crew* act for themselves, where possible. Judge Clack's niece, Amy, who joins the sisters on the road, has run away from an undesirable marriage. In performance, much of the comedy here lay in the fear and caution of the clerk who steals her, Martin, whose attitude on the road contrasted with the fearless enthusiasm of Amy. The actor Rhys James took on a very mealy-mouthed and petulant delivery, which costume designer Melanie Liertz emphasised by giving him ridiculous yellow gloves and sunglasses. Grace Maddern as Amy used the stage boldly and led the way on the journey, appearing later in a leather jacket, thus 'toughening up' for the road. Even if they are living downstairs, Brome's women take advantage of the apparent freedom given to them by being lower in the foodchain. De Certeau, in writing about systems and the flexibility of subjection to them, has defined these tactics as 'ways of using':

> [he] creates for himself a space in which he can find *ways of using* the constraining order of the place or of the language ... he establishes within it a degree of *plurality* and creativity. By an art of being in between, he draws unexpected results from his situation. (De Certeau 1988: 30)

The beggar crew using the road in *A Jovial Crew* are all on the run from city living, as evidenced by a begging soldier, poet and lawyer who are living creatively. My students related to the in-between nature of the characters, the blend of poverty and music in the play, and especially to running away from home and adopting a position of rejection of society's rules and values. Cave et al. suggest of *A Jovial Crew* that the road offers both the characters and their audiences a lens to examine issues of freedom and bondage:

> If [the play] has a unifying object for its relentless interrogating, it lies in traditional social relations as practised within Caroline communities (marriage, paternity, employment, land tenure and rental systems, justice, estate management) and the play encourages an investigative spirit in audiences by presenting all these incidences in contrast with the workings of a community that rejects all such inherited value-systems in the pursuit of personal liberty (beggardom). (Cave et al. 2010: 2)

This 'investigative spirit' is evident in the way Brome ridicules those in power and temporarily elevates those who are downtrodden. Taking my cue from the songs sprinkled liberally throughout the play, I interpreted this liberty on stage as that form of free living embodied by professional rock and pop musicians. My young actors took their research both from the seventeenth century and online, in images from famous rock stars and the pages of *Rolling Stone* magazine (a very apt title, given the lives of the characters on the road).

I also drew a conceptual link between our location and this play. The regional city of Ballarat is seen by some as the crucible for modern Australian democracy, because it is where a rebel uprising enshrined the rights of the common man against oppression. At Bakery Hill in 1854, rebel gold miners swore an oath by the Southern Cross constellation, an image that became their symbol, and refused to pay a government mining tax, leading to a bloody battle between soldiers and miners. They erected a barricade at Eureka Lead. Their rebel flag was sprinkled with the stars of the Southern Cross. The Eureka Rebellion in Ballarat is reputed to mark the beginning of an Australian democratic movement, as described here by Clare Wright:

> The diggers lined up to throw their licences upon a bonfire – an act of communal defiance of the law ... When committing their licences to the flames, the diggers swore to defend any unlicensed digger from arrest, with armed force if necessary. (Wright 2013: 379)

A Museum of Democracy in Ballarat opened the month before we performed *A Jovial Crew*, and it is the site where the original Eureka flag hangs on display. The Eureka story is one well known to my actors.[6] The beggars of Brome's play, arrested as vagrants and held in captivity, are forced to adopt the identity of travelling players, not just begging on the road, but begging favour by providing entertainment in a rich man's house in order to survive. The beggar-poet Scribble takes the lead in proposing themes, and his vision for his play sounds to me like an uncannily direct description of this most famous uprising in Australia:

> SCRIBBLE I would have the country, the city, and the court be at great variance for superiority. Then would I have Divinity and Law stretch their wide throats to appease and reconcile them. Then would I have the soldier cudgel them all together and overtop them all. (*AJC*, 4.2.813)

As Rosemary Gaby has suggested, a moment of reality arrives in the centre of the entertainment. She celebrates what I believe is the democratic perspective of a play that does not settle for a single view of events: 'Brome's comedy makes us view the beggar's community from many different perspectives, thus encouraging us to question its significance' (Gaby 1994: 409).

Contextualising the politics of Scribble's play in rehearsal led the acting company to a shift of tone. Initially the actors described it as a '*Sesame Street* scene' and they reported feeling silly playing the action of catcalling and encouraging, until I suggested Scribble's call to arms related to our (then current) Australian federal election. This shift awakened the cast to the potential for radicalism in the original text. This part of Act 5, scene 1 was eventually staged as a boozy party, with band-leader Scribble inspiring his crew whilst balanced on the band's road case. The beggar crew of *A Jovial Crew* in some respects echoes the broad social mix of the Australian convict and gold-digging population. For the local population of Ballarat today, many are descendants of those early gold diggers and soldiers, and are thus viewed as important people, lauded as descendants of the stars of their time. So for my season of *A Jovial Crew* in 2013, I conceptualised the beggar crew as a starry rock band and showed them eking out an existence on the road, complete with instruments, road cases and photographers recording their every move. The 'road' in the Helen Macpherson Smith Theatre was an open space with multiple entrances. The floor was painted with hippy-style flowers, creating a natural space for dancing and begging. This space was later criss-crossed with a red cloth, to form a chamber for Judge Clack's house and thus an inevitable barrier to free movement.

The 'road' in our thrust theatre was not characterised by signposts or scenic details, filled instead by the invisible diagonal lines running between the vomitories that determined the travellers' floor-path. Sometimes it was filled with the photographic and music equipment of the beggars' 'tour', and sometimes it was an open, democratic space. The interesting dramaturgical pattern in this play of the stage filling and then emptying is a characteristic of Brome's work that I have noted in staging the plays, such as Springlove's soliloquy in Act 1 being interrupted by the beggars' song and dance (1.1.71–84). The dramaturgy of *A Jovial Crew* requires a lot of space, including, for Ballarat, an upper galley where the band played live for the beggars' celebrations. Stage directions are not always clear-cut in Brome. For example, Tim Fitzpatrick's spatial analysis of *A Jovial Crew*, a document I examined after the event of my production, is peppered with reflections on the action, such as 'Where has Patrico been? What does it mean that the beggars "look out"? Are they still within or behind one of the doorways?' I shared Fitzpatrick's questions. I am sorry I missed this, for example:

> Time lapse, change of location: here we have the four 'slumming it' as beggars, at an unspecified 'outwards' location . . . Evidence of split-staging techniques: Springlove instructs men on begging (67) as the ladies plan their demeanour before conversing with the men. (Fitzpatrick 2011: 3)

Fitzpatrick's suggestion that Vincent and Springlove are still on stage is clear, but Brome's textual action implies that the pursuing gentlemen characters are 'searching' the local area and thus need to cover some ground. This scene was hard to direct, especially dealing with the 'horses' (we used Razor scooters). The 'road' is easy to portray on an open stage, due to the lack of scenic impingement. I took these visual questions into rehearsal, splitting the staging between upstage, where the sisters are recovering after a night on the boards, and downstage, where their men are learning how to become beggars. They are outdoors, but not yet 'on the road', only 'rehearsing' for it. The stage may be seen to operate here as a meta-theatrical location for the lovers 'scripting' their relationship, with the steward Springlove 'directing' them in how to beg to the gentry. Their perambulations back and forth create the world; in de Certeau's words, 'it thus seems possible to give a preliminary definition of walking as a space of enunciation' (de Certeau 1988: 98).

Brome's plays, as staged in Ballarat to date, have proven to be entertaining in good measure, with genuine comic strengths that have been celebrated by cross-generational and cross-class audiences. I have witnessed Brome's downstairs dramaturgy being well received by Ballarat audiences, many of whom are working-class people, with their children the first ever to go to university. They have laughed broadly at the 350-year-old jokes and commented favourably on the quality and the tone of the works. Brome's writing was valued for this by the director of the only contemporary Shakespeare's Globe revival of *The Antipodes*, Gerard Freeman:

> Brome created a world of antic humour and anarchic suspension of expectations that makes for a screwball comedy. The viewer is left wondering: who are the doctors and who the patients? . . . His imagination, energy and theatrical suspense are unflagging. (Kastan and Proudfoot 2000: viii)

I suggest that the glossing over of Brome's repertoire may constitute a significant omission to our understanding of the early modern canon because, as Hill suggests, it articulates a view of the world from below. I believe that it is here, downstairs in the kitchen and the cellar, or on the road (or, indeed, in our extreme 'downstairs' location, the southern hemisphere), that the democratic tone of Brome's unique voice can be heard most resonantly. This early modern road trip has echoes of the contemporary 'road movie' that we are familiar with. Like many famous road movie heroes and heroines (think the boys in *Priscilla, Queen of the Desert*, *Thelma and Louise*, even Dorothy in *The Wizard of Oz*), Brome's characters leave their homes to see the world and are changed by their on-road experiences. Road movie characters may be travelling the open road for a variety of reasons, as suggested by Murphy et al.:

> The impetus for this particular notion of 'journeying' is generally triggered by: the Escape *motive* – from country, from the city, the past, family, 'home', authority or enemies; the Quest *motive* – for people, places, 'home', objects or understanding of self. (2001: 75)

In *A Jovial Crew*, Brome combines these suggested triggers of 'Escape' and 'Quest', using the device of the road trip to provide a new perspective on the nature of the early modern family: disobedient daughters, servants and lovers are under threat (as usual in any road movie) from figures of power and authority, in this play symbolised by a judge. The road is *jovial* in this play because of its fellowship, expressed in the music that the beggars sing, and, as Randall the groom suggests, because of its capacity to nurture, a place to 'stroll and beg till their bellies be full, and then sleep till they be hungry' (1.1.65). Brome appears to present a picture of the English highways and commons as places of freedom and meditation, perhaps even of sanity. Yet the play changes its attitude constantly; as Tiffany Stern describes, even the title of the play may contain a double meaning:

> 'Jovial', the first word of the title, and a theme of the play throughout, is a loaded adjective. It derives from Jove, or Jupiter, king of the classical gods – and thunder. 'Jovial', then, might equally signify 'happy' or 'turbulent and ungovernable' . . . For Brome, joviality and distress were closely allied. (Stern 2014: 6)

Begging with those whose lives are 'sweetened by delights such as we find by shifting place and air' (*AJC*, 1.1.52) is a life or death proposition for Springlove, whose analogy heads this chapter; namely, that he 'must abroad or perish!' (*AJC*, 1.1.54). His name underlines the literal nature of his attraction to the road; hearing the nightingale, he pleads: 'O sir, you hear I am called' (*AJC*, 1.1.40). When the daughters of the household follow, they inadvertently create havoc both at home and abroad. Rachel and Meriel push the boundaries, and likewise assert control over their own time, by taking to the road to discover freedom away from their father's household demands, and this wish binds them to both their servant and the beggars on the road in short-lived democratic harmony, when mistresses and masterless men are brought into equal circumstances but their roles are inverted. Brome has a merry time in all his plays when he provides characters with inverted circumstances. The young lover Hilliard is at first full of admiration for the roving beggars' life:

> Beggars! They are the only people can boast the benefit of a free state in the full enjoyment of liberty, mirth, and ease, having all things in common and nothing wanting of nature's whole provision within the reach of their desires. Who would have lost this sight of their revels? (*AJC*, 2.1.120)

The runaways soon come to see that the outdoor life of freedom has less to recommend it than might be imagined:

> MERIEL I am sorely surbated with hoofing already though, and so crupper–cramped with our hard lodging and so bumfiddled with the straw that –
> RACHEL Think not on't. I am numbed i'the bum and shoulders too a little. And have found the difference between a hard floor with a little straw and a down bed with a quilt upon't. (*AJC*, 3.1.380–1)

The road keeps changing its meaning: it is nominated to be a playground by the lovers; a battleground for the gentlemen seeking the runaways Amy and Martin; a temptation to freedom from responsibility for Springlove; a location for sexual congress with beggar-wenches for the young blade Oliver; and a threat to both civil and domestic harmony for the parent figures Judge Clack and Oldrents. Clack's niece has rejected the suitor chosen for her and run away with her uncle's clerk, Martin, who is threatened with hanging by his employer thus:

> And you, in assisting her, furthering, and conveying her away, did not only infringe the law, in an unlawful departure from your master, but in a higher point; that is to say, top and topgallows high. I would ha' found a jury should ha' found it so. (*AJC*, 5.2.860)

But Brome soon has the judge drunk on his own wine and the disaster is comically averted.

I find it surprising that Brome has not found his theatrical champions in contemporary times, apart from two professional productions (and some student shows).[7] In England, it is not possible to walk on a Richard Brome trail. William Shakespeare gives us, by comparison, the example of Bardolatry, and any road, public building, garden, outlook and theatre can use his identity or image, his face and meaning, symbolised and woven into the fabric of the landscape to create a giant literary pilgrimage site. As Terry Eagleton observes, 'Shakespeare is the quintessential commodity, at once ever-new and consolingly recognisable' (cited in Holderness 1988: 206). By comparison, the Brome trail is very faint and does not have the same cultural meaning, despite his capacity to open the picture of the lot of the common man. Brome's reputation received favour from a seminal text by Martin Butler that shifted the view on his work:

> The most striking thing about *A Jovial Crew*, then, is that it should be there, that at a major moment of crisis in English history a dramatist should evoke so completely the continuity, the particularity and the presence of English life, and Brome reinforces the effect theatrically ... which makes the play read as if casting back to the very earliest days of the English stage (with its specially close relationship with the country) and taking stock of the whole great achievement of the English theatre too. (Butler 1984: 275–6)

But since Butler renovated Brome's reputation, only *A Jovial Crew* and *The Antipodes* (in the White and Red season at Shakespeare's Globe, 2000) have received fully professional productions. In England, when reviewing the reviews of the 1992 Royal Shakespeare Company production, I was intrigued to see that responses were split down the middle in their enthusiasm for the Jeffreys version or the original Brome, which was either known about or speculated upon. Apart from its chiaroscuro and autumnal prettiness, I noted many aspects of this well-acted and successful production that I could admire, especially a very strong energy and drive, with a running time of 172 minutes. Randall seemed to be the favourite of the audience, even though only one speech of his was written by Brome. Much of the play worked, but then, to me, there would be longueurs, or else I was uncertain about how the characters had been interpreted. Frequently the play did not read as a comedy at all, especially in its humourless representation of the Lord of the manor Oldrents, to the point where I began to wonder how director Max Stafford-Clark saw the character. The judge was genuinely frightening. This interpretation of his character was supported by an additional 'arrest' scene, which worked to underline the social divide between masters and their men as they trudged along the road to their judgement. This was not Brome's image of the free and redemptive road. The Act 2 beggar ritual in the barn contained an extended ecstatic dance (complete with female toplessness that I found unnecessary, a point emphasised by a couple of female critics), which reminded me of Caryl Churchill's play *Light Shining in Buckinghamshire*. Given that Churchill's play was also developed by Stafford-Clark, I could feel a definitive desire in this version of *A Jovial Crew* for radical politics to be embraced and uplifted in an early British vision of Utopia. The editors of Richard Brome Online have noted that this kind of adaptation has been a continual part of its stage history:

A Jovial Crew, or *The Merry Beggars* is the one play by Brome that has a sustained stage history which spans several centuries; however, the play has almost always been radically adapted by those producing and performing it. There seems to be something about *A Jovial Crew* that inspires theatre practitioners, but which does not quite fit their agendas, or their estimation of what their contemporary audiences want to see in the theatre. (Cave et al. 2010: n.p.)

To me, Richard Brome takes a radically different view. The play-within-a-play that the idealist (and satirical) poet Scribble describes is indeed radicalised and utopian, but the eventual play performed by the lovers and their friends is a self-referential re-enactment of the daughters' story, bringing the adventure to a harmonious close. We do not witness them reject Scribble's plot, yet the play-titles they offer to Judge Clack all focus on fathers and daughters (so different from Jeffreys's 1992 choice for one daughter to stay on the road). Martin White has investigated the way that Stephen Jeffreys's version of Brome's text sharpens up the lyrics of the beggars' songs to underline their social position (White 1998: 222). In fact, I see that Jeffreys *reverses* the playwright's perspective by portraying the misery of the beggars, rather than their cheerful joviality as written by Brome. I believe that this dramaturgical choice tends to weaken the role of the beggars in the play, undermining the generosity of Oldrents and the centrality of the beggars' freedom and autonomy, the very qualities that justify Springlove's escape to the road, which is the action that sets the plot in motion. The beggars sing:

> Enough is our feast, and for tomorrow
> Let rich men care; we feel no sorrow.
> No sorrow, no sorrow, no sorrow, no sorrow.
> Let rich men care; we feel no sorrow. (*AJC*, 1.1.78)

This repetition of 'no sorrow' (so useful to my rock star production of the play) is instructive. Brome underlines the democratic autonomy of those who choose to ramble and to reject society. Oldrents asks Springlove, 'Can there no means be found to preserve life in thee but wandering like a vagabond?' (*AJC*, 1.1.47), and Springlove answers this question in his greeting of the beggars sheltering in the barn: 'You are a jovial crew, the only people whose happiness I admire' (*AJC*, 1.1.111). Brome presents happiness as a legitimate goal, whether sought by Amy, rejecting her arranged marriage, or Oldrents, finally brought to an acknowledgement of an earlier transgression with a beggar-maid and surprised to be claiming the King of the Beggars as both his illegitimate son and legitimate heir. I think the 1992 production offered several misreadings of the actions at the end of the play because it failed to focus on Brome's determination to bring the lost family of the play together. The daughters vote with their feet when they take to the road, but the road eventually takes them home again. The healing involved in claiming Springlove mirrors the mending of the travel-crazy Peregrine in *The Antipodes*. It is an open-ended and democratic shift: when Springlove is revealed to be Oldrents's unknown son, and thus the inheritor of the estate, everything may be inverted and realigned, but the beggars do not stop travelling.

It was challenging to conceive an Australian production, given that we are an infamous offshoot of English culture and society that has developed its own colour and texture. But I concluded that the continual status play in Brome's work, emphasising the conflict between the classes, would have been understood in gold-rush-crazy Ballarat. Even now, the city always harks back to its past to illuminate the present and is, as such, a place where the remounting of historical drama should be able to find acceptance. Before departure from Australia to visit the Royal Shakespeare Company archives in Stratford-upon-Avon for research into the 1992 production of the play, I held auditions and a first reading of *A Jovial Crew* with my student actors. They read the play quite well but stumbled repeatedly on unfamiliar words, as they accessed the text from Richard Brome Online on phones and iPads. There was frequent (attempted) singing, a visible lift in energy from the appearance of the beggars, pleasure at repetition, and some of our eventual audience's favourite lines such as 'He is no snail, sir' (*AJC*, 4.1.614) were immediately funny. They loved it, describing it as 'rad', 'fresh' and 'frantic'. They did not know how to perform this play but were prepared to believe that it could be played well, as we set about creating the mechanics and the poetics of a contemporary approach to the Brome canon in a rural Australian setting. It is certainly fair to say that Brome is unknown in Australia. Whenever I have told anyone here about my research into the plays of Richard Brome, I am asked to explain who he is, and, out of many, I have only met three people who can place him. The average theatregoer cannot call to mind specific quotations or images from the plays. I also started rehearsals in relative ignorance. When I staged my first Brome play, *The City Wit*, in 2007, I did not have the benefit of Richard Brome Online.

Through staging practice I have investigated the dramaturgical devices in these plays, mainly Brome's use of theatrical space and his consistent deployment of meta-theatricality, as especially indicative of a democratised dramaturgy that resists favouritism. A play-within-a-play is a repeated plot device that Brome uses boldly to bring events to a head. There is a wedding masque in *The City Wit* that leads to gender-shock in the unmasking of truth, and a musical masque at the end of *The Antipodes* that creates harmony, forgiveness and healing from madness. In these examples, characters become an inner audience, and watching the play through their responses shifts the perspective from the auditorium. I suggest that Brome sees the theatre itself as a device for revelation to his audience. In staging these plays, I have also accepted the invitation issued by Brome's use of inversion to reveal his democratic inclination, whether this is viewed as the characters' status drops and ascends in *The City Wit* as they switch tactics; the creation of anti-London in *The Antipodes* where statuses are reversed; or the training of masters as beggars in *A Jovial Crew*. These actions have a dramaturgical purpose: as de Certeau has described, 'the space of a tactic is the space of the other' (1988: 37).

I have collaborated openly with the Brome actors and valued their insights built from their experience of the rehearsal-room floor. I prefer to underscore Brome's characteristic balance by giving my actors freedom to interpret their roles in the rehearsal process: I give them 'space' to explore and draw conclusions rather than determining the result beforehand. For example, we found it extraordinary that in the original text the fortune-teller Patrico offers Master Oldrents his choice of virgins for entertainment. The Ballarat *A Jovial Crew* cast encouraged me to keep the offer of the doxies, but turn them into men for our female Oldrents – a Bromian inversion that seemed to make this action work properly. These games, experiments and reversals in interpretation have exposed a characteristic fluidity in Brome's writing and storytelling, or, in my terms, a democratically dramaturgic construction of Self and Other that has opened itself successfully to a feminist director's gaze.

Performative evidence thus suggests that the form of Brome's democratised dramaturgy lives in this blended 'upstairs' and 'downstairs' scenario, and on the open road; further, that the class meditation of these plays, whilst not documentary in nature, needs to be taken more seriously. There is a delicate trajectory that could be drawn between, firstly, the plot and characters of this play written on the brink of an English civil war; secondly, the young gold miners of an Australian rebellion; and, finally perhaps, our current questions about the rights and survival of asylum seekers. To a twenty-first-century practitioner, the view of beggars who dance, eat, marry, give birth and sing together seems compassionate and detailed, even as they struggle to be free. Together with women and servants, these allies in Brome's meta-theatrical scene feature within an imaginative and reflexive dramaturgy that could refresh Richard Brome's reputation as a dramatist if recognised as valuable. By providing new insights into a production of this play for the stage, and grounds for a reconsideration of the democratic form and reputation of the dramatist, I hope that I have successfully shared my enthusiasm for and relish of this early modern 'road movie'.

Notes

1. All quotations from *A Jovial Crew* (*AJC*) in this chapter are from Brome 2010.
2. Jeffreys explains his dramaturgical decision in his introduction to *A Jovial Crew* (Brome 1992a: n.p.). For a stage history of *A Jovial Crew*, see <https://www.hrionline.ac.uk/brome/history.jsp> (last accessed 20 May 2019).
3. Thanks to Dr Rob Conkie for this suggestion.
4. For more on this, see the textual note to 1.1.50 in Cave et al. 2010.
5. The cities of Ballarat (115 km from Melbourne) and Bendigo (151 km) are the two most well-known 'gold' towns in regional Victoria, their broad streets and gracious buildings established during the rush for gold that attracted many international citizens of the early 1800s. An example of this history is the setting for my site-specific production of *The Antipodes*. The Ballarat Mining Exchange in Lydiard Street, which was built in 1836, was the place where the gold prices were called, and gold was traded. In the twentieth century, it was reused variably as an antiques emporium and a bus depot. It is currently administered by the City of Ballarat for community use, weddings and functions. The Ballarat population is estimated at 157,485 at the time of writing.
6. The museum closed in 2018 and has since been renamed the Eureka Centre.
7. See Richard Brome Online for a comprehensive stage history: <https://www.dhi.ac.uk/brome/history.jsp?play=JC> (last accessed 7 June 2019).

Works cited

Bonnemaison, Joël (2005), *Culture and Space: Conceiving a New Cultural Geography*, London: I. B. Tauris.
Brome, Richard (1992a), *A Jovial Crew*, ed. Stephen Jeffreys, London: Warner Chappell.
—— (1992b), *A Jovial Crew*, Royal Shakespeare Company, Stratford-upon-Avon, dir. Max Stafford-Clark, DVD, Shakespeare Institute RSC Archives, Stratford-upon-Avon (last accessed 10 July 2013).
—— (2000), *The Antipodes*, ed. David Scott Kastan and Richard Proudfoot, London and New York: Nick Hern Books.
—— (2010), *A Jovial Crew*, ed. Helen Ostovich, Richard Brome Online, <https://www.dhi.ac.uk/brome> (last accessed 20 May 2019).
—— (2014), *A Jovial Crew*, ed. Tiffany Stern, London: Arden Bloomsbury.
Butler, Martin (1984), *Theatre and Crisis 1632–1642*, Cambridge: Cambridge University Press.
Cave, Richard, Brian Woolland, Helen Ostovich and Elizabeth Schafer (2010), '*A Jovial Crew*: Critical Introduction', Richard Brome Online, <https://www.

dhi.ac.uk/brome/viewOriginal.jsp?play=JC&type=CRIT> (last accessed 7 June 2019).
Certeau, Michel de [1984] (1988), *The Practice of Everyday Life*, trans. Steven F. Rendell, Berkeley and Los Angeles: University of California Press.
Elliott, Stephan (dir.) (1994), *The Adventures of Priscilla, Queen of the Desert*, film, Australia: Gramercy Pictures.
Eureka Centre, <http://www.ballarat.vic.gov.au/lae/attractions/eureka-centre-home-of-the-eureka-flag.aspx> (last accessed 20 May 2019).
Fitzpatrick, Tim (2011), '*A Jovial Crew*: Spatial Analyses of 80 Elizabethan and Jacobean plays', University of Sydney, <http://hdl.handle.net/2123/7809> (last accessed 20 May 2019).
Gaby, Rosemary (1994), 'Of Vagabonds and Commonwealths: *Beggars' Bush*, *A Jovial Crew*, and *The Sisters*', *Studies in English Literature, 1500–1900* 34.2, Elizabethan and Jacobean Drama, pp. 401–24.
Hill, Christopher (1996), *Liberty against the Law*, London: Allen Lane, Penguin.
Holderness, Graham (ed.) (1988), *The Shakespeare Myth*, Manchester: Manchester University Press.
Ingram, R. W. (1976), 'The Musical Art of Richard Brome's Comedies', *Renaissance Drama*, New Series, 7, Drama and the Other Arts, pp. 219–42.
Kastan, David Scott, and Richard Proudfoot (eds) (2000), *The Antipodes* by Richard Brome, London and New York: Nick Hern Books.
Khouri, Callie (1991), *Thelma and Louise*, film, dir. Ridley Scott, USA: Metro-Goldwyn-Mayer.
Langley, Noel, et al. (1939), *The Wizard of Oz*, film, dir. King Vidor, USA: Metro-Goldwyn-Mayer.
Loomba, Ania (1989), *Gender, Race, Renaissance Drama*, Manchester and New York: Manchester University Press.
Murphy, Ffion, Rama Venkatasawmy, Catherine Simpson and Tanja Visosevic (2001), 'From Sand to Bitumen, from Bushrangers to "Bogans": Mapping the Australian Road Movie', *Journal of Australian Studies* 25.70, pp. 73–84.
Stern, Tiffany (ed.) (2014), *A Jovial Crew* by Richard Brome, London: Arden.
Walsham, Alexandra (2011), *The Reformation of the Landscape: Religion, Identity, and Memory in Early Modern Britain and Ireland*, Oxford: Oxford University Press.
White, Martin (1998), *Renaissance Drama in Action*, London: Routledge.
Wright, Clare (2013), *The Forgotten Rebels of Eureka*, Melbourne: Text Publishing Company.

III. Writing the Road

Chapter 10

Staging the Road: Walking, Talking, Footing

Robert Stagg

How do actors and characters walk roads on stage? And how, even in a theatre uncommitted to absolute realism, are actors supposed to travel along an onstage road without it appearing ludicrously foreshortened or abbreviated? How, that is, did the early modern stage handle the problem of representing pedestrian travel? One (good) answer to this question might be: it didn't. The 'vocabulary of the unactable journey' (Holland 1996: 160) abounds in the choruses of early modern drama, from Queen Henrietta's Men bemoaning how 'Our stage so lamely can express a sea / That we are forc'd by Chorus to discourse / What should have been in action' (*The Fair Maid of the West I*, 4.5.1–3) to the Lord Chamberlain's Men repeatedly acknowledging 'Th'abuse of distance' in *Henry V* (2.0.32). Even outside its choruses, early modern theatre often sought to obscure onstage travel by, for example, switching rapidly between different locations: one group of characters leaves the stage as, or shortly before, another enters and – plausibly enough – the freshly arrived characters are in a new setting. This is a drama that tends to evoke travel rather than presenting it, hoping to avoid a stage with 'Asia of the one side' and 'Afric of the other' (in Philip Sidney's scoffing phrase (2002: 243)).

In the first part of Christopher Marlowe's *Tamburlaine the Great* (1587) – a play of 'geographic sweep' (Shapiro 1991: 36), 'perhaps the most geographically and geopolitically extensive of the era' (Hutchings 2005: 190) – we hear Cosroe, Menaphon, Ortygius, Ceneus and other soldiers talk of how 'far are we towards Theridamas / And valiant Tamburlaine' (Marlowe 2003: 2.1.1–2) at the start of one scene, as they make their way to 'the river Araris' (63), only to leave the stage seventy lines later as they are replaced by Mycetes, Meander and others 'having passed Armenian deserts now' (2.2.14). By the next scene, Cosroe and company have reached 'worthy Tamburlaine' (2.3.1). Indeed, 2.2 features a spy who has 'viewed the army of the Scythian' (41) upon 'these champian plains' (40), attesting in choric manner to the travel occurring beyond an audience's purview.

It is possible to imagine each of these scenes as a series of static declamations, with distance verbalised rather than visualised – such that the play's 'exuberant sprinkling of exotic, alien names' (Hopkins 1996: 8) becomes a placeholder for places that are scarcely represented (or representable). Yet this risks yielding to a somewhat narrow account of Marlowe as a dramatist of 'audacious rant' (Altman 1978: 10), 'huffe-snuffe bombast' (Eliot 1932: 88) and 'epic rumble' (Levin 1954: 40), writing characters who furiously vociferate instead of doing anything or going anywhere. In fact, there are plenty of suggestions in these scenes that Marlowe's characters are speaking on the move. The scenes throng with deictic gestures to their characters' progress – 'Thus far are we' (2.1.1), 'having passed Armenian deserts now' (2.2.14) – and commands to immediate onstage action: 'direct me straight' (2.1.68), 'let us to this gear' (2.2.1), 'Go on my lord' (2.2.57), 'Strike up the drum, and march courageously!' (2.2.72). While these indications of movement tend to occur at the start and end of scenes, possibly suggesting action that has taken place or will predominantly take place off stage, they might just as well frame speech delivered while walking – hence why the play can seem, to some of its readers, 'like a triumphal pageant' (Marlowe 2003: xvii). In other words, the characters in these scenes might be like those in Book 2 of Spenser's *The Faerie Queene* (1590/6): 'So talked they, the whiles / They wasted had much way, and measured many miles' (2.9.8–9), recording distance in speech as well as steps. Marlowe and other early modern dramatists may have found a means to combine walking with talking which allowed the latter to distract from the potential absurdity of the former, or to somehow realise the act of walking in the art of talking.

Stephen Greenblatt notices how 'Marlowe is drawn to the idea of physical movement' – though note that it is the 'idea' of movement as much as, or more than, the thing itself – and especially 'to the problem of its representation within the narrow confines of the theatre' (Greenblatt 2005: 194). If the *Tamburlaine* plays were first or eventually performed at the Rose, this representational problem would have been acute. The first Rose (c. 1587) was only around 490 square feet, and the second (c. 1592) was barely any larger. It is at first hard to imagine the *Tamburlaine* plays taking place within these relatively small confines; for Greenblatt, then, the plays figure forth and occupy a 'transcendental homelessness' (Greenblatt 2005: 196). The first Rose stage nevertheless made the most of its intimacy; by being 'tacked onto the inner wall of the [structure's] frame' (Bowsher 2012: 73), it offered five planes from which onstage action could be viewed. Even (or especially) if not heavily schematised, the onstage movement across those planes of vision could have hinted at a considerable fictional distance: Asia in one plane, Afric in another. It is also important that the Rose's playing space would have been thought of, then as now, in terms of 'feet' – it allowed performers to 'act walking', in John Kerrigan's suggestive phrase (2018: 44), by considering their bodies' feet in relation to the square feet of the stage below them (it is likewise sometimes said that Edmund Kean's only rehearsal for *Richard III* was to measure out his paces on stage at Drury Lane). If Marlowe – the son of a Canterbury shoemaker – found, or had, a way to correspond the feet of the stage space with the feet of his performers, he may have not only overcome the Rose's putative limitations but made those limitations into some of the enabling conditions for his dramaturgy. By allowing the dimensions of the Rose stage to become part of the play's 'distributed cognition', in Evelyn Tribble's terms, where 'dialogue and stage movement can *potentiate* space' (Tribble 2011: 35) even when it is ostensibly cribbed and inert, Marlowe fashioned 'a rhetoric of space' (Mullaney 1988: 1) that was never merely or straightforwardly rhetorical.

Early modern players were notorious walkers, especially off stage. English legislation has long associated vagrancy with 'bards, rhymers, and other idlers'; by the middle of the sixteenth century (in statutes of 1545 and 1572) 'players' were legally grouped with mendicants and vagabonds (Pugliatti 2003: 2). Actors were members of 'the unsettled' culture or class identified by Patricia Fumerton, part of a 'wandering trade' (that last phrase coming from a touring company, claiming the patronage of Sir William Waller, in a lawsuit brought by a Kentish justice of the peace to the Privy Council in 1583). Richard Brome's *A Jovial Crew* (1641–2) has its 'merry beggars' perform a play in the final act, almost as a tribute to the itinerant status of early modern drama (Brome's was probably the last play to be performed on the public stage before the 1642 closure of the theatres): when the landlord Oldrents asks if there is 'a play to be expected and acted by beggars', Clack replies, 'That is to say, by vagabonds; that is to say, by strolling players' (5.1.289–92). Julie Sanders has recorded the play's expansive diction of walking – 'gadding', 'pilgrimage', 'wandering', 'journey', 'stroll-the-land-over', 'motion', 'ramble', 'progress', 'tramplings', 'hoofing' (Sanders 2011: 139) – while noting its friction alongside and within the play's rather static, conservative conclusion in which each character ends up 'knowing one's place' (Sullivan 1998: 159). Shakespeare shows us itinerant players in *Hamlet* (2.3.32–4) and *The Taming of the Shrew* (Ind. 1), while in Ben Jonson's *Poetaster* (1601–2) Tucca jokingly promises the actorly figure of Histrio that he will not need 'to travel with [his] pumps full of gravel anymore' (3.4.144–5) should he allow a 'gent'man parcel-poet' (3.4.137–8) to write for him.

Jonson had himself undertaken a 'foot voyage' from London to Edinburgh in 1618 on which he encountered a 'shake-rag errant' and 'three minstrels' (Jonson 2017: 39–40), although these vagabondish, theatrical figures are gradually vanished from the journey, repudiated in favour of something more regal (Jonson's travels emulate one of James I's royal progresses to the land of his birth). They also emulate, as Jonson knew, the 'nine days' wonder' of William Kemp, the Lord Chamberlain's Men clown who danced from London to Norwich in 1599. In his published account of the dance, Kemp similarly dissociates himself from vagrant balladeers and their theatrical kin. He endeavours to 'satisfy his friends the truth against all lying ballad-makers' (Kemp 1840: 2) and excoriate those 'notable shakerags' who 'can understand nothing but what is knocked into [their] scalps' (Kemp 1840: 20). Like Jonson, Kemp was following the route of a royal progress (this time Elizabeth's). These texts do not therefore 'endorse the unfettered movement of commoners' (and, within that category, actors), preferring instead to 'insist that something special about the journey or the journeyer legitimises the enterprise' (McRae 2009: 164). The 'intentional wandering' of royal progresses (Cole 1999: 122) had its more shapely counterpart in coronation pageants and processions, typically featuring contributions by playwrights, that restrained royal travel to London and its immediate environs; taken together, these may have helped circumscribe the seemingly disciplined 'urbane walking' (Sanders 2011: 172) of Brome's earlier drama (see for instance the managed peripatetic business of *The Sparagus Garden* (1635)).

Early modern drama was therefore 'a territorial art' (Mullaney 1988: 7) in at least two senses: it found itself having to formally apply for territory when touring in the provinces, while perennially dealing with the theatrical difficulties involved in the representation of territory on stage. Nor was touring antithetical to the territorial. The Earl of Oxford's players began their touring career – a word that in this context must be a verb as well as a noun – in the south and south-east of England, apparently because those regions constituted 'the principal sphere of influence' for the de Vere family (MacLean 1993: 9). Even when mostly confined to London, plays would travel between multiple venues: plays were 'on the move' (McGavin 2015: 111) between 'Shakespeare's two playhouses' (the Globe and the Blackfriars), for example, with some having more 'migratory potential than others' (McGavin 2015: 114), and with that migratory potential a way of marking out, as well as bridging, territory.

Scholars have increasingly conceived of *The Tempest*, for instance, in terms of a Globe *Tempest* and a Blackfriars *Tempest*, emphasising the ways in which the play evokes the distinctive territorial qualities of each venue (Dustagheer 2018). Territory is itself a concern of early modern drama – we have the 'mapmindedness' of *Lear* (Gillies 2001: 118), the 'land and soil' of *Hamlet* (de Grazia 2007), and we also have the less cartographic, more general or 'placial' (Gillies 2001: 125) claims of the 1599 Globe to 'bring forth / So great an object' as the 'two mighty monarchies' of France and England (*Henry V*, Prol. 10–11, 20).

The emerging application of linear perspective to theatrical space, particularly indoors in the form of periaktoi and perspective scenery, may have elided or reduced the representation of travel between locations (all of which could now be figured within a new paradigm of accuracy) – though even with these developments, such scenery was only ever a 'background' which, David McInnis argues, demanded 'further interpretation and engagement' (2013: 163) with the theatrical space before (and around) it. These visual representations of space typically exist alongside an acoustic 'sounding out' of the stage, often performed or facilitated by the sonic properties of the stage itself (which could be, in Bruce Smith's reconstructive hearing of the Globe, 'the largest, airiest, loudest, subtlest sound-making device fabricated by the culture of early modern England' (1999: 207–8)). As such, the prologue to *Henry V* concludes with a plea or prayer for the audience to 'Gently . . . hear' the play (Prol. 34), proceeding to imply that its sounds can evoke not only the individual detail of Agincourt or London but also the movement between them, via the sea roads across 'The perilous narrow ocean' (Prol. 22); when Shakespeare uses the word 'road' literally, he often does so with reference to maritime travel – see the 'road' as 'a sheltered piece of water near the shore where vessels may lie at anchor' (*OED sb.* 3a, in *The Two Gentlemen of Verona*, 1.1.53 and *The Merchant of Venice*, 5.1.288).

One of Shakespeare's less literal locutions of the word 'road' suggests how this might be accomplished – not by a sort of travelling ekphrasis, whereby a moment of voyage is pictured in sound or speech, but by designing the poetic metre of a verse line to yield the experience of a journey. In *Much Ado About Nothing* (c. 1598), Benedick talks of names that 'run smoothly in the even road of a blank verse' (5.2.32–3). Like a road, early modern blank verse could have a sense of direction: at least three-quarters of Marlowe's lines end with a stressed tenth syllable, signalling their point of destination (when we listen to the pioneers of English blank verse, Henry Howard and George Gascoigne, we can hear a stressed tenth syllable at the conclusion of 90 to 95 per cent of their lines). In some of his plays Shakespeare stresses over 90 per cent of his tenth-position syllables – albeit increasingly adding an extra unstressed syllable to coax the line over its typographical endpoint, something his predecessors were loath to entertain: the conclusions of their lines were part road and part barricade (Tarlinskaja 2014: 'Appendix', Table B.1). We can therefore travel along or across a blank verse line, rather as we might a road (though we must also attend to the differences between these kinds of travel, and the tenuousness of the simile we use to compare them: 'no simile runs on all four legs,' Coleridge reminds us, whether we be running on a road or on a series of metrical feet (Coleridge 1976: 86)). We do indeed travel through a verse line on its feet – the prosodic feet, whether iambs or trochees or spondees, that constitute its particular metrical arrangement – such that our experience of metre, at least in the language we use to convey it, is fundamentally pedestrian.

For Michel de Certeau, the 'production of space' (that forked phrase of his contemporary Henri Lefebvre) is very often achieved by a combination of walking and talking; we have already seen – or, better, heard – a similar act of combination being forged in Marlowe's *Tamburlaine* plays. In de Certeau's account, *un espace propre* is always 'a practised place' rather as a street is 'transformed into a space by walkers' not by the 'geometric definition' of urban planners (de Certeau 1988: 117). It 'seems possible' to de Certeau – possible only because he has the language for the possibility, and the willingness to reiterate that language until its possibility is secured – 'to give a preliminary definition of walking as a space of enunciation' (de Certeau 1988: 98). He quickly takes that 'preliminary' definition for a stroll: cities, he states, are produced by 'pedestrian speech acts', with 'The act of walking' bearing the same relationship 'to the urban system' as the 'speech act [does] to language or to uttered statements' (de Certeau 1988: 97). We might equivalently think of Shakespeare, Marlowe and other early modern dramatists as authors of pedestrian speech acts, in the context of the theatre as well as the city, with metred 'speech' here construed as variously accompanying and actuating pedestrian activity.

The footing metre acquires on stage can make the 'traffic' of a play (*Romeo and Juliet*, Prol. 12) both its dramatic business, its 'bargaining; trade' (*OED* n.2a), and also 'A trading voyage or expedition' (*OED* n.1b), a sense available in the language from at least the middle of the sixteenth century. In an especially smooth blank verse, such a journey would be as 'even' as Benedick (quite sardonically) makes out. But we can imagine choppier voyages through a verse line in which the feet jerk or stamp or scurry; if blank verse is a relatively 'even' road, there are other metres (and more discrepant forms of blank verse) that can compose or evoke 'by-paths and indirect crooked ways' (*2 Henry IV*, 4.3.313). Outside the theatre, though not outside the theatrical, William Kemp found himself perplexed by what he was speaking when he danced through Mile End, as the movement of his anatomical feet wrenched something peculiar from his tongue: '*Congruity*, said I? how came that strange language in my mouth?' (Kemp 1840: 4).

The double meaning of 'foot', its being a prosodic as well as a physical phenomenon, is historically and linguistically long-standing. In Latin the words *pes* and *pedis* can be applied to metrical and material feet so that, compiling his etymologies in the early 600s, Isidore of Seville could adduce the connection between the two senses: clusters of syllables 'are called "feet" because in using them the metres walk' (Isidore of Seville 2006: 47). The double meaning is alive and kicking in Renaissance England. In a letter to Spenser, Gabriel Harvey judges a poem's metrical feet 'deformed' and recommends that 'one of the feet be sawed off with a pair of syncopes' (Harvey 1816: 97). Roger Ascham criticises the Earl of Surrey's 'benumbed feet . . . unfit for a verse . . . deformed, unnatural, or lame' (Ascham 1761: 331). He conceives of trochees 'standing upon two syllables, the one long, the other short' while dactyls 'rather stumble than stand upon monosyllables' (Ascham 1761: 328). George Puttenham writes of the 'feet whereupon [classical] measures stand' (Puttenham 2007: 95). There is everywhere a 'similarity – sometimes seeming to border on a distinct identity – of animal-feet (what we walk on) with verse-feet (what we speak on)' (Shell 2015: 20).

This identity was realised in performance. Renaissance dances assumed metrical names and terms. John Davies, author of the 'dancing poem' *Orchestra* (1594), writes of dance measures with 'only spondees, solemn, grave and slow' (Davies 2004: 66.7), corantos that 'run' on 'a triple dactyl foot' (69.2) and lavoltas in which 'An anapest is all their music's song' (70.6). The music master Thomas Morley tells his young charges of a galliard that 'goes by a measure which the learned call *trochaieam rationem*, consisting of a long and short stroke successively: for as the foot *trochaeus* consists of one syllable of two times and another of one time, so is the first of these two strokes double to the latter' (Morley 2002: 184). Fabritio Caroso's *Nobilità di Dame* (1600) lists metrical dance steps like the 'Dactylic step' (Caroso 1995: 93) and the 'Spondaic step', both of which can be 'done to the verses of Virgil or Ovid' (Caroso 1995: 130). There was an entire dance called the pyrrhic, performed at the wedding of Lucrezia Borgia in Ferrara in 1502 as well as at Henri II's entry into Lyon in 1548, although, unlike Caroso's steps, its etymology is not drawn explicitly from classical prosody (McGowan

2008: 122–6). There were even Renaissance dances that wrote, in which the protagonists spelled names with their feet. The final dance of *Cupid's Banishment* (1617) traced the names 'Anna Regina' and 'Jacobus Rex' in front of the seated monarchs, a practice that was established on the Continent as early as the 1580s and which may have been inspired by the dancing of the names 'Elisabeth' and 'Friderich' in a Württemberg court ballet of 1616 (McGowan 2008: 118).

Shakespeare's theatrical feet are fleshed out by speed and movement. For Shakespeare 'foot' can be a verb (appropriately for audiences wedged against the Globe stage, since actors' feet would have been at eye- and ear-level). Cloten says he'll 'foot' Innogen 'home again' (*Cymbeline*, 3.5.143) and Ariel's song instructs its listener to 'Foot it featly here and there' (*The Tempest*, 1.2.381). Feet make something happen. In a *3 Henry VI* stage direction, Warwick 'stamps with his foot and the soldiers show themselves' (1.1.171), this being in a play where other stage directions are usually thought authorial (especially 3.1.12 and 4.3.27). Hubert issues a similar instruction in *King John*: 'When I strike my foot / Upon the bosom of the ground, rush forth' (4.1.2–3). One of Shakespeare's most rousing calls to action, directed at the 'band of brothers' in *Henry V* (4.3.18–67), is made under the aegis of St Crispin, the patron saint of cobblers.

There are feet in acting as well as action. Hamlet advises the players to 'Speak the speech, I pray you, as I pronounced it to you – trippingly on the tongue' (3.2.1–2). 'Tripping' is typically dancing (as in *A Midsummer Night's Dream*, 5.2.26) but it is also footing featly, working daintily across the feet in a verse line. When Nestor tells Agamemnon about the crude pageants Achilles and Patroclus have been staging, he goads him with the details of how they parade 'like a strutting player' with 'stretched footing' (*Troilus and Cressida*, 1.3.153, 156). The 'strutting', 'stretched footing' is the wide bombastic movement and posture made by a ham actor (many plays for child actors mocked the 'apish' activity of the older 'stalking-stamping player, that will raise a tempest with his tongue, and thunder with his heels' (Marston, *Antonio's Revenge*, 1.5.77–80)). But Nestor's anecdote additionally speaks to the way the verse lines might be delivered – with every metrical foot afforded a dull protracted aplomb, perhaps accompanied by a 'strutting' stamp of the physical foot. Hamlet recommends a lighter, nimbler performance of the verse.

On the other hand (or foot), a number of early modern plays feature lame or crippled characters and thereby test the relationship between the prosody and anatomy of 'feet': do those personages who walk oddly also speak oddly or, as Frank Golding wonders when disguising himself as a cripple in *The Fair Maid of the Exchange* (1607), why is it that he should be 'Crooked in shape *and* crooked in my thoughts' (Anon. 1963: 4.2.55, my emphasis), with the one seeming to incur the other? The anonymously authored *A Larum for London* (1602) bodies forth a different relationship between metrical and material feet. The soldiers besieging Antwerp make much of their feet – Sancto Danilo longing for them to 'Tread a virtuous measure in their streets' (1.69), Cornelius wanting to 'run with the hare' when the town falls (3.498) – but it is actually the play's cripple who speaks its most metrically regular verse lines. Indeed, the prologue of *A Larum* seeks to wrongfoot our prejudices in this regard: it begins with the hobbled figure of Time enjoining its audience to 'Laugh at my lameness', only for her then to reproach such cruelty as 'the mischief of degenerate minds' (Prol. 17, 21). The play's distribution of metrical regularity to both able-bodied and disabled characters hints that Stump is no less a soldier than his unhobbled counterparts, even as it must also hint that he is no less a ruthless sadist.

In other words, we might wonder whether metrical feet simply mimic material feet or (more interestingly) whether verse lines can take anatomical feet for a walk. With the vision of a dagger fresh from his eyes, Macbeth walks to Duncan's chamber – and his paces eke out an answer to that vexed question:

> and withered murder
> Alarmed by his sentinel, the wolf,
> Whose howl's his watch, thus with his stealthy pace,
> With Tarquin's ravishing strides, towards his design
> Moves like a ghost. Thou sure and firm-set earth,
> Hear not my steps, which way they walk, for fear
> The very stones prate of my whereabout,
> And take the present horror from the time,
> Which now suits with it. (2.1.52–60)

Macbeth's steps seem to move of their own accord; 'they' walk him as much as he walks them (as in the Folio's 'hear not my steps, which they may walk'). He appears, or wants it to appear that he is, led by something outside his volition, whether that be 'withered murder', 'the wolf', 'Tarquin' or Tarquin's 'ghost'. Yet his own feet are not printless (like a ghost's) or stealthy (like a wolf's), but all too loud. They do not require an adjective or adverb because we hear them make their way across the verse: 'Hear not my steps, which way they walk' has the audible tread of an 'even' blank verse 'road'. We can imagine an actor combining Macbeth's tentative footsteps with the line's insistent stresses to suggest that he is pulled along by the verse in a prosody of tragic teleology; or that he speaks a spurious rhythm – a metrical alibi – for his already plotted movements.

When Ben Jonson disparaged 'the Tamerlanes and Tamerchams of the late age' (Jonson 1892: 27), he did so for both their 'furious vociferation' and their 'scenical strutting' (he may have also had Hamlet, who 'strutted and bellowed' (3.2.32), in mind). By yoking together these seemingly discrete criticisms, Jonson suggests that they might not be different after all; in fact, furious vociferation might be the necessary or preferred complement of scenical strutting. The *Tamburlaine* plays throng with feet, spoken and trodden, and those feet come to indicate hierarchies of power and command (Tyrone Guthrie's 1951 production thus had its Tamburlaine stamp across the Old Vic stage, which sported a giant map beneath his feet). Bajazeth declares that Tamburlaine will not 'set his foot in Africa' (3.1.28), while Tamburlaine insists he will (3.3.59–60). When Tamburlaine proves to be right – he has the play's most 'conquering feet' (3.3.230) – Bajazeth becomes his footstool (4.2). Tamburlaine's scenical strutting continues in the second part, one reason why the two plays can seem like 'a huge drama in ... ten acts' (Jusserand 1906–9: 3.135) rather than separate entities with individual concerns. Having ended the first part 'Conquering the people underneath our feet' (4.4.141–2) and leaving his rivals 'breathless at my feet' (5.1.469), in the second he 'treadeth Fortune underneath his feet' (3.4.52) and – one difference between the plays – loses his footing as a result. The plays' 'processional spectacle' (Parr 2018: 27), their 'ambulatory construction' (Levin 1954: 51), is audible in the mouths of the characters, in the mightiness of Marlowe's line; it was probably audible too in the 'stalking steps' and 'thundering threats' of Edward Alleyn, playing Tamburlaine for the Admiral's Men (at least in Joseph Hall's probable remembrance of Alleyn's performance for the *Virgidemiarum* 3.16–17).

For Tamburlaine and the world he inhabits, feet are a testament of character (as when, in Marlowe's *Dido, Queen of Carthage* (c. 1586), Aeneas knows the disguised Venus 'by the movings of her feet' (1.2.241)). Tamburlaine talks of his 'kingly feet' (1.3.116) crowned by a mental resilience more than a physical toughness; he tells Calyphas, 'Thou shalt not have a foot, unless thou bear / A mind courageous and invincible' (1.3.72–3). Marlowe accordingly eschews one important aspect of Tamburlaine's relationship to the historical figure of Timur the Lame (the fourteenth-century founder of the Timurid Empire). Menaphon describes Tamburlaine as 'Of stature tall, and straightly fashioned, / Like his desire, lift upwards and divine' (2.1.7–8); unlike Timur, his body is unlamed and thereby ready to realise his ambitions.

If the prosody of these plays can sometimes seem bombastic or stiff – the drawbacks of a Marlovian mightiness – it is because it resounds to Tamburlaine's tune, in which the sturdiness of his physical feet sets the pace for the plays' prosodic feet (even at the risk of laming them).

In *Coriolanus* (1608), Shakespeare issues his version of the Marlovian foot fetish (appropriately so, because the play's eponymous character is very often a more quizzical, jaded Tamburlaine). Feet compose its strange penultimate stage direction, almost a tableau: 'The Conspirators draw, and kill Martius, who falls; *Aufidius stands on him*' (5.6.131–2 s.d., my emphasis). In fact, the play begins and ends with a body. In Menenius's fable of the belly, he calls Rome's citizens 'the great toe of this assembly' (1.1.153), and in one of his earliest lines Coriolanus filches feet from the fable: the plebeians 'feebling such as stand not in their liking / Below their cobbled shoes' (1.1.193–4). Unlike the frail part-feet of the citizens, 'he moves like an engine and the ground shrinks before his treading' (5.4.18–20). The play's battles are fought in terms of feet. When Coriolanus's forces retreat, one of the senators calls them a 'cloven army' (1.4.21). When the battle changes course, the citizens are 'Following the fliers at the very heels' (1.5.20). Toward the end of Act 1, Aufidius tells Coriolanus to 'Fix thy foot' in single combat (1.9.5), and Coriolanus is praised for his 'loving motion to the common body' (1.9.53). Yet within one hundred lines Cominius has begun to tilt the praise into criticism: 'Our spoils he [Coriolanus] *kick'd* at, / And look'd upon things precious as they were / The common muck of the world' (1.9.124–6, my emphasis). Coriolanus mistakenly assumes the tribunes' foot-language, talking about how he wants to 'o'erleap' the popular celebratory customs (1.9.138). Feet are now an instrument for stepping over and kicking at the populace, rather than standing with or alongside them.

This is partly the vocabulary of social standing, an implication alive in the early seventeenth century (*OED* 2a). Feet can be grubby when covered in 'The common muck of the world', whether that be the mud of the city or the soil of the tilling field. The grubbiness of the foot is exacerbated when it is trod over the 'unworthy scaffold' of the public playhouse (*Henry V*, Prol. 10) – as the anti-theatricalist John Northbrooke rails, 'they that go with clean unpolluted foot into the church of God must utterly altogether abstain from ungodly and profane places, as these [theatres] are' (Northbrooke 2004: 6). In Thomas Dekker's *The Shoemaker's Holiday* (1599) the apprentice Simon Eyre never refers to himself as a cobbler, preferring the more distinguished 'cordwainer' (4.110), and the shoemakers' union in scene 18 desperately makes the trade out to be a 'Gentle [i.e. noble] Craft' (169). The Lord Mayor of

Dekker's play is furious at his daughter running off with 'A Fleming butter-box, a shoemaker! / Will she forget her birth' (16.43–4).

In Act 3 *Coriolanus*'s language of feet reaches its metrical stomping ground. The tribunes lambast Coriolanus: 'The service of the foot, / Being once gangren'd, is not then respected / For what before it was' (3.1.308–10). Yet Menenius does not yield to this. He warns the tribunes about their own feet: their 'tiger-footed rage' will 'Tie leaden pounds to's [Coriolanus's] heels' (3.1.313, 315). The ominous 'heels' reappear – previously the heels of Aufidius's unexpectedly vanquished army – as if to imply that the tribunes' assault is already latently a defeat. For the 'unscann'd swiftness' of the tribunes is metrically dangerous too. 'Unscann'd' hints at 'scan' in *OED* 1a's sense, 'To analyse (verse) by determining the nature and number of the component feet' (first recorded usage 1398). Earlier in the scene Brutus warns Coriolanus of his rhetorical 'over-measure' (3.1.142), likewise glimpsing at the prosodic meaning of 'measure' (*OED* 14, 'Metrical or rhythmical sound or movement'). In the next scene, Volumnia joins these prosodist politicians and rebukes her son with the language of metre: he should speak 'such words that are but roted in / Your tongue, though but bastards and syllables / Of no allowance to your bosom's truth' (3.2.55–7). Interestingly, the play's metrical texture does not much change as its two types of feet coalesce. The metre does not disintegrate, unravel or straighten out. Its prosody remains neutral; it does not commit to any particular character or argument. This prosodic neutrality allows Shakespeare to stage what de Certeau calls a 'poaching' of territory ('everyday life invents itself by *poaching* in countless ways on the property of others' (de Certeau 1988: xii)), whereby the shuffling of 'feet' and its meaning(s) indicate transfers of power and authority, in which power can be 'poached' by those who take ownership of the play's pedestrian language.

The play ends with a '"reverse" discourse' of its feet (Foucault 1976: 101). Coriolanus goes through the motions about standing in Aufidius's house and fixing his foot there (4.5.25), but other characters have by now appropriated the play's (diction of) feet. Brutus praises the tribunes for having 'stood to't in good time' (4.6.10) and Aufidius tricks Coriolanus to avoid '[laming] the foot / Of our design' (4.7.8–9). Finally we reach the play's perplexing stage direction: Aufidius 'stands on' the knifed Coriolanus. In Thomas North's translation of Plutarch (1579), which Shakespeare used for this and other plays, the conspirators 'all fell upon [Coriolanus], and killed him in the market place, none of the people once offering to rescue him' (Plutarch 2001: 367) – so Coriolanus is never stood upon. Productions flinch from the stage direction. David Thacker's 1994 RSC production had the onstage characters 'form a "cage" over Coriolanus and the others lean in to try and get him'.[1] David Farr's 2002–3 Old Vic production saw Aufidius yank out Coriolanus's heart. Laurence Olivier famously leapt from the Royal Shakespeare Theatre's balcony before being stabbed, and Ralph Fiennes's filmic Coriolanus was enveloped by a cloud of assassins. Of all recent productions, only Greg Doran's (2007) directed Aufidius to 'stand on COR back' and then, half-jealously, 'push boys off him'.

The original stage direction seems absurd, the kind of clunky motion that risks sniggers in an audience (partly because it seems an unjust reversal of the characters we have seen thus far, as though Hamlet had conquered Fortinbras). However, there is manifold rationale for the stage direction. J. L. Styan notes Volumnia's ironical words about Coriolanus at 1.3.47–8 – 'He'll beat Aufidius' head below his knee, / And tread upon his neck' – and remarks upon how Shakespeare 'has translated simple stage business into a repercussive symbol' (Styan 1976: 62). The stage business is more repercussive and complicated than Styan realises. 'Aufidius stands on him' takes up and takes on the Second Lord's appeal to 'Stand, Aufidius, / And trouble not the peace' (5.6.126–7). The Second Lord is speaking in defence of Coriolanus such that Aufidius's posture, standing atop Coriolanus, is one of defiance to 'the lords of the city' (5.6.61) as well as a sarcastic fulfilment of the lord's appeal (since the peace will, Aufidius implies, not be troubled now that he is standing on the dead troublemaker Coriolanus: like Christ trampling the serpent's head, evil has been pacified (Luke 10: 19)). Aufidius, remember, has not killed Coriolanus. It was the 'conspirators' who did that. By standing on Coriolanus's body, Aufidius assumes an undeserved responsibility for his death (in all three Folios the stage direction starts to grammatically winnow the conspirators from several to one, as though yielding to Aufidius's claims: 'Draw both the Conspirators, and *kil[l]s* Martius' (my emphasis)). This is a play in which 'Action is eloquence' (3.2.76) and eloquence action.

Thomas Campion complained of actors 'in comedies, when if they did pronounce *Memini*, they would point to the hinder part of their heads; if *Vides*, put their finger in their eye'. For Campion this was a 'ridiculous' and 'childish observing of words' (Campion 1903: 5). In the 'gestic poetry' (Styan 1976: 56) of Marlowe, Shakespeare and their contemporaries, we find a more sophisticated alignment of stage action with verse activity, mediated through the 'foot' and its movements of speech and body. David Bevington is not quite right to call these gestures 'the unspoken language of the theatre' (1984: viii) since they are spoken in the corresponding and corresponsive feet of verse lines, a kind of performative or illocutionary utterance not normally detailed by speech-act theorists (although J. L. Austin thinks performative language 'hollow or void' (Austin 1978: 22) when spoken by an actor, he does not wonder what should happen if a performer or character notices the physical implications of metrical feet but chooses to reject them).

These early modern verse lines play out something richer than the obvious gestural acting described by Campion or its concomitantly crude performance of space on stage. They suggest that onstage roads are not only travelled but 'read', in the sense that prosody is dramatically readable, and that we can profitably regard a road's 'rhythm' as the means by which it could be materialised in the early modern theatre. On a stage where feet could 'speak' (*Troilus*, 4.6.57), we might wonder whether we are experiencing something like 'travel writing' – that 'named and accepted category', 'ubiquitous, popular, unavoidable, and, most importantly perhaps, unremarkable' (Hadfield 1998: 1) – or something more like travel *speaking*, a kind of journeying that can only be conveyed once the voice has begun to co-operate with the feet. When Richard Brome's Springlove sings of his pleasure in vagrancy, of walking to and fro and around the country, he concludes that 'in all this / Only one sense is pleased: mine ear is feasted' (*A Jovial Crew*, 1.1.369–70). This is the 'Movement's Song' (Lorde 1992) of the early modern theatre, a matter of metre as well as motion, forever singing as it goes, and going precisely because it sings.

Note

1. See 'Works Cited' for all prompt book references. My thanks to the Shakespeare Birthplace Trust for providing a Jubilee Education Fund grant which enabled me to consult the RSC's prompt book archive.

Works cited

Altman, Joel (1978), *The Tudor Play of Mind: Rhetorical Inquiry and the Development of Elizabethan Drama*, Berkeley: University of California Press.

Anon. (1913), *A Larum for London*, ed. W. W. Greg, Oxford: Oxford University Press.

Anon. (1963), *The Fair Maid of the Exchange*, ed. Peter H. Davison, Oxford: Oxford University Press.

Ascham, Roger (1761), *The Schole Master*, in *The English Works of Roger Ascham*, ed. James Bennett, London: R & J Dodsley.

Austin, John Langshaw (1978), *How to Do Things with Words*, ed. J. O. Urmson and Marina Sbisa, Oxford: Oxford University Press.

Bevington, David (1984), *Action Is Eloquence: Shakespeare's Language of Gestures*, Cambridge, MA: Harvard University Press.
Bowsher, Julian (2012), *Shakespeare's London Theatreland: Archaeology, History and Drama*, London: Museum of London Archaeology.
Brome, Richard (2014), *A Jovial Crew*, ed. Tiffany Stern, London: Arden.
Campion, Thomas (1903), *Book of Airs*, in *Songs and Masques; with Observations in the Art of English Poesy*, ed. A. H. Bullen, London: A. H. Bullen.
Caroso, Fabritio (1995), *Courtly Dance of the Renaissance: A New Translation and Edition of the Nobilità di Dame*, trans. and ed. Julia Sutton, New York: Dover Publications.
Certeau, Michel de (1988), *The Practice of Everyday Life*, trans. Steven Rendall, Berkeley: University of California Press.
Cole, Mary Hill (1999), *The Portable Queen: Elizabeth I and the Politics of Ceremony*, Amherst: University of Massachusetts Press.
Coleridge, Samuel Taylor (1976), *On the Constitution of the Church and State*, ed. John Colmer, Princeton: Princeton University Press.
Davies, John (2004), *Orchestra*, Whitefish, MT: Kessinger Library Reprints.
Doran, Gregory (2007), Prompt book for 2007 RSC *Coriolanus*, Shakespeare Centre, Stratford-upon-Avon, RSC/SM/1/2007/COR1.
Dustagheer, Sarah (2018), *Shakespeare's Two Playhouses: Repertory and Theatre Space at the Globe and the Blackfriars, 1599–1613*, Cambridge: Cambridge University Press.
Eliot, T. S. (1932), 'The Blank Verse of Marlowe', in *The Sacred Wood: Essays on Poetry and Criticism*, London: Methuen & Co., pp. 86–94.
Foucault, Michel (1976), *The Will to Knowledge*, trans. Robert Hurley, London: Penguin.
Fumerton, Patricia (2006), *Unsettled: The Culture of Mobility and the Working Poor*, Chicago: University of Chicago Press.
Gillies, John (2001), 'The Scene of Cartography in *King Lear*', in A. Gordon and B. Klein (eds), *Literature, Mapping and the Politics of Space in Early Modern Britain*, Cambridge: Cambridge University Press, pp. 104–37.
Grazia, Margreta de (2007), *Hamlet without Hamlet*, Cambridge: Cambridge University Press.
Greenblatt, Stephen (2005), *Renaissance Self-Fashioning: From More to Shakespeare*, Chicago: University of Chicago Press.
Hadfield, Andrew (1998), *Literature, Travel, and Colonial Writing in the English Renaissance 1545–1625*, Oxford: Oxford University Press.
Hall, Joseph (1598), *Virgidemiarum*, London: Richard Bradocke.
Harvey, Gabriel (1816), *Three Proper, and Witty, Familiar Letters* (1580), in Joseph Haslewood (ed.), *Ancient Critical Essays upon English Poets and Poesy*, 2 vols, London: T. Bensley.
Heywood, Thomas (1968), *The Fair Maid of the West, Parts 1 and 2*, ed. Robert Kean Turner, London: Edward Arnold.
Holland, Peter (1996), '"Travelling Hopefully": The Dramatic Form of Journeys in English Renaissance Drama', in J. Maquerlot and M. Williams (eds), *Travel and Drama in Shakespeare's Time*, Cambridge: Cambridge University Press, pp. 160–78.

Hopkins, Lisa (1996), '"And Shall I Die, and This Unconquered?": Marlowe's Inverted Colonialism', *Early Modern Literary Studies* 2.2, <https://extra.shu.ac.uk/emls/02-2/hopkmarl.html> (last accessed 21 May 2019).
Hutchings, Mark (2005), '"And Almost to the Very Walls of Rome": 2 *Tamburlaine*, II.ii.9', *Notes and Queries* 52.5, pp. 190–2.
Isidore of Seville (2006), *Etymologies*, trans. and ed. Stephen A. Barney, W. J. Lewis, J. A. Beach and Oliver Berghof, Cambridge: Cambridge University Press.
Jonson, Ben (1892), *Timber: or, Discoveries Made upon Men and Matter*, ed. Felix E. Schelling, Boston: Ginn & Company.
—— (2012), *The Cambridge Edition of the Works of Ben Jonson*, vols 1–7, ed. David Bevington, Martin Butler and Ian Donaldson, Cambridge: Cambridge University Press.
—— (2017), *Ben Jonson's Walk to Scotland: An Annotated Edition of the 'Foot Voyage'*, ed. James Loxley, Anna Groundwater and Julie Sanders, Cambridge: Cambridge University Press.
Jusserand, Jules (1906–9), *A Literary History of the English People*, 3 vols, London: T. F. Unwin.
Kemp, William (1840), *Kemps Nine Daies Wonder: Performed in a Dance from London to Norwich*, ed. Alexander Dyce, London: John Bowyer Nichols and Son.
Kerrigan, John (2018), *Shakespeare's Originality*, Oxford: Oxford University Press.
Lefebvre, Henri (1991), *The Production of Space*, trans. Donald Nicholson-Smith, Oxford: Blackwell.
Levin, Harry (1954), *Marlowe the Overreacher*, London: Faber & Faber.
Lorde, Audre (1992), *Undersong: Chosen Poems Old and New*, New York: W. W. Norton.
McGavin, John (2015), 'Plays on the Move', in E. Dutton and J. McBain (eds), *Drama and Pedagogy in Medieval and Early Modern England*, Tübingen: Narr Francke Attempto, pp. 111–29.
McGowan, Margaret (2008), *Dance in the Renaissance: European Fashion, French Obsession*, New Haven: Yale University Press.
McInnis, David (2013), *Mind-Travelling and Voyage Drama in Early Modern England*, Basingstoke: Palgrave Macmillan.
MacLean, Sally-Beth (1993), 'Touring Routes: "Provincial Wanderings" or Traditional Circuits?', *Medieval and Renaissance Drama in England* 6, pp. 1–14.
McRae, Andrew (2009), *Literature and Domestic Travel in Early Modern England*, Cambridge: Cambridge University Press.
Marlowe, Christopher (2003), *The Complete Plays*, ed. Frank Romany and Robert Lindsey, London: Penguin.
Marston, John (1966), *Antonio's Revenge*, ed. G. K. Hunter, London: E. Arnold.
Morley, Thomas (2002), *A Plain and Easy Introduction to Practical Music*, ed. Ben Byram-Wigfield, Great Malvern: Cappella Archive.
Mullaney, Steven (1988), *The Place of the Stage: License, Play and Power in Renaissance England*, Chicago: University of Chicago Press.
Northbrooke, John (2004), *A Treatise against Dicing, Dancing, Plays, and*

Interludes, with Other Idle Pastimes, in Tanya Pollard (ed.), *Shakespeare's Theater: A Sourcebook*, Oxford: Blackwell.

Parr, Anthony (2018), '"For his Travailes Let the Globe Witnesse": Venturing on the Stage in Early Modern England', in C. Jowitt and D. McInnis (eds), *Travel and Drama in Early Modern England: The Journeying Play*, Cambridge: Cambridge University Press, pp. 21–38.

Plutarch (2001), 'The Life of Caius Martius Coriolanus', repr. in William Shakespeare, *Coriolanus*, ed. Philip Brockbank, London: Arden.

Pugliatti, Paola (2003), *Beggary and Theatre in Early Modern Europe*, Aldershot: Ashgate.

Puttenham, George (2007), *The Art of English Poesy*, ed. Frank Whigham and Wayne A. Rebhorn, New York: Cornell University Press.

Sanders, Julie (2011), *The Cultural Geography of Early Modern Drama, 1620–1650*, Cambridge: Cambridge University Press.

Shakespeare, William (2005), *The Complete Works*, ed. John Jowett, William Montgomery, Gary Taylor and Stanley Wells, Oxford: Oxford University Press.

Shapiro, James (1991), *Rival Playwrights: Marlowe, Jonson, Shakespeare*, New York: Columbia University Press.

Shell, Marc (2015), *Talking the Walk and Walking the Talk: A Rhetoric of Rhythm*, New York: Fordham University Press.

Sidney, Philip (2002), *The Defence of Poesy*, in *The Major Works*, ed. Katherine Duncan-Jones, Oxford: Oxford University Press.

Smith, Bruce (1999), *The Acoustic World of Early Modern England: Attending to the O-Factor*, Chicago: University of Chicago Press.

Spenser, Edmund (1987), *The Faerie Queene*, ed. Thomas P. Roche Jr, London: Penguin.

Styan, J. L. (1976), *Shakespeare's Stagecraft*, Cambridge: Cambridge University Press.

Sullivan, Garrett (1998), *The Drama of Landscape: Land, Property, and Social Relations on the Early Modern Stage*, Stanford: Stanford University Press.

Tarlinskaja, Marina (2014), *Shakespeare and the Versification of English Drama, 1561–1642*, Farnham: Ashgate.

Thacker, Davis (1994), Prompt book for 1994 RSC *Coriolanus*, Shakespeare Centre, Stratford-upon-Avon, RSC/SM/1/1994/COR2.

Tribble, Evelyn (2011), *Cognition in the Globe: Attention and Memory in Shakespeare's Theatre*, New York: Palgrave.

Chapter 11

The Road to Damascus and the Road to Hell in Philip Massinger's *The Renegado*: Islamic England and the Pauline Crossroads

Paul Frazer

This is not an essay about literal, material roads, but rather about how the metaphor of the road was used to think about inward concerns, especially in relation to religious and political identity. Specifically, this chapter explores Saint Paul's conversion (from Judaism to Christianity) on the Road to Damascus. I read this in relation to Philip Massinger's treatment of changeable religious identity in *The Renegado* (1623–4) – a tragicomic travel play famed for its portrayal of Christians turning Turk, and Turks turning Christian. I analyse the play's layered interest in mobility in light of its outspoken preoccupation with the movement, atonement and transformation of Saint Paul. The relationship between Saint Paul and religious conversion is, moreover, explored in relation to Islam. I argue that in *The Renegado* the conversion of Paul is recognised as an important crossroads between Massinger's understanding of Protestant and Muslim belief – and that critics have generally underestimated this text's knowledge of (and interest in) the latter.

The plotline of *The Renegado* might seem tangential to the study of roads, but this is a play that explores abstract forms of mobility and directionality along a range of imaginative pathways, in relation to a prominent series of turnings; and it does so in a city-setting with a complex history of Islamic-Christian occupation, conflict and conversion. The play considers the theological transition of its renegade protagonist, Antonio Grimaldi – a pirate who has converted to Islam, and who loses everything when he kidnaps a Venetian noblewoman named Paulina and attempts to sell her to the Viceroy of Tunis. Grimaldi finds his way back to Christianity in a Pauline transformation in one of the play's set-pieces in Act 4. *The Renegado* also details the near-conversion (to Islam) of Paulina and her brother Vitelli, the Christian conversion of Donusa (niece to the Ottoman Sultan), and the comical transition of the clown Gazet, from Christian poverty to a fleeting illusion of Muslim riches. Crucially, the narrative action is orchestrated by the Jesuit Father, Francisco, who leads Grimaldi to his conversion, is the architect of Donusa's baptism, and engineers the escape of the Christian (Catholic) characters at the end of the play.

The comic resolution of *The Renegado* has – quite conventionally – prompted readings which value the protagonists as goodies, and the Muslim infidels as baddies; Vitelli and company do, after all, infiltrate, outwit and escape their Muslim opponents, and, crucially, they convert two lost souls to Christianity along the way.[1] But this positive portrayal of Catholicism is problematic, because Massinger wrote the play during the ill-fated marriage negotiations of Prince Charles and the (Hapsburg) militant Spanish-Catholic Infanta, Maria Anna, in 1623.[2] The marriage talks were, of course, unpopular with England's Protestant subjects and they triggered a flood of anti-Catholic political commentary, in which the demonisation of the figure of the Jesuit priest was as consistent as ever in wider textual forms. To date, critical readings have struggled to reconcile this polemical context with the narrative of the play, and have argued that audiences would have adopted some curious interpretive strategies. Doris Adler and Benedict S. Robinson have, for instance, argued that the Catholics were in fact read 'as Protestants', and the Muslims as 'stand-ins for Catholics' – a reversal that Robinson terms 'allegorical displacement' (Adler 1987: 57; Robinson 2006a: 129). Michael Neill, however, finds this 'improbable', arguing instead that the play's doctrinal (Catholic-ish) attitudes are more compatible with Arminianism, a connection made possible by 'the exceptional fluidity and complexity of English religious politics at the time' (Neill 2018: 37–8).[3]

In contrast, I argue that the Catholics are Catholics, and that the play encourages us to view them as the hell-bound baddies we ought to expect from an English play from this period, despite their comic and seemingly victorious escape-finale. It does this, perhaps more surprisingly, by encouraging audiences to relate to the Muslim characters of the play, in part by engineering connections between Islam and Englishness – connections drawn from recent political and distant mythological histories. Crucial to how the play does this is the narrative of Saint Paul's conversion, which functions as a conceptual crossroads between Christianity and Islam. From the perspective of the play's Islamic characters (a perspective we are encouraged several times to adopt), *The Renegado*'s obsessive deconstructions and mutations of Paul's conversion become evidence of the Catholic characters' damned soteriological pathways. They think they walk on the Road to Damascus, but instead we are encouraged to laugh at their descent down the road to hell. I conclude by returning to the question of this play's political context, and how we might rethink Anglo-Islamic literary representations in this period in relation to broader concerns about religious and political conversion and change.

Tunis turned: an Islamic England?

As is well known, Massinger adapted the plotline of *The Renegado* from the writings of Miguel de Cervantes, which return repeatedly to the author's experiences of being taken captive by Barbary pirates and transported to the city of Algiers (Neill 2018: 54–8). Massinger's relocation of these narratives to Tunis is generally read in relation to the play's other borrowings from Robert Daborne's *A Christian Turned Turk* from 1612 (which was also set in Tunis).[4] The city does, however, carry important connections to England and Englishness in this period which might bear more relevance to *The Renegado*'s political satire than is generally recognised.

Tunis is located in North Africa in the centre of the Mediterranean, and its way-point location, between the busy ports of Algiers, Tripoli and Alexandria, was enhanced by the North African network of Roman roads, and the busy naval trade-routes between Europe, Africa and the Middle East. In the popular English imagination, Tunis was inextricable from the histories and legacies of the city which it had replaced, its close neighbour (which now lay in ruins), the ancient city of Carthage.[5] The region encompassing Tunis and Carthage had been associated with religious conversion for centuries, beginning with Christianity: after Rome's conquest of Carthage in the Third Punic War (149–146 BCE) the city became a key refuge for early persecuted Christians, fostering Saints Tertullian (c. 160–240 CE), Cyprian (c. 200–258 CE) and Augustine of Hippo (354–430 CE). Thereafter, the region was conquered by the Vandals (435 CE), the Byzantines (533 CE) and then Ottoman Islam (698 CE). Subsequently, Tunis was ruled by a number of Muslim Berber dynasties (both Shi'a and Sunni), and was the capital city of the Hafsid dynasty from the thirteenth to the early sixteenth century, before becoming embroiled in the power struggle between the Ottoman-supported Corsairs (so-called Barbary pirates) and Christian Spain (Masri 2017: 93–121). Tunis fell to the Spanish in 1535, was retaken by the Ottomans in 1569, changed hands again after the Battle of Lepanto in 1571, before being occupied more decisively by the Islamic Ottoman Empire in 1574. In short, just as England had swung between Catholicism and

Protestantism in the sixteenth century, Tunisian history had experienced (and was associated with) a similar pendulum-like trajectory – but between the Church of Rome and Islam.

The conflict with Spain made Tunis a logical site of interest for the English, but other aspects of the city's history and wider mythology posed more specific connections to Englishness. To begin with, the mythic origins story of neighbouring Carthage was connected to England's history by the name and narrative of its founding queen, Dido – spurned lover of the Trojan Aeneas, whose great-grandson (Brutus) was believed, by some, to have founded ancient Britain. Dido's Punic name was Elissa. In lieu of this, Dido was elevated to the summit of Elizabeth I's mythological personas, and prompted imaginative political critique on the Elizabethan stage – most infamously through Christopher Marlowe's (and, according to its 1594 title page, Thomas Nashe's) *Dido, Queen of Carthage* (c. 1584–8).[6] In Dido's Virgilian narrative of Trojan/Roman abandonment and isolation, the city of Carthage echoed aspects of the public reputation and personal mythologies of the last Tudor monarch; and, according to Lisa Hopkins, 'Marlowe's Dido could in different ways look like both Elizabeth I (because of her other name of Elissa) and Mary, Queen of Scots (because of her reckless willingness to sacrifice political power for love)' (Hopkins 2008: 157).[7] Looking back to Elizabeth in particular, the diplomatic ties between England and Islamic places like Tunis should not, moreover, be overlooked. According to Nabil Matar, throughout Elizabeth's reign (from at least as early as 1561), the Ottoman Empire proved to be an important military ally, because of the shared campaigns against Catholic Spain, and the threatening activities of Spanish and French missionaries to the East. Walsingham in particular 'pressed hard for coordinating military policy with the Turks' (the byword for all Islamic subjects in the period), and in pursuing the pact, Elizabeth emphasised the continuity that could be imagined between English Protestants and the wider Islamic world: 'as a Protestant Christian, she rejected the veneration of idolatrous images which the Pope and the Spanish king practised. Her Christianity, she implied, was closer to Islam than was Catholicism' (Matar 1998: 123). Through this prolonged period of political posturing between Elizabeth and the Ottomans, the political intimacy – or, at least, adjacency – of English and Islamic subjects was becoming part of England's international reputation: 'European Catholics were saying in Istanbul that "the English lack nothing to make them sound Mussulmans, and need only stretch out a finger to become one with the Turks in outward appearance, in religious observance and in their whole character"' (cited in Matar 1998: 124, n. 18). Links between Englishness and the port of Tunis, in particular, were also heightened after James's accession, when peace with Spain changed the complexion of English maritime culture. For, according to Robinson, after James brokered the peace treaty of 1604, the English privateers that Elizabeth had encouraged, paid and protected ('a large population') were 'apparently left without legal means of support . . . [and resultantly] many of these privateers turned pirate in North Africa' (Robinson 2006b: 222). A logical base for maritime smugglers and raiders (whose livelihoods centred, at least in part, in disrupting and intercepting Spanish galleons), multicultural and mercantile Tunis became a haven for English privateers during James's reign. Because *The Renegado* is very obviously an English play about piracy, Islam and Islamo-Catholic conversions, which is set on the part of the North African coast to which English privateers had fled, and which carried ready links to theatrical treatment of English political history (via Dido), it makes sense to read it in light of these contexts and concerns.

Links between Tunis, Islam and Englishness surface in *The Renegado* in a number of ways, and usually in proximity to female identity. In an aside from the opening scene, for instance, Gazet recalls a story about 'An English pirate's whore' who was publicly stripped naked by a Muslim religious authority ('one of their muftis') for wearing the colour green (1.1.50–8) – because green is the sacred colour of Muhammad (Neill 2018: 93, n. 56). It is worth noting that this is one of a number of occasions in which the audience are invited to think about Tunis in relation to Islamic law and culture, rather than as a thin foil for London, as we see in other plays from the period.

The only other direct reference to England is the play's eunuch, Carazie, who was 'born in England' (1.2.22), and who works in the service of Donusa, niece to the Ottoman Sultan. In lieu of her status, Donusa is treated as royalty by the other Muslim characters of the play, and her dialogue and characterisation echo the association between Islam and England in a number of ways. This participates in what Jonathan Burton notes as *The Renegado*'s interest 'in women's power and the weakness of English men abroad' (Burton 2005: 106). The play established a link between Donusa and Englishness early, by having her be curious about English custom. In 1.2, Donusa probes Carazie for information about English women: 'what's the custom there / Among your women?' (1.2.22–3), and he replies that they 'For the most part live like queens' (1.2.28), such is their liberty. In the following act, after she has become infatuated with Vitelli, the link between Donusa and Elizabeth is suggested by the servant Manto, who describes Donusa as appearing 'Like Cynthia in full glory, waited on / By the fairest of the stars' (2.1.14–15), using another of Elizabeth's infamous nicknames. In the speech that follows, Donusa alludes to the mythologies of both Dido and Elizabeth:

> What magic hath transformed me from myself?
> Where is my virgin pride? How have I lost
> My boasted freedom? What new fire burns up
> My scorched entrails? What unknown desires
> Invade and take possession of my soul,
> All virtuous objects vanished? Have I stood
> The shock of fierce temptations, stopped mine ears
> Against all siren notes lust ever sung
> To draw my bark of chastity – that, with wonder,
> Hath kept a constant and an honoured course –
> Into the gulf of a deserved ill fame? (2.1.23–33)

As I have noted elsewhere, 'vanish' was a word made famous by Marlowe, and the reference here to Donusa's 'scorched entrails' certainly seems to echo the fate of the playwright's Carthaginian queen, who '*Casts herself into the flames*' in the play's finale (5.1.313 s.d.).[8] (Pygmalion of Tyre, brother to Dido, is also instanced in relation to Donusa at 1.3.133–6, where Vitelli describes one of his paintings as so 'perfect in all parts that, had Pygmalion / Seen this, his prayers had been made to Venus / To have given it life'.)

Donusa's wavering chastity also echoes the fabled (and often lampooned) abstentions of Elizabeth which critics have long noted within Marlowe's *Dido*. And the conflict that Donusa describes with her sexual appetite certainly complicate if not subvert the crude contemporary stereotype of the insatiable Islamic female.[9] When, for instance, Donusa describes her desire for Vitelli to her servant Manto, she does so bashfully: 'Thus then I whisper / Mine own shame to you [*Whispers to Manto*] – Oh, that I should blush / To speak what I so much desire to do' (2.1.65–7). Then, after the fact, she worries excessively about the corruption of her virginal public image: she asks Manto, 'could thy friends / Read in thy face, thy maidenhead gone?', to which Manto replies, 'No, indeed. I passed / For current many years after' (3.1.12–15). In her subsequent rejection of Mustapha's advances, Donusa's changed demeanour is similarly reminiscent of England's shrewish queen: 'Come you here to stare? / If you have lost your tongue and use of speech, / Resign your government' (3.1.35–7). And among the barrage of insults she heaps upon poor Mustapha in this scene, her comment on his 'tadpole-like complexion' (50) certainly could echo the protracted courtship of the Duke Anjou, whom Elizabeth had nicknamed her frog.[10] It is worth remembering the context of royal marriage that Massinger's play was written against, which make echoes like this one (of Protestant England's most famous near-miss with a Catholic marriage project) all the more likely.

As has been noted by David Hawkes, moreover, Donusa's behaviour in the marketplace also connects her to Protestantism, through her iconoclasm in 1.3 (Hawkes 2010: 157). In this earlier scene, the disguised Donusa rejects Vitelli's false/deceptive paintings – paintings which, we learn in the opening lines of the play, are of the 'bawds and common courtesans in Venice' (1.1.13), but which are being hawked by the pair as masterpieces 'of Michelangelo' (1.3.131). In a furious reaction, Donusa '*unveils herself*' and '*Breaks the glasses*' (1.3.143–4 s.d.), in an important scene which Hawkes reads as 'a Muslim iconoclast confronting Christian idolaters' (Hawkes 2010: 157). This is, again, in keeping with the memory of Elizabeth's diplomacy with the Ottoman East, as supplementing the continuities she traced between the English and Islam, she also accompanied messages with 'fragments of broken images' to the Muslim potentate (Matar 1998: 123–4). Iconoclasm became a key ideological site of dialogue between England and the Ottoman Empire during Elizabeth's reign, and it otherwise makes sense that Massinger's play might find more in common between Englishness and Islam through this female character. As Bernadette Andrea illustrates, England's pursuit of 'unorthodox diplomatic, economic, and military ties with the Ottoman empire' (which began during Elizabeth's reign) was propelled by English women, and their communications with Muslim sovereigns, 'including the Ottoman queen mother or the *valide sultan*' – indeed, it was primarily via female correspondence that the English-Ottoman dialogue continued throughout the seventeenth century (Andrea 2007: 1). This tandem link between England's recent political past and the Islamic Tunisian present of Massinger's play should guide our reading of Pauline references, because it is through the saint's roadside conversion that the concept of religious turning is animated and opened up for scrutiny.

The road to Damascus: a Christian-Islam crossroads

Paul's legacy was tied to the Road of Damascus, and along with it the development of the early Church and its writings. The saint's legacy as a martyr was also specific to two other major roads leading south of Rome: the Appian Way, where Paul was met by crowds of zealous Christians after his third mission (Acts 28: 15 KJV), and the Ostian Way, the apocryphal site of his execution and possibly burial.[11] According to the Acts of the Apostles, sometime after the death of Christ, Paul (or

Saul of Tarsus as he was then known) was struck blind on the road from Jerusalem to Damascus, and was there instructed by the voice of Christ to cease his persecutions: 'he fell to the earth, and heard a voice saying unto him, Saul, Saul, why persecutest thou me? And the Lord said, I am Jesus whom thou persecutest: *it is* hard for thee to kick against the pricks' (Acts 9: 4–5 KJV). Led by the hand to Damascus, Paul remained without sight for three days – days spent in fasting and prayer – before Ananias of Damascus laid his hands upon Paul (in the house of Judas): 'And immediately there fell from his eyes as it had been scales: and he received sight forthwith, and arose, and was baptized' (Acts 9: 18 KJV). Hereafter, Paul became the fulcrum evangelist of the Christian mission, eventually co-founding the Church of Rome, and spreading the word of God throughout the territories of Jerusalem, Antioch, Corinth, Galatia, Phrygia, Ephesus and Macedonia. In Paul's writings, the gruelling onward (missionary) journey became an important narrative synthesis of bodily and spiritual kineses: 'We are hard pressed on every side, but not crushed; perplexed, but not in despair; persecuted, but not abandoned; struck down, but not destroyed. We always carry around in our body the death of Jesus, so that the life of Jesus may also be revealed in our body' (2 Cor. 4: 8–10); 'But one thing I do: Forgetting what is behind and straining toward what is ahead, I press on toward the goal to win the prize for which God has called me heavenward in Christ Jesus' (Phil. 3: 14; Meeks and Fitzgerald 2007: 93).[12] And from the vantage point of Massinger's Tunis, Paul holds especial geopolitical significance.

Though he never visited Tunis, Carthage or any other part of Africa, the Cult of Paul flourished there among early Christian refugees and converts in the early days of Roman persecution. Paul's writing and wider mythologies became crucial to the region's experience of persecution, and inhabited many of its earliest martyrologic writings (Eastman 2011: 156–86). In other words, the figure and writings of Paul became a model for the North African Christian martyr tradition – and, importantly, this tradition was reported in English print. For example, William Caxton's 1485 *The story and life of the Noble and Christian Prince Charles the great of France* recounted how the remains of the North African martyr 'saint Speratus' were gifted to Charlemagne by Aaron King of the Persians; and the 1627 *The Roman Martyrology* named the same saint among the twelve holy martyrs beheaded at Carthage (the Scillitan Martyrs) (Catholic Church 1627: 224–5). Similarly, the story of the African saints Perpetua and Felicity uses Pauline pathway imagery (of the perilous ladder) to describe the passage that the persecuted Christian convert must follow. From the account 'Of Saint Saturnyne' in Caxton's 1483 edition of Jacobus de Voragine's *Golden Legend*:

'I saw', said she, 'a ladder of gold of a marvellous height, erect to heaven, and was so straight that no man might go but one alone. And cutlers and swords of iron sharp were fixed on the right side and left side, so that he that went up might neither look here nor there but byhoued [i.e. in want] always to behold right up to heaven. And a dragon of horrible great form lay under the ladder, which made every man to dread and fear to mount up'; and she saw Satyre ascending by the same unto above and looking towards us, and [he] said 'doubt ye no thing this dragon, but come up surely that ye may be with me'. And when they heard this vision they all gave thanks to our lord [G]od, for they knew then that they were called to martyrdom. (Jacobus de Voragine 1483: CCCxxxx^v–CCClxxxxi^r)

This metaphor of the perilous, narrow pathway has genesis in the story of Paul's blinding and conversion, where the spiritual quest for salvation is corporealised along the straight lines reminiscent of the Roman roads which connected Damascus and Jerusalem, and places like Carthage to the wider trading world. Roman roads were typically built in straight lines, and Andrew McRae records how the straightness of roads in early modern England was conceived, within contemporary civic discourse, as analogous to the orderly behaviour of the subjects who travelled them (McRae 2009: 74–5). In terms of the European Christian mindset, Carthage's and Tunis's locations were liminal, between the desert and the sea at the junction of three continents, and their early relationship with Saint Paul was fitting (and known).

From start to finish, *The Renegado* abounds with pathway imagery, usually in relation to warped Pauline combinations of the sensory (especially blindness/sight) and transformation. We witness, for instance, Vitelli refer to Francisco as 'stay of my steps in this life / And guide to all my blessed hopes hereafter' (1.1.64–5). In the market scene, Mustapha guides Donusa ('you may please to keep your way') by dismissing the wares as 'toys and trifles not worth your observing' (1.3.104–5). In her temptation of Vitelli, Donusa speaks of his obedient 'fainting steps', buffered by her servants 'Not daring to look' on him (2.4.133); and Vitelli (having questioned 'May I believe my senses?' (2.4.25)) describes Donusa's chamber as 'this forbidden place, / Where Christians yet ne'er trod' (2.4.32–3), before giving himself over to Donusa's charms: 'though the Devil / Stood by and roared, I follow!' (2.4.134–5); when, moreover, Vitelli is arrested by the Sultan's Janizaries, he asks, 'Under what law / Am I to fall that set my foot upon / Your statutes and decrees?' (3.5.97–9). Elsewhere, the Master and Boatswain recall the unusual detail of the city of Venice 'Joined in devotion . . . with barefoot steps' (4.1.20) during their story of Grimaldi's desecration of the Host; this is chief among the many crimes Grimaldi considers remedying with 'An eye's loss with an eye' (4.1.60), before voicing his fantasy of prolonged (redemptive) self-harm:

> I would do a bloody justice on myself,
> Pull out these eyes that guided me to ravish
> Their sight from others, lop these legs that bore me
> To barbarous violence, with this hand cut off
> This instrument of wrong, till nought were left me
> But this poor bleeding limbless trunk, which gladly
> I would divide among them. (4.1.66–72)

This is, in part, a deconstruction of an important passage from Paul's Letter to the Ephesians, in which Paul ruminates on how Christ had 'ascended on high' and 'took many captives', thereby anchoring his unmoored converts to Christianity:

> we will no longer be infants, tossed back and forth by the waves, and blown here and there by every form of teaching ... speaking the truth in love, we will in all things grow up into him who is the head, that is, Christ. From him the whole body, joined and held together by every supporting ligament, grows and builds itself up in love, as each part does its work. (Eph. 8: 14–16)

Furthermore, Grimaldi's impulse to amputate his 'instrument of wrong' could certainly imply castration – often conflated with circumcision, a perennial focus for the writings of Paul (both were firmly associated with Islam); and the pirate's use of 'ravish' here is also significant (the word recurs with unusual frequency in this play: twelve times in total).[13] According to Carol Mejia LaPerle, 'ravish' denotes 'a potentially violent transport, drawing a person "forcibly into some condition or action"' – and we might remember that the name of the person Grimaldi has transported is a variation of Paul (Paulina) (Mejia LaPerle 2017: 82). When Paulina is on stage the concentration of Pauline allusions increases. Asambeg (Viceroy of Tunis), for instance, expresses his desire for her in Pauline terms ('For now I only walk a loving dream ... And am yet blind' (2.5.116–18)) and later tells her that 'No fee'd spies wait upon your steps' (4.2.5), explaining a change in her treatment that she greets as a 'wondrous strange ... alteration' – just lines before she affirms that her 'chastity' is 'built upon' the Petrine 'rock of my religion' (4.2.29–30). The play captures echoes and distortions of Paul's journey into its dialogue, through almost every scene, and these become unusually concentrated in the final act.

Patricia Parker describes *The Renegado*'s closing scenes as 'filled with Pauline biblical echoes, of the "end of the race" and of movement forward (in the "right" direction)' (Parker 2002: 25). Parker reads this in relation to a wider pattern of what she terms 'the preposterous', whereby the play's obsession with 'turning' helps to destabilise binary oppositions (of, in this case, Christian and Turk). This is a helpful and sophisticated reading, but we can advance and sharpen Parker's conclusion in relation to the Islamic perspective (and the connections with Englishness) that the play seems to promote. For whilst the figure of Christ represents a crossroads for Islam and Christianity – because Islam regards Christ as a prophet (who prefigured Muhammad) – the writings of Saint Paul represent a crucial bifurcation of Muslim and Christian belief. Where Christians sacralise Paul's journeys and conversions, Islam holds the missions of the early Church as genesis of Christianity's corruption and misinterpretation of Allah's message – thereby framing Paul as the chief and original instrument of Christianity's error and damnation. Indeed, in the Islamic versions of Paul, his conversion is persistently returned to as false and calculated: 'Paul is not only by origin but also by religious conviction a Jew who sides with the Jews against Jesus' followers. Consequently, his conversion to Christianity was not genuine, but rather out of guile and cunning' (Sjoerd van Koningsveld 1996: 207). *The Renegado* narrows the divide between its Muslim characters and their English audience by relating Islam to Protestant Englishness, and generally presenting its Muslim characters as stoic, honourable and merciful: not only is Donusa depicted sympathetically, Asambeg twice shows mercy and restraint to Vitelli and Donusa (at 3.5.106–7 and 4.3.163–6); and as well as resisting his urges towards Paulina throughout the play, he actually instructs her to 'forever be deterred / From yielding basely' at 4.2.40–1. By making its Islamic characters more humane and ostensibly 'Christian' than their Catholic insurgents, and, crucially, by building continuities between Donusa, Tunis and (Protestant) England, the play's finale invites us to question and reverse the comic resolution with which the play closes – including, and especially, in relation to Donusa's conversion, and any prospect she might have of salvation.

Whilst references to forms of communal Pauline resolve occur often within contemporary comedies, especially those of Shakespeare, by the final act of *The Renegado* these occur with such unusual frequency that it starts to feel rather more subversive than reverent.[14] And whilst the exchange between Vitelli and Francisco (the Jesuit) initially seems heroic, a range of Francisco's actions undermine his supposed superiority over the Muslims he outwits. Arguing against a critical grain which generally accepts the hero-status of this character, Claire Jowitt questions 'the extent of Massinger's support of this figure' (Jowitt 2003: 182). Pointing out a range of his actions including superstitious practices, prohibited Catholic sacraments, deception and manipulation, Jowitt places him 'in the role of an untrustworthy machiavel' – a role more in keeping with the 'standard anti-Jesuit propaganda of the time' (Jowitt 2003: 182). I think this reading is correct, and we might well read it against Vitelli's self-identification as 'a sinful man' (1.1.60), who then goes on to sleep with Donusa and almost converts to Islam, and Grimaldi's later acknowledgement that 'I must downward, downward! Though repentance / Could borrow all the glorious wings of grace, / My mountainous weight of sins would crack their pinions' (3.2.69–71). These are not supposed to be virtuous characters.

This also rings true if we think about Francisco's forgiveness (enacted via auricular confession) and re-conversion of Grimaldi the pirate. Grimaldi enters the play a known renegade, murderer and slave-trader, and only finds his way back to Christianity through Francisco after he has been stripped of his wealth by Asambeg. (In another of the play's subversions of Islamic fury and violence, Asambeg punishes him, rather than rewarding him, for the abduction of Paulina.) Grimaldi refers to Francisco as his 'religious creditor' (5.2.13), and is then instructed by the Jesuit to simulate and deceive: 'Borrow your late distracted looks and gesture: / The more dejected you appear, the less / The Viceroy will suspect you' (5.2.35–7). Lying to the infidels may be all well and good when it serves the (Pauline) commonwealth, but there is little reason for us to view Grimaldi as a convert with any hope of salvation – even a strict predestinarian reader would struggle to see symptoms of the elect in Grimaldi, beyond his quite brief (and financially motivated) repentance.

Similar issues surround the character Vitelli (Paulina's brother). In a comical scene from the opening of 4.3, Vitelli is imprisoned in the lower hell-space (under the stage), and Francisco bribes the gaoler for his release:

> FRANCISCO I come not empty-handed: I will purchase
> Your favour at what rate you please. There's gold.
> [*Gives Gaoler gold.*]
> GAOLER 'Tis the best oratory. I will hazard
> A check for your content. [*Opens the trapdoor*]
> Below there!
> VITELLI (*under the stage*) Welcome.
> Art thou the happy messenger that brings me
> News of my death? [*Vitelli's head appears*]
> GAOLER Your hand.
> [*Vitelli* [*is*] *plucked up by the Gaoler*]. (4.3.1–7)

Couched within the comedy, there are clear hints of Vitelli's damnation here, and the notion of a Jesuit purchasing his salvation cannot but emphasise the hopelessness of Vitelli's plight. The gaoler's words, moreover, that he 'will hazard / A check', combine a word derived from Arabic, meaning 'a gambling game with two dice' (*OED*, 'hazard', *n*. and *adj*. etym. and A*n*.1), with a word meaning, ironically, to 'arrest, stop, or retard the onward motion or course' of a person' (*OED*, 'check', *v*.II.3). The word 'check' is also used in the game of chess, of course ('to attack the opponent's King', *OED*, *v*.I.1.a), which echoes rather suggestively against the site of Vitelli's imprisonment in Act 5, 'The Black Tower', given Thomas Middleton's near-contemporary association of the colour black with Spanish deviance in *A Game at Chess* (1624).[15] From the Black Tower-imprisonment in Act 5, Vitelli remarks that he had won Donusa's affections 'not with / Loose lays, poor flatteries, apish compliments, / But sacred and religious zeal' (5.1.21–3), but he cannot really mean Christian zeal, because none of their courtship was on his terms; rather, he was seduced by her, bedded in her palace, and briefly turned Turk when he appeared in 2.5 dressed in the '*fine*', and presumably Islamic, '*clothes*' he received from her – clothes that cause Gazet to mistake him for a 'Turk' (2.5.9) and Francisco to term him 'strangely metamorphosed' (2.5.20).

And whilst the play connects Donusa with Elizabeth, there is no convincing suggestion that her conversion to Christianity should be taken seriously, nor indeed that it might assure her salvation – rather the contrary. Aesthetically, the scene of her surprise-baptism (which interrupts Vitelli's supposed real conversion to Islam) bears zero dramatic jeopardy for the audience, because in 5.2 Francisco basically spells out what will happen (see 5.2.19–40), albeit the means of her baptism is not clarified. Then, when Vitelli follows up his bombastic and overblown entrance to the ceremony by suddenly throwing water in the unwitting Donusa's face, the scene holds her baptism up for ridicule. For her response rings ridiculously against Francisco's immediate leading questions: 'Feel you no alteration? No new motives? / No unexpected aids that may confirm you / In that to which you were inclined before?' (5.3.118–20). More confidence-trickster than spiritual saviour, Francisco prompts a reaction from Donusa that smacks of absurdity:

> I am another woman – till this minute
> I never lived, nor durst think how to die.
> How long have I been blind! Yet on the sudden,
> By this blest means, I feel the films of error
> Ta'en from my soul's eyes. O divine physician,
> That hast bestowed a sight on me which death,
> Though ready to embrace me in his arms,
> Cannot take from me! Let me kiss the hand
> That did this miracle, and seal my thanks
> Upon those lips from whence these sweet words vanished

That freed me from the cruellest of prisons –
Blind ignorance and misbelief. False Prophet,
Imposter Mahomet! (5.3.121–33)

Only onlooking Paulina gets the joke: 'Ha, ha, ha! . . . Who can hold her spleen, / When such ridiculous follies are presented – / The scene, too, made religion?' (5.3.140–2). And, in an aside, Gazet underscores the falsity of these Pauline moments by referring to 'a damned whore's false epistle' (5.3.159) – a barbed line that harks back to an earlier remark from Vitelli, when he tried to sell Donusa '*Corinthian* plate studded with diamonds' which 'Concealed oft deadly poisons' (1.3.122–3, my emphasis). False epistles and poisonous Corinthians rather suggest that in this context reversions to Paul are not to be trusted. For a Protestant English audience, be they Calvinist, some degree of Laudian/Arminian, or somewhere in the middle, Donusa's status as fallen is therefore reasonably assured, and the sins of being a Muslim and seducing and having sex with Vitelli outside of marriage seem unlikely to be washed away by an unexpected splash of Jesuit-blessed water, administered by the dubious Catholic layman Vitelli.

Similarly, where we might more usually equate a protagonist's rescue and escape (in comedy) with their salvation on some level – especially in the context of a Christian escaping from a foreign, Muslim imprisonment – Vitelli's prison-break is rather more suggestive of his damnation. For despite the play's (too) remarkably positive handling of Catholic references elsewhere in the narrative, the stage directions of 5.7 must surely read as anti-Catholic: Vitelli enters above and '*Cuts open the bake-meat*' (echoing Acts 9: 18: 'And when he had received meat, he was strengthened') to reveal a secret 'scroll bound up in pack-thread'; the scroll spells out directions for his escape. Then:

[*lets down the thread*]
O best of men! He that gives up himself
To a true religious friend leans not upon
A false deceiving reed, but boldly builds
Upon a rock, which now with joy I find
In reverend Francisco, whose good vows,
Labours and watchings in my hoped-for freedom
Appear a pious miracle. [*Pulls up the rope.*] I come,
I come, good man, with confidence: though the descent
Were as steep as hell, I know I cannot slide,
Being called down by such a faithful guide.
[*Descends by the rope.*] *Exit.* (5.7.11–22)

Regardless of the shifting political sands of the Stuart court, no political transformation had as yet occurred that would render these lines about a Jesuit priest as anything other than ludicrous. Yes, Vitelli believes that he is saved, as did many Catholics, Protestants and for that matter Muslims, but the text invites us to question the validity of those claims by holding them up for scrutiny and ridicule. His praise of Francisco is too outspoken ('best of men', 'a true religious friend', 'reverend Francisco', 'good man'), and his model of faith is too externalised. Vitelli descends physically and eschatologically, and though he thinks (much like the converts Grimaldi and Donusa) that he follows the road of Paul, he in fact follows the road to hell.

Read in this way, such is *The Renegado*'s antipathy towards religious turning that we should certainly continue to read it in relation to the marriage that King James I/VI was attempting to broker between his son, the future King of England, and the Spanish Infanta. However, *The Renegado* distorts and resituates Paul's Road to Damascus trope in ways that clearly cannot be read as pious or reverent – and must be seen as critical of the Catholic match. Demonising notions of Catholic turning, and rendering the use of Pauline discourse to justify and sacralise religious conversion as ludicrous (and wrong), sets this play more logically at odds with the dominant political context of its inception. Furthermore, that Massinger used his knowledge of Islam to do this is notable. The Qur'an was not translated into English until 1649, but clearly subjects were learning about Islamic dis/continuities with Christianity long before this date. Since the beginning of Elizabeth's reign, we know that 'Islam left its mark on Britain in a way that was unparalleled by any other non-Christian civilisation which Britons encountered' (Matar 1998: 184). So we should be unsurprised to see curious intellectuals like Philip Massinger using Islam (and its connections to England) to write about political issues. In this period, the roads that most Islamic and English subjects walked may well have been far removed; but perhaps the conceptual pathways of their beliefs were being understood as more proximate and familiar than is often assumed.

Notes

1. Because of the perceived sympathy in his dramatic works towards the history and practices of the Roman Church, Massinger was once considered to be a crypto-Catholic; see Gifford 1813 and Gardiner 1876.
2. See Jowitt 2004, Jowitt 2006, and her earlier treatment of the play in Jowitt 2003: 175–90.
3. All quotations from *The Renegado* in this chapter are from the 2018 edition edited by Michael Neill.

4. Among the best work on these and other 'Turk plays' is still Daniel Vitkus's trailblazing *Turning Turk* (2003) and his introduction and notes to *Three Turk Plays* (2000).
 5. Glover, for example, referred to 'Carthage, near where Tunis stands, (famous for Dido and Hannibal)' (Glover 1637: 41). Similarly, John Leo (Africanus) described how the 'kingdom of Tunis . . . containeth Byzacium, which by *Strabo* is accounted a part of Africa propia. The head of this province in times past was Carthage, whereof at this present there are nothing but ruins extant' (Leo 1600: 7).
 6. On the dating of the play, and the related debate about Nashe's contributions, see Wiggins 2008.
 7. On the intersecting mythologies of Dido and Elizabeth, see also Williams 2006 and Stump 2000.
 8. The death of Marlowe's Dido was a loose adaptation of Virgil's, for in *The Aeneid* Dido climbs atop the funeral pyre and stabs herself with a Trojan blade (IV: 664–707). On Marlowe's 'vanish', see Frazer 2015: 46–7.
 9. Vitelli, for instance, voices his own prejudice against 'these Turkish dames' who will 'run a course the fiends themselves would shake at / To enjoy their wanton ends' (1.3.11, 13–14).
10. According to Doran, 'pejorative references to "frogs" or "toads" proliferated in all kinds of published works from 1579 to 1581, acting as a coded form of hostility to the match' (Doran 1996: 168).
11. See Eastman's chapter 'The Pauline Cult in North Africa' in *Paul the Martyr* (Eastman 2011: 15–114).
12. All references to Paul's writings here are from Meeks and Fitzgerald 2007.
13. For a brief but informative discussion of castration in *The Renegado*, see Gil Harris 2004: 136–62 (chapter 6).
14. See Hassel 1971. Reinhard Lupton 2014 also reads Saint Paul (in Shakespeare) as the prototypical figure of the citizen.
15. Without speaking to its wider significance, Neill notes that George Sandys's *Relation of a Journey begun Anno Domini 1610* locates a 'Black Tower' in Constantinople: the castle guarding the Bosphorus north (Massinger 2018: 224, n. 170).

Works cited

Adler, Doris (1987), *Philip Massinger*, Boston: Twain.
Andrea, Bernadette (2007), *Women and Islam in Early Modern English Literature*, Cambridge: Cambridge University Press.
Burton, Jonathan (2005), *Traffic and Turning: Islam and English Drama, 1579–1624*, Newark: University of Delaware Press.
Catholic Church (1627), *The Roman Martyrology according to the reformed calendar*, trans. G. K. of the Society of Jesus, London.
Doran, Susan (1996), *Monarchy and Matrimony: The Courtships of Elizabeth I*, London: Routledge.
Eastman, David (2011), *Paul the Martyr: The Cult of the Apostle in the Latin West*, Atlanta: Society of Biblical Literature.

Frazer, Paul (2015), 'Moving with Marlowe (& Co.): Relocation, Appropriation and Personation in Thomas Dekker's *Shoemaker's Holiday*', *Marlowe Studies: An Annual* 5, pp. 37–60.
Gardiner, S. R. (1876), 'The Political Element in Massinger', *Contemporary Review* 28, pp. 495–507.
Gifford, William (ed.) (1813), *The Plays of Philip Massinger*, 4 vols, London: W. Bulmer.
Gil Harris, Jonathan (2004), *Sick Economies: Drama, Mercantilism and Disease in Shakespeare's England*, Philadelphia: University of Philadelphia Press.
Glover, George (1637), *The Arrival and Entertainments of the Ambassador Alkaid Jaurar Ben Abdella, with his associate Mr Robert Blake from the High and Mighty Prince, Mulley Mahamed Sheik, Emperor of Morocco*, London.
Hassel, R. Chris (1971), 'Saint Paul and Shakespeare's Romantic Comedies', *Thought* 46.3, pp. 371–88.
Hawkes, David (2010), 'Islam and the Economy of the Senses in Renaissance English Literature', *The Senses and Society* 5.1, pp. 144–59.
Hopkins, Lisa (2008), *Christopher Marlowe: Renaissance Dramatist*, Edinburgh: Edinburgh University Press.
Jacobus de Voragine (1483), *Legenda aurea sanctorum, sive, Lombardica historia*, London.
Jowitt, Claire (2003), *Voyage Drama and Gender Politics, 1589–1642*, Manchester and New York: Manchester University Press.
—— (2004), 'Massinger's *Renegado* (1624) and the Spanish Marriage', *Cahiers Élisabéthains* 65, pp. 45–54.
—— (2006), '"I Am Another Woman": The Spanish and French Matches in Massinger's *The Renegado* (1624) and *The Unnatural Combat* (1624–5)', in Alexander Samson (ed.), *The Spanish Match: Prince Charles's Journey to Madrid, 1623*, London and New York: Routledge, pp. 151–72.
Leo, John [Africanus] (1600), *A Geographical History of Africa*, London.
McRae, Andrew (2009), *Literature and Domestic Travel in Early Modern England*, Cambridge: Cambridge University Press.
Marlowe, Christopher, and Thomas Nashe (1999), *Dido, Queen of Carthage*, in *Christopher Marlowe: The Complete Plays*, ed. Mark Thornton Burnett, London: Everyman.
Masri, Safwan M. (2017), *Tunisia: An Arab Anomaly*, New York: Colombia University Press.
Massinger, Philip (2018), *The Renegado, or The Gentleman of Venice*, ed. Michael Neill, London: Arden Bloomsbury.
Matar, Nabil (1998), *Islam in Britain, 1558–1685*, Cambridge: Cambridge University Press.
Meeks, Wayne A., and John T. Fitzgerald (eds) (2007), *The Writings of Paul*, New York and London: W. W. Norton.
Mejia LaPerle, Carol (2017), '"Unclothe Me of Sin's Gay Trappings": Foreign Ornaments and Plain English in Philip Massinger's *The Renegado*', *Cahiers Élisabéthains* 94.1, pp. 74–92.
Neill, Michael (2018), 'Introduction', in Philip Massinger, *The Renegado, or The Gentleman of Venice*, ed. Michael Neill, London: Arden Bloomsbury, pp. 1–71.
Parker, Patricia (2002), 'Preposterous Conversions: Turning Turk and its

"Pauline" Rerighting', *Journal for Early Modern Cultural Studies* 2.1, pp. 1–34.
Reinhard Lupton, Julia (2014), *Citizen-Saints: Shakespeare and Political Theology*, Chicago: University of Chicago Press.
Robinson, Benedict S. (2006a), *Islam and Early Modern English Literature: The Politics of Romance from Spenser to Milton*, New York: Palgrave Macmillan.
—— (2006b), 'The "Turks", Caroline Politics, and Philip Massinger's *The Renegado*', in Adam Zucker and Alan B. Farmer (eds), *Localizing Caroline Drama: Politics and Economics of the Early Modern Stage, 1625–1642*, Basingstoke: Palgrave Macmillan, pp. 213–37.
Sjoerd van Koningsveld, Pieter (1996), 'The Islamic Image of Paul and the Origin of the Gospel of Barnabas', *Jerusalem Studies in Arabic and Islam* 20, pp. 200–28.
Stump, Donald (2000), 'Marlowe's Travesty of Virgil: *Dido* and Elizabethan Dream of Empire', *Comparative Drama* 34, pp. 79–107.
Virgil (1991), *The Aeneid: A New Prose Translation*, trans. David West, London: Penguin.
Vitkus, Daniel (ed.) (2000), *Three Turk Plays from Early Modern England*, New York and Chichester: Columbia University Press.
—— (2003), *Turning Turk: English Theater and the Multicultural Mediterranean*, Basingstoke: Palgrave Macmillan.
Wiggins, Martin (2008), 'When Did Marlowe Write *Dido, Queen of Carthage*?', *RES* 59.241, pp. 521–41.
Williams, Deanne (2006), 'Dido, Queen of England', *ELH* 73.1, pp. 31–59.

Chapter 12

How Margaret Cavendish Mapped a Blazing World

Marion Wynne-Davies

The process of mapping during the first years of the seventeenth century imagined a vista that superimposed a spiritual road map on to topographical journeys. The English Civil War changed the conception of roads and geographical environments completely, demanding that a hard-edged understanding of the material realities of travel took precedence over the old allegorical passageways. Yet even this is too simplistic. For if men travelled across Europe after the war in terms of expediency and political manoeuvring, for women the necessity of leaving their home and beginning again in a new country was fraught with danger. As the Royalists abandoned England for exile in France, the Netherlands and Spain, gendered narratives diverged and women increasingly came to identify road travel, not as a spiritual journey, but as a terrifying experience fraught with very real dangers. Of course, most women did not record in print this new understanding of what 'travel' had come to mean and, even when they did, it is often couched in fiction – a semi-autobiographical flight in verse or prose. This is why Margaret Cavendish's writing is so important; she was a prodigious author, composing prose, poetry and drama as well as philosophical treatises, often drawing upon her own personal experience to explain historical events, scientific hypotheses, moral dilemmas, and even how to avoid wrinkles. Unsurprisingly, therefore, Cavendish's various discourses on travel are both illuminating and proactive. They challenge us to think about how the Civil War changed the idea of mapping: interrogating gender difference and creating dramatic analogies with geographical exploration and material geography that demanded allegory be questioned, if not abandoned altogether. This shift may be contextualised by the history of maps in Michel de Certeau's *The Practice of Everyday Life* (1984) in which he explains the transition from itineraries to road maps. More significantly, de Certeau links travel to narrative, allowing for the exploration of spatial syntaxes and the modalities that may transform and disrupt expected paths, both geographical and literary. This chapter, therefore, sets out to explore these new and gendered forms of travel on England's roads by establishing traditional forms both of mapping and of early modern prose, before exploring Cavendish's unsettling use of geographical space, primarily in *The Blazing World* (1666).

To begin, it is informative to consider an example of early seventeenth-century mapping: John Speed's *A Prospect of the Most Famous Parts of the World* (1627), which was the first world atlas to be compiled by an Englishman. This was a path-breaking work of its time, yet to present-day readers the spiritual tone of Speed's opening sentence can appear anachronistic for a cartographical text. The opening passage, however, demonstrates the period's understanding of the link between material and spiritual journeys:

> Heaven was too long a reach for man to recover at one step and therefore God first placed him upon the earth, that he might for a time contemplate upon his inferior workes, magnifie them in his Creator: and receive here a hope of a fuller blisse, which by degrees he should at last enjoy in his place of rest. (Speed 1627: 1)

The purpose of this early modern atlas is, therefore, to allow the viewer to 'contemplate' the 'earth' as an inferior replica of heaven and, by so doing, begin to appreciate God's power and munificence, thereby preparing him/herself for the 'place of rest' at the end of life's journey. As such, maps were not only useful tools for navigation on earth, but also a guide on the spiritual path to 'heaven'. Thus for Speed and his readers the material and spiritual spheres merge inextricably on the page. In literary texts, such a journey is exemplified in the medieval morality play *Everyman*, in Spenser's *The Faerie Queene* and in Bunyan's *The Pilgrim's Progress*, all of which use travel across a terrain to represent an allegorical spiritual journey to salvation.

Yet, in *A Prospect*, Speed obfuscates any simple allegory through a representation of God's diverse 'workes', as he amplifies the charts with seemingly material facts: historical descriptions of the continents, intriguing vignettes about the peoples and areas of the various countries, and a series of border engravings depicting the costumes and cities of the regions. For example, 'The Description of Africa' presents a debate between the Christian understanding that 'Africa as it lay neerest the seate of the first people [Adam and Eve], so questionlesse it was the next inhabited' and, therefore, the indigenous history: 'give the people their owne asking, and they will have the glory of the first Inhabitants of the World' (Speed 1627: 5).

The chart itself is similar to current maps of Africa, although the framework depicts a King of Madagascar with a fanciful headdress, as well as a series of ports whose plans recall European towns, rather than African cities. Finally, Speed adds further intriguing pieces of information such as that one of the Canary Islands 'hath no water but from a cloud, that hangs over a tree, and at noone dissolves' (Speed 1627: 5–6). As such, *A Prospect* combines cartography, history, spiritual treatise, characterisations, narrative accounts, travel writing and anything else John Speed happened to believe about a particular location. This places Speed's maps as one of the itineraries described by de Certeau:

> The first medieval maps included only the rectilinear marking out of itineraries (performative indications chiefly concerning pilgrimages), along with the stops one was to make (cities which one was to pass through, spend the night in, pray at, etc.). (De Certeau 1984: 120)

Like his medieval forebears, therefore, Speed conceives of his map as a 'pilgrimage' or itinerary with interesting 'stops' and curiosities along the road. Moreover, as de Certeau suggests, we may identify the similarities between the road and the text since, while we can accept, from its title, the classification of the book as an atlas, *A Prospect* may be identified as a typical work of early modern prose, albeit one illustrated with pictures. And this, I think, is the intriguing link, because the traditional method of mapping was, in many ways, analogous to early seventeenth-century prose writing.

Early modern prose texts are characterised by a yoking together of a range of seemingly disconnected information and representations; they are, if you like, a rag-bag genre, and critics have long recognised this diversity. Rob Maslen points out that,

> Throughout the sixteenth century, prose fiction seems consistently to have been regarded, by its authors as well as its readers, as the most slippery of literary mediums. Its slipperiness lay partly in the difficulty of defining what it was. Prose fiction refused to conform to any of the generic categories by which contemporary textbooks charted the hegemony of what is written: tragedy, comedy, history, epic, satire, and the rest. It masquerades as anything but fiction. (Maslen 1997: 11–12)

Similarly, Roger Pooley comments that

> a history of seventeenth-century prose is a history of paradigms, of images, as well as of styles, of rhetorics, of ideas, of faiths often in conflict. It is also a history of genres – autobiography, history, sermons, essays as well as fiction. (Pooley 1992: 7)

Maslen's description of the 'slipperiness' of sixteenth-century prose with its list of 'generic categories' is echoed by Pooley's inventory of 'paradigms ... [and] genres'. Therefore, in order to comprehend prose writing in Early Modern England we have to accommodate a confusing mass of often divergent and inconsistent genres, styles and forms. For readers accustomed to twenty-first-century novels, with their solid generic foundations (even when those are challenged), the earlier prose works appear overly complex and made almost impenetrable with these multiple parts. Yet it is precisely here that John Speed's atlas might be able to help.

If we imagine a work of Renaissance prose, not as a modern map, but as an itinerary across a hugely detailed and varied plan, then the process of reading becomes more manageable. This plan must be contemplated at intervals so that the reader will be able to follow the correct road to the journey's end. In the same way, the narrative line of the prose work must be halted at regular intervals so that theme may be considered as a contemplative point on the way to a final sense of knowledge and understanding. And in each case, proceeding along the road or, as de Certeau puts it, the spatial syntax, one finds one's way with the aid of an array of thematic paradigms, from spiritual quest to political satire. Indeed, the image of the medieval map is particularly apt since the first Elizabethan prose fictions were often set in distant or imaginary lands, such as John Lyly's *Euphues* (1578 and 1580) and Philip Sidney's *Arcadia* (1590). In each case the foreign location offered the opportunity to comment upon the author's own society, and the adventures of the main characters in both works represent the concerns of the late sixteenth-century courtier. Geographical distinction was further suggested by the fact that Lyly and Sidney were influenced by English translations of the Italian pastoral romances of Boccaccio, Ariosto and Tasso. The Spanish picaresque form also proved influential, resulting in, among other works, Thomas Nashe's *The Unfortunate Traveller* (1594), which itself depicts a road trip across Europe.

There is, however, a distinct difference between reading Speed's map and reading an early modern prose work. Imagine, if you like, unfolding a map from the particular place you are focusing upon so that you can see the whole of the region, and then compare that act with trying to tear out and paste together all the pages of a prose work so that you can see every chapter laid out from start to finish. Yet I would like to argue that there is a similarity. The process of understanding a map requires the reader to undertake two simultaneous yet antithetical positions. First, she or he must have a static and elevated overview of the whole and a sense of the final goal in order to plan the journey. Yet at the same time, the map-reader must also be aware of the material conditions of movement along the actual route, recognising features from their symbolic replication upon the chart so that they may attain their as-yet-unseen destination. As such, the map-reader appears to be both stationary and moving, aware of, and yet distant from, the conclusion. While this doubled process of map reading can never exactly mirror reading an early modern prose work, there are useful similarities. And, here, de Certeau's explanation of the post-medieval comes into play, since he describes how by the seventeenth century formal 'maps [were] constituted as proper places in which to exhibit the products of knowledge' while 'stories about space exhibit on the contrary the operations that allow it, within a constraining and non-"proper" place, to mingle its elements' (de Certeau 1984: 121). Therefore, an initial overview of the text might well incorporate a kaleidoscopic range of referents (genres, themes and styles), yet the method of understanding them demands movement through the text and the recognition of – sometimes drastic – shifts of meaning. That linear journey through sequential literary features is a familiar one for readers of the novel, yet to understand early modern prose we must be ready to halt occasionally along the way and consider what de Certeau refers to as modalities that indicate a 'kind of passage' between points on the road (de Certeau 1984: 115). These modalities are essential because the elements that seem unfamiliar and jarring are constructed precisely to make the reader study the broader compass of the road map and so appreciate the difficulties we must encounter before reaching our destination – both cartographic and spiritual. That 'slipperiness' described by Maslen is, therefore, an intrinsic aspect of both early modern maps and prose fiction demanding a bifurcated view of the world in which material linear travel on the lines of the itinerary is inextricably linked to a more modern cartographic overview.

These early seventeenth-century traditions of mapping and prose fiction provide the foundations for Margaret Cavendish's *The Blazing World*, which sets a complex fictional narrative and philosophical treatise in a seemingly allegorical new world. The work has been criticised as 'tedious chaos' presenting the reader with a contradictory hodge-podge of ideas that supposedly reflect, as Virginia Woolf judged, the author's 'crack-brained and bird witted ideas' (Bowerbank 1984: 402; Woolf 1925: 87). This 'hodgepodge' characteristic, however, makes Cavendish's work typical of early modern prose – albeit a late example in a period when the genre was changing. But this is something I want to question, because while Speed, in 1627, had been able to allege that maps led the traveller to a heavenly conclusion, by the 1660s such certainties were no longer in place. Indeed, by the mid seventeenth century English authors, like their cartographic counterparts, were inevitably influenced by the Civil War (1642–51), the defeat of Charles I, and the subsequent exile in France and the Netherlands of many of the nobility. For Margaret Cavendish, therefore, any fictional accounts of travelling derived not from a sense of exploration or a quest for knowledge, but from political necessity and harsh personal experience. In exploring her 'blazing world', therefore, it becomes necessary to consider the traditions of early modern prose, as well as the diversity and the double necessity of the stasis necessary for the itinerary and the movement demanded by scientific cartography. However, these elements need to be set alongside Margaret Cavendish's material experience of space in both its political and personal evocations.

First, then, what were Cavendish's experiences of road travel? The young Margaret Lucas was Maid of Honour to Charles I's consort, Henrietta Maria, and accompanied her when the Queen escaped to Paris in 1644 under threat from the Parliamentarian troops. While in Paris, Margaret met William Cavendish, the Duke of Newcastle, who was similarly exiled, and despite the difference in their ages (she was in her twenties and he was a widower in his fifties) they appear to have fallen in love. The couple were married in 1645 and moved to Antwerp, where they lived in relative poverty until the restoration of the monarchy in 1660, when they returned to England and retired to a secluded life at Welbeck Abbey on one of the Duke's estates. William Cavendish authored a number of poems and plays, and he certainly encouraged his daughters in their literary activities, so it is likely it was he who first supported Margaret in her own attempts to write. She soon surpassed her husband's output, however, and in the space of twenty years (1653–73) produced a range of texts covering poetry, drama and prose, as well as focusing upon an array of topics from courtly wit to scientific research. However, a woman, particularly one of her social standing, writing with serious intent and publishing her own works at considerable personal expense was uncommon, and Margaret Cavendish became an object of ridicule on the occasions she and her husband returned to London society. If Virginia Woolf's judgement of the Duchess as 'crack-brained and bird witted' seems harsh, it was more than echoed by Cavendish's seventeenth-century contemporaries. Dorothy Osborne noted that 'there are many soberer people in Bedlam', and Samuel Pepys recorded in his diary that 'all the town-talk is nowadays of her extravagancies' (Cavendish 1994: xiii; Salzman 1985: 293). It is hardly surprising therefore that Paul Salzman prefaces his edition of her prose work with the hope that it 'will give readers the opportunity to judge for themselves whether *The Blazing World* is readable' (Salzman 1991: xviii). It is possible to negotiate a path through Cavendish's work, but, I would like to suggest, only if you come prepared with the right road map.

The prose fiction was first published as *The Description of a New Blazing World* in 1666 and was appended to the quasi-scientific treatise *Observations upon Experimental Philosophy*. In the latter work Cavendish sets out to challenge Robert Hooke's *Micrographia* (1665), which promotes the use of a telescope, with an analysis of how the human eye is more suited to the study of moving objects. This explains why Cavendish's address to the reader of her fictional piece notes that 'I join a work of fancy to my serious philosophical contemplations', and she goes on:

> And this is the reason why I added this piece of fancy to my philosophical observations, and joined them as two worlds at the ends of their poles, both for my own sake, to divert my studious thoughts which I employed in the contemplation thereof, and to delight the readers with variety, which is always pleasing. (Salzman 1991: 252)

The diversity necessary to early modern prose is immediately apparent – that 'variety, which is always pleasing' – but she also signals the use of another world and conjures an image of two globes attached at 'their poles'. Moreover, the 'fiction' allows us to travel from one world to another, revealing on the way almost excessive 'variety', while at the same time allowing for sharp and accurate cartographic details. The narrative outline of *The Blazing World* is as tortuous and fantastical as that of any Elizabethan romance; therefore, in the subsequent analysis, I intend to follow the text sequentially through its labyrinthine shifts, while at the same time highlighting the elements of the text that are embedded in material experience of travel and knowledge of travel literature and geography. Importantly, it is at these points that we may identify the various modalities noted by de Certeau, which serve to destabilise the dominant patriarchal road maps of both geography and literature.

To begin, an anonymous young lady is abducted by a foreign merchant while she 'gather[s] shells upon the shore' and is carried away on a craft that suggests a reasonably accurate knowledge of shipping: 'a little light vessel, not unlike a packet-boat' (Salzman 1991: 253). Packet-boats were small craft used to carry regular mail services and also able to take a few passengers in cramped conditions. The key point here, however, is that they became popular in the mid seventeenth century with the Dutch East India Company and would have been seen by Cavendish as they sailed regularly along the Scheldt river in Antwerp. This is the first instance where Cavendish inserts a destabilising element into the romance narrative, so that instead of the expected linear narrative, the reader's attention is diverted to a maritime detail. The allusion to shipping is, subsequently, underlined when the vessel is blown off course and sails to the North Pole, where the merchant and his crew freeze to death and the ship itself is transported, via the adjoining polar regions, to a new world – the 'blazing world' of the title. There are two further modalities of this part of the narrative worth noting: first, Cavendish's experience of travelling aboard ship, and second, the siting of this journey in polar waters.

Cavendish describes how 'Heaven ... raised such a tempest as they knew not what to do or whither to steer their course' (Salzman 1991: 253). Such 'tempests' recur in Cavendish's writing, most notably in the short story 'Assaulted and Pursued Chastity' (1656), which is commonly seen as a precursor to *The Blazing World* (Cavendish 1994: xvi). At the start of the narrative,

> a Lady, amongst the rest, enriched by Nature, with Virtue, Wit, and Beauty; in her returning-voyage, felt the spight of Fortune, being cast by a storm, from the place she steered to, upon the Kingdom of Sensuality. (Cavendish 1656: 396)

Yet the most telling aspect of the journey comes immediately before the storm where the reason for the lady's voyage is explained, since she chooses as other women do

> to venture their Lives with the hazards of Travels, rather than their Honours and Chastities, by staying at home amongst rough and rude Soldiers. (Cavendish 1656: 396)

While the narrative evokes an allegorical 'storm' that deposits the lady in the 'Kingdom of Sensuality', the 'hazards of Travels' and the reference to being raped by 'rough and rude Soldiers' are embedded in the realities of the English Civil War and Cavendish's own fears. These concerns are made more explicit in *Sociable Letters* (1664):

> But since our Wars some are Necessitated and Forc'd to Travel into Forein Countreys, being Banish'd out of their Native Countrey, and the Wives of Banished men are forced to Travel to and from their Husbands, to seek for Means and Subsistence, to Maintain or Relieve their Necessitated lives, wanting Meat to feed on and Cloaths to cover them. (Cavendish 1664: 196–7)

Here Cavendish draws upon personal experience: the English Civil War had 'Forc'd' her to travel to France with Queen Henrietta Maria and later to Antwerp with her husband, William Cavendish, who was indeed 'Banish'd'. Moreover, since they were so impoverished, Cavendish undertook a journey to London in 1651 to petition Parliament in the hope of obtaining some 'Means and Subsistence' from William Cavendish's estates. The claim that she lacked 'Meat to feed on and Cloaths' adds a typical Cavendish rhetorical flourish, but William Cavendish was heavily indebted and, as Katie Whitaker points out in her biography *Mad Madge*, 'the royalist émigrés were near to destitution' (Whitaker 2002: 134). A similar claim is made in 'The Claspe. Phantasmes Masque' (1653), where an autobiographical narrative is embedded in the 'Similizing [of] a young Lady to a Ship' (Cavendish 1653: 155). In describing how the Ship/lady must cross 'the troubled Seas of Misery' until into the 'Haven of great France she got', where 'a Nobel Lord this Ship did buy', Cavendish reworks her own journey to France and her marriage to William (Cavendish 1653: 155). The metaphor of marriage as a financial transaction is apt within its historical context, although both Margaret's and William's writings suggest genuine love and attraction (Whitaker 2002: 80–2). The next lines in the poem reveal, however, that money is an overwhelming issue for the Ship/lady:

> At last a storm of Poverty did rise,
> And showers of Miseries fell from the Skies,
> And Thundering Creditors a Noise did make,
> With threatning Bills, as if the Ship would break. (Cavendish 1653: 156)

For Margaret Cavendish, therefore, travel was seen as dangerous and should only be undertaken if deemed necessary because of threats such as rape and poverty. Thus the second modality emerges from the romance narrative, backed up by Cavendish's other works: the regendering of travel narratives in which the spatial syntax of the road is broken by penury, danger and rape. Unsurprisingly, for men Cavendish describes a very different experience.

In *Natures Pictures Drawn by Fancies Pencil to the Life*, the same work that includes 'Assaulted and Pursued Chastity', Cavendish includes the story of 'a Traveller' who

> fitted himself to travel into Forreign Countreys, to see their Varieties and Curiosities, and to learn the Customs and Laws thereof, going into all places and Companies of note and recourse. (Cavendish 1656: 516)

Unlike female travellers, the man seeks 'Varieties and Curiosities' and is allowed into 'places and Companies' that establish his own social standing as being 'of note'. This is a mild comment in comparison to her sharp critique in *Orations of Divers Sorts Accommodated to Divers Places* (1662), where she advises:

> You think your Sons not well Bred, unless you send them to Travel into Forein Nations, to see and understand Fashions, Customs, and Manners of the World, by which they may Learn the better to Know themselves, and to

Judge of others; but though you send your Sons abroad, in Hope they will Profit by their Travels, yet you are for the most part Deceived in your Hopes and Expectations. (Cavendish 1662: 73–4)

Again, there is a sense that men travel to learn about the 'Varieties' of 'Customs, and Manners of the World', yet she goes on to point out that, rather,

> Our Travelling Gallants bring home only Vanity and Vice, as more Prodigality than Frugality, more Luxury than Temperance, more diseases than Health, more Extravagancy than Discretion, more Folly than Experience, and more Vice than Vertue, it were better they should stay at Home, than Travel as they do. (Cavendish 1662: 74)

This is again typical of Cavendish's ornate and convoluted prose style, but the allusion to 'diseases' and 'Vice' refers to the Gallants' use of prostitutes and the very real threat of venereal disease, an infection that would, in turn, have drastic consequences for the man's future wife. Cavendish describes post-Civil-War travel not only as dangerous for women as they fled sexual assault and battled for income, but also from the impact of men's voyages that were undertaken out of curiosity and mainly for pleasure. When the lady in *The Blazing World* gets abducted by the captain of the packet-boat, she is about to set off on an allegorical journey, yet she simultaneously represents the material plight of the exiled Royalist women and Cavendish herself.

At this point, however, I would like to return to Cavendish's autobiographical masque 'The Claspe', where immediately after the threats from the 'Thundering Creditors' make the Ship/lady almost 'break', there is a surprise shift because, instead of going to London, as Cavendish did, 'This Ship was forc'd towards the Northern Pole, / There Icy Wants did on this Ship take hold' (Cavendish 1653: 156). The allegory shows how poverty – 'Wants' – makes the lady cold, suggesting a loss of sustenance and fuel, but the reference to the North Pole and 'Icy' suggests that Cavendish is bringing in a second aspect of travel and a third modality: polar exploration. And, of course, this is exactly where the lady in *The Blazing World* travels to:

> The vessel . . . was carried as swift as an arrow out of a bow towards the North Pole, and in short time reached the icy sea, where the wind forced it amongst huge pieces of ice. (Salzman 1991: 253)

Why, then, does Cavendish use travel to the North Pole twice in very similar narratives? Perhaps an explanation may be ascertained from Letter CXC in *Sociable Letters*, where she confesses,

> I know not how Cold it is at the Poles, for I never was there in Person, but in my Imagination yet ... Cold with all its Potent Strength, as an Army of Flakes of Snow, with Ammunition of Hail for Bullets, and Wind for Powder, also Huge Ships of Ice, which Float in the Main Sea, and Stop up all the Narrow Rivers; also Cold and its Army Shooting forth the Piercing Darts, which fly so Thick and Fast, and are so Sharp, as they Enter into every Pore of the Flesh of all Animal Creatures, whereby many Animals are Wounded with Numbness, and Die Insensibly, although Mankind bring what Strength they can get against Cold, as an Army of Furs. (Cavendish 1664: 396–7)

As is common in Cavendish's work, war is used as a metaphor, for battling 'Cold' with its 'Army of Flakes of Snow', yet alongside this military allusion she invokes the discourse of polar exploration. Indeed, the descriptions of 'Huge' ice floes that 'Stop up all the Narrow Rivers', the freezing to death of 'many Animals' and the use of 'Furs' by 'Mankind' suggest that although she has not visited the 'Poles' herself, she can imagine what it is like. Her 'Imagination' was, I believe, stimulated by one particular book: Gerrit de Veer's *A true Description of three Voyages by the North-East towards Cathay and China, undertaken by the Dutch in the Years 1594, 1595, and 1596* (published in Dutch in 1598 and translated into English in 1609). The clue comes two letters later, where she writes about how William Cavendish has taken her to see ice skaters in Antwerp: 'Men Slide upon the Frozen Moat, or River, which Runs, or rather Stands about the City Walls' (Cavendish 1664: 400). This detail places her interest in the cold and ice firmly in Antwerp and possibly around 1650, when the Little Ice Age began, and which was depicted by Barent Avercamp in his painting *Skating on a Frozen River* (c. 1650). While de Veer's work was little known in England, it went through numerous editions in the Netherlands, partly because it tells the story of Dutch polar exploration and partly because it proved a riveting story that was graphically illustrated.

De Veer recounts the three voyages of the Dutch navigator Willem Barentsz as he attempted to discover a North-East passage. De Veer did not accompany Barentsz on the first expedition, so the narrative is told in the third person, but he was present on the second and third journeys and kept a detailed diary on both occasions. He points out that the only animals living in the polar regions are 'beares and foxes' and recounts how they ate the latter and had to fight off the former as 'the beares rose up upon their hinder feete to see us' (de Veer 2010: 5, 90). He also describes the ice floes:

> there we found so great store of ice, that it was admirable: and wee sayled along through it, as if wee had past betweene two lands ... [and how the ship became] inclosed with flakes of ice. (De Veer 2010: 74, 21)

Indeed, because the ship became trapped in the ice, Barentsz, de Veer and fifteen other crew members were forced to spend the winter on the ice, where they suffered from extreme cold and continual blizzards and freezing fog. The following summer they escaped on two small boats, were rescued by a Russian merchant ship and finally returned to Amsterdam on 1 November. Barentsz died on the journey home and only twelve men survived. Although some of de Veer's text covers details of maritime exploration such as distance and fathoms, the discursive prose sections are full of danger and suspense, so it is not surprising that the book ran to several editions and that, even today, the location of that stranded winter is a tourist destination. It is not improbable that either William or his brother, Charles Cavendish, would have purchased or borrowed de Veer's *A true Description*, since, as Whitaker points out, 'Sir Charles was an avid reader, and the latest philosophical and scientific works poured into the Cavendish household' (Whitaker 2002: 118). Cavendish's description of ice floes and snow could, therefore, have been taken from de Veer's diary. Indeed, there are further similarities in other works. In *Observations upon Experimental Philosophy*, which precedes *The Blazing World* in the same publication, Cavendish notes that

> great shelves of Ice, do not expand cold beyond their icy bodies; but the air patterns out the cold, and so doth the perception of those Seaman that sail into cold Countries . . . [where] some Beasts, as Foxes, Bears, and the like, are not so much sensible of cold, as Man. (Cavendish 1666: 107, 111)

She later goes on to discuss massive ice floes:

> *Quest. 7.* What produces those great Precipices and Mountains of Ice which are found in the Sea, and other great waters? I answer: That Snow, as also thick Fogs and Mists, which are nothing but rarified water, falling upon the Ice, make its out-side thicker, and many great shelves and broken pieces of Ice joyning together, produce such Precipices and Mountains as mentioned. (Cavendish 1666: 129)

In her philosophical works Cavendish makes specific reference to 'Seamen' on polar expeditions, refers to the same two creatures noted by de Veer (polar bears and arctic foxes), describes the huge ice 'Mountains' and ice floes that accord with de Veer's report, and also refers to the 'fogs and mists' also noted in the diary. Nevertheless, it seems unlikely that Cavendish would have acquired sufficient Dutch to read de Veer's account, but what she could do was look at the plates. If anything, the illustrations are more dramatic than the text, and two in particular could have influenced Cavendish: the first, 'How a frightful, cruel, big bear tare to pieces two of our companions', and the fourth, 'How our ship stuck fast in the ice, whereby three of us were nearly lost', since they show the polar bear, ice mountains and ice floes. Indeed, *The Blazing World* includes its own 'bear-men' and 'fox-men' who act, respectively, as the lady's 'experimental philosophers' and 'politicians' (Salzman 1991: 261). Indeed, de Veer's illustrations reach back to the medieval itineraries in which the cartographic road map is abandoned for the sensational sites along the route. While Cavendish's interest in polar navigation does not gender the concept of travel in the same way that her depiction of post-Civil-War voyages does, the key elements of material danger and an evasion of scientific discourse recur. The women blown off course in 'The Claspe' and *The Blazing World* face, therefore, not only the hardships of life in exile but also the threat of isolation and attack in strange lands, and in both cases the terms used to describe their situations eschew philosophical allegories for hard and immediate reality.

In bringing together danger and isolation, Cavendish is, in many ways, identifying the fundamental experiences of the exiled Royalists, a point that is made again when she describes in *The Blazing World* how the lady is rescued and taken by the inhabitants of the blazing world to their capital city through the waterways of a delta:

> a great number of vast and large rivers, all ebbing and flowing into several islands of unequal distance from one each other, which in most parts were as pleasant, healthful, rich and fruitful as nature could make them and, as I mentioned before, secure from all foreign invasions, by reason that there was but one way to enter and that like a labyrinth. (Salzman 1991: 258)

The delta is based upon Antwerp and Cavendish could well have been drawing on Speed's map of the Netherlands, with its clear depiction of the 'large rivers' and the islands of 'unequal distance'. At the same time, she would also have drawn upon her own personal experience of visiting Rotterdam and living in Antwerp. The most telling aspect of this seemingly fictional delta is, however, that it is 'secure'. Indeed, as an exiled Royalist, she, like her husband and Prince Charles, would have been grateful of the protection that the delta provided. In a wider context, Emma Rees points out that both '*Assaulted and Pursued Chastity* and *Blazing World* relate directly to the experiences and affiliations of the [Royalists] during the Interregnum' (Rees 2003: 15). As such, at the beginning of the journey to the blazing world, the description of location is, within Cavendish's contemporary knowledge, accurate. But the material aspects of personal experience and knowledge of cartography and polar exploration must be set alongside the fantastical diversity of the fiction, with its bear-men and fox-men.

It is almost as if, when the lady reaches the blazing world, she enters Cavendish's imagination and acts out the author's 'philosophical fancies'. In this return to imaginative prose fiction, it is not surprising that the Emperor of the blazing world falls in love with the lady and she is elevated to the position of Empress, nor that, from this elevated position, she is able to develop her own cabbala, or system of philosophical knowledge. Indeed, it is the cabbala that allows Cavendish to draw further away from the earlier material realities of the text. The Empress realises that she will require someone to write down her words and so asks the spirits of the blazing world to provide her with a scribe; they reply, 'there's a lady, the Duchess of Newcastle, which although she is not one of the most learned, eloquent, witty and ingenious, yet she is a plain and rational writer' (Salzman 1991: 306). Thus, in a convoluted narrative stratagem, Cavendish the author introduces into *The Blazing World* a fictional second self, 'the Duchess of Newcastle', who will enable another Cavendish persona, the Empress, to write her own philosophical treatise that, of course, espouses exactly the same cabbala as Cavendish herself. To add to these contortions, the Empress determines that by choosing a female scribe the Emperor will have no cause for jealousy, to which the spirit replies, 'In truth ... husbands have reason to be jealous of Platonic lovers, for they are very dangerous, as being not only very intimate and close, but subtle and insinuating' (Salzman 1991: 306). Platonic female relationships are foregrounded in the text as 'dangerous' and the spirit's warning of a possible erotic attachment is reinforced as the Empress salutes her scribe with 'a spiritual kiss' (Salzman 1991: 307).

The possible eroticism of the female relationships further complicates the assemblage of authorial selves (Cavendish, the Empress and the 'Duchess of Newcastle') who must now represent the similitude of a single authorial identity, as well as the difference of two sexually attracted women. In so doing Cavendish steps back from the harsh realities of travelling and re-enters the omnipresent overview seen in Speed's maps where material and spiritual spheres merge on the page. Indeed, the real Duchess of Newcastle is transposed into a soul so that she may commune with the spirit of the fictional and philosophical Empress. Moreover, as an authorial second self merges with the protagonist of a romantic narrative and the fantastical utopia turns into a philosophical treatise, it is apt to recall Maslen's assertion that early modern prose is 'slippery' and Pooley's comment that it uses multiple 'genres'.

It is at this internal moment, however, when authors and texts almost unite as a lone author in a single interior world, that Cavendish alters the focus and draws us back to the material realities of her road map, because in the next section of the book the Duchess takes the Empress to visit her own world, mid-seventeenth-century England. The following accounts of the 'majesty and affability' of the King and Queen and the lamentable ruin and destruction of the Civil War (Salzman 1991: 317–18) are predictable within the historical context, but they are brief. Rather, Cavendish focuses upon the journey north 'some 112 miles off' to

> Nottinghamshire (for that was the place the Duke [of Newcastle] did reside), passing through the forest of Sherwood, the Empress's soul was very much delighted with it, being a dry, plain and woody place, very pleasant to travel in both in Winter and Summer, for it is neither much dirty nor dusty at no time. At last they arrived at Wellbeck, a house where the Duke dwelled, surrounded all with a wood so close and full that the Empress took great pleasure and delight therein. (Salzman 1991: 318)

And, of course, Cavendish is right. The distance between London and Nottinghamshire is about 120 miles and the description of Sherwood Forest was – and is – accurate. Again, we can look at one of Speed's map of Nottinghamshire and trace how the two women would have travelled through Sherwood Forest to Welbeck Abbey, following roughly the route the A60 takes today. Moreover, when the Empress and Duchess arrive at Welbeck they describe it as surrounded by a wood, again an accurate fact evidenced by a contemporary engraving of the house in William Cavendish's *A New Method and Extraordinary Invention to Dress Horses* (1667) and Margaret's own comments in *The Life of William Cavendish, Duke of Newcastle* (1667) that,

> Of eight parks, which my Lord had before the wars, there was but one left that was not quite destroyed, viz. Welbeck Park. Of about four miles' compass. (Cavendish 1906: 70–1)

Similarly, when they see William Cavendish come 'into the court to see his horses of manage' she depicts an accurate event in which her husband did inspect his 'manage', or management of his stable, as is again evidenced by an engraving in *A New Method and Extraordinary Invention to Dress Horses*. Finally, when the Duchess describes her Lord's other residence, Bolsover Castle, as 'a naked house and unclothed of all furniture', she again describes the actual state of the castle after the plundering of the Parliamentarian troops during the Civil War. These material instances provide the reader almost with a map of Nottinghamshire that focuses upon Sherwood Forest, Welbeck Abbey and Bolsover Castle. Indeed, the two women are envisaged, not travelling along the roads in a coach, but floating above the whole country as 'two female souls' who are made of 'the purest and finest sort of air and of a human shape' (Salzman 1991: 318), who see the roads, forests and houses laid out beneath them.

However, the arrival of the 'souls' at Welbeck predicates a shift, once again, from material reality to internal quest. As the Empress and Duchess watch William Cavendish riding and fencing, the latter expresses a common-sense concern about her husband's digestion and immediately enters his body. This astonishing merging of soul and flesh is further complicated when the Empress joins her friend, so that 'the Duke had three souls in one body' (Salzman 1991: 319). William Cavendish is so 'wise, honest, witty, complaisant and noble' that the Empress and he soon become 'enamoured of each other' (Salzman 1991: 319), making the Duchess, his wife, a little jealous. But she pacifies herself on realising that since they are all souls and Platonic lovers 'no adultery could be committed' (Salzman 1991: 319). Since the spirits have already warned of the dangers of Platonic love, however, the possibility of a dangerous erotic attachment remains, allowing Cavendish to explore a different perspective within this section of the text. In the fantastical narrative the Empress and Duchess, both authorial second selves, via the movement of their 'souls', inhabit the single material form of William Cavendish, in which a battle between friendship and erotic attraction is enacted. Moreover, it is only by accepting the possibilities of a fictional world that such fluidity becomes realisable. The rational perspective of cartography is invoked, therefore, precisely so that it may be set alongside the inner journey of Cavendish's own creation that is then sustained until the end of the narrative. There is, however, one final twist along the road back from the Blazing World.

At the end of the fictional narrative Cavendish adds an 'Epilogue to the Reader' in which she analyses her own text:

> By this poetical description you may perceive that my ambition is not only to be Empress but authoress of a whole world ... For concerning the philosophical world, I am Empress of it myself, and as for the Blazing World, it having an Empress already who rules it with great wisdom and conduct, which Empress is my dear Platonic friend. (Salzman 1991: 347–8)

As such, the Duchess of Newcastle is both the author of the 'philosophical world', that is, the scientific *Observations upon Experimental Philosophy*, and therefore Margaret Cavendish, while at the same time being the Empress's 'Platonic friend', in other words, a fictional character, the Duchess of Newcastle. The Epilogue makes perfect sense as an address to the reader by the actual author, who refers to the earlier scientific treatise, acknowledging the employment of a formal literary technique of parallel worlds. Yet, at the same time, the Epilogue also has substance as a continuum of the literary prose in which Cavendish retains the guise of a fictional second self. The rational view of the text may thus move outwards to an overview of authorial presence and contemporary relevance, while at the same time using the 'natural eye' of the imagination to suggest a journey of the philosophical soul in search of truth.

Margaret Cavendish's *The Blazing World* may, at first, appear to be an almost nostalgic yearning for the past forms and certainties of the medieval itinerary. Correspondingly, at times it seems like a typical example of early modern prose, combining that excessive use of diversity, strangeness and disconcerting multiplicity Rob Maslen describes as 'slippery'. Then again, it recalls the scientific skills of mapmaking, as the lady's and Duchess's travels merge into a spiritual quest of the soul across a fraught and unknown landscape that must lead to a philosophical truth. But Cavendish creates potholes along her fantastical and philosophical roads. These are the destabilising modalities along her spatial syntax. For in her post-Civil-War world the road has become dangerous, women travellers face rape, destitution and venereal disease, while scientific exploration challenges the Christian overview of cartography. Even as Cavendish creates the feminised and philosophised utopia in the Blazing World, she cannot help but respond to the radical changes that have blazed through the real world, making it a much more dangerous place to travel through, especially if you're a woman. Perhaps, then, when we read *The Blazing World* today, we should not look back to early modern prose and Speed's spiritual certainties, but recognise the work as a precursor of the next stage of prose fiction. Strange creatures, polar exploration, the dangers of science, fraught sexual relationships, and a woman's take on all these – *The Blazing World* is not so much a last-ditch example of early modern prose fiction as a signpost along the road from Cavendish's 'blazing world' to the 'frozen wastes' of Mary Shelley's *Frankenstein*.

Works cited

Bowerbank, Sylvia (1984), 'The Spider's Delight: Margaret Cavendish and the Female Imagination', *English Literary Renaissance* 14, pp. 392–408.
Cavendish, Margaret (1653), *Poems and Fancies*, London.
—— (1656), *Natures Pictures Drawn by Fancies Pencil to the Life*, London.
—— (1662), *Orations of Divers Sorts Accommodated to Divers Places*, London.
—— (1664), *Sociable Letters*, London.
—— (1666), *Observations upon Experimental Philosophy; To which is added The Description of a New Blazing World*, London.

—— (1906), *The Life of William Cavendish Duke of Newcastle*, London: Routledge.
—— (1994), *The Blazing World and Other Writings*, ed. Kate Lilley, London: Penguin.
Cavendish, William (1667), *A New Method and Extraordinary Invention to Dress Horses*, London.
Certeau, Michel de (1984), *The Practice of Everyday Life*, trans. Steven Rendall, Berkeley: University of California Press.
Maslen, R. W. (1997), *Elizabethan Fictions: Espionage, Counter-Espionage and the Duplicity of Fiction in Early Elizabethan Prose Narratives*, Oxford English Monographs, Oxford: Clarendon Press.
Pooley, Roger (1992), *English Prose of the Seventeenth Century 1590–1700*, London: Routledge.
Rees, Emma (2003), *Margaret Cavendish: Gender, Genre, Exile*, Manchester: Manchester University Press.
Salzman, Paul (1985), *English Prose Fiction, 1558–1700: A Critical History*, Oxford: Clarendon Press.
—— (ed.) (1991), *An Anthology of Seventeenth-Century Fiction*, Oxford: Oxford University Press.
Speed, John (1627), *A Prospect of the Most Famous Parts of the World*, London.
Veer, Gerrit de (2010), *A true Description of three Voyages by the North-East towards Cathay and China, undertaken by the Dutch in the Years 1594, 1595, and 1596*, ed. Charles T. Beke, Farnham: Ashgate.
Whitaker, Katie (2002), *Mad Madge: Margaret Cavendish, Duchess of Newcastle, Royalist, Writer and Romantic*, London: Chatto & Windus.
Woolf, Virginia (1925), *The Common Reader*, London: Hogarth Press.

Chapter 13

'The King's Highway': Reading England's Road in *The Pilgrim's Progress, Part I*

Martha Lynn Russell

Much scholarship has been focused on the religious, spiritual and theological components of John Bunyan's *The Pilgrim's Progress*, but although this lens is consistent with Bunyan's stated goal of writing his hero's journey as a religious allegory, it proves to be too narrow in understanding the complexities of the enduring work. This chapter continues the history of studying Bunyan's masterpiece by taking scholarship to a new, understudied area: seventeenth-century infrastructure. I argue that Bunyan's world, from the City of Destruction to the Celestial City, is not only a metaphorical journey, but also the real landscape of England; therefore, Bunyan's roads are not just spiritual paths, but very much literal roads reminiscent of roads and road systems in seventeenth-century England. The material reality of these roads reveals Bunyan's religious and political views on English Puritanism and the reign of Charles II.

There is no dearth of scholarship on *The Pilgrim's Progress*. Though academic interest in the text has fluctuated, about fifty years ago there was a large resurgence of Bunyan scholars and publications. In 1971, Stanley Fish published his argument about Bunyan's fictional journey, entitled 'Progress in *The Pilgrim's Progress*', in which he argued that though Christian makes physical progress to the Heavenly City, he makes no progress spiritually. Fish suggests that, throughout the whole book, Christian is stuck in a cycle of repeating sins, learning nothing from his journey and making no real progress (Fish 1971: 261). Since Fish's publication, other scholars have both praised and critiqued his argument. For example, Edward Philips believes that Stanley Fish's view of the journey metaphor is flawed because Fish has only one view of journey as progress; Philips disagrees by quoting the *Oxford English Dictionary*'s definition of progress as the act of travelling – neither physical nor spiritual, and, importantly, not directional (Philips 1980). More recent scholarship has taken an interest in the international influence of *The Pilgrim's Progress*. In *The Portable Bunyan: A Transnational History of The Pilgrim's Progress*, Isabel Hofmeyr called Bunyan's book a 'transnational and translingual text', taking up residency in a multitude of different countries, including India and China, with eighty of the translations taking place in Africa (Hofmeyr 2004: 3). It has taken many forms such as abridged versions, children's illustrated classics, print episodes in newspapers, radio adaptations, drama, films, and been rewritten into poetry.

This chapter adds to this vast conversation on travel and geography by refocusing it in a different direction: England's topography and infrastructure. I am still working with the book's foundational theme of progress, but instead of viewing progress as spiritual or theological, which has been studied by scholars such as David Walker (1998), I am studying progress as a physical act, set in physical places in the locale of England. My local focus on the text is not new, as both Albert Foster and Vera Brittain have written about the correlation of the landmarks of Elstow, the town nearest Bunyan's home, to the places in *The Pilgrim's Progress* (Foster 1911; Brittain 1949). However, since the publication of these books, further geospatial studies on early modern England have been made, and these earlier readings are in need of re-evaluation. But I also want to deviate from Foster's and Brittain's works by focusing not on landmarks but rather on infrastructural systems, such as the highway systems, drainage systems and the fair system. Though there are several landmarks that correlate to the landmarks of Christian's world in seventeenth-century England, I am far more interested in studying how Bunyan is influenced by his environment, both the landscape and politics of seventeenth-century infrastructure – and is thus, in effect, writing the road of England.

This chapter will first discuss how *The Pilgrim's Progress* fits into the tradition of road narratives through the lens of the travel narrative theory in order to understand England's system of denizens as the basis from which Bunyan gets his ideas for his pilgrim's citizenship. Next, it will argue that Bunyan's road, from the City of Destruction to the Celestial City, is not just a spiritual journey: Bunyan's road is also a literal journey along the seventeenth-century Great North Road. Lastly, it will examine three particular English systems along the roads of England – turnpike, drainage and fairs – in order to compare them to Bunyan's world and determine how Bunyan uses these systems to offer political and religious commentary on the role of government and on his Dissenting views.

'Writing of the way': travel narrative theory

Although the road that takes Christian from spiritual death to spiritual life is assuredly the controlling metaphor of Bunyan's novel, I contend he also intertwines the classical travel narrative and England's process of denization to create a metaphor that functions on multiple levels, one far more complex than the simple metaphor of life-as-a-journey. With this lens, scholars should see this not merely as a religious and metaphorical work, but as a work that allows the intersection of the spiritual with the practical and the metaphorical with the political, specifically in the way it merges physical and spiritual travel narratives and the political and spiritual denization and citizenship of Bunyan's time. Bunyan's work should not be studied only as a religious text, but as a text that intersects with the politics of Bunyan's day, with genre theory, and with material reality.

One of the most prominent, and most discussed, metaphors in *The Pilgrim's Progress* is the book's obvious metaphor for the Christian life. The book is laden with characters whose names represent Christian virtues, sins and spiritual places. On a large scale, the road that takes Christian from the City of Destruction to the Celestial City is John Bunyan's perspective on the progress from unbelieving, to salvation, and finally to heaven – a path that takes Christian from spiritual death to spiritual life.

Obviously, Bunyan chooses the medium of narrative to create his story. In recent scholarship, narrative theorists such as Jim Phelan, David Herman and Brian McHale have analysed this form to better understand how and why humans use written narratives. Narrative theory seeks to distinguish story from other written works such as lists, documents, poems, arguments and so on by defining it as its own unique agent for coming to terms with the human experience. This theory helps literary scholars make sense of the author's social, historical and spiritual world, as well as make sense of the nature of story. Bunyan's most remembered – and arguably most powerful – text, *The Pilgrim's Progress*, is written in narrative form, the story coming from his physical experiences, such as his imprisonment, travels as a preacher, and physical locations of residence, as well as his spiritual experiences of conversion, confession and testimony; therefore, through Bunyan's masterful interweaving of his physical and spiritual experiences, he understands his spiritual self in terms of his physical reality, using various common life experiences along the road of England to understand and communicate complex religious and political concepts.

But Bunyan's allegory is not merely a narrative, it is a travel narrative; and along with the genre of travel narrative comes certain reader expectations. In medieval and classical literature, for example, the travel narrative takes the form of epics, quests, odysseys and adventures, serving as a master-plot trope in early British literature. In these travel narratives, generally there is an overall arching plot of departure, voyage, encounters on the road, and return: Beowulf travels to the country of Hrothgar and returns having killed Grendel, and Sir Gawain leaves his homeland to encounter the Green Knight but eventually returns home a true knight (Mikkonen 2007). As for Christian, he leaves his home of the City of Destruction, voyages through the countryside, encounters people and beasts along the way – but he does not return to his original space, as do heroes like Beowulf and Gawain.

It would seem that *The Pilgrim's Progress* is breaking from the travel narrative tradition of Bunyan's time. Travel narrative (also called travel writing) was a popular commodity of the day; for example, Sir Thomas Herbert's *Some Years Travels into Divers Parts of Africa and Asia the Great* was published in 1634 and was widely read by English readers. Herbert was a low-ranking member of the court under the reign of Charles I who travelled to India and Persia to meet Shah Abbas I, King of Persia. The book recounts his experiences travelling through the Parthian desert to the Caspian Sea, then finally his return home. Another source of travel writing comes from almanac travel diaries, written by authors such as Lady Isabella Twysden and Anthony Wood, as well as the famed writer John Taylor, who travelled 200 miles around England before his death in 1653 and published over 400 lines of couplets in pamphlet form to record his journey (Ambrose 2013). Many of the travel narratives during the seventeenth century, regardless of whether they recounted domestic or international travel, ended with the author's return home. Christian's story does not seem to fit the mould of a travel narrative, since Christian ends in the Celestial City, not the City of Destruction, the place where he began.

Though it might seem that Christian's story is not a true travel narrative, I assert that he does embrace the travel metaphor as a true traveller through the use of the word 'home'. In the beginning of the book, Christian claims the City of Destruction as his home; one of his neighbours tells Christian, 'You dwell in the City of Destruction, the place also where I was born, I see it to be so' (Bunyan [1678] (2005): 18, hereafter page numbers only). Later in the allegory Christian faces Apollyon, who questions Christian's place of belonging and allegiance to the City of Destruction, to which Christian responds, 'I have given him [God] my Faith, and sworn my Allegiance to him, How then can

I go back from this, and not be hanged as a Traitor?' (66). Christian is saying here that if he goes back to the City of Destruction, he will be a traitor to the Celestial City – his true home, rejecting his allegiance to the City of Destruction in place of his true belonging to the Celestial City.

Therefore, though Christian leaves home, he also goes home, which by definition completes the travel narrative structure. This is significant because Bunyan's use of the travel narrative structure is not just a tribute to classical literature, it is a tribute to biblical language. In the New Testament, Paul tells the church at Philippi that '*our citizenship is in heaven*, and from it we await a Saviour, the Lord Jesus Christ', and in Peter's first letter to churches in Asia Minor, he pens, 'Dear friends, I urge you, *as foreigners and exiles*, to abstain from sinful desires, which wage war against your soul' (Philippians 3: 20; 1 Peter 2: 11, emphases mine). Both of these examples link the binary of heaven and hell to the language of citizenship and foreigner in much the same way that Christian identifies himself as a traitor to the City of Destruction and as belonging to the Celestial City.

In the text, Christian and Hopeful are able to enter the gates at the Celestial City because they both have their certificates. Here, Bunyan is no longer linking his work to other classical texts but is rather incorporating the laws of England within the road narrative. When Bunyan was writing his allegory, the Alien Act of 1705 and the 1707 Act of Union had not yet been written, so Bunyan's England would still have been functioning under thirteenth-century rules about citizenship. Under this tradition, citizens received their status in two different ways: through being born in England or through denization. The process of denization required a person not born in England to obtain letters patent from government officials, pay a small fee, and take the oath of allegiance to the monarch in power. If a person became a denizen, he had the ability to own land, vote, and make his permanent residence in England, but without the paperwork, oath and fee, he lacked citizenship and legal rights.

This concept of denization is evidenced in the character of Christian. Though he is not a natural citizen of the Celestial City, he is a denizen of the Celestial City, having all of the privileges of a citizen. Ignorance, meanwhile, is neither a citizen nor a denizen. When he comes to the gates of the Celestial City, he claims, 'I have eat and drank in the Presence of the King, and he has taught in our streets' (177), but the angels at the gate question him: 'Then they asked him for his Certificate, that they might go in and shew it to the King; so he fumbled in his bosom for one, and found none' (177). Though many scholars view this scene as a metaphor for Ignorance's lack of salvation, it is also reflective of the rules and laws of England at the time of Bunyan's writing. Since Ignorance does not have his legal denization or citizenship, he is not permitted to enter the gates. Though Bunyan spent twelve years in prison, his groundbreaking work views citizenship as positive. Bunyan believed in a heavenly government more than the flawed earthly government that put him in prison, yet he praises the patriotism of an earthly government because one's citizenship to heaven was a patriotism to a perfect ruler. And though Bunyan's views of the government changed from ruler to ruler, he still believed in a type of national pride and belonging to one's nation that intersects with his faith and loyalty to his God, even when an individual was not a natural born citizen to the nation or religion.

'Make a traveller of thee': England's Great North Road

Much scholarship has been completed on Bunyan's metaphorical road in *The Pilgrim's Progress*, but little research has been carried out into how Bunyan's roads are not only metaphorical but also literal. Christian's road is not simply a metaphor for life but also the literal road of England in the seventeenth century. His road takes him through gates, bogs and fairs which are generally studied in a metaphorical sense, but I argue that these are not just Bunyan's devices for religious commentary but actual experiences from his life of travel, intersecting with his religion, the geography of England, and his personal politics to provide commentary on the local and national roles of government.

In the beginning of *The Pilgrim's Progress*, Christian starts his one-path journey to the Celestial City. This one-path concept is not only an allegory for the path to heaven but is also reminiscent of one of England's major roads, the Great North Road, which was the main road out of London, spanning about 376 miles. It left London from two locations, Holborn and Shoreditch, and eventually merged in the town called Alconbury and headed north to the northern counties of England, ending in Berwick-upon-Tweed (Albert 1972: 33). During the seventeenth century, the Great North Road was the longest and most heavily travelled road in all of England, so it is virtually certain that Bunyan used this road as a travelling pastor. His home town of Elstow near Bedford was about eight miles from the road, so he probably used it often, as did his fellow businessmen and travellers.

A study of the Great North Road's geography can clear up a metaphorical controversy. Many scholars have debated whether Bunyan's metaphorical road is cyclical or linear. For example, in Thomas Hyatt Luxon's article 'The Pilgrim's Passive Progress' he argues that *The*

Pilgrim's Progress is cyclical because there is no spiritual progress in the book; Christian makes the same errors over and over again; and when he does make progress, it is God who actively progresses him forward, not Christian's own will (Luxon 1986). On a metaphorical level, Luxon and others have argued that Christian by the end has not made any spiritual progress forward; he keeps doubting and questioning his faith and travels throughout the whole narrative.

This idea that the physical road to the Celestial City has many roads that lead into the main one parallels the actual Great North Road. For example, though the Great North Road is one road that goes strictly north from London, it does not begin in once place. As mentioned, it begins in both Holborn and Shoreditch, then goes north to eventually converge into one road around Alconbury, so these two roads extend for about sixty miles before converging into one road; therefore, according to the road map of the seventeenth century, Hopeful's and Christian's beginnings at two different sites would be in linear accordance with the actual road of England.

In addition to shedding light on the linearity of Christian's journey, a study of the Great North Road as the literal road of England in his allegory illuminates Bunyan's political views about English tolls. One of the main functions of the Great North Road was the transportation of goods. During this period, the transportation of a company's or farm's products could increase the selling price by 66 per cent or, in some cases, seven times the local price (Albert 1972: 10). One of the reasons why the transportation cost was so high was due to poor roads that caused delayed travel, so in 1555 Parliament passed laws delegating road maintenance to local parishes. At this time, the parish repair system could adequately fix the road's problems because traffic was light and generally local. A century later, the financial burden of repairing the road became so great that parishes petitioned the government to be able to establish a toll. The Turnpike Act of 1663 temporarily gave parishes government support to enact a toll on the roads the parishes thought particularly busy, such as Wadesmill, Caxton and Stilton (Albert 1972: 20). In addition to the statute labour required by the parishes, Parliament established nine surveyors for each county to decide on the repairs needed for their particular portion of the road and also to designate toll-collectors and report receipts to Parliament (Albert 1972: 20).

By the time Bunyan wrote his work, the Turnpike Act of 1663 was well established, so Bunyan probably had to pay these tolls, especially as a travelling pastor. These tolls were generally collected at gates, where the gate-tender would take the wage for using the road and then open the gate to let travellers by. In *The Pilgrim's Progress*, Christian uses the Wicket Gate. There may be some humour in the choice of the word 'wicket' since it resembles the word 'wicked', which is possibly what Bunyan thought of the gate and toll systems of England. When Christian is on his way to the gate for the first time, he chooses to leave the path due to Mr Worldly Wiseman's counsel, but when he mends his error and finally reaches the Wicket Gate, all he needs to do is knock and the door will be open to him (32). This is of course a reference to the biblical passage in Matthew 7: 7, but I argue that Bunyan is also offering political commentary, because when Goodwill opens the gate, he does not require a toll. Christian simply asks, 'Since I am informed that by this Gate is the Way thither, know if you are willing to let me in?' to which Goodwill responds: '"I am willing with all my heart," he said; and with that he opened the Gate' (32). Here Bunyan is intertwining his belief that salvation is a choice, not a financial price, with the actual gates of England. Since Goodwill is the gatekeeper, he would be receiving the toll, yet he asks nothing but for travellers to knock, which reflects Bunyan's belief that salvation is free to humanity and that the physical gates of England should also be free to the people of England. By allowing the intersection of theology and politics, Bunyan is able to give commentary on both simultaneously. Walker argues that too much scholarship has focused on Bunyan's work as merely religious, which devalues the complexities of the book. He argues that Bunyan's pamphlets, specifically *The Doctrine of Law and Grace Unfolded*, document Bunyan's empowerment of the people to oppose authoritarian powers. And though Bunyan never mentions in this connection the actual government of England, Walker believes he greatly implies it. Though Walker's article does not prove that Bunyan despised the gate fee of the seventeenth century, it does open the door for analysing Bunyan as giving more commentary on the state of his world and government, not just religion (Walker 1998).

'This lusty fair': fair days in England

Bunyan integrates not only England's road system but also its system of fairs into his allegory. During this period, fairs were prominent means of selling goods to locals about once a year, as opposed to markets that sold on a weekly basis. The increase of fairs during this period was partly the result of readers' interest in almanacs prior to 1569, where almanacs were primarily read by educated Englishmen who were interested in astronomy, astrology, medicine and law (Hodgen 1942: 390). In 1560, Joachim Hubright published an almanac for the English traveller that listed various roads and fairs in England and in Wales. These almanacs were sold for a penny and became some of the most widely read books in the English language (Hodgen 1942: 390).

With the accessibility of the almanacs and the number of fairs in England, it is likely that Bunyan attended one in his home town. In Margaret Hodgen's comprehensive study of Elizabethan fairs in various towns in England and Wales, she documents the different fairs and fair sites by month, county and region. According to her study, the town of Bedford had eleven fair sites with a total of twenty-nine fairs per year, with most fairs occurring in the months of March, May, August and October (Hodgen 1942: 395). In addition, her research documents that the highest percentage of fairs – 21 per cent, exactly 212 fairs, of all of England and Wales – happened in the cities of Middlesex, Bedfordshire, Hertfordshire and Cambridgeshire, so it can be concluded that Bunyan was well aware of England's culture of fairs and most likely had attended several of them (Hodgen 1942: 392).

In many ways, Vanity Fair is much like the fairs of Bunyan's England. According to David Cameron in *The English Fair*, the nature and role of a fair changed very little from the medieval period up to the seventeenth century (Cameron 1988). Caravans and merchants were the chief sources of wholesale products for chapmen and peddlers, and for the most part were the only means of trading because conditions were so primitive, and due to the lack of banking developments (Cameron 1988: 21). Almost all fairs in England were located in towns much like the Town of Vanity. Though many readers of *The Pilgrim's Progress* read Vanity Fair as a town, it is actually a fair within a town: 'They presently saw a Town before them, and the name of that Town is *Vanity*, and at the Town there is a Fair kept, call *Vanity-Fair*' (98). Later, when the narrator tells the reader how the fair came into existence, he says that Beelzebub, Apollyon and Legion wanted to create a fair on the way to the Celestial City that 'sold all Sorts of Vanity' (99). And of course, as readers know, one of the reasons why Christian and Faithful are arrested is because they want to buy 'the Truth', while all the fair sells is vanity (101).

Bunyan keeps to the tradition of an English fair by having his fictional fair sell goods: 'The Town where it is kept, is lighter than Vanity; and also, because all that is there sold, or that cometh thither, is *Vanity*' (98–9). This was in accordance with English fairs that sold to its patrons merchandise such as food, household products and working tools, similar to what Vanity Fair sells to its customers: 'houses, lands, trades, places' (99). The list does not stop here, but rather continues to list other merchandise: 'kingdoms, lusts, pleasures; and delights of all sorts, as whores, bawds, wives, husbands, children, masters, servants, lives, blood, bodies, souls, silver, gold, pearls, precious stones, and what not' (99). Obviously, Bunyan goes beyond the typical merchandise of a common fair, ironically putting the common currency of the time, silver, next to the word 'souls'. He could be commenting on two aspects of English life; he could be commenting on his perception of the debauchery that sometimes happened at fairs, but he could also be commenting on the apparently demonic belief that souls and money are worth the same, or of no worth at all. This could be Bunyan's commentary on the physical fair's devaluing of human life, equating it to commercialisation and nascent capitalism, and also on what Bunyan believed evil valued – power over human worth. And in terms of Bunyan's belief that his fellow Englishmen should not have to pay for tolls, he also appears to suggest that items at a fair should be either fairly priced or not sold at all. Bunyan's ideal toll and fair would place Englishmen themselves of ultimate value – not capitalistic hunger for money and power that devalues and defaces human worth.

Bunyan also deviates from the standard English fair in Vanity Fair's length. About 51 per cent of almanacs printed during this time described one-day fairs, 26 per cent of fairs were listed as two-day fairs, and 22 per cent of fairs were three days in duration. Occasionally, there are documented fairs that lasted from ten to fifteen days, especially in the northern counties where fairs were scarce. For example, the county of Kent has a record of forty-two fairs of ten days' length or more, and the county of Essex has a record of eight fairs that lasted for more than ten days (Hodgen 1942: 397). Fairs were of a periodic and discontinuous nature and were usually in accordance with different harvest times of the year; they were almost never scheduled during the months of December and January due to the extreme weather conditions.

Yet Bunyan wants his readers to understand that his fictional fair runs all year long, which would have been unheard of during this time in England, stating the fact twice in the text. When it is first introduced to the reader, the narration states, 'At the Town there is a Fair kept, called Vanity-Fair: it is kept all year long' and when the narrator is speaking about its history, he says that Beelzebub, Apollyon and Legion meant to have the fair run all year long: 'They contrived here to set up a Fair; a Fair, wherein should be sold all Sorts of Vanity, and that it should last all the year long' (98–9). In other words, Vanity Fair does not just happen to run all year long; the town's establisher meant it to run all year long. The fact that this year-long fair did not exist in seventeenth-century England seems to suggest a commentary on capitalism, commerce and money. The fair serves as an intersection between politics and religion by suggesting human life is of equal or less value than money. Just as the founders of Vanity Fair did not care that they were marginalising and exploiting people, so Bunyan suggests that the people of his era cared more about making money and advancing commerce than they valued human life and freedom. Therefore, Vanity Fair functions as an object of commentary on both the religious and political beliefs of Bunyan's day.

'This plat is not mended': Bunyan's bogs and politics

Not only are Bunyan's roads and fairs based heavily on the actual systems of seventeenth-century England, but so are his bogs, such as the seemingly allegorical Slough of Despond. In both sixteenth- and seventeenth-century Europe, wetland reclamation projects were in their heyday. They started in Italy, then moved to the Dutch Republic and Germany, and then eventually came to France and England in the seventeenth century. Though there are numerous reasons for this interest in drainage, these projects were mostly driven by demographic growth that caused grain prices to rise and large-scale export commerce to become more expensive, resulting in the need for more workable soil and shorter passageways to sell the harvest. Prior to 1500, drainage was an endeavour by local landlords, but after 1500, drainage projects became more wide-scale, generally funded by the country's government; these government-run projects were sometimes unwelcomed by lords, cities and religious institutions and sometimes occasioned riots, sabotage and costly litigations (van Cruyningen 2015: 421–2).

During this time, England was having its own drainage problems. James I implemented the General Drainage Act of 1600 which was meant to aid in draining the Fens; later, Charles I enacted a large-scale drainage project in the 1620s, but because he was not willing to negotiate and compromise with the commoners, he was met with much opposition, thus all seventeenth-century drainage projects in the Fenlands, Hatfield Chase and the Somerset Levels were confronted by riots and litigations. Under Charles I's rule, all drained wetlands were converted into government property because Charles believed that technological improvements were more important than property rights, so he would send in teams of surveyors to drain these bogs.

The political problems of bogging and surveyors appear in Christian's adventure with the Slough of Despond. When Christian comes to the slough, the narrator gives his readers some commentary about the reason why the slough is still a slough:

> It is not the pleasure of the King that this place should remain so bad; his labourers also have, by the directions of his Majesties Surveyors, been for above the sixteen hundred years employ'd about this patch of ground, if perhaps it might have been mended: Yea, and to my knowledge, said he, here hath been swallowed up at least twenty thousand cart loads. (22–3)

As evidenced here, Bunyan is using the general seventeenth-century drainage system to describe whether the bog can be fixed. What is interesting about this passage is that the King of the Celestial City does not have the power to fix the Slough of Despond. The text later mentions that the 'Lawgiver' places 'good and substantial Steps' so that travellers can get through the 'Midst of this Slough', but the slough itself is completely unfixable (23).

On a theological level, this unfixable Slough of Despond represents the doubts that a Christian would go through after conversion. In David Alff's article 'Why No One Can Mend the Slough of Despond', he discusses how roads were prone to bogging, which means that Christian's Slough of Despond is more realistic than hyperbolic (Alff 2013). Since bogging was quickly fixed, Alff concludes that the Slough of Despond was unfixable because otherwise it would have already been fixed by this time, and further argues that Bunyan's irredeemable Slough of Despond represents the doubts after one converts to Christianity; therefore, by making the bog unfixable, Bunyan communicates that everyone must go through doubts after conversion – there is no way to avoid the bog.

Bunyan's slough makes sense on a theological level but also on a material level. Why would he have the King of the Celestial City, a King he admires and loves, complete the same duties as the King of England, a government that Bunyan so ardently hates? The answer lies within the account of history. During England's Civil War, drainage projects collapsed and were abandoned so many villagers were able to gain back their stolen land. Though many people associate drainage projects with monarchists like Charles I, Cromwell (under whom Bunyan served) actually supported drainage projects, only with much less coercive state power, and when Charles II ascended the throne during the Restoration, he re-established drainage projects and agreed with Cromwell that people should not have to give up property for their wetlands to be drained (van Cruyningen 2015: 436).

We generally view Bunyan as anti-government, but he actually approved of Puritan Cromwell – sending a Bedfordshire document to the Lord Protector lauding his actions and suggesting two magistrates for the Assembly (Sadler 1979: 20–1). If he did hate a government, it would be the Royalist government. His father was an Anglican Royalist who frustrated Bunyan by conceding so placidly to the national government.

Even Bunyan's long imprisonment, though he was punished for unlicensed preaching, was due in part to his anti-Royalist views; when Charles II ascended the throne, freeing many prisoners all over England, Bunyan was not one of them (Sadler 1979: 20–1).

So with Cromwell starting the drainage projects near Bunyan's town, the writer might not have been as angry when Charles II picked up where Cromwell left off. Specifically in the town closest to Bunyan's home, Parliament passed the 1663 Act for the Bedford Level Corporation which established the Commissioners of Sewers of the Great Level. These commissioners were dedicated to resolving government and civilian disputes about wetland drainage; in some cases, these officials had the authority to give financial compensation for past years of damaged or stolen property. Because of this system, litigations and riots were few and far between. According to van Cruyningen, 'The Act for the Bedford Level Corporation seems to have functioned well. It gave the drainage for the Fens the secure legal grounding that it had previously lacked and established processes to resolve disputes in what remained an insecure and fragile environment' (van Cruyningen 2015: 436). He also notes that although this act worked well, other drainage acts throughout England did not follow Bedford's example, and thus drainage riots were still prevalent in other counties throughout England up until the late eighteenth century (van Cruyningen 2015: 436).

Though it is peculiar, given Bunyan's Dissenting views, that Bunyan has the King of the Celestial City take on a similar role to England's king, it could be inferred that if Bunyan approved of the 1663 Act, then he might have approved of the Celestial King trying to fix the bogs, especially since the English government was trying to compensate people for what they had done – which might have pleased Bunyan because, in this, the government is admitting its previous mistake. And if this assumption is correct, then Bunyan's depiction of the King as similar to the King of England would not be a contradiction of Bunyan's political beliefs. The Heavenly King and the King of England are trying to mend the bogs out of concern for their subjects, not to exploit them.

In conclusion, these studies in the roads of England bring new meanings and clarity to Bunyan's layered metaphor. Although this chapter covers the relationship of Christian's journey to national roads, bogs, tolls and fairs, other infrastructure correlations were outside the scope of this project, and I did not analyse the road correlations in Christiana's story, nor how they compare to Christian's roads. As English infrastructure and literature become a new avenue of scholarship for *The Pilgrim's Progress*, so will the road traditions and political controversies of England be further revealed in the pages of this masterpiece.

Works cited

Albert, William (1972), *The Turnpike Road System in England 1663–1840*, Cambridge: Cambridge University Press.
Alff, David (2013), 'Why No One Can Mend the Slough of Despond', *Eighteenth Century: Theory and Interpretation* 54.3, pp. 375–92.
Ambrose, Laura Williamson (2013), 'Travel in Time: Local Travel Writing and Seventeenth-Century English Almanacs', *Journal of Medieval and Early Modern Studies* 43.2, pp. 419–43, <https://doi.org/10.1215/10829636-2082023> (last accessed 23 May 2019).
The Bible (2009), English Standard Version, Oxford: Oxford University Press.
Brittain, Vera (1949), *In the Steps of John Bunyan*, London: Rich & Cowan.
Bunyan, John [1678] (2005), *The Pilgrim's Progress*, Uhrichsville, OH: Barbour.
Cameron, David Kerr (1988), *The English Fair*, Stroud: Sutton.
Crisp, Peter (2003), 'Allegory, Maps, and Modernity: Cognitive Change from Bunyan to Forster', *Mosaic* 4, pp. 49–64.
Cruyningen, Piet van (2015), 'Dealing with Drainage: State Regulation of Drainage Projects in the Dutch Republic, France, and England during the Sixteenth and Seventeenth Centuries', *Economic History Review* 68.2, pp. 420–40.
Dunan-Page, Anne (2006), *Grace Overwhelming: John Bunyan, The Pilgrim's Progress and the Extremes of the Baptist Mind*, Bern: Peter Lang.
Fish, Stanley Eugene (1971), 'Progress in *The Pilgrim's Progress*', *English Literary Renaissance* 1.3 (Autumn), pp. 261–93.
Foster, Albert J. (1911), *Bunyan's Country: Studies in the Topography of Pilgrim's Progress*, London: H. Virtue.
Hodgen, Margaret T. (1942), 'Fairs of Elizabethan England', *Economic Geography* 18.4, pp. 389–400.
Hofmeyr, Isabel (2004), *The Portable Bunyan: A Transnational History of The Pilgrim's Progress*, Princeton: Princeton University Press.
Luxon, Thomas Hyatt (1986), 'The Pilgrim's Passive Progress: Luther and Bunyan on Talking and Doing, Word and Way', *ELH* 1, pp. 73–98.
Maclean, Margaret (2015), '17th Century Adventures in Travel Writing', University of Leicester Library Special Collections, 7 January 2015, <http://staffblogs.le.ac.uk/specialcollections/2015/01/07/17th-century-adventures-in-travel-writing/> (last accessed 23 May 2019).
Mikkonen, Kai (2007), 'The "Narrative Is Travel" Metaphor: Between Spatial Sequence and Open Consequence', *Narrative* 15.3, pp. 286–305.
Philips, Edward (1980), 'The Journey in *The Pilgrim's Progress*', in Vincent Newey (ed.), *The Pilgrim's Progress: Critical and Historical Views*, Liverpool: Liverpool University Press, pp. 111–17.
Sadler, Lynn Veach (1979), *John Bunyan*, Boston: Twayne.
Walker, David (1998), '"Heaven Is Prepared for Whosoever Will Accept of It": Politics of the Will in Bunyan's "Doctrine of Law and Grace Unfolded" (1659)', *Prose Studies* 21.3 (December), pp. 19–31.
Znojemska, Helen (1999), 'From Bunyan's *Pilgrim's Progress* to Hawthorne's "Celestial Rail-Road"', *Litteraria Pragensia* 10.19, pp. 16–22.

Conclusion
Lisa Hopkins and Bill Angus

It is no surprise that the essays in this volume collectively show that while a road in early modern literature might sometimes be an actual road, it was never *just* a road. Todd Borlik and Laurie Johnson both pay attention to the practicalities of road travel, with Borlik reminding us that for early modern audiences and readers roads were inextricably connected with horses, and Johnson considering the experience of travelling along the road which led to the Newington Butts playhouse. But Borlik traces ways in which the price of oats has metaphorical and literal consequences and Johnson shows that the road was also an edge, staking out territorial demarcations in the present and memorialising older geographies. The road as edge is an idea also taken up in the chapters by Lisa Hopkins, Bill Angus, Jennifer Allport Reid and Paul Frazer, all of which reveal that roads can be places where quotidian space borders the otherworld.

Karalyn Dokurno and Alice Equestri both draw attention to the important link between roads and vagrancy, which is especially resonant for drama because actors themselves might be construed as vagrants. The fact that one might meet fools or homeless wanderers on roads made them potentially dangerous; Dokurno, Kim Durban, Sharon Emmerichs and Marion Wynne-Davies remind us both that roads were experienced differently by women and by men and that roads are also spaces in their own right and places in which things happen. Finally Wynne-Davies and Martha Lynn Russell develop further ways in which literal roads acquire metaphorical meanings, showing how spiritual overtones accrue to physical journeys.

At the same time, though, roads in drama and prose often *were* real roads: Robert Stagg explores how the march of a foot along the road is echoed in the marching feet of verse, Wynne-Davies, Hopkins, Angus, Reid and Russell all relate fictional roads to actual ones which can still be traced today, and Durban's mapping of Brome's imagined Antipodes on to the real thing shows some surprising points of correspondence. All roads run in two directions, and these essays show that roads in early modern literature similarly have two separate but coterminous existences, as real places which are also simultaneously symbolic spaces. In this sense, roads are the perfect image for the ways in which early modern prose and plays offer to transport readers and audiences from the place they occupy to places they are invited to imagine. We hope the highways and crossways of these essays have enabled readers also to take up this invitation to imagine another world.

Notes on Contributors

Bill Angus is Lecturer in Early Modern Literature at Massey University in New Zealand. He has written extensively on metadrama and the informer figure in early modern drama. His first two monographs are *Metadrama and the Informer in Shakespeare and Jonson* (2016) and *Intelligence and Metadrama in the Early Modern Theatre* (2018), both with Edinburgh University Press, and he has published articles on early modern drama, music and material culture. He is currently finishing his fourth book, on the physical crossroads in early modern literature and culture, encompassing histories of place magic, judicial execution, burial regulation, wandering spirits, religious ritual, and transformative and binding power.

Todd Borlik is Senior Lecturer in Renaissance Literature at the University of Huddersfield. He is the author of *Ecocriticism and Early Modern English Literature* (Routledge), *Literature and Nature in the English Renaissance: An Ecocritical Anthology* (Cambridge), and over a dozen articles in journals such as *Shakespeare*, *Shakespeare Quarterly*, *Shakespeare Survey* and *Medieval and Renaissance Drama in England*. He is currently at work on a monograph about the environmental politics of Shakespeare's late plays.

Karalyn Dokurno is a PhD candidate in the Department of English, Theatre, Film & Media at the University of Manitoba. Her research focuses on representations of early modern British women's travel c. 1590–1670, from Shakespeare to the early Quakers.

Kim Durban trained as a teacher in South Australia, then as a director at the Victorian College of the Arts. Over the last thirty-three years she has built a strong reputation as a director of both new plays and classic texts for theatres across Australia, including Melbourne Theatre Company,

State Theatre of South Australia, Queensland Theatre Company, Playbox, La Mama Theatre and Red Stitch Theatre. In 2001, Kim was appointed Senior Lecturer in Performing Arts at Federation University Australia, situated in the regional city of Ballarat. There her productions have included *Margaret of Anjou*, *Machinal*, *Ant + Cleo*, *The Tempest*, *A Little Touch of Chaos*, *Much Ado About Nothing*, *Murder on the Ballarat Train*, *The Hatpin* and *Kiss Me, Kate*. She is currently the Program Coordinator of the Bachelor of Acting for Stage and Screen and Bachelor of Contemporary Performance Practice undergraduate degrees. Kim is the winner of a 2015 Vice Chancellor's Citation for Teaching Excellence, the 2012 EJ Barker Fellowship, a 2010 Australian Learning and Teaching Council Citation, the Yvonne Taylor Award for Directors in 2002 and joint winner of the 1990 Ewa Czajor Memorial Award. She has a current entry in the *Who's Who of Australian Women*, and her PhD on Caroline playwright Richard Brome, completed at La Trobe University, included Australian premieres of Brome's plays *The City Wit*, *The Antipodes*, *A Jovial Crew* and *Covent Garden Weeded* (renamed for Australian audiences as *Garden City Weeded*.)

Sharon Emmerichs is an Assistant Professor at the University of Alaska Anchorage and specialises in early modern drama, poetry and prose, with specific emphases on Shakespeare, feminist theory and ecocritical studies. Her secondary area of specialisation is medieval literature and her research spans everything from Beowulf to Milton. She received her MA and PhD from the University of Missouri and holds two bachelor's degrees, one in Speech-Language Pathology/Communicative Disorders from the University of New Mexico and the other in English Literature from the University of Oregon. Her published research focuses on landscape in Shakespeare's plays and examines how, when Shakespeare's characters transgress the culturally known and accepted meanings of various landscapes, they suffer moral degradation. She explores the link between humankind and its environments in the context of early modern culture and belief. Her publications include 'Shakespeare and the Landscape of Death: Crossing the Boundaries of Life and the Afterlife' (*Shakespeare: Journal of the British Shakespeare Association*, 2012) and 'Playing God: The Landscape of Resurrection in *Romeo and Juliet*' (*Cahiers Élisabéthains*, 2013).

Alice Equestri is Marie Skłodowska-Curie Fellow at the University of Sussex. She previously held fellowships in English Literature at the Universities of Venice Ca' Foscari and Padua. She received her PhD from the University of Padua in 2014. She was awarded the AIA/Carocci

Doctoral Dissertation Prize 2015. Her research interests include folly in early modern English literature, Robert Armin's works, Shakespeare's last plays, English verse translations of Italian *novelle* and connections between medieval and early modern English literature. She has published the monograph *'Armine . . . thou art a foole and knaue': The Fools of Shakespeare Romances* (Carocci, 2016), as well as articles in *Renaissance Studies*, *Notes and Queries*, *Cahiers Élisabéthains* and several book chapters.

Paul Frazer is a Senior Lecturer in Early Modern Literature at the University of Northumbria in Newcastle upon Tyne. He is currently writing a monograph under the working title of 'Mobility and Inwardness in Early Modern Tragedy', and has published numerous essays on themes relevant to mobility studies in relation to the works of Shakespeare, Marlowe, Dekker and Webster. Paul co-edited the Arden Bloomsbury *Critical Companion to The White Devil* (2016), and is also co-editing a Manchester Revels edition of *Gorboduc, or the Tragedy of Ferrex and Porrex*.

Lisa Hopkins is Professor of English at Sheffield Hallam University and co-edits *Shakespeare* (the journal of the British Shakespeare Association) and Arden Early Modern Drama Guides. Her most recent publications are *From the Romans to the Normans on the English Renaissance Stage* (ARC Humanities Press, 2017), *Shakespearean Allusion in Crime Fiction: DCI Shakespeare* (Palgrave, 2016), *Renaissance Drama on the Edge* (Ashgate, 2014) and *Drama and the Succession to the Crown, 1561–1633* (Ashgate, 2011).

Laurie Johnson is Professor of English and Cultural Studies at the University of Southern Queensland. He is author of *Shakespeare's Lost Playhouse: Eleven Days at Newington Butts* (2018), *The Tain of Hamlet* (2013) and *The Wolf Man's Burden* (2001), and editor of *Embodied Cognition and Shakespeare's Theatre: The Early Modern Body-Mind* (with John Sutton and Evelyn Tribble, 2014) and *Rapt in Secret Studies: Emerging Shakespeares* (with Darryl Chalk, 2010). He has also published more than forty articles and book chapters, is the current President of the Australian and New Zealand Shakespeare Association, and is a member of the editorial board on the journal *Shakespeare*.

Jennifer Allport Reid is currently completing a PhD at Birkbeck, University of London, exploring how customary culture intersects with popular forms in the early modern period, and the relationship of mutual influence between folklore and performed genres such as the theatre, sermons and ballads. She has published on the relationship between early modern customary drama and Anthony Munday's Robin Hood plays (*The Wenshan Review of Literature and Culture*, June 2017) and on hunting customs in popular culture and Shakespearean comedy in *The Routledge Handbook of Shakespeare and Animals*, edited by Karen Raber and Holly Dugan. She is particularly interested in the place of the early modern subject within their environment, and especially how early modern folklore and popular culture reflect the interactions between humans, animals and the landscape.

Martha Lynn Russell is an English instructor at Bryan College and a PhD student at Old Dominion University. She holds a master's degree from the University of South Florida in English Literature, where her thesis title was '"The King's Highway": Reading the Road in *The Pilgrim's Progress, Part 1*', which was partially presented at the 2019 Northeast Modern Language Association Conference (NeMLA). Her research areas include early modern geo-spatial relationships between land and identity as well as early modern issues surrounding sovereignty and social class.

Robert Stagg is Lecturer in English Language and Literature at St Anne's College, Oxford. He has published work in *Shakespeare Survey*, *Essays in Criticism* and various edited collections, and is currently completing a monograph about Shakespeare's blank verse. He has been a Wolfson Visiting Fellow at the New York Public Library, a Tom Jarman Research Fellow at Gladstone's Library, and will be Pforzheimer Visiting Research Fellow at the Harry Ransom Center, Austin, in 2019–20. He won the University of Oxford's Charles Oldham Shakespeare Prize, for original research on a Shakespearean subject, in 2012.

Marion Wynne-Davies holds the Chair of English Literature in the School of Literature and Languages at the University of Surrey. Her main areas of interest are early modern literature and women's writing. She has published two editions of primary material, *Renaissance Drama by Women: Texts and Documents* (with S. P. Cerasano) and *Women Poets of the Renaissance*, as well as several collections of essays in the same field. She has written four monographs: *Women and Arthurian Literature*, *Sidney to Milton*, *Women Writers of the English Renaissance: Familial Discourse* and *Margaret Atwood*.

Index

Page numbers in *italics* refer to illustrations.

Aaron, King of the Persians, 209
Act for the Punishment of Vagabonds (1572), 109, 131
Act of Union (1707), 242
'Acte for Punyshment of Rogues, Vagabondes and Sturdy Beggars' (1597), 77–8
Adler, Doris, 203
Admiral's Men (playing company), 39, 120, 152, 194
Agas Map, 57, 118, *166*
Albanactus, 19
Albania, 19–20
Alff, David, 249
  'Why No One Can Mend the Slough of Despond', 249
Alien Act (1705), 242
Alleyn, Edward, 113, 194
Al-Qaeda, 32
Andrea, Bernadette, 208
Andrew, Saint, 20
Anglicus, Bartholomeus, 139–40
Animal Studies, 35
Anjou, Francis, Duke of, 207
Anne of Denmark, 192
Aquinas, Saint Thomas, 58
Arden, Edward, 51–2
Arden, Mary, 52
Ariosto, Ludovico, 223
Aristotle, 31, 39, 88, 96
Armin, Robert, 4, 8, 129, 131–2, 134–5
  Foole upon Foole, 134–5
Armstrong clan, 17
Arthur, King, 17
Arthur, Prince (heir to Henry VII), 118
Ascham, Roger, 191
Aubrey, John, 61
Augustine of Hippo, Saint, 58, 204
Austin, John Langshaw, 198
Avercamp, Barent, 230
  Skating on a Frozen River, 230

Awdeley, John, 139–40
  The Fraternity of Vagabonds, 139–40
Aztecs, 34

Bakhtin, Mikhail, 42, 138, 140
Bandello, Matteo, 110–11
  Certaine tragicall discourses written out of Frenche and Latin (trans. Geffray Fenton), 110–12
  see also Fenton, Geffray
Barclay, Alexander, 130–1
  Ship of Fools, 8, 130, 138
Barentsz, Willem, 10, 230–1
Battle of Solway Moss, 17
Beaumont, Francis, *The Knight of the Burning Pestle*, 36
The Beggar's Opera (John Gay), 169
Beier, A. L., 92, 95
Bennett, J. M., 95
Beowulf, 241
Bethlem, 128
Bevington, David, 197
'Black Act' (1723), 51
Blackfriars Theatre, 44, 108, 188–9
Blatherwick, Simon, 109
Boccaccio, Giovanni, 223
Boehrer, Bruce, 35, 46
Bolsover Castle, 234
Bonnemaison, Joël, 2, 7, 127–8, 169
Borgia, Lucrezia, 191
Borlase, William, 65
Bradshaw, John, 55
Brant, Sebastian, 130, 138–9; see also Barclay, Alexander: *Ship of Fools*
Brayne, John, 117–19, 122
Brecht, Bertolt, 31, 39, 46
Brewer, Anthony, *The Lovesick King*, 18
Brittain, Vera, 239
Brome, Richard, 9, 167–80, 188
  The Antipodes, 168–70, 174, 177, 179–80, 252–3

The City Wit, 169, 179–80
Covent Garden Weeded, 169
A Jovial Crew, 3–4, 8–9, 167–71, 173, 175–80, 187, 198: Ballarat production, 170, 172–3, 179–81; Stephen Jeffreys's adaptation, 167, 169, 177–9
Richard Brome Online, 169–70, 177–9
The Sparagus Garden, 188
Brown, Eric C., 34
Brown, Ivor, 90, 93–4
Brownlow, Frank Walsh, 53
Bruegel, Pieter, the Elder
The Cripples, 140
Sloth, 42
Brutus, King, 20
Bunyan, John, 1, 2, 10–11, 238–50
The Doctrine of Law and Grace Unfolded, 245
The Pilgrim's Progress, 3–4, 10–11, 221, 238–50
Bunyan, Thomas, 249
Burbage, James, 119, 122
Burghley, William Cecil, Lord, 37
Burton, Jonathan, 206
Butler, Martin, 177

Calvin, John, 58
Camden, William, 17, 18
Britannia, 17
Cameron, David Kerr, 246
The English Fair, 246
Camino de Santiago, 27–8
Campion, Thomas, 197–8
Carey, Henry, Lord Hunsdon, 19, 21
Carey, Sir John, 22
Carey, Philadelphia, 23
Carey, Robert, 16, 19, 21–3, 26, 28
Memoirs, 16, 21–2, 26
Carlson, Susan, 83
Caroso, Fabritio, 191
Nobilità di Dame, 191
Carroll, William, 73–4
Casimir, John, Prince Elector Palatine, 132
Cave, Richard, Brian Woolland, Helen Ostovich and Elizabeth Schafer, 171
Cavendish, Sir Charles, 231
Cavendish, Margaret, 220–1, 224–9, 231–6
Assaulted and Pursued Chastity, 232
The Blazing World, 3–4, 10, 221, 224–7, 229, 231–6
'The Claspe. Phantasmes Masque', 228–9, 232
The Life of William Cavendish, Duke of Newcastle, 234
Natures Pictures Drawn by Fancies Pencil to the Life, 228

Observations upon Experimental Philosophy, 226, 231, 235
Orations of Divers Sorts Accommodated to Divers Places, 228–9
Sociable Letters, 227, 229–30
Cavendish, William, 225, 227–8, 230–2, 234–5
A New Method and Extraordinary Invention to Dress Horses, 234
Caxton, William, 15, 19–20
Golden Legend (Jacobus de Voragine), 209–10
The story and life of the Noble and Christian Prince Charles the great of France, 209
Cervantes, Miguel de, 204
Challoner, Richard, 54
Chamberlain's Men (playing company), 121
Chambers, Edmund Kerchever, 108–9
The Elizabethan Stage, 109
Chapman, George, *All Fools*, 44
Charlemagne, 209
Charles I, King, 55, 203, 216, 224, 234, 241, 248–9
Charles, Prince (later King Charles II), 232, 238, 249–50
Châteauneuf, Guillaume de L'Aubépine, Baron de, 16
Cherokee Trail of Tears, 1
Churchill, Caryl, *Light Shining in Buckinghamshire*, 177
Civil War, The, 220, 224, 227, 234, 249
Cock Lorell's Bote, 138–9
Coghill, Nevill, 152
Coleridge, Samuel Taylor, 61, 190
Collins, Marie, 15, 19
The Contention of Liberality and Prodigality, 43
Corfield, Cosmo, 159
Cortez, Hernan, 34
Cottam, John, 52
Cottam, Thomas, 51–2
Cresswell, Tim, 2
Cromwell, Oliver, 55, 59, 249–50
crossroads, 5–6, 8, 24, 52–6, 59–60, 62–6
Cruyningen, Piet van, 250
Cupid's Banishment (Robert White), 192
Curtain (playhouse), 122
Cyprian, Saint, 204

Da Monte, Gianbattista, 129
Daborne, Robert, *A Christian Turned Turk*, 204
Daley, Stuart, 73
'Where Are the Woods in *As You Like It*?', 73
Darlington, Ida, 116–17

Davies, Sir John, 191
  Orchestra, 191
Day, John, William Rowley and George Wilkins, 132
  The Travailes of the Three English Brothers, 132
De Certeau, Michel, 1–2, 9, 168, 171, 174, 180, 190, 196, 220–4, 226
  The Practice of Everyday Life, 220
De Ornellas, Kevin, 37
De Veer, Gerrit, 230–1
De Vere family, 188
Dekker, Thomas, 95, 136–7
  The Gull's Hornbook, 136–7
  The Shoemaker's Holiday, 195–6
Della Porta, Giambattista, 140
  A true Description of three Voyages by the North-East towards Cathay and China, undertaken by the Dutch in the Years 1594, 1595, and 1596, 230–2
Dibdale, Robert, 51–3
Dillon, Janette, 2–3
Doran, Greg, 197
Douglas, Archibald Douglas, 4th Earl of, 37
Drainage Act (1600), 11
Draney, John, 119
Drayton, Michael, 39
  'How many paltry, foolish painted things / That now in coaches trouble ev'ry street', 44
Drury Lane Theatre, 187
Dunn, Caroline S., 94, 96
Dutch East India Company, 226
Dyer, Sir James, 56

Eagleton, Terry, 176
ecocriticism, 4–5, 31–46
Edinburgh, 16, 19, 22, 27–8
Edwards, Peter, 35
Elen Luyddog (Helen of the Ways), 15
Elizabeth I, Queen, 16, 21–3, 46, 52, 74, 94–5, 107–9, 118, 132, 188, 205–8, 214, 216
  'Declaration of the Queen's Proceedings since her Reign', 74
Elizabeth Stuart, Queen of Bohemia, 192
Elstrack, Renold, 130
Erasmus, Desiderius, 8, 131
  Praise of Folly, 130
Eshu Elegba (Yorùbá god), 65
Everyman, 221

The Famous Victories of Henry V, 40–1
Farr, David, 197
Federation University Australia, 169–70
Felicity, Saint, 209

Fellheimer, Jeannette, 112
Fenton, Geffray, 110–12; see also Bandello, Matteo; Guicciardini, Francesco
Fiennes, Ralph, 197
Fish, Stanley Eugene, 238
  'Progress in *The Pilgrim's Progress*', 238
Fisher, Will, 80–1
Fitter, Chris, 80–1
Fitzpatrick, Tim, 173–4
Fletcher, Laurence, 19
folklore, 146–62
folly, 127–41, 252
Forbes, Thomas R., 59
Forman, Simon, 62
Foster, Albert, 239
Frazer, Paul, 38
Frederick V, Elector Palatine, 192
Freeman, Gerard, 174
Fripp, Edgar, 53
Fumerton, Patricia, 74–5, 81, 91, 187

Gaby, Rosemary, 172–3
Gascoigne, George, 189–90
General Drainage Act (1600), 248
General Drainage Act (for the Bedford Level Corporation, 1663), 250
Gennep, A. Van, 56
ghosts, 60–4
Gittings, Clare, 51, 55, 58–9, 63
Globe Theatre, 81, 108, 188–9, 192; see also Shakespeare's Globe (contemporary reconstruction)
Goodey, C. F., 131, 137
Grady, Hugh and Cary DiPietro, 44
Grant, Allison, 81, 83
Great North Road, 4, 10, 239, 243–4
Green, Father Hugh, 55
Greenblatt, Stephen, 186
Greene, Robert, 18–19, 88–90, 92, 95, 135–7
  Friar Bacon and Friar Bungay, 152
  James the Fourth, 16–17, 18–19, 27
  'A Notable Discouery of Coosinage: Now daily practised by sundry lewd persons, called Connie-Catchers, and Crosse-Biters', 88–92
  The Third and Last Part of Cony-Catching, 135–7
Grissold, Robert, 54–5
Guicciardini, Francesco, *Historia d'Italia* (translated by Geffray Fenton), 112; see also Fenton, Geffray
Gurr, Andrew, 109, 112–13, 117
  Shakespearian Playing Companies, 109
Guthrie, Tyrone, 194

Hales, Sir James, 56
Hall, Edward, 110

The vnion of the two noble and illustre famelies of Lancastre [and] Yorke, 110–11
Hall, Joseph, 194
 Virgidemiarum, 194
Harley MS, 131
Harman, Thomas, 95, 135
 A Caveat or Warning for Common Cursetors, Vulgarly Called Vagabonds, 74, 78
Harrison, William, 129
Harsnett, Samuel, 62, 64–5
 A Declaration of Egregious Popish Impostures, 53, 61–5
Harte, Jeremy, 66
Harvey, Gabriel, 191
Hathaway, Anne, 53
Hawkes, David, 208
Henri I, Prince of Joinville, Duke of Guise, 52
Henri II, King, 191
Henrietta Maria, Queen, 225, 227, 234
Henry IV, King, 35, 46, 89
Henry VI, King, 89
Henry VII, King, 118
Henry VIII, King, 118, 131, 138
Henslowe, Philip, 110, 152
Herbert, Sir Thomas, 241
 Some Years Travels into Divers Parts of Africa and Asia the Great, 241
Herman, David, 240
Herrick, Robert, 60
 'To Perilla', 60
Hertel, Ralf, 40
Heywood, Thomas
 The Fair Maid of the Exchange, 192–3
 The Fair Maid of the West I, 185
Hill, Christopher, 9, 169, 174
Hippocrates, 42
Hodgen, Margaret T., 246
Hofmeyr, Isabel, 239
 The Portable Bunyan: A Transnational History of The Pilgrim's Progress, 239
Holland, Aaron, 119
Hooke, Robert, *Micrographia*, 226
Hopkins, Lisa, 205
Housesteads, 17
Howard, Henry, Earl of Surrey, 189–91
Howard, Jean E., 97
Howitt, William, 119
 The Northern Heights of London, 119–20
Hubright, Joachim, 245
Hutton, Ronald, 148

ignis fatuus, 8, 146–8, 151, 156, 158, 161–2
Ingram, R. W., 170
Ingram, William, 37, 117
 The Business of Playing, 117
intellectual disability, 127–9, 131, 134–41
Iraq War, 32
Ireton, Henry, 55
Isidore of Seville, 191
Islam, 202–6, 208, 211–16
 The Qur'an, 216

Jack of Dover, 128–9
Jacobite rising (1745), 18
James I and VI, King, 16–17, 18, 19, 20, 21–3, 27–8, 188, 192, 206, 216, 248
James, Rhys, 171
James, Saint, 27–8
Jeffreys, Stephen, 167; *see also* Brome, Richard: *A Jovial Crew* (Stephen Jeffreys's adaptation)
Jesus, Christ, 11, 38–9, 197, 208–9, 212, 242
Johnson, Nora, 135
Johnson, Robert, 65
Johnson, Samuel, 38
Johnston, S. I., 64
Jonson, Ben, 17, 18, 20–1, 23, 188, 194
 Bartholomew Fair, 137
 The New Inn, 73
 Poetaster, 187–8
Jonson, Ben and John Marston, *Eastward Ho!*, 44
Jowitt, Claire, 212–13
Jutte, Robert, 73

Kaeuper, Richard, 91
Kean, Edmund, 187
Kemp, Will, 4, 8, 131–4, 138, 188, 191
 Nine Daies Wonder, 133–4
Ker, Sir Robert, 21, 26
Kerrigan, John, 187
Kimbrough, Robert, 76
King's New School, Stratford, 52
Klause, John, 53
Knollys, Sir Francis, 74

Lady Elizabeth's Men (playing company), 16
Lander, Jesse, 148
Landon, John, 34
A Larum for London, 193
Lefebvre, Henri, 1–2, 5, 6, 7, 8, 33, 73, 88, 107–8, 122, 146, 161, 190
 'Space and the State', 108
Leicester's Men (playing company), 132
Leland, John, 19
Liertz, Melanie, 171
Lodge, Thomas, 121
 Rosalynde, 75–6
Londinium (Roman city), 116
Loomba, Ania, 168
Loomis, Catherine, 22–3

Lord Chamberlain's Men (playing company), 120, 185, 188
Lord Chandos's Men (playing company), 8, 132, 134–5
Lord Strange's Men (playing company), 107, 112
Loxley, James, Anna Groundwater and Julie Sanders, 18, 23, 25, 27; see also Sanders, Julie
Luther, Martin, 58, 111
Luxon, Thomas Hyatt, 244
  'The Pilgrim's Passive Progress', 243–4
Lydgate, John, 139
Lyly, John, 44, 223
  Euphues, 223

MacDonald, Michael, 56–8
McElroy, Mary and Kent Cartwright, 121–2
McHale, Brian, 240
McInnis, David, 189
McRae, Andrew, 2, 6, 9, 33, 71, 91, 210
  Literature and Domestic Travel in Early Modern England, 71
Maddern, Grace, 171
Magnus Maximus, 15
Malone, Edmond, 108
  'Historical Account of the English Stage', 108
Margary, Ivan, 116
Maria Anna, Infanta, 203, 216
Marlowe, Christopher, 186–7, 189–90, 194–5, 197, 207
  Dido, Queen of Carthage, 194, 205, 207
  1 Tamburlaine, 185–6, 190, 194–5
  2 Tamburlaine, 186, 190, 194–5
Marshall, Peter, 59, 148
Marston, John, *Antonio's Revenge*, 192; see also Jonson, Ben and John Marston: *Eastward Ho!*
Martin Marprelate tracts, 51
Mary, Queen of Scots, 17, 21–2, 28, 52, 74, 205
Maslen, Rob, 222, 224, 233, 236
Massinger, Philip, 10, 202–4, 212, 216
  The Renegado, 3–4, 10, 202–4, 206–16
Matar, Nabil, 205
Matthew, Gospel of, 245
Maxfield, Father Thomas, 55
Mejia LaPerle, Carol, 211
men, and roads, 88–91
Merleau-Ponty, Maurice, 2
The Merry Devil of Edmonton, 152
Middleton, Thomas, 214
  A Game at Chess, 214
  The Puritan, 44
Milton, John, 61

Moffat, Alistair, 19
Molmutius (King of the Britons), 15
monstrosity, 88–91, 93, 96–9
Moorman, F. W., 61
Morgan, Thomas, 16
Morley, Thomas, 191
Muhammad, The Prophet, 212, 215
Munday, Anthony, 112, 161–2
  Amadis of Gaule (translation), 112
  John a Kent and John a Cumber, 3–4, 8, 146, 152–7, 160–1
Murad III, Sultan, 208
Murphy, Ffion, Rama Venkatasawmy, Catherine Simpson and Tanja Visosevic, 175
Murray, John Tucker, 109
  English Dramatic Companies 1558–1642, 108–9

Nashe, Thomas, 41–2, 51, 205
  The Unfortunate Traveller, 223
Neill, Michael, 203
Newington Butts (playhouse), 7, 107, 110, 112–13, 115, 116–17, 120–2, 252
Newton, Isaac, 147
Nicholl, Charles, 16
Norris, Francis, 1st Earl of Berkshire, 58
North, Thomas, *The Lives of the Noble Grecians and Romanes* (translation of Plutarch), 196
Northbrooke, John, 97, 195
Northerne poems congratulating the Kings majesties entrance to the crowne, 27
Northumberland, Henry Percy, 9th Earl of, 39

Old Vic Theatre, 194, 197
Oldridge, Darren, 148
Olivier, Laurence, 197
On the Road (Kerouac), 1
'Oram's Grave' (Maddington, Wiltshire), 66
Ortelius, Abraham, 19
  Theatrum, 19
Osborne, Dorothy, 225
Ovid, 62, 191
The Oxford Companion to Shakespeare (Michael Dobson and Stanley Wells, eds), 109
Oxford's Men (playing company), 188

Paracelsus, 129
  De generatione stultorum, 129
Parker, Patricia, 211–12
Paul, Saint, 4, 10, 42, 202–3, 208–13, 215–16, 242
Peele, George, *Edward I*, 23
Pembroke's Men (playing company), 121

Pepys, Samuel, 225
Perpetua, Saint, 209
Peter, Saint, First Epistle of Peter, 242
Phelan, Jim, 240
Philip II, King, 205
Philips, Edward, 238
Platter, Thomas, 93–4
Poley, Robert, 16
Pooley, Roger, 222–3, 233
Pope, 205
Powell, Father Philip, 55
Preiss, Richard, 132–3
presentism, 44
Priscilla, Queen of the Desert, 175
Privy Council, 16, 107, 110, 112, 120, 187
Pryme, Abraham, 158–9
Prynne, William, 97
Puck (or Robin Goodfellow), 148–51, 157
Pugliatti, Paola, 138
Puttenham, George, 191

Queen Henrietta's Men (playing company), 185
Queen's Men (playing company), 131

Raber, Karen, 35
Red Bull (playhouse), 119–20
Red Lion (playhouse), 7, 117, 119
Rees, Emma, 232
Renwick, W. L., 18–19
Reivers, 18–19, 21
Richard II, King, 118
Robinson, Benedict S., 203, 206
Rolling Stone (magazine), 172
The Roman Martyrology (1627), 209
The Rose (playhouse), 107, 110, 112, 121, 186–7
Rosenfeld, Nancy, 61
Rous, Francis, 64
Royal Shakespeare Company, 167, 177, 179, 196–7

St Albans, 89
  Battle of St Albans, 89
Salgādo, Gāmini, 93
Salzman, Paul, 225
Sanders, Julie, 2–3, 9, 25, 73, 187
  The Cambridge Introduction to Early Modern Drama, 1576–1642, 109
  see also Loxley, James, Anna Groundwater and Julie Sanders
Sarn Helen, 15–16, 17
Savage, Jerome, 120, 122
Saxton, Christopher, 19
Schafer, Elizabeth, 170
Schoenbaum, Samuel, 33, 113, 117
Scrope, Henry, 9th Baron Scrope of Bolton, 16, 74

Scrope, Thomas, 10th Baron Scrope of Bolton, 16, 21
Segal, Janna, 75, 78, 81
Seneca, 61
Seven Deadly Sins, 42
Shah Abbas I, King of Persia, 241
Shakespeare, John, 36
Shakespeare, William, 1, 2, 3–7, 15, 19, 21, 27–8, 31–2, 34–9, 41–4, 46, 51–4, 56, 58, 61, 65, 66, 72–3, 75–6, 79, 81, 83, 87–8, 89–90, 93–4, 96–9, 108, 129, 132, 149, 152, 159, 161–2, 167, 169, 176, 187, 189–90, 192, 195–7, 212
  All's Well That Ends Well, 27–8, 53–4
  As You Like It, 3–4, 6, 71–83, 88, 91–3, 95–9
  The Comedy of Errors, 35
  Coriolanus, 9, 195–7
  Cymbeline, 3–4, 15, 192
  Hamlet, 3–4, 7, 36, 53, 58–60, 62–3, 66, 121, 187, 192, 194, 197
  1 Henry IV, 3–5, 32–3, 36–44
  2 Henry IV, 19, 89–90, 191
  Henry V, 40, 54, 185, 189, 192, 195
  3 Henry VI, 52, 192
  King John, 192
  King Lear, 53, 129, 189
  Love's Labour's Lost, 54
  Macbeth, 3–4, 16, 17, 21, 22–8, 39, 61, 193–4
  The Merchant of Venice, 189
  A Midsummer Night's Dream, 3–6, 8, 25, 60, 63–4, 146, 149–55, 159–62, 192
  Much Ado About Nothing, 189–90
  Othello, 28
  Richard II, 18, 38, 54–5
  Richard III, 40, 79, 187
  Romeo and Juliet, 190
  Sonnet 44, 46
  Sonnet 50, 46
  The Taming of the Shrew, 34, 37, 187
  The Tempest, 3–4, 8, 9, 61, 146, 155–60, 162, 189, 192
  Titus Andronicus, 3–4, 7, 88, 94, 98, 120–1
  Troilus and Cressida, 9, 192, 198
  Twelfth Night, 3, 97–9, 129
  The Two Gentlemen of Verona, 189
  The Winter's Tale, 62, 137–8, 159
Shakespeare's Globe (contemporary reconstruction), 174, 177
Shaughnessy, Robert, 42
Shell, Alison, 147, 150
Shelley, Mary, *Frankenstein*, 236
Sherwood Forest, 234
Sidney, Philip, 111, 185, 223
  An Apology for Poetry, 111, 185
  Arcadia, 223

Sindercombe, Miles, 59
Siôn Cent, 152
Sir Gawain and the Green Knight, 241
Sir John Oldcastle, 39
Siward, Earl of Northumbria, 17
Slack, Paul, 77
Smith, Bruce, 189
Society of London Bowmen, 118
Somerville, John, 51–2, 56, 59
Speed, John, 10, 221–2, 224, 236
  A Prospect of the Most Famous Parts of the World, 10, 221–3, 232
Spenser, Edmund, 42, 191
  The Faerie Queene, 42, 186, 221
Speratus, Saint, 209
S.R., 'Martin Markall, Beadle of Bridewell', 74
Stafford-Clark, Max, 177
Stainton, Tim, 128
Stapylton, Robert, 64
Stern, Tiffany, 175
Stewart, Alan, 33
Stockwood, John, 121
Stokes, Amy, 59
Stopes, Charlotte Carmichael, 52
Stow, John, 44, 116
  Annales, or a Generall Chronicle of England, 116–17
Stubbes, Phillip, 97
Styan, J. L., 197
suicide, 5, 51, 56–60, 66
Sullivan, Garrett A., 147
Sussex's Men (playing company), 121
Swan, John, 147–8, 151, 158
Swirski, Peter, 88

Tarlton, Richard, 131–2
  Tarlton's Jests, 131–2
Tarocchi Cards of Mantegna, 130–1
Tasso, Torquato, 223
Taylor, John, 20, 25, 241
  The World Runs on Wheels, 44, 45, 241
Tertullian, Saint, 204
Thacker, David, 196–7
The Theatre, Shoreditch (playhouse), 7, 108, 112–13, 119, 121–2
Thelma and Louise, 175
Theodore of Cyprus, Saint, 64
'Thomas the Rhymer' (folk tale), 17–18, 24
Throckmorton, Francis, 51

Throckmorton, Mary, 52
Timur the Lame, 194
Traister, Barbara, 156
treason, 51–5, 59
Tribble, Evelyn, 120–1, 187
Tuan, Yi-Fu, 25
Turnpike Act (1663), 11, 244
Twysden, Lady Isabella, 241
Tyburn, 52–5
Tyndale, William, 111, 148

Ungus, King of the Picts, 20

vagrancy, 4, 6–8, 11, 37, 62, 71–83, 91–3, 95–9, 127–31, 162, 167–80, 187–8, 198, 252
Van Hoogstraten, Dirk, 130
Vindolanda, 17
Virgil, 191

Walker, David, 239, 245
walking, 9, 185–8, 190–4, 198
Waller, Sir William, 187
Walsham, Alexandra, 3, 168
Walsingham, Francis, 16, 21, 205
War of the Roses, 89
Watson, Robert, 44
Weever, John, 59–60
Weimann, Robert, 62
Welbeck Abbey, 225, 234–5
Whitaker, Katie, 228, 231
  Mad Madge, 228
White, Martin, 178
Wickham, Glynne, 110
Wilbraham, Thomas, 59
Wilson, Rawdon, 73–4
  'The Way to Arden: Attitudes toward Time in *As You Like It*', 73–4
Wilson, Richard, 28, 53
Winehouse, Amy, 65
  Back to Black, 65
The Wizard of Oz, 175
women
  and roads, 87–99
  and travel, 6, 9, 71–83
  see also vagrancy
Wood, Anthony, 241
Woodbridge, Linda, 74, 78, 81–3
Woodliffe, Oliver, 37
Woolf, Virginia, 224–5
Wright, Clare, 172

Zijderveld, Anton C., 128

EU representative:
Easy Access System Europe
Mustamäe tee 50, 10621 Tallinn, Estonia
Gpsr.requests@easproject.com

www.ingramcontent.com/pod-product-compliance
Lightning Source LLC
Chambersburg PA
CBHW071830230426
43672CB00013B/2805